# FROMMER'S

## COMPREHENSIVE TRAVEL GUIDE

# PHILADELPHIA
## '93-'94

by Jay Golan

T5-AFQ-105

**PRENTICE HALL TRAVEL**

NEW YORK • LONDON • TORONTO • SYDNEY • TOKYO • SINGAPORE

**FROMMER BOOKS**

Published by Prentice Hall General Reference
A division of Simon & Schuster Inc.
15 Columbus Circle
New York, NY 10023

ISBN 0-671-84666-3
ISSN 0899-3211

Design by Robert Bull Design
Maps by Geografix Inc.

**FROMMER'S PHILADELPHIA '93-'94**
Editor-in-Chief: Marilyn Wood
Senior Editors: Judith de Rubini, Alice Fellows
Editors: Thomas F. Hirsch, Paige Hughes, Sara Hinsey Raveret, Lisa
Renaud, Theodore Stavrou
Assistant Editors: Margaret Bowen, Peter Katucki, Ian Wilker
Managing Editor: Leanne Coupe

**Special Sales**
Bulk purchases of Frommer's Travel Guides are available at special discounts. The publishers are happy to custom-make publications for corporate clients who wish to use them as premiums or sales promotions. We
can excerpt the contents, provide covers with corporate imprints, or create
books to meet specific needs. For more information write to Special Sales,
Prentice Hall Travel, Paramount Communications Building, 15 Columbus
Circle, New York, NY 10023

Manufactured in the United States of America

# CONTENTS

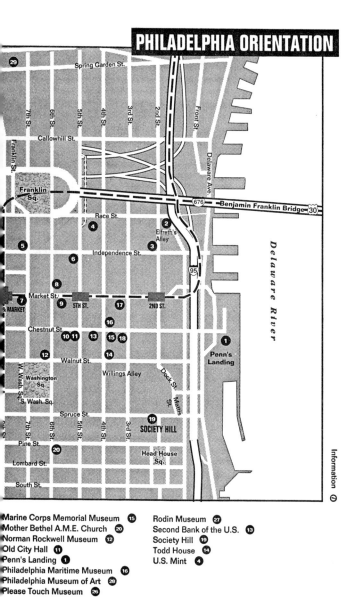

# PHILADELPHIA ORIENTATION

Spring Garden St.

Callowhill St.

Franklin Sq.

Race St.

Elfreth's Alley

Independence St.

Market St.   5TH ST.   2ND ST.

Chestnut St.

Walnut St.

W. Wash. Sq.   Washington Sq.   Willings Alley

S. Wash. Sq.

Spruce St.   SOCIETY HILL

Pine St.

Lombard St.   Head House Sq.

South St.

Penn's Landing

Delaware River

Benjamin Franklin Bridge

676   30

95

Delaware Ave.

Front St.

Information ①

7th St.   6th St.   5th St.   4th St.   3rd St.   2nd St.

Dock St.   Mattis St.

Commerce Square at Market and 21st streets (tel. 567-8630) and at 205 S. 38th Street (tel. 382-5700).

## THE JOSEPH FOX BOOKSTORE, 1724 Sansom St. Tel. 563-4184.

This bookstore has choice selections in art, graphic design, architecture, photography, and current and classic fiction.

## PENNSYLVANIA ACADEMY OF FINE ARTS, Broad and Cherry sts. Tel. 972-7633.

A wonderful collection of books on all facets of American arts and architecture, from the 1500s to the present, can be found here. There's also a selection of children's books and construction projects.

**ROBIN'S BOOK STORES, 1837 Chestnut St. Tel. 567-2165.**

Robin's prides itself on carrying a wide range of serious and popular books, shelved in pleasant surroundings. The store at 108 S. 13th Street (tel. 735-9600) was an old counterculture hangout.

**TOWER BOOKS, 425 South St. Tel. 925-9909.**

Tower Books has extended the concept of massively stocked, discounted merchandise from recordings into books and magazines. It's open every night until midnight.

**UNIVERSITY OF PENNSYLVANIA BOOKSTORE, 3729 Locust Walk at 37th Street. Tel. 898-7595.**

Obviously, the store stocks the complete readings for every one of thousands of courses, but it also includes excellent selections of quality fiction and nonfiction.

## CARDS

**SEALED WITH A KISS, 137 S. 13th St. Tel. 925-7474.**

The most witty and esoteric cards around can be found here; in fact, it's a bit skimpy on the traditional variety. There's also a selection of small gifts and paper goods.

## CHINA, SILVER & GLASS

**KEYSTONE SILVER, Hopkinson House, Washington Square South. Tel. 922-1724.**

About 50% of the business here is repair—replating, polishing, or replacing parts—but Keystone also sells plate and sterling and antique and modern reproductions. Hours are 10am to 4pm weekdays, and 10am to 1pm Saturday (except July and August).

**NIEDERKORN SILVER, 2005 Locust St. Tel. 567-2606.**

Antique baby items, dressing-table adornments, napkin rings, picture frames, and jewelry are featured here. Also on display is Philadelphia's largest selection of period silver, including works of such fine crafters as Jensen and Tiffany.

## COLONIAL REPRODUCTIONS

**FRIED BROTHERS, 467 N. 7th St. Tel. 627-3205, or toll free 800/356-5050.**

Near the Edgar Allan Poe House, Fried Brothers specializes in hardware suitable for Colonial buildings and furnishings. If you admire the doorknobs in Society Hill, you'll see the like here.

## CRAFTS

Philadelphia artisanry has always commanded respect. The tradition lingers on, in both small individual workshops and cooperative stores. The Olde City section, north of Society Hill, has seen a mushrooming of contemporary crafts and design stores. The Craft Show held every November is one of the top five in the country.

For outdoor crafts vendors, check **Independence Mall** during

# LIST OF MAPS

## INVITATION TO THE READERS

In researching this book, I have come across many wonderful establishments, the best of which I have included here. I am sure that many of you will also come across appealing hotels, inns, restaurants, guest houses, shops, and attractions. Please don't keep them to yourself. Share your experiences, especially if you want to comment on places that have been included in this edition that have changed for the worse. You can address your letters to:

Jay Golan
*Frommer's Philadelphia '93–'94*
c/o Prentice Hall Travel
15 Columbus Circle
New York, NY 10023

## A DISCLAIMER

Readers are advised that prices fluctuate in the course of time and travel information changes under the impact of the varied and volatile factors that affect the travel industry. Neither the author nor the publisher can be held responsible for the experiences of readers while traveling. Readers are invited to write to the publisher with ideas, comments, and suggestions for future editions.

## SAFETY ADVISORY

Whenever you're traveling in an unfamiliar city or country, stay alert. Be aware of your immediate surroundings. Wear a moneybelt and keep a close eye on your possessions. Be particularly careful with cameras, purses, and wallets, all favorite targets of thieves and pickpockets.

# INTRODUCING PHILADELPHIA

Old history and new excitement— these are Philadelphia today. When you scratch the surface of William Penn's "Greene countrie town," you find a wealth of pleasures and pastimes. Don't take just my word for it: The city has become a popular and charming center for tourism on the East Coast, and thousands of impressed visitors are spreading the news.

Try these descriptions on for size: Philadelphia is the largest Colonial district in the country, with dozens of treasures plus Independence National Historical Park. It boasts the most historic square mile in America, where the United States was conceived, declared, and ratified—and you can touch the Liberty Bell to prove it. It offers some of the best dining values and several of the finest restaurants in America. It's a stroller's paradise of restored Georgian and Federal structures that are integrated with smart shops and contemporary row-house courts to create a working urban environment. Philadelphia is a center of professional and amateur sports, with over 7,000 acres of parkland within the city limits. And it's a city filled with art, crafts, and music for every taste, with boulevards made for street fairs and parades all year long.

Between postwar urban-renewal efforts and sprucing up for America's bicentennial in 1976, the city's 300th birthday in 1982, and the Constitution's bicentennial in 1987, Philadelphia turned itself into an ideal vacation city. From row-house boutiques to the Second Continental Congress's favorite tavern, from an Ivy League campus to street artists and musicians, from gleaming skyscrapers to Italian marketplaces, Philadelphia is a city of gentle and easy living.

Even geographically, Philadelphia sits pretty. Some 60 miles inland, it's the country's busiest freshwater port, controlling the Delaware Valley. It's a natural stopping place between New York and Washington, D.C., with easy access by rail and road. And the casinos and beaches of Atlantic City, the Revolutionary War sites of Valley Forge and Brandywine, Pennsylvania Dutch Country, and the great duPont family mansions all lie about an hour away. In fact, 38% of the nation's population is within a 4½-hour drive from the city.

Economically, Philadelphia's a great deal too. A 1989 study of corporate travel showed that the city's average daily cost of lodging and meals was 70% of New York's and 90% of Boston's and Washington. Family-style travel is even more of a bargain.

# WHAT'S SPECIAL ABOUT PHILADELPHIA

## Architectural Highlights

☐ Independence Hall (1732), with its classic, quiet magnificence, a very important building in American history.
☐ The Liberty Bell, always visible and always visited, in its own pavilion across from Independence Hall.
☐ Furness Library (1890), with its gargoyles, on the University of Pennsylvania's campus at 34th Street and Locust Walk—newly restored by the firm of Venturi, Rauch, and Scott Brown.
☐ Christ Church (1744), at 2nd and Market, with its Palladian altar window—the wonder of the 1740s.
☐ Logan Square fountain, brilliantly landscaped.

## Museums

☐ The Philadelphia Museum of Art and the Barnes Foundation, housing the world's strongest collection of impressionist art outside Paris.

## Streets/Neighborhoods

☐ Society Hill and Independence National Historical Park, a square-mile chronicle of U.S. birth pangs.
☐ Boathouse Row, where the toy-village boathouses along the Schuylkill River adorn weekend rowing regattas and twinkle every night.
☐ Olde City, with a working stone drinking fountain, "Presented by a Lady," for horses at the curb in front of the Arch Street Friends Meeting House at 3rd Street.

☐ Head House Square, a covered market for provisions and crafts since the 1740s.
☐ South Philadelphia, the home of Rocky Balboa of the movies and "pasta with red sauce."

## Events/Festivals

☐ The Mummer's Parade, up Broad Street on New Year's Day.
☐ Freedom Week, just before July 4, with outdoor events of all types.

## For the Kids

☐ The Zoo, the Please Touch Museum, and the rejuvenated Franklin Institute (see Chapter 7, "Cool for Kids").

## Shopping

☐ Shops at Liberty Place, a gleaming new urban mall.
☐ Franklin Mills, off I-95, the world's largest outlet and entertainment center.

## Natural Spectacles

☐ Along the Schuylkill River behind the Philadelphia Museum of Art, a springtime burst of thousands of azaleas and rhododendrons.
☐ Fairmount Park, 4,000 acres of greenery that make up an extraordinary city parkland.

## After Dark

☐ The world-famous Philadelphia Orchestra, based at the Academy of Music.

## Literary Shrine

☐ The Rosenbach Museum, featuring original manuscript of James Joyce's *Ulysses* and first editions of Herman Melville.

# 1. CULTURE, HISTORY & BACKGROUND

## GEOGRAPHY/PEOPLE

Philadelphia occupies a tongue of land at the confluence of the Delaware River—one of the largest U.S. rivers feeding into the Atlantic—and the Schuylkill River. The original settlement, and the heart of Center City today, is the band about 5 miles north that didn't dwindle into marshland in the 1600s. Since then, of course, the city has drained and used the entire tongue to the south and has exploded into the northeast and northwest.

The city and its region are flat and fertile ground. Philadelphia has traditionally looked south, with shipping and manufacturing along the Delaware, and west, with produce being brought across the Schuylkill from inland Pennsylvania. In the 19th century, the city improved on nature's fortunes through extensive canals and rail links that made it central to hundreds of miles of coal and oil fields, timber lands, and farms.

The waves of settlement and immigration witnessed by the area now known as Philadelphia are fascinating, starting with the Delaware or Lenape branch of the Algonquian Indians, who were found by the first European settlers from Sweden in the 1640s. Unusual tolerance, personified by Quakers, led to two separate strains of immigrants between this period and 1800. One was made up of entire European families of almost every sort—English, Scottish, Sephardic Jews, and German (*Deutsch* in German—whence the term Pennsylvania "Dutch")—who often made the decision to immigrate based on promises of cheap farmland. The other included thousands of London-based craftsmen, servants, and sailors who wanted to dwell in America's premier city.

After 1800, immigration was a push-pull thing; English commoners fled the industrialization of their countryside in the 1820s, Irish escaped from the 1840s potato famine, and waves of Germans and other central Europeans sought peace and stability throughout the 1870s. From the 1880s to the 1920s, Russians and Jews from eastern Europe, Italians, and free blacks from the American South all migrated in record numbers to the city. In recent years, Asian and Hispanic inflows have balanced the suburban outflow of descendants of earlier immigrants, creating a more multicultural Philadelphia than ever before. The classic pattern of these groups has been to stake out a section of the city as "home turf" in the first generation—South Philadelphia for Italians, South Street for Russian Jews, and North Philadelphia for blacks—and to move away from that section in later generations.

These various influences have shaped the modern city. To cite just one example, the Mummer's Parade mixes an English country-fair tradition with music of the black South of a century ago. The Philadelphia experience has not always been happy, however. The city has suffered from riots, protests, and bigotry along racial, religious, and economic lines. These have been most pronounced in times of economic distress.

# HISTORY/POLITICS

Although Philadelphia may conjure up thoughts of William Penn and the Revolutionary period in the minds of most Americans, it was in fact a tiny group of Swedish settlers who first established a foothold here in the 1640s. (You can see models of the two ships that brought them over in the Gloria Dei Church.) Queen Village commemorates Queen Christina, who appointed the 400-pound Johan Printz as the first of the colonial governors. The Native American name for Printz meant "Big Belly," and in his behavior in dealing with the Dutch, whose territories extended south from New Amsterdam (New York), he seemed equally Falstaffian—much bluff and no bloodshed. The Swedes could hardly afford battling, as their relations with the Delaware Indians (soon to die out) were never excellent and their farming was even more precarious.

## COLONIAL PHILADELPHIA

Where does William Penn fit in? Well, his father had been an admiral and a courtier under Charles II of England. The king was in debt to Admiral Penn, who died in 1670, and the younger Penn asked to collect the debt through a land grant on the west bank of the Delaware River, a grant that would eventually be named Pennsylvania, or "Penn's forest." At the time, Penn was in prison. His Quaker religion, anti-Anglican Church attitudes, and contempt for authority had gotten him expelled from Oxford and arrested for conspiracy and "tumultuous assembling" numerous times. The chance for him to set up a utopia in the New World, based on Quaker principles, was too good to pass up. Since Swedish farmers owned most of the lower Delaware frontage, he decided to settle upriver, where the Schuylkill met the Delaware. The name he chose was Philadelphia—the City of Brotherly Love.

In 1982 Philadelphia celebrated its 300th anniversary, and—incredibly—Penn's original city plan still adequately described the Center City, down to the public parks and the site for City Hall. Because of London's terrible 1666 fire, exacerbated by narrow streets and semidetached wooden buildings, the founder figured that broad avenues and city blocks arranged in a grid were the safest answer here. As he intended to treat Native

Americans and fellow settlers equally, he planned no city walls or neighborhood borders. Front Street, naturally, faced the Delaware, as it still does, and parallel streets were numbered until 24th Street and the Schuylkill. Streets running east to west were named after trees and plants (Sassafras became Race Street, for the horse-and-buggy contests run along it). To attract prospective investors, Penn promised bonus land grants in the "Liberties" (outlying countryside) to anyone who bought a city lot; he took one of the largest for himself, now Pennsbury Manor, (26 miles north of town). Colonies were in the business of attracting settlers in those days, and Penn had to wear a variety of hats—those of financier, politician, religious leader, salesman, and manufacturer.

Penn's city before the "Greene countrie town" plan was a jumble of farms and coves along the Delaware. Homes and public buildings filled in the map, but slowly—that's why all the colonial row houses of Society Hill and Elfreth's Alley (continuously inhabited since the 1690s) are so near the Delaware docks. When he wrote the Declaration of Independence in 1776, almost a century later, Thomas Jefferson could still say of his boarding house on 7th and Market that it was away from the city noise and dirt! The city spread west to Broad Street even later, around 1800. One big problem in the 18th century, though, was that Philadelphia grew along the river and not west as Penn had planned. Southwark, to the south, and the Northern Liberties, to the north, housed the less affluent, including most of the rougher sailors and their taverns set up in unofficial alleys. These were Philadelphia's first slums—unpaved, without public services, and populated by those without enough property or money to satisfy voting requirements.

Although Philadelphia had been founded after Boston and New York, manufacturing, financial services, excellent docking facilities, and fine Pennsylvania farm produce soon propelled it to the first city of the colonies—the largest English-speaking city in the British Empire except for London. Some 82 ships docked in 1682, in a cove that Dock Street has filled in and along docks at Front Street up to Vine. By 1770 the figure was 880 ships along 66 wharves.

Despite its urban problems, Colonial Philadelphia was a thriving city in virtually

## DATELINE

- **1765** Mass protests on news of English Parliament's passage of the Stamp Act, with boycotts of imports and office "strikes."
- **1774** First Continental Congress held in the State House (now Independence Hall).
- **1776** Declaration of Independence debated and adopted on July 2.
- **1777** General Howe, moving up from Maryland, takes Germantown on October 4 and occupies Philadelphia soon after; members of the Continental Congress, with the Liberty Bell, flee to Lancaster.
- **1778** British troops abandon Philadelphia in June to advance on New York City.
- **1780** Pennsylvania becomes the first state to abolish slavery, calling for general emancipation by 1827.
- **1782** Bank of North America opens on the corner of Chestnut and 3rd streets.
- **1787** Constitutional Convention meets in the State House.
- **1790–1800** Philadelphia is the capital of the United States.
- **1799** Private (continues)

### DATELINE

bathing becomes a fashion. Elizabeth Drinker writes, "I bore it better than expected, not having been wet all over once in my life."

• **1805** First permanent bridge spans the Schuylkill, connecting the city to Pennsylvania's rich farmlands.

• **1812–15** English blockade of international trade shuts down Philadelphia shipping, though its Navy Yard outfits most of U.S. Navy.

• **1820s** Transformation of the seaport city into America's first major industrial city.

• **1832** Railroad to Germantown built.

• **1844** Riots over rail laying through Kensington for the Trenton route.

• **1840s** Anti-Catholic (Irish) riots; troops guard churches against "Know-Nothing" bigots.

• **1854** Consolidation Act expands Philadelphia tremendously, creating a city of 154 square miles.

• **1857–61** Bank panic, stagnation, and depression burden city until Civil War.

• **1860** First baseball game played in Philadelphia.

• **1861** Civil War begins. City elite, *(continues)*

every way, boasting public hospitals and streetlights; cultural institutions and newspapers; stately Georgian architecture and Chippendale furniture; imported tea and cloth; and, above all, commerce. William Penn put the stamp of his rough genius on the young city. However, the next generation turned away from his vision of brotherly love geographically, politically, and religiously, re-creating the institutions they had known in English towns. But in the third and fourth generations men like James Logan, the first Biddles, and David Rittenhouse proved even more influential in determining a distinct Philadelphia style— genial, cooperative, and relaxed, though without the later Main Line inbred gentility. Alexander Graydon, a journalist, wrote in 1811, "of all the cities in the world, Philadelphia was for its size, perhaps, one of the most peaceable and unwarlike."

One man will always be linked with Philadelphia—multitalented, insatiably curious Benjamin Franklin. Franklin had an impulse to set things right, whether it be stoves, spectacles, or states. It sometimes seems that his hand appears in every aspect of the city worth exploring! The colonial homes with the four-hand brass plaques were protected by his fire-insurance company; the post office at 3rd and Market streets was his grandson's printing shop; the Free Library of Philadelphia, the University of Philadelphia Hospital at 8th and Pine streets, and the American Philosophical Society all were begun through Franklin's inspiration. He was an inventor, a printer, a statesman, a scientist, and a diplomat—an all-round genius.

## FROM REVOLUTION TO CIVIL WAR

Like most important Philadelphians, Franklin considered himself a loyal British subject until well into the 1770s, though he and the other Colonists were increasingly subject to what they considered capricious English policy. Philadelphia lacked the radicalism of New England, but after Lexington and Concord and the meeting of the First and Second Continental Congresses, whose delegates were housed all over Philadelphia, tremendous political debate erupted. William Allen said, "We are to be England's Milch Cow, but if they are not prudent . . . we shall turn dry upon their hands." The moderates—wealthy citizens with friends and relatives in England—held out as long as they could. But with the April 1776 decision in Independence Hall to consider drafting a declaration of independence, revolutionary fervor became unstoppable.

"These are the times that try men's souls," wrote Thomas Paine in *The Crisis*—and they certainly were for Philadelphians, with so much to lose in a war with Britain. Thomas Jefferson and John Adams talked over the situation with George Washington, Robert Morris, and other delegates at City Tavern by night and at Carpenter's Hall and Independence Hall by day. On July 2, their declaration was passed by the general Congress; on July 6, it was read to a crowd of 8,000 who tumultuously approved.

Your visit to Independence National Historical Park will fill you in on the Revolution's effect on the City of Brotherly Love. Of the major colonial cities, Philadelphia had the fewest defenses. The war came to the city itself because British troops occupied Patriot homes during the harsh winter of 1777 to 1778. Woodford, a country mansion in what is now Fairmount Park, hosted many Tory balls, while Washington's troops drilled and shivered at Valley Forge. Washington's attempt to crack the British line at Germantown ended in a confused retreat. The city later greatly benefited from the British departure and the Peace of Paris (1783), which ended the war.

Problems with the new federal government brought a Constitutional Convention to Philadelphia in 1787. This body crafted the Constitution the United States still follows. It's hard to say whether Philadelphia had an effect on the beautifully and strongly worded sessions that fostered both the Declaration of Independence and the Constitution, but its native tolerance and acuity must have stood the young country in good stead.

In the years between the ratification of the Constitution and the Civil War, Philadelphia prospered. For ten of these years, 1790 to 1800, the U.S. government operated here, while the District of Columbia was still marshland. George Washington lived in an Executive Mansion where the Liberty Bell is now; the Supreme Court met in Old City Hall; Congress met in Congress Hall; and

## DATELINE

made wealthy through Southern trade, are against the war, despite strong popular anti-slavery sentiment.

• **1862** Philadelphia is an armed camp, with tremendous demand for locomotives, uniforms, and supplies manufactured here.

• **1863** Battle of Gettysburg in July saves city from Confederate attack but with the loss of thousands of local troops.

• **1865** Antiblack riots culminate in an ordinance forbidding blacks to ride in the horsecars; Jim Crow laws persist until the 1870s. Lincoln's body lies in state in Independence Hall on its way to burial in Illinois.

• **1860–90** Rise of the saloon (6,000 by 1887) as a focus of German and Irish immigrant society.

• **1866–72** Chestnut Street bridge spurs the quick development of West Philadelphia; University of Pennsylvania moves there in 1872.

• **1874** Groundbreaking on July 4 for both City Hall and the Centennial Exhibition in Fairmount Park.

• **1876** President Grant and the emperor of Brazil open *(continues)*

**DATELINE**

the Centennial Exhibition; 38 nations and 39 states and territories are represented. First public demonstration of the telephone and other wonders of the age.

• **1878** First use of electric lighting for houses and offices; first Bell telephone exchange at 400 Chestnut Street.

• **1890** Drexel University founded at 32nd and Chestnut streets.

• **1892** First trolley car, on Catharine and Bainbridge streets.

• **1893** Reading Terminal built for Reading Railroad.

• **1894** Cobblestones replaced by asphalt on Broad Street.

• **1899** First motor car arrives in Philadelphia, brought from France by a local merchant.

• **1900** More people own houses in Philadelphia than in any other city in the world; a middle-class house with seven rooms rents for $15 per month. City's population is over 1.25 million, with 25% foreign-born.

• **1901** First Mummer's Parade marches up Broad Street on New Year's Day. It's taken from English traditions but quickly becomes a city insti-
*(continues)*

everybody met at City Tavern for balls and festivals.

In general the quality of life was high, despite a disastrous 1793 yellow fever epidemic. The legacies of Benjamin Franklin flourished, from printing and publishing to fire-insurance companies (you can still visit the period headquarters of the Contributionship and the Mutual Assurance Company). The resources of the Library Company became available to the public, and both men and women received "modern" educations—that is, with more emphasis on accounting and less on classics. The 1834 Free School Act established a democratic public school system, but such private academies as Germantown Friends School and Friends Select are still going strong today. The Walnut Street Theater, founded in 1809, is the oldest American theater still in constant use, and the Musical Fund Hall at 808 Locust Street (now apartments) hosted operas, symphony orchestras, and chamber ensembles. The 1805 Pennsylvania Academy of Fine Arts, now at Broad and Cherry streets, taught such painters as Washington Allston and the younger Peales. Charles Willson Peale, the eccentric patriarch, set up the first American museum in the Long Hall of Independence Hall; its exhibits included a portrait gallery and the first lifelike arrangements of full-size stuffed animals.

It makes sense that Philadelphia retained the federal charter to mint money, build ships, and produce weapons even after the capital moved to Washington. The transportation revolution that made America's growth possible was fueled by the city's shipyards, ironworks, and locomotive works. Philadelphia vied with Baltimore and New York City for transport routes to agricultural production inland. New York eventually won out as a shipper, thanks to its natural harbor and the Erie Canal. Philadelphia, however, was the hands-down winner in becoming America's premier manufacturing city, and it ranked even with New York in finance. The need to harness Philadelphia's neighborhoods better for large-scale enterprises, in fact, led to the 1854 incorporation of outlying suburbs into one 154-square-mile city.

During the Civil War, Philadelphia's manufacturers weren't above supplying both Yankees and Confederates with guns and rail equipment. Fortunately for the city, the Southern offensive met with bloody defeat at Gettysburg, not far away. With the end of the Civil War in 1865, port activity rebounded, as Southern cotton was spun and shipped from city textile looms. Philadelphia became the natural site for the first world's fair held on American soil: the Centennial Exposition. It's hard to imagine the excitement that filled Fairmount Park, with 200 pavilions and displays. There's a scale model in Memorial Hall, one of the few surviving structures in the park; it gives a good idea of how seriously the United States took this show of power and prestige. University City in West Philadelphia saw the establishment of campuses for Drexel University and the University of Pennsylvania, and public transport lines connected all the neighborhoods of the city.

## 20TH-CENTURY PHILADELPHIA

In the 20th century Philadelphia's fortunes have been checkered. While port and petroleum-refining operations bolstered its position as an industrial center until the 1980s, manufacturing in general has moved out of the city and the region. As industry has moved out, the city has tried to develop a tax base around service businesses. Tourism has become a major revenue source, and public and private efforts coordinate to create the relaxed but efficient attitude you'll find all over Center City. Major corporate headquarters in Philadelphia now include SmithKline Beecham (pharmaceuticals); ARA Services (food and hospitality); CoreStates, Meridian, and Mellon banks; and CIGNA (insurance).

Politically, the city in 1900 was controlled by a small core of moderate Republican bosses, most with old-Philadelphia pedigrees. Immigrant populations united behind President Franklin D. Roosevelt to swing the city Democratic in the 1930s, and in the name of unions and the liberal state, they grew their own form of abuses of government. The period 1949 to 1962, under mayors Joseph Clark (later a U.S. senator) and Richardson Dilworth, was the height of "good government" reform. It was succeeded in the 1970s by the controversial "law-and-order" administration of Frank Rizzo, who rose to fame as police commis-

# 10 · INTRODUCING PHILADELPHIA

## DATELINE

- **1929–37** Great Depression in the United States; Democratic Party strength in popular vote replaces traditional Republicanism in Philadelphia.
- **1934** With repeal of Prohibition, establishment of state liquor stores (as opposed to those privately owned). Opening of 30th Street Station, the city's main railroad terminus.
- **1936** Special June Mummer's Parade entertains Democratic Party National Convention.
- **1944** Due to World War II labor shortages, black workers make substantial gains, despite union opposition.
- **1946** First computer, ENIAC, developed at University of Pennsylvania for the U.S. Army.
- **1950** Restoration and renovation of Society Hill begins.
- **1951** National Park Service establishes Independence National Historical Park.
- **1954** Philadelphia International Airport dedicated.
- **1958** Pennsylvania Railroad merges with New York Central.
- **1950s** Pop singing stars like Fabian, Frankie Avalon, and *(continues)*

sioner trying to control the anti-Vietnam War and racial disturbances of the 1960s. Ironically, one of Rizzo's successors, Wilson Goode, is linked to the highly criticized leveling of a city block in West Philadelphia in order to protect public safety.

In terms of urban homeowners—an area in which Philadelphia led the world for decades—there have been good reasons for successful citizens to leave for pleasanter suburban areas. The urban-renewal projects at Society Hill, the commercial developments at Penn Center, the boom period of expansion along the Parkway, and the establishment of Independence National Historical Park have combated the out-migration somewhat. After a rather disappointing 300th anniversary in 1982, the city boomed during a splendid bicentennial celebration of the 1787 drafting and signing of the U.S. Constitution.

## TODAY & TOMORROW

The early 1990s have brought mixed fortunes to Philadelphia. Many of the problems that plague urban centers throughout America—homelessness, drugs, crime, and inadequate resources for public services—have hit Center City. The city was technically bankrupt in 1990, as dwindling tax revenues lagged behind bond obligations, and it remains on shaky ground. Budget balancing by new Mayor Ed Rendell and the City Council has produced pain; for example, the loss of $560,000 from the annual appropriation to the Museum of Art will mean closing many of its galleries during selected hours.

A number of projects, however, will continue the upward sweep of construction and big thinking for city improvement. In the public sector, most of the main thoroughfares leading in and out have been reconstructed, and it is now possible to get from Scranton to Independence Park without encountering any traffic lights. The below-ground Vine Street Expressway, finally reconstructed, connects Interstates 95 and 76 (along the two rivers) with plenty of easy entrances and exits. Terminal A (Dilworth Terminal) provides easier connections for international visitors, and the airport is also benefiting from a $40-million facelift and a new runway.

No one can ignore that Philadelphia has finally entered the age of the superskyscraper with One Liberty Place, the energetic and gracious 945-foot spire. In fact, the northwest side of Center City, spurred by private finance and developments, has quietly become the central axis of Philadelphia's regional prestige. The 150,000-square-foot Shops at Liberty Place are the true flagship of city merchandising, after a decade of retrenchment in such institutions as Wanamaker's and Bonwit Teller. Other megaliths planned or completed are the 58-story Two Liberty Place, the 54-story One Mellon Center at 18th and Market streets, 1919 Market Street, the Bell Atlantic Building, and a second tower at Commerce Square. What all these projects have done, however, is leave the fabled Rittenhouse Square area, especially Chestnut Street, looking a bit seedy by comparison, and these locations must redevelop to maintain their cachet.

Development along the waterfront area has similarly bypassed grandiose urban-renewal plans on either side of the 37-acre city-owned Penn's Landing at the foot of Market Street. If building happens—and the location and views would be terrific—it will be private and piecemeal. Most of the excitement is happening well north of the Benjamin Franklin Bridge (several clubs and restaurants) or well south of South Street. In addition, the Philadelphia Maritime Museum will take over the Port of History Museum right on the waterfront, and the Delawhale ferry to the new Camden Aquarium should boost traffic.

A private partnership has also leased 30th Street Station and is spending some $80 million to add a new 450-car underground garage and a food court and to install air conditioning. The station gleams anew as of 1992. Further in the future, the aim is to build office buildings connecting directly to the station over 66 acres of tracks north of the station, providing a state-of-the-art business complex midway between New York City and Washington, D.C. Meanwhile, Rittenhouse Square, South Street, and South Broad Street are all developing more services and places for the visitor to Philadelphia. The John F. Kennedy Stadium has been demolished; there's a new Spectrum II to house the 76ers and Flyers in luxury, and the

## DATELINE

Chubby Checker emerge from Philadelphia neighborhoods.

• **1960** Dr. John Gibbons invents heart-lung machine at Jefferson Medical Center.

• **1964, 1967** Racial disturbances, said to have been aggravated by Police Commissioner Frank Rizzo, who would serve as mayor from 1972 to 1980.

• **1964** Society Hill Towers, symbolic of old and new in the neighborhood, constructed to design of I. M. Pei.

• **1974** Chestnut Street urban mall project built; seen as a failure by 1980.

• **1975** Philadelphia Flyers win National Hockey League's Stanley Cup.

• **1976** Liberty Bell moved from Congress Hall to the new Independence Mall; America's Bicentennial celebrated.

• **1980** Phillies win their first World Series championship.

• **1982** Philadelphia's 300th anniversary celebration. Tall ships line Penn's Landing.

• **1984–92** Administration of Wilson Goode, Philadelphia's first black mayor, tainted by the 1985 MOVE bombing of a city

*(continues)*

**DATELINE**

block in West Phila-
delphia in the name
of law and order.
• **1987** Bicentennial
of U.S. Constitution
celebrated at Inde-
pendence Hall.

old Spectrum will host more concerts, truck pulls, and one-of-a-kind events.

Pride in the past and measured optimism for the future are now the predominant attitudes in Philadelphia. William Penn couldn't have wished for anything more.

# FAMOUS PHILADELPHIANS

**Richard Allen** (1760–1831) Born enslaved to a Pennsylvania attorney general, he became an itinerant Methodist preacher and eventually the founder and first bishop of the original African Methodist Episcopal Church, still at 419 S. Sixth Street.

**Marian Anderson** (b. 1902) A noted contralto, she began her career in the Union Baptist Church Choir and broke operatic racial barriers throughout America. In 1955 she both made her Metropolitan Opera debut and served as a U.S. delegate to the United Nations.

**Nicholas Biddle** (1786–1844) Born of old Philadelphia stock, he was a scholar and literary figure until the War of 1812 and was drawn into a directorship of the Second Bank of the United States. Thanks to his hard work and talent, he became president of the Second Bank from 1823 to 1839, resigning after the controversy with President Andrew Jackson over the bank's right to a national charter. His home in Andalusia is still an attraction.

**David Brenner** (b. 1945) A comedian with a B.A. from Temple University, he was a producer at KYW–TV before going solo. His 1983 autobiography, *Soft Pretzels with Mustard,* is a minor Philadelphia classic.

**Mary Cassatt** (1845–1926) An Impressionist painter from an old Philadelphia family (her brother, president of the Pennsylvania Railroad, lived on the current site of the Rittenhouse Hotel), she lived in Paris from 1874. A protégée of Degas, Cassatt is noted for figures of washerwomen and domestic scenes in pastels, oils, and especially etchings.

**John Coltrane** (1926–67) A jazz musician and composer who spent his adolescence in North Philly, practicing at the AME Zion Church at 12th and Oxford streets, he joined the Miles Davis Quintet in 1955. He later struck out on his own, with African and Indian-influenced, highly cerebral and arpeggioed jazz.

**Bill Cosby** (b. 1937) An entertainer, a comedian, an actor, and an author born in Germantown, he has a B.A. from Temple. After winning several Emmys, he ended eight years on the hugely popular "Cosby Show" in 1992. He then moved on to a new show, "You Bet Your Life."

**Thomas Eakins** (1844–1916) He was the quintessential painter and teacher and was generally considered, with Winslow Homer, to be a leading American artist of the 19th century. Eakins spent his life in Philadelphia, except for study trips to Europe, rising from student to teacher. Eventually, he was forced to resign from the Pennsylvania

## IMPRESSIONS

*I have never observed such a wealth of taverns and drinking
establishments as are in Philadelphia. . . . There is hardly a street
without several and hardly a man here who does not fancy one
his second home.*
—THOMAS JEFFERSON, LETTER TO A VIRGINIA FRIEND, 1790

*The question eagerly put to me by every one in Philadelphia is,
'Don't you think the city greatly improved?' They seem to me to
confound augmentation with improvement. It always was a fine
city, since I first knew it; and it is very greatly augmented.*
—WILLIAM COBBETT, *A YEAR'S RESIDENCE IN THE UNITED STATES OF
AMERICA*, 1817–19

---

Academy of Fine Arts. His work emphasizes the human figure and
the dignity of common things; his *Clinic of Dr. Gross* (1875) is a
well-known masterpiece.

**W. C. Fields**   (1880–1946) He ran away from home at 11 to
perfect his vaudeville skills, then moved on to the theater, the
Ziegfeld Follies, and the movies. His best-known film roles were in
*The Bank Dick* (1940) and as Mr. Micawber in *David Copperfield*
(1935).

**Benjamin Franklin**   (1706–90) He was a ubiquitous talent as a
statesman, a printer, a citizen, a scientist, and an inventor. There
probably wouldn't have been a United States without him; he
shepherded American interests at home and abroad for 60 years.

**Kelly Family**   Patriarch John Kelly (1889–1960) championed
the rise of the Irish by becoming an Olympic rowing medalist, the
Democratic Party chairman from 1934 to 1941, and a multimillion-
aire construction contractor. His son Jack also won an Olympic
rowing medal, and his daughter Grace (1929–80) rose to stardom in

---

## IMPRESSIONS

*It is a handsome city, but distractingly regular. After walking about
it for an hour or two, I felt that I would have given the world for a
crooked street. The collar of my coat appeared to stiffen, and the
brim of my hat to expand, beneath its Quakery influence. My hair
shrunk into a sleek short crop, my hands folded themselves upon
my breast of their own calm accord, and thoughts of taking
lodgings in Mark Lane over against the Market Place, and of
making a large fortune by speculations in corn, came over me
involuntarily.*
—CHARLES DICKENS, *AMERICAN NOTES*, 1842

*The vast extent of the streets of small, low, yet snug-looking
houses. . . . Philadelphia must contain in comfort the largest
number of small householders of any city in the world.*
—LONDON *TIMES* REPORTER WILLIAM RUSSELL, *MY DIARY NORTH
AND SOUTH*, 1850

theater and films (such as *Rear Window* and *The Country Girl*, both 1954) before marrying Prince Rainier of Monaco.

**Patti LaBelle**   (b. 1944) Born Patricia Louise Holte, she began with the Bluebelles and has sung and acted solo since 1977. Her 1986 album "Winner In You" went platinum, and her film roles include *A Soldier's Story* (1985).

**Eugene Ormandy**   (1899–1981) Born in Hungary, he led the Philadelphia Orchestra for over 40 legendary years, giving its string and brass sections an instantly recognizable sheen and richness. He was a pioneer in orchestral recordings.

**Charles Willson Peale**   (1741–1827) A portrait painter and naturalist, he moved to Philadelphia in 1776, just in time to establish a career painting official portraits of the U.S. founders. An accomplished collector with 16 children, he also established the first American museum in Independence Hall. He helped found the Pennsylvania Academy of Fine Arts in 1805.

**Teddy Pendergrass**   (b. 1950) A singer with a romantic, rich bass, he recorded many hits including "If You Don't Know Me By Now." He now lives and works out of suburban Bala Cynwyd.

**William Penn**   (1644–1718) The founder of Philadelphia, Penn had a nature in many ways combining doses of peevishness and idealism that led to his personal tragedies. (See the description in this chapter.)

**Betsy Ross**   (1752–1836) She was a seamstress and an upholsterer with important relatives. It is said she made the first flag of the United States at the request of George Washington. A visit to her modest house at 239 Arch Street is recommended.

**Benjamin Rush**   (1745–1813) The most influential doctor and public-health figure in the colonies and the young United States, he also promoted Thomas Paine to agitate for American independence. His theory of treatment by purging blood proved disastrous during the 1793 yellow fever epidemic, yet his clinical analyses set standards for American medicine.

**Owen Wister**   (1860–1938) This dilettante member of an old Philadelphia family defined the Western hero in his novel *The Virginian* (1902), an influence on innumerable movie plots.

# 2. RECOMMENDED BOOKS & FILMS

## BOOKS
### HISTORY

It is impossible to read about the transition from the Colonies to the United States and the first 50 years of independence without learning about Philadelphia. Carl Bridenbaugh's *Rebels and Gentlemen* (Oxford University Press, 1965) is a good summary of events leading

## IMPRESSIONS

*Of all goodly villages, the very goodliest, probably, in the world;
the very largest, and flattest, and smoothest. . . . The absence of
the note of the perpetual perpendicular, the New York, the
Chicago note, . . . seemed to symbolize exactly the principle of
indefinite level extension and to offer, refreshingly, a
challenge . . . to absolute centrifugal motion.*
—HENRY JAMES, *THE AMERICAN SCENE*, 1905

---

up to independence. Catherine Drinker Bowen's *Miracle at Philadelphia* (Atlantic–Little, Brown, 1960) is a vivid retelling of the 1787 Constitutional Convention. A Bancroft Prize–winner is Thomas Doerflinger's *A Vigorous Spirit of Enterprise: Merchants and Economic Development in Revolutionary Philadelphia* (University of North Carolina Press, 1986).

E. Digby Baltzell's *Puritan Boston and Quaker Philadelphia* (Free Press, 1980) is a thoughtful and amusing comparison between these two preeminent colonial cities, explaining why their histories turned out so differently—in particular, why the emphasis placed on keeping a civil society dampened outstanding individual achievements in Philadelphia. Baltzell's first classic effort here was *Philadelphia Gentlemen: The Making of a National Upper Class* (Free Press, 1958).

The transformation from ideal seaport to ideal manufacturing city is covered in *Civil War Issues in Philadelphia 1856-1865* by William Dusinberre (University of Pennsylvania Press, 1965). *Magee's Illustrated Guide of Philadelphia and the Centennial Exhibition* (1876) is a treat of civic pride, with wonderful lithographs throughout.

W. E. B. Du Bois's *The Philadelphia Negro* (University of Pennsylvania Press, 1899) is a classic analysis of racism and its social effects in the North since the Civil War. Jean Seder has edited *Voices of Another Time: 3 Memories* (Institute for the Study of Human Issues, 1985), three oral histories of Afro-American women who were born in the South but who spent their lives in Philadelphia, complete with recipes, cures, and proverbs.

Edwin Wolf II's *Philadelphia: Portrait of an American City* (Stackpole Books, 1975) is one of the more engaging recent histories, with beautiful and appropriate illustrations. The building of the Benjamin Franklin Parkway, a swath like the Champs Elysées in the midst of a colonial grid, is covered in David Bruce Brownlee's *Building the City Beautiful* (Philadelphia Museum of Art catalog, 1989).

Philadelphia in the Mayor Rizzo years is covered in Conrad Weiler's *Philadelphia: Neighborhood, Authority and the Urban Crisis* (Praeger, 1974). Of the three books on the MOVE tragedy, try Charles Bowser's *Let the Bunker Burn* (Camino Books, 1989).

## THE ARTS

There is a surfeit of material on Philadelphia's architecture; try *Philadelphia Architecture* (MIT Press, 1984), which goes into environmental issues as well, or George B. Tatum's *Penn's Great Town* (University of Pennsylvania Press, 1981) for a survey of historic houses. Roslyn Brenner's *Philadelphia's Outdoor Art: A Walking Tour* (Camino Books, 1987) has a makeshift text but contains good photography. *Center City Philadelphia: The Elements of Style* (University of Pennsylvania Press, 1984) examines artistic works involving views of Philadelphia.

The collection of essays gathered in *In This Academy* (Philadelphia Academy of Fine Arts, 1976), the bicentennial catalog of the academy, is an excellent introduction to the historic preeminence of the city's classical art tradition. The *Treasures of the Philadelphia Museum of Art* (1973) is stunning but less complete than one might expect. The catalog of the museum's 1982 Thomas Eakins exhibition, by Darrel Sewell, is outstanding.

Fredric Miller has put together two superb photographic histories of the city: *Still Philadelphia*, covering 1890 to 1940, and *Philadelphia Stories*, covering 1920 to 1960—both published by Temple University Press. Robert Llewellyn has also assembled a sensitive book of contemporary photographs *Philadelphia* (Thomasson-Grant, 1986).

## FICTION, TRAVEL & BIOGRAPHY

**FICTION**   Try Pete Dexter's *God's Pocket* (Warner Books, 1990) for a gritty contemporary look at the city by a former newspaper reporter turned big-league novelist and scriptwriter. Donald Zochert's *Murder in the Hellfire Club* (Holt, Rinehart & Winston, 1978) is an amusing historical mystery, with Colonists framed in London of the 1770s and Ben Franklin on hand to solve the case. S. Weir Mitchell's *Hugh Wynne, Free Quaker* and *The Red City* are verbose but gain from being almost family history, written about the 1790s in the 1910s.

**TRAVEL**   If you find old guidebooks fascinating, consult *Magee's Illustrated Guide* for the 1876 city (see "History," above) or the *Federal Writer's Project Guide to Philadelphia* (1937; Scholar Press, reprint 1978). Witty and perceptive is Christopher Morley (1890–1957), the Haverford-born author of *Kitty Foyle* and recent subject of a Rosenbach Museum show; a selection from his *Travels in Philadelphia* has been published as *Christopher Morley's Philadelphia* (Fordham University Press, 1990). *Bicentennial City: Walking Tours of Historic Philadelphia* (Pyne Press, 1974), by John Francis Marion, is fine, although it's definitely dated and presupposes a real "inside" knowledge of the city's history and personages.

In terms of geography, a look at Richard Saul Wurman's *Manmade Philadelphia: A Guide to Its Physical and Cultural Environment* (MIT Press, 1972) is eye-opening. Wurman, now an innovative travel writer, sharpened his eye with this project.

**BIOGRAPHY**   John Lukacs's *Philadelphia: Patricians & Philistines 1900–1950* (Farrar, Straus & Giroux, 1981) is a charming, slightly offbeat collection of profiles of seven colorful figures who flourished during this period and have faded into obscurity since. The book opens and concludes with wonderful ruminations on what made Philadelphia so different—its geniality and datedness.

One of those chronicled by Lukacs, Albert C. Barnes of the legendary Barnes Foundation and its Reniors, is further examined in Howard Greenfield's *The Devil and Dr. Barnes: A Portrait of an American Art Collector* (Viking, 1987).

The Kelly family—John, Jack, and Grace—receives a hagiographic and slightly dated treatment in John McCallum's *That Kelly Family* (A.S. Barnes, 1957). Another "immigrant-made-good" story, although more measured, is the biography of former Mayor Frank Rizzo, Joseph Daughen's *The Cop Who Would Be King* (Little, Brown, 1977).

## FOR KIDS

Robert Lawson's classic *Ben and Me* (Houghton Mifflin, 1939) tells of Ben Franklin's career through a mouse's view of the telescope. Katherine Milhous's *Through These Arches: The Story of Independence Hall* (Lippincott, 1965) is illustrated and engaging. For younger readers there's Elvajeen Hall's *Today in Old Philadelphia* (Children's Press, 1975), combining historic buildings and sights with daily life. In *The Treasure Code* by Milton Dank (Delacorte, 1985), six junior-high students search for a dragonring, a valuable treasure buried somewhere in the city; included are lots of clues and comments. John Loeper's *The House on Spruce Street* (Atheneum, 1984) concentrates on Philadelphia history during the restoring of a grand old Society Hill house.

Elizabeth Gray Vining's *The Taken Girl* (Viking, 1972) is a lovely story of an orphan girl taken on as a helper in the 1840s Quaker household of John Greenleaf Whittier and how she becomes involved in the antislavery movement. In Susan Lee's *The Fall of the Quaker City* (Children's Press, 1975), a Quaker family must decide whether to support the American Revolution.

## FILMS

The classic *The Philadelphia Story* (1940), adapted from a play by Philip Barry, involves a headstrong Philadelphia socialite who learns to find love with her first husband, on the eve of her wedding to a very proper second husband. The film stars Katharine Hepburn, Cary Grant, and Jimmy Stewart (who won a Best Actor Oscar). Alfred Hitchcock's psychological study *Marnie* (1964) is partly set in Philadelphia.

Films of the 1970s and 80s include Sylvester Stallone's *Rocky* (1976), in which the young South Philadelphia boxer jogs through the Italian Market at 9th and Catharine and up the Art Museum steps, as well as its sequels; *Blowout* (1983), in which John Travolta as a sound technician hears mysterious noises when a presidential candidate's car runs off a Wissahickon Creek bridge; and *Witness* (1985), in which Harrison Ford plays a Philadelphia detective forced to go undercover in Amish country.

# CHAPTER 2

# PLANNING A TRIP TO PHILADELPHIA

1. **INFORMATION & MONEY**
- **WHAT THINGS COST IN PHILADELPHIA**
2. **WHEN TO GO**
- **PHILADELPHIA CALENDAR OF EVENTS**
3. **TIPS FOR THE DISABLED, SENIORS, SINGLES, FAMILIES & STUDENTS**
4. **GETTING THERE**
- **FROMMER'S SMART TRAVELER: AIRFARES**

This chapter is devoted to the where, when, and how of your trip—the advance-planning issues required to get it together and take it on the road.

After deciding where to go, most people have two fundamental questions: What will it cost? and How do I get there? This chapter will answer both questions and also resolve other important questions, such as when to go, what insurance coverage is necessary, and where to obtain more information about Philadelphia for special needs.

---

## 1. INFORMATION & MONEY

---

**INFORMATION** The **Philadelphia Visitors Center**, 16th Street and John F. Kennedy Boulevard, Philadelphia, PA 19102 (tel. 215/636-1666, or toll free 800/537-7676), should be your first resource. They offer a wealth of publications, from seasonal calendars of events to maps; knowledgeable volunteers staff their phones. If you obtain nothing else, request the "Official Visitors Guide," an annual compendium. Guest Informant, an outfit that places upscale city guides in hotel rooms, has recently started **"Quick City Guide,"** a 40-page brochure that provides the basics and is issued every four months. It's dropped in lobbies all over town, but you can write or call for a copy at 1700 Walnut St., Suite 1025, Philadelphia, PA 19103 (tel. 215/546-5155).

**MONEY** Except for truly deluxe experiences, you will find moderate prices in Philadelphia: less than those in New York and on a par with or slightly above those in Washington, D.C. Expenses for a family of four staying in a hotel, with meals in restaurants and a healthy dose of sightseeing in Independence Park (all free) and museums, should run about $200 per day.

Minimal cash is required, since credit cards are accepted universally and automatic-teller machines linked to national networks are strewn around tourist destinations and increasingly within hotels. To get more specific information on the **Cirrus** network, call toll free 800/424-7787; for the **Plus** system, call toll free 800/843-7587. If you're planning to explore Philadelphia in unusual neighborhoods, at unusual hours, or in a style that will make you conspicuous, you would be well advised to carry cash in the form of traveler's checks. Center City has recently responded to visible signs of urban distress, including tourist crime, with a combination of police staffing and specially identified "Community Ambassadors," so incidents are rare under normal circumstances. Should anything occur, the three major traveler's check agencies are **American Express** (tel. toll free 800/221-7282); **BankAmerica** (tel. toll free 800/227-3460); and **VISA** (tel. toll free 800/227-6811).

| WHAT THINGS COST IN PHILADELPHIA | U.S. $ |
|---|---|
| Taxi from the airport to Center City | 25.00 |
| Airport train to Center City (cash on board) | 5.75 |
| Local telephone call | .25 |
| Double at Ritz-Carlton Philadelphia (deluxe) | 205.00 |
| Double at Philadelphia Hilton and Towers (expensive) | 145.00 |
| Double at Holiday Inn–Independence Mall (moderate) | 113.00 |
| Double at Comfort Inn at Penn's Landing (budget) | 75.00 |
| Two-course lunch for one at The Garden (expensive) | 15.00 |
| Two-course lunch for one at the Food Court at Liberty Place (budget) | 6.00 |
| Three-course dinner for one at Dilullo Centro (expensive) | 40.00 |
| Three-course dinner at The Magnolia Café (moderate) | 27.00 |
| Three-course dinner at Marabella's (inexpensive) | 18.00 |
| Bottle of beer | 2.50 |
| Coca-Cola | 1.50 |
| Cup of coffee | 1.25 |
| Roll of ASA 100 Kodacolor film, 36 exposures | 5.00 |
| Admission to Philadelphia Museum of Art | 6.00 |
| Movie ticket | 7.50 |
| Concert ticket at the Academy of Music | 15.00–40.00 |

# 2. WHEN TO GO

Philadelphia has four distinct seasons with temperatures ranging from the 90s (F) in summer to the 30s (F) in winter, although below-zero (F) temperatures normally hit only one out of every four winters. Summers tend to be humid, so pack lightweight, comfortable clothes in light colors if you plan to be in the sun. In the fall, the weather becomes drier; heavier cottons, light knits, and wools are the best bet, with a sweater or jacket for the evening. Winter wear requires more layers with heavier wools. Spring is variable; count on comfortable breezes and keep a jacket on hand.

## AVERAGE TEMPERATURE AND PRECIPITATION IN PHILADELPHIA

|       | High (°F) | Low (°F) | Precipitation (Days) |
|-------|-----------|----------|----------------------|
| Jan   | 40        | 26       | 11                   |
| Feb   | 41        | 26       | 9                    |
| Mar   | 50        | 33       | 11                   |
| Apr   | 62        | 43       | 11                   |
| May   | 73        | 53       | 11                   |
| June  | 81        | 63       | 10                   |
| July  | 95        | 68       | 9                    |
| Aug   | 95        | 66       | 9                    |
| Sept  | 80        | 60       | 8                    |
| Oct   | 66        | 49       | 8                    |
| Nov   | 54        | 39       | 10                   |
| Dec   | 43        | 29       | 10                   |

# PHILADELPHIA CALENDAR OF EVENTS

You'll probably want to time your visit to Philadelphia to coincide with some merrymaking or special celebration. That isn't hard—in fact, you'll almost always find something awaiting you! For more details, contact the **Convention and Visitors Bureau,** 1515 John F. Kennedy Blvd., Philadelphia, PA 19106 (tel. 215/636-1666).

## JANUARY

✪ **MUMMER'S PARADE** *Starting in late morning and lasting most of the day, spangled strutters march with feathers and banjos in a celebration that must have been pagan in origin. If you go to the Mummer's Museum, the gaudiness and elaborateness of the costumes won't amaze you quite so much. But the music (everyone ends up humming "Oh, Dem Golden Slippers" sooner or later) and gaiety will have you entranced.*

*Where: Broad Street, from South Philadelphia up to City Hall. When: January 1; the following Saturday in case of poor weather. How: Just line up on Broad Street, dressed for winter. If you want reserved seats, they're available from early December at the Convention and Visitors Bureau for $2.*

☐ **Benjamin Franklin's Birthday,** The Franklin Institute. Call 215/448-1200 for details. Mid-month Sunday.

## FEBRUARY

☐ **Chinese New Year.** You can enjoy dragons and fireworks at 11th and Arch streets, traditional 10-course banquets, or a visit to the Chinese Cultural Center at 125 N. 10th Street. Call 215/923-6767 for details. Between late January and mid-month.

☐ **Black History Month.** The Afro-American Museum, 7th and Arch streets offers a full complement of exhibitions, lectures, and music. Call 215/574-0380 for details. All month long.

☐ **George Washington's Birthday.** Valley Forge Historical Park holds a Cherries Jubilee weekend. Call 215/783-7700 for details. Third Sunday and Monday.

☐ **Spectator Presidential Jazz Weekend.** More than 90 events are held around the clock, from concerts to screenings and meals. Call 215/636-1666 for details. Presidents' Day weekend.

☐ **U.S. Pro Indoor Tennis Championships.** This event features some of the world's best players. At the Spectrum. Call 215/947-2530 for particulars. Third weekend.

## MARCH

☐ **Philadelphia Flower and Garden Show,** at the Civic Center, 34th Street and Civic Center Boulevard. It's the largest in the country, with acres of gardens and rustic settings. There are usually tickets at the door, but the Pennsylvania Horticultural Society at 325 Walnut Street sells them in advance. Call 215/625-8253 for information. First half of month.

✪ *THE BOOK AND THE COOK FESTIVAL* For the past several years, Philadelphia has combined the love of reading and eating into this festival. For five days, eminent food critics, cookbook authors, and restaurateurs are invited to plan dream meals with participating city restaurants. If you're a "foodie," you know that the chance to stroll through Reading Terminal Market with Alice Waters, or to dine on what she turns up, is not to be declined. The festival has recently expanded into wine and beer tastings.
*Where: All over town. When: Usually the third week in March. How: Call 215/686-7602 for a schedule and to make a reservation.*

☐ **St. Patrick's Day Parade.** The parade starts at noon on 20th Street and the Parkway. Call the Visitors Bureau for details. The Irish Pub at 2007 Walnut Street will be packed. March 17.

## APRIL

☐ **Philadelphia Antiques Show.** Started in 1961, this is probably the finest in the nation. 103rd Engineers Armory, 33rd and Market streets. Call 215/687-6441 for information. First weekend.

☐ **Valborgsmassoafton** (St. Walpurgis Night). This welcomes the arrival of spring, aided by the American Swedish Museum. Call 215/389-1776 for information. Second half of month.

☐ **American Music Theater Festival.** In its tenth year in 1993, this festival offers premieres of music-theater works by major American artists, ranging from traditional Broadway-bound musicals to avant-garde works. Call 215/988-9050 for information. Through June.

☐ **Easter Sunday.** This day brings fashion shows and music to Rittenhouse Square. The Easter Bunny usually makes an appearance at Wanamaker's and the Gallery. Call 215/686-2876 for details. April 11 in 1993, April 3 in 1994.

☐ **Spring Tour of Fairmount Park.** The dogwoods and cherry trees along both sides of the Schuylkill are in blossom. Trolleybuses make a special run along Wissahickon Creek, a lovely woodland minutes away from Center City. Call 215/636-1666 for details. Last Sunday (or first in May).

## MAY

☐ **Philadelphia Open House.** These tours—35 in 1992!—give you a rare chance to see Germantown, Society Hill, and University City mansions. Call 215/928-1188 for information. Late April to early May.

☐ **Rittenhouse Square Flower Market.** This has been an annual event since 1914. Plants, flowers, baked goodies, and lemon sticks are some of the irresistibles for sale. Call 215/525-7182 for details. Third Thursday.

Also, the azaleas behind the Museum of Art literally stop traffic with their brilliance—there are over 2,000 azaleas and rhododendrons exhibiting their finery, and you have to look at them to believe the splendor.

☐ **Mozart on the Square.** Also around Rittenhouse Square, this festival brings about 20 chamber performances of good younger talent to town. Performances cost $5 to $15; for information contact P.O. Box 237, Merion Station, PA 19006 (tel. 215/668-1799). All month.

☐ **International Theater Festival for Children.** Another new tradition, this takes place on or near the University of Pennsylvania campus, based at 3680 Walnut Street. Call 215/898-6791 for programs and prices. Last week of month.

☐ **Israel Independence Day.** This holiday brings a Center City parade and daylong Israeli bazaar to the Parkway. Call 215/922-7222 for details. Sunday in mid-May.

☐ **Jambalaya Jam.** This was cooked up as a way for Philadelphia to pay homage to New Orleans and to use its own waterfront better. It's based at the Great Plaza at Penn's Landing, and the best of Dixieland and zydeco and Cajun and Creole cuisine are in full force. In recent years, Dr. John and the Preservation Hall Jazz Band have been in attendance. Call 215/636-1666 for particulars. Late May.

☐ **Devon Horse Show,** Route 30, Devon. This event outside Philadelphia includes jumping competitions and carriage races and a great country fair, with plenty of food stalls under cheerful awnings. Call 215/688-1312 for details. End of month.

☐ **Dad Vail Regatta.** This is one of the largest collegiate rowing events in the country. You can picnic on East River Drive near Strawberry Mansion. Call 215/582-7844 for details. Second weekend.

## JUNE

☐ **Rittenhouse Square Fine Arts Annual.** Philadelphia moves outdoors with this event, in which hundreds of professional and

student artworks go on sale. Call 215/634-5060 for details. First two weeks.
- ☐ **Head House Square.** Local craftspeople, food vendors, and street artists set up shop on Saturday from noon to midnight, Sunday from noon to 6pm. Throughout summer.
- ☐ **Elfreth's Alley Days.** The row-house dwellers, many in colonial costumes, open up their homes for inspection and admiration. First weekend.
- ☐ **CoreStates Pro Cycling Championships.** The 156-mile-long course starts and finishes on the Parkway. First weekend.
- ☐ **Betsy Ross House.** Flag Day festivities are held here. June 14.
- ☐ **Mellon Jazz Festival.** A top-drawer collection of artists are featured in the Mann Music Center and the Academy of Music. Second or third week.
- ☐ **Bloomsday.** The Irish Pub at 2007 Walnut Street celebrates the 24-hour time span of James Joyce's novel, *Ulysses.* June 16.

## JULY

✪ *FREEDOM FESTIVAL  The whole town turns out for this festival to celebrate America's birthday with fountains, theater, free entertainment, and assorted pageantry.*
   ***Where:*** *Principal locations are the terrace by the Philadelphia Museum of Art, John F. Kennedy Plaza, Rittenhouse Square, and Independence Mall.* ***When:*** *Week before July 4. The Fourth of July brings special ceremonies to Independence Square, including a reading of the Declaration of Independence and a parade. There's also a Schuylkill regatta on the Fourth.* ***How:*** *Call 215/636-1666 for information.*

- ☐ **Philadelphia Orchestra Summer Concerts,** Mann Music Center in Fairmount Park. The concerts are free on Monday, Wednesday, and Thursday through August. Also, there are pop concerts at low prices at Robin Hood Dell East and dance at Art Museum Terrace.
- ☐ **Sound-and-Light Show.** Independence Square. Nightly through Labor Day.
- ☐ **Riverblues.** Annual blues festival on Penn's Landing. Call 215/636-1666 for details.

## AUGUST

- ☐ **Philadelphia Folk Festival,** Suburban Poole Farm, Schwenksville. This festival has a national reputation and brings major crowds. Call 215/242-0150 for details. Late month.
   Even more authentic (and unpronounceable!) is the **Goschenhoppen Folk Festival** in East Greenville, one hour away—call 215/754-6013 for the scoop.
- ☐ **Pennsylvania Dutch Festival.** Reading Terminal Market venue for quilts, music, food, crafts, and such. Daily throughout month.

## SEPTEMBER

- ☐ **Fairmount Park Festival.** This festival includes the Harvest

Show at Memorial Hall and parades of varying themes down the Parkway almost every weekend. Through November.

☐ **Penn's Landing In-Water Boat Show.** This show features yachts and boats of all shapes and sizes. $5 admission. Second weekend.

☐ **Philadelphia Distance Run.** One of the nation's premier tests, it's a half-marathon through Center City and Fairmount Park. In town, it's bigger than the November marathon and gets plenty of national running figures. Call 215/665-8500 if you wish to join the field of 7,500. Usually the third Sunday.

## OCTOBER

☐ **Battle of Germantown Reenactment.** The disastrous defeat for Washington is reenacted each autumn at Cliveden, 6401 Germantown Avenue. Early in month.

☐ **Columbus Day Parade.** Parkway. Also look for South Philadelphia fairs. Second Monday.

✪ *SUPER SUNDAY Think of a party for an entire city—that's Super Sunday, held on the Parkway from Logan Circle to the Museum of Art. There are clowns, jugglers, mimes, rides, craft vendors, and a flea market. The museums and academies along the Parkway have sponsored this since 1970, rain or shine, and most have reduced admissions and special events. This is one day when parking on the grass won't get you a ticket.*
    ***Where:*** *Benjamin Franklin Parkway.* ***When:*** *Third Sunday.* ***How:*** *Call 215/665-1050 for information.*

## NOVEMBER

☐ **Philadelphia Marathon.** The finish line is at Independence Hall. Sunday at mid-month.

☐ **Virginia Slims Women's Tennis Championships,** Spectrum. Call 215/568-4444 for details. Second week.

☐ **Thanksgiving Day Parade.** This parade features cartoon characters, bands, floats, and Santa Claus. Fourth Thursday.

## DECEMBER

☐ **Holiday Activities Around Town.** It's not surprising that Christmas occasions lots of activities in Center City, beginning with the tree-lighting in City Hall courtyard. The Gallery at Market East, "A Christmas Carol" at Strawbridge and Clothier, a Colonial Christmas Village at Market Place East, and Wanamaker's all host elaborate extravaganzas, with organs and choruses. The Society Hill and Germantown Christmas walking tours are lovely, with the same leafy decorations as Fairmount Park. All month long.

☐ **Christmas Tours of Fairmount Park and Germantown.** Colonial mansions sparkle with wreaths, holly, and fruit arrangements donated by local garden clubs. Call 215/763-8100 or 215/848-1777 for details. From mid-month.

☐ **Dickens Christmas Party.** The Ebenezer Maxwell Mansion in Chestnut Hill hosts an annual party with Wassail bowls, readings, and Victorian toys and dolls. Admission is $4 for adults, $2 for children. Call 215/438-1861 for information. Two Sundays before Christmas.

☐ **Private Lights.** For an unusual Christmas experience, visit the 2700 block of South Colorado Street, south of Oregon Avenue, between 17th and 18th streets. The sight of some 40 houses bathed in interconnected strands of holiday lights is not to be believed. All month long.

☐ **Lucia Fest,** Old Swedes' Church. It sounds Italian, but the Lucia Fest is a Swedish pageant held by candlelight. First weekend.

☐ **Nutcracker Ballet.** The Pennsylvania Ballet performs Tchaikovsky's classic at the Academy of Music. Call 215/893-1935 for details. Most of month.

☐ **New Year's Eve.** Fireworks are held at the Great Plaza of Penn's Landing. December 31.

# 3. TIPS FOR THE DISABLED, SENIORS, SINGLES, FAMILIES & STUDENTS

**FOR THE DISABLED** Philadelphia is accessible to the disabled in favorite tourist areas. Even though many streets in Society Hill and bordering Independence National Historical Park have uneven brick sidewalks and Dock Street itself is paved with rough cobblestones, all curbs are well-cut at intersections. The same is true for Chestnut Street, the Parkway, and the University of Pennsylvania campus. Virtually all theaters and stadiums accommodate wheelchairs. Call ahead to plan routes. To aid the hearing impaired, the Academy of Music provides free infrared headsets for concerts; the Annenberg Center rents them for $2.

A national resource, the **Travel Information Service** at Moss Rehabilitation Hospital, 1200 W. Tabor Rd., Philadelphia, PA 19141 (tel. 215/329-5715, ext. 2233) charges $5 for a full kit of information for Philadelphia (or any other destination).

For basic information, contact the **Mayor's Commission on People with Disabilities,** Room 143, City Hall, Philadelphia, PA 19107 (tel. 215/686-2798). SEPTA publishes a special "Transit Guide for the Disabled"; you can request it from **SEPTA Special Services,** 130 S. 9th St., Philadelphia, PA 19107 (tel. 215/580-7365). The most popular bus routes are accessible; the subway is not.

The Free Library of Philadelphia runs a **Library for the Blind and Physically Handicapped,** very conveniently located at 919 Walnut Street (tel. 925-3213); it's open Monday to Friday from 9am to 5pm. It adjoins the **Associated Services for the Blind,** which offers transcriptions into braille for a fee.

If you travel with Amtrak or Greyhound/Trailways, be aware that on the former you can receive a 25% discount and a special seat with advance notification (tel. toll free 800/523-6590) and on the latter a free seat for a companion (tel. toll free 800/345-3109).

**FOR SENIORS** Seniors should bring some form of photo ID

because many city attractions grant special discounts, especially during weekdays. Some hotels, too, will shift their rates, particularly on weekends. The Convention and Visitors Bureau publishes "Seniors on the Go," which lists dozens of specific benefits around town—from flat taxi fares to museum admissions; write ahead or pick it up at the Visitors Center. They'll also give you a "Ben's Pass for Senior Citizens," good for a calendar year.

If you haven't already done so, think about joining the **American Association of Retired Persons (AARP),** 1909 K St. NW, Washington, DC 20049 (tel. 202/872-4700). Their Purchase Privilege Program unlocks an incredible chest of discounts.

Many seniors prefer places with convenient local transportation between sites, and Philadelphia is wonderful in this regard. Seniors might consider the SEPTA DayPass ($4), available at the Visitors Center at 16th Street and John F. Kennedy Boulevard, which offers unlimited on-off rides; or the Ben Frankline, which goes from Society Hill up to the Art Museum ($1.50 per ride).

You can pick up a **Golden Age Passport** at Independence National Historical Park if you are 62 or over. Since this park is free, it won't matter there, but the passport provides free admission to all parks, monuments, and recreation areas operated by the National Park Service.

Some of the educational programs run by **Elderhostel** are in the Philadelphia area. You must be over 60 (and your spouse or companion over 50) to participate. The cost of the program itself averages $350 per person; for information contact them at 80 Boylston St., Suite 400, Boston, MA 02116 (tel. 617/426-7788).

**FOR SINGLES** The main problem for single travelers can be meeting other people. There is, of course, the bar scene (see Chapter 10). You might consider signing up for one of the many tours through parts of Independence National Historical Park at their Visitors Center or join tours of Fairmount Park and other city areas at the Visitors Center at 16th Street and John F. Kennedy Boulevard. The Friday Philadelphia *Inquirer* "Weekend" section lists many other participatory events. You might also consider staying in a smaller hotel, such as Independence Park Inn, or in a hotel with a health club.

**FOR FAMILIES** Planning is essential for success here in Philadelphia—I know from personal experience! If your kids are old enough to appreciate the destination, let them read something ahead of time; for a brief list of literature for children see "Recommended Books and Films" in Chapter 1.

If you are traveling by air or train, be aware that the airlines and Amtrak both let children under two travel free and offer discounts for children and/or families. Once you arrive, children under 12 (in some cases 18) can stay free in the same room as their parents in virtually all Philadelphia hotels. Be sure to reserve cribs and playpens if needed in advance. Restaurants all over the country are increasingly aware of the need to provide the basics, and "Cool for Kids" in Chapter 6 will cover some favorites.

The best current resource for family travel in Philadelphia is *Metrokids,* a bimonthly newspaper available at the Visitors Center at 16th Street and John F. Kennedy Boulevard. It lists all special cultural attractions geared to families, along with theme issues on factory tours, the new Camden aquarium, and the like. Call 215/735-7035 with specific questions.

**FOR STUDENTS** It's not well known, but there probably are more colleges and universities in and around Philadelphia than any other city in the country. So accredited students will find a warm reception from area vendors and sites. To be accredited, the key is to have an **International Student Identity Card (ISIC),** available to any full-time high-school or university student. Contact your own campus or the **Council on International Educational Exchange (CIEE),** 205 East 42nd St., New York, NY 10017 (tel. 212/661-1450). While in Philadelphia, students might head for the **University of Pennsylvania,** 34th and Walnut streets (tel. 898-5000); **Temple University,** Broad Street and Montgomery Avenue (tel. 787-8561); or **International House,** 3701 Chestnut Street (tel. 387-5125). All publish free papers listing lectures, performances, films, and social events.

# 4. GETTING THERE

## BY PLANE

All flights into and from Philadelphia use **Philadelphia International Airport** (tel. 215/492-3181), at the southwest corner of the city. There are flights to more than 100 cities in the United States and more than 1,000 arrivals and departures daily.

### THE MAJOR AIRLINES

You can check flight schedules and make reservations on the following domestic airlines. **American Airlines** (tel. 215/365-4000, or toll free 800/433-7300); **Continental Airlines** (tel. toll free 800/525-0280); **Delta Air Lines** (tel. 215/667-7720, or toll free 800/221-1212); **Midway Airlines** (tel. toll free 800/866-9000); **Northwest Airlines** (tel. toll free 800/225-2525 domestic, 800/447-4747 international); **TWA** (tel. 215/923-2000, or toll free 800/221-2000 domestic, 800/221-4141 international); **United Airlines** (tel. 215/568-2800, or toll free 800/241-6522); and **USAir** (tel. toll free 800/428-4322).

International carriers include **Air Jamaica** (tel. toll free 800/523-5585); **British Airways** (tel. toll free 800/247-9297); **Lufthansa** (tel. toll free 800/645-3880); **Mexicana** (tel. toll free 800/531-7921); and **Swissair** (tel. toll free 800/221-4750).

### AIRFARES

Airfares these days shift quickly, depending on the date and day of week, advance reservations, prepayment, nonstop or transfer status, competition for the flight among carriers, and length of stay, just for starters. If this sounds confusing, that's why it's imperative to shop around or have a friendly travel agent do so for you. *Note:* In mid-1992 airfares were undergoing considerable changes, the ultimate result of which was unclear.

The various price classes on flights range from first class—the most expensive—through business class to economy—which carries no special restrictions. The cheapest direct-flight option usually is the **APEX (Advance Purchase Excursion)** fare, which typically is valid from 7 to 60 days and must be purchased at least 14 to 21 days in advance. Any round-trip fare will be lower still if it includes a Saturday-night stay.

There's always less demand, and consequently greater seat availability and lower prices, for off-peak hours of travel, especially after 7pm. Monday, Thursday, and Friday are the heaviest travel days. Holidays generally are the worst times of year to travel.

The two domestic airlines that use Philadelphia International Airport as a hub are Midway Airlines and USAir, so look for competitive fares from cities in which they both have stops.

Shuttle service up and down the east coast can be high-priced, and flights from the southwest are limited. International rates are best to and from Mexico, London and Jamaica and some other Caribbean islands.

There aren't too many super-budget options to and from Philadelphia by air. Because of the vagaries of routing, domestic airlines may make it cheaper to fly via larger New York or Atlanta hubs, with a switch onto a plane that is stopping in Philadelphia on its way to another destination. Bucket shops, or ticket discounters, may be able to deliver a rate lower than anything advertised by the airlines; try **Access International,** 101 West 31st St., New York, NY 10001 (tel. 212/333-7280).

## BY TRAIN

Philadelphia is a major Amtrak stop. It's on the Boston–Washington, D.C., northeast corridor, which has extensions south, west to Pittsburgh and Chicago, and east to Atlantic City. The Amtrak terminal is Penn (30th Street) Station, about 15 blocks from City Hall. Regular service from New York City takes 85 minutes; Metroliner service is 15 minutes faster. Philadelphia is 5 hours from Boston and 100 minutes from Washington, D.C., by Metroliner. Tel. toll free 800/USA-RAIL.

SEPTA commuter trains also connect 30th Street Station and

---

 **FROMMER'S SMART TRAVELER:
AIRFARES**

1. Shop all airlines that fly to Philadelphia.
2. Ask for the lowest fare, not just a discount fare, and be prepared to transfer mid-route.
3. Keep calling the airline to check fares. As a departure date draws nearer, more seats are sold at lower prices, so keep checking if you can cope with the uncertainty.
4. Ask about senior-citizen discounts (usually 10%).
5. Check reputable bucket shops for last-minute discount fares that are even cheaper than advertised fares.
6. Look for special promotions offered by major carriers trying to protect hubs or gain a foothold in the Philadelphia market.

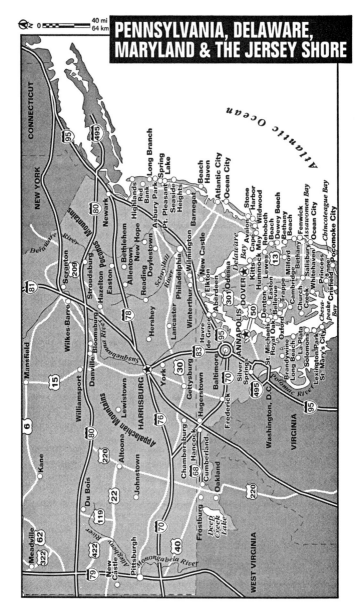

several Center City stations to Trenton, N.J., to the northeast, Harrisburg to the west, and directly to airport terminals to the south.

These are sample round-trip fares on Amtrak: New York City to Philadelphia, $60 regular, $47 excursion (not valid Friday from 11am to 7pm); Washington to Philadelphia, $68 regular, $51 excursion; and Chicago to Philadelphia, $212 regular, $156 excursion.

Keep in mind that Philadelphia trips can be much cheaper if you take **Transport of New Jersey (TNJ)** commuter trains out of

Penn Station in New York City or Newark to Trenton, then switch across the platform to a Philadelphia-bound SEPTA commuter train that makes several Center City stops before heading out to Chestnut Hill. Total one-way cost is $17; tel. 215/569-3752.

## BY BUS

**Greyhound/Trailways,** the chief U.S. intercity operator, operates a terminal at 10th and Filbert streets (tel. 215/931-4000). Bus travel is definitely cheaper than train travel, but it's generally slower and more cramped. Depending on advance purchase and length of stay, a round-trip ticket to or from New York City is $32 or $30 for the 140-minute trip. The same conditions to Washington, D.C., produce fares of $42 or $35.70. Transport of New Jersey (TNJ) (tel. 215/569-3752) also operates buses out of Philadelphia, with terminals at Camden, Atlantic City, and other nearby destinations.

## BY CAR

Philadelphia is better served than ever before by a series of interstate highways that circle or pass through the city. I-95 whizzes by the southern and eastern side of the city. The Pennsylvania Turnpike (I-276) is just north of the city, but I-76 splits off and snakes along the Schuylkill River into town. A branch, I-676, leads to adjacent Camden, N.J., via the Ben Franklin Bridge over the Delaware. I-276 and I-76 are connected with I-95 by I-476 (the "Blue Route") about 15 miles west of the city. Philadelphia is some 300 miles (6 or so hours) from Boston, 100 miles (2 hours) from New York City, 135 miles (3 hours) from Washington, D.C., and 450 miles (9 hours) from Montreal. Tolls between either New York City or Washington come to about $10.

# CHAPTER 3

# FOR FOREIGN VISITORS

**1. PREPARING FOR YOUR TRIP**

**2. GETTING TO & AROUND THE UNITED STATES**

**• FAST FACTS: FOR THE FOREIGN TRAVELER**

The entire world knows American pop entertainment and culture—but a first visit to the United States will quickly bring you into contact with different and complex lifestyles. Philadelphia, as a first destination, is slightly easier to take than most other cities, especially if you have been to or live in London; after all, the city was the second city of the British Empire for 100 years. Nevertheless, you will encounter many uniquely American situations.

## 1. PREPARING FOR YOUR TRIP

Any American city can be a bit bewildering for a foreign tourist on first arrival, even a city that has accepted as many immigrants throughout its history as Philadelphia. The City of Brotherly Love wants to make the foreigner feel at home, so it has set up an **International Visitors Center** at the Civic Center, 34th Street and Civic Center Boulevard, Philadelphia, PA 19104 (tel. 215/823-7261). This center offers special services to visitors from overseas, including foreign-language assistance and information. The Language Bank puts the foreign visitor in touch with linguistic resources in the city (call 215/879-5248, 24 hours a day).

Another option is the **Nationalities Service Center,** 1300 Spruce St., Philadelphia, PA 19107 (tel. 215/893-8400). This center serves the needs of immigrants and families and is thus geared to "permanent" visitors, but they can also help with translation and interpreters. Call 215/893-8418, ext. 116. For 24-hour (fee charged) help in any foreign language, call the **NSC Interpreter Service** hotline at 215/893-8410, ext. 115, during business hours and 215/735-7022 at other times.

### ENTRY REQUIREMENTS

**DOCUMENT REGULATIONS** Canadian citizens may enter the United States without visas; they need only proof of residence. British, Dutch, French, German, Italian, Japanese, Swedish, and Swiss citizens traveling on valid national (or EC) passports do not need visas for holiday or business travel in the United States of 90 days or less if they hold round-trip or return tickets and if they enter the United States on an airline or cruise line that participates in the no-visa travel program.

*Note:* Citizens of these visa-exempt countries who first enter the United States may then visit Mexico, Canada, Bermuda, and/or the Caribbean islands and then reenter the United States, by any mode of transportation, without needing a visa. Further information is available from any U.S. embassy or consulate.

A citizen of a country other than those above requires a valid **passport,** with an expiration date at least six months later than the scheduled end of his or her visit to the United States; and a **tourist visa,** available without charge from the nearest U.S. consulate. The traveler must submit a completed visa application form (either in person or by mail) with a passport photograph attached. If applying in person you will generally receive your visa at once or within 24 hours at most; try to avoid the summer rush from June to August, however. If applying by mail, enclose a large self-addressed stamped envelope and expect an average wait of two weeks. Visa application forms are available at airline offices or from travel agents as well as from U.S. consulates. The U.S. tourist visa (visa B-2) is theoretically valid for a year and for any number of entries, but the U.S. consulate that issues the tourist visa will determine the length of stay for a multiple- or single-entry visa. However, there is some latitude here, so if you are of good appearance and can give the address of a relative, friend, or business connection living in the United States (useful, too, for car rental, passage through Customs, and so forth), you have an excellent chance of getting a longer permit if you want one.

**MEDICAL REQUIREMENTS** No inoculations are needed to enter the United States unless you are coming from areas known to be suffering from epidemics, especially of cholera or yellow fever.

If you have a disease requiring treatment with medications containing controlled drugs, carry a valid, signed prescription from your physician to allay any suspicions that you are smuggling illegal drugs. The same applies to syringes.

## TRAVEL INSURANCE — BAGGAGE, HEALTH & ACCIDENT

All insurance is voluntary in the United States. Given the very high cost of U.S. medical care, however, I strongly advise every traveler to arrange for appropriate coverage before setting out. There are specialized insurance companies that will, for a relatively low premium, cover loss or theft of baggage; trip-cancellation costs; guarantee of bail in case of arrest; sickness or injury costs (medical, surgical, and hospital); and costs of an accident, repatriation, or death. Insurance packages (for example, Europ Assistance, 252 High St., Croydon, Surrey CR0 1NF, England; tel. 01/680-1234) are sold by automobile clubs at attractive rates, as well as by banks and travel agencies.

# 2. GETTING TO & AROUND THE UNITED STATES

Travelers from overseas can take advantage of the **APEX (Advance Purchase Excursion) fares** offered by major U.S. and European carriers. Aside from these, attractive values are offered by **Icelandair** on flights from Luxembourg to New York or Orlando and by **Virgin Atlantic** from London to New York–Newark or Miami.

Some large airlines (for example, TWA, American, Northwest, United, Delta) offer transatlantic and transpacific travelers special discount tickets under the name **Visit USA,** allowing travel between U.S. destinations at minimum rates. They are not on sale in the United States. This system is the best way to see the United States at low cost. You should obtain information well in advance from your travel agent or the office of the relevant airline, since conditions attached to these discount tickets can change at any time.

For information on transportation to Philadelphia from elsewhere in the United States, see "Getting There" in Chapter 2.

# FAST FOR THE
## FOREIGN TRAVELER

**Accommodations**   See Chapter 5.

**Automobile Organizations**   Auto clubs can supply maps; recommended routes; guidebooks; accident and bail-bond insurance; and, most important, emergency road service. The leader, with some 850 offices and 28 million members, is the **American Automobile Association (AAA),** with national headquarters at 1000 AAA Dr., Heathrow, FL 32745 (tel. 407/444-7000). The local office is **Keystone AAA,** 2040 Market St., Philadelphia, PA 19103 (tel. 215/864-5000).

**Auto Rentals**   To rent a car, you will need a major credit card or you'll be required to leave a sizable cash deposit ($100 or more for each day). Minimum driver age is usually 21, and you'll need a valid driver's license.

The majors are **Hertz** (tel. toll free 800/654-3131), **Avis** (tel. toll free 800/331-1212), **National** (tel. toll free 800/227-7368), **Budget** (tel. toll free 800/527-0700), and **Dollar** (tel. toll free 800/421-6868). Also check smaller local companies and **Rent-A-Wreck** (tel. toll free 800/535-1391).

**Business Hours**   Public and private **offices** are usually open Monday through Friday from 9am to 5pm.

**Banking hours** are generally Monday through Friday from 9am to 3pm, in some cases Friday until 6pm and Saturday morning.

**Post offices** are open Monday through Friday from 8am to 5:30 or 6pm, Saturday from 8am to noon.

**Store hours** are Monday through Saturday from 9 or 10am to 5:30 or 6pm, though often Thursday until 9pm in Philadelphia. Most shopping centers, drugstores, and supermarkets are open Monday through Saturday from 9am to 9pm, with some open 24 hours a day.

**Museum hours** vary widely. The norm for big cities is six days a week from 10am to 5pm (closing day is usually Monday).

**Climate**   See "When to Go" in Chapter 2.

**Currency**   The U.S. monetary system has a decimal base—one **dollar** ($1) = 100 **cents** (100¢).

The commonest **bills** (all mostly green, all the same size) are the $1 ("a buck"), $5, $10, and $20 denominations. There are also $2 (seldom encountered), $50, and $100 bills (the latter two are not welcome when paying for small purchases).

There are six denominations of **coins:** 1¢ (one cent, a penny); 5¢ (nickel); 10¢ (dime); 25¢ (quarter); 50¢ (half dollar); and the rare $1 (both older, larger silver dollars and newer, smaller, many-sided Susan B. Anthony coins).

**Traveler's checks** denominated in U.S. dollars are accepted without demur at hotels, motels, restaurants, and large stores. The best place to change foreign-denominated traveler's checks is at a bank.

The payment method most widely used is the **credit card**— VISA (BarclayCard in Britain), MasterCard (EuroCard in Europe, Access in Britain, Diamond in Japan), American Express, Discover Card, Diners Club, and Carte Blanche. You can save yourself trouble by using "plastic money," rather than cash or traveler's checks, in 95% of all hotels, motels, restaurants, and retail stores. A credit card can serve as a deposit when renting a car; as proof of identity (often carrying more weight than a passport); or as a "cash card," enabling you to draw money from automatic-teller machines and at banks.

**Currency Exchange** For major foreign currencies, the following Philadelphia institutions in Center City provide exchange service: **American Express Travel Service,** 2 Penn Center Plaza (tel. 587-2342 or 587-2343); **Continental Bank,** 1201 Chestnut Street (tel. 564-7188); **Thomas Cook Currency Services, Inc.,** 16 N. 17th Street (tel. 563-5544); **CoreStates First Pennsylvania Bank,** 16th and Market streets, which issues foreign drafts and wire transfers as well (tel. 786-8880 or 786-8881); **Fidelity Bank,** Broad and Walnut streets (tel. 985-7068); **Mellon Bank,** Broad and Chestnut streets (tel. 585-2145); **Meridian Bank,** 1700 Arch Street (tel. 854-3549); **Philadelphia National Bank,** 5th and Market streets (tel. 629-4402); and **Provident National Bank,** Broad and Chestnut streets (tel. 585-5000).

**Customs & Immigration** Every adult visitor may bring in, free of duty: 1 liter of wine or hard liquor; 200 cigarettes or 100 cigars (but *no* cigars from Cuba) or 3 pounds (1.35kg) of smoking tobacco; and $400 worth of gifts. These exemptions are offered to travelers who spend at least 72 hours in the United States and who have not claimed them within the preceding six months. It is forbidden to bring into the country foodstuffs like cheese, fruit, cooked meats, and canned goods and plants (vegetables, seeds, tropical plants, and so on). Foreign tourists may bring in or take out up to $10,000 in U.S. or foreign currency with no formalities; larger sums must be declared to Customs on entering and leaving.

The visitor arriving by air, no matter what the port of entry— New York, Boston, Miami, Honolulu, Los Angeles, or the rest— should cultivate patience and resignation before setting foot on U.S. soil. The U.S. Customs and Immigration services are among the slowest and most suspicious on earth.

In contrast, for the traveler arriving by car or by rail from Canada, the border-crossing formalities have been streamlined to the vanishing point. And for the traveler by air from Canada, Bermuda, and some points in the Caribbean, you can go through Customs and Immigration at the point of *departure,* which is much quicker and less painful.

**Drinking Laws** As with marriage and divorce, every state, and sometimes every county and community, has its own laws governing the sale of liquor. The only federal regulation (based on a judgment of the U.S. Supreme Court on June 23, 1987) restricts the consumption of liquor in public places anywhere in the country to persons aged 21 or over (states not respecting this rule may be penalized by a withdrawal of federal highway funds). In Philadelphia, establishments may serve alcoholic beverages from 9am to 2am (private clubs may serve to 4am).

**Electric Current** U.S. wall outlets give power at 110–115 volts, 60 cycles, compared to 220 volts, 50 cycles, in most of Europe. Besides a 110-volt converter, small appliances of non-American manufacture, such as hairdryers and shavers, will require a plug adapter with two flat, parallel pins.

**Embassies/Consulates** All embassies are located in Washington, D.C., as it's the nation's capital, and many consulates are located there as well. Among the embassies are those for **Australia,** 1601 Massachusetts Ave. NW, Washington, DC 20036 (tel. 202/797-3000); **Canada,** 501 Pennsylvania Ave. NW (tel. 202/682-1740); **France,** 4100 Reservoir Rd. (tel. 202/944-6000); **Germany,** 4645 Reservoir Rd. (tel. 202/298-4000); **Netherlands,** 4200 Linnean Ave. NW (tel. 202/244-5300); **United Kingdom,** 3100 Massachusetts Ave. NW, Washington, D.C. 20008 (tel. 202/462-1340). You can obtain the telephone numbers of other embassies and consulates by calling "Information" in Washington (dial 202/555-1212).

**Emergencies** In all major cities (including Philadelphia) you can call the police, an ambulance, or the fire brigade through the single emergency telephone number **911.** Another useful way of reporting an emergency is to call the telephone-company operator by dialing **0** (zero, *not* the letter "O"). Outside major cities, call the county sheriff or the fire brigade at the number you will find in the local telephone book.

If you encounter such travelers' problems as sickness, accident, or lost or stolen baggage, it will pay you to call the **Travelers Aid Society** at 546-0571 or 386-0845. It's an organization that specializes in helping distressed travelers, whether American or foreign.

**Gasoline [Petrol]** One U.S. gallon equals 3.75 liters, while 1.2 U.S. gallons equals one imperial gallon. You'll notice several grades (and price levels) of gasoline at most gas stations. And you'll also notice that their names change from company to company. The unleaded grades with the highest octane are the most expensive, but most rental cars take the least expensive "regular" unleaded. Leaded gasoline is rarely used anymore.

**Holidays** On the following national legal holidays, banks; government offices; post offices; and many stores, restaurants, and museums are closed.

January 1 (New Year's Day)
Third Monday in January (Martin Luther King Day)
Third Monday in February (Presidents Day, marking Washington's and Lincoln's birthdays)
Last Monday in May (Memorial Day)
July 4 (Independence Day)
First Monday in September (Labor Day)
Second Monday in October (Columbus Day)
November 11 (Veterans Day/Armistice Day)
Fourth Thursday in November (Thanksgiving Day)
December 25 (Christmas Day)

The Tuesday following the first Monday in November is Election Day. It is a legal holiday in presidential-election years (1992, 1996).

**Legal Aid**   The foreign tourist will probably never become involved with the American legal system. If you are cited for a minor infraction (for example, of the highway code, such as speeding), never try to pay the fine directly to a police officer; you may wind up arrested on the much more serious charge of attempted bribery. Pay fines by mail or directly to the clerk of a court. If you're accused of a more serious offense, it is wise to say and do nothing before consulting a lawyer. Under U.S. law, an arrested person is allowed one telephone call to a party of his or her choice. Call your embassy or consulate.

**Mail**   Generally found at major road or street intersections, mailboxes are blue with a red-and-white stripe and carry the inscription "U.S. MAIL." If your mail is addressed to a U.S. destination, don't forget to add the five-figure postal code or ZIP code after the two-letter abbreviation of the state to which the mail is addressed (CA for California, MA for Massachusetts, NY for New York, PA for Pennsylvania, and so on).

Philadelphia's **main post offices** are located at 9th and Market streets and across from Penn Station at 30th Street.

**Newspapers/Magazines**   National newspapers include *The New York Times, USA Today,* and *The Wall Street Journal.* There are also several national news weeklies including *Newsweek, Time,* and *U.S. News & World Report.* For information on local Philadelphia periodicals, see "Newspapers/Magazines" in "Fast Facts: Philadelphia," in Chapter 4.

**Radio/Television**   Audiovisual media, with three coast-to-coast networks—ABC, CBS, and NBC—joined in recent years by the Public Broadcasting System (PBS) and the Fox Broadcasting Network and the cable network CNN, play a major part in American life. In big cities like Philadelphia, televiewers have a choice of about a dozen channels, most transmitting 24 hours a day, without counting the pay-TV channels showing recent movies or sports events. All options are indicated on your hotel TV. You'll also find a wide choice of local radio stations, each broadcasting particular kinds of talk shows and/or music, punctuated by news broadcasts and frequent commercials.

**Safety**   Whenever you're traveling in an unfamiliar city, stay alert. Be aware of your immediate surroundings. Wear a moneybelt—or, better yet, check valuables in a safety deposit box at your hotel. Keep a close eye on your possessions and be sure to keep them in sight when you're seated in a restaurant, theater, or other public place. Don't leave valuables in your car—even in the trunk. Every city has its criminals. It's your responsibility to be aware and be alert even in the most heavily touristed areas.

**Taxes**   In the United States there is no VAT (value-added tax) at the national level. Every state, and each city in it, can levy its own local tax on purchases, including hotel and restaurant checks, airline tickets, and the like. It is automatically added to the price of certain services, such as public transportation, cab fares, phone calls, and gasoline. It varies from 4% to 10%, depending on the state and city, so when you are making major purchases such as photographic equipment, clothing, or high-fidelity components, it can be a significant part of the cost. Philadelphia's sales tax is 7%.

Each locality can levy its own separate tax on hotel occupancy. Since this tax is in addition to any general sales tax, taken together these two taxes can add a considerable amount to the cost of your accommodations. In Philadelphia, in addition to your hotel rate, you pay 7% sales tax plus a 5% surcharge.

**Telephone/Telegraph/Telex** You will find **pay phones** an integral part of the American landscape. They are almost everywhere—at street corners; in bars, restaurants, public buildings, stores, and service stations; along highways; and on and on. Telephones are provided by private corporations, which perhaps explains the high standard of service. In Philadelphia local calls cost 25¢.

For **long-distance** or **international calls,** stock up with a supply of quarters; the pay phone will instruct you when, and in what quantity, you should put them into the slot. For direct overseas calls, first dial 011, followed by the country code and then by the city code and the number of the person you wish to call. For calls to Canada and long-distance calls in the United States, dial 1 followed by the area code and number.

Before calling from a hotel room, always ask the hotel phone operator if there are telephone surcharges. These are best avoided by using a public phone, calling collect, or using a telephone charge card.

For **reversed-charge** or **collect calls,** and for **person-to-person calls,** dial 0 (zero, *not* the letter "O") followed by the area code and number you want; an operator will then come on the line, and you should specify that you are calling collect, or person-to-person, or both. If your operator-assisted call is international, ask for the overseas operator.

For local **directory assistance** ("information"), dial 411; for **long-distance information,** dial 1, then the appropriate area code and 555-1212.

Like the telephone system, **telegraph** and **telex** services are provided by private corporations, such as ITT, MCI, and above all, Western Union, the most important. You can bring your telegram in to the nearest Western Union office (there are hundreds across the country) or dictate it over the phone (a toll-free call, 800/325-6000). You can also telegraph money or have it telegraphed to you very quickly over the Western Union system.

**Telephone Directory** See "White and Yellow Pages," below.

**Time** The conterminous United States is divided into four **time zones** (six, if Alaska and Hawaii are included). From east to west, these are: Eastern Standard Time (EST), Central Standard Time (CST), Mountain Standard Time (MST), Pacific Standard Time (PST), Alaska Standard Time (AST), and Hawaii Standard Time (HST). Always change time zones in your mind if you are traveling (or even telephoning) long distances in the United States. For example, noon in New York City (EST) is 11am in Chicago (CST), 10am in Denver (MST), 9am in Los Angeles (PST), 8am in Anchorage (AST), and 7am in Honolulu (HST). Philadelphia is on EST.

**Daylight saving time (DST)** is in effect from the first Sunday in April through the last Saturday in October (actually, the change is made at 2am on Sunday) except in Arizona, Hawaii, part of Indiana, and Puerto Rico. Daylight saving time moves the clock one hour ahead of standard time.

**Tipping** This is part of the American way of life, on the principle that you must pay for any service received. Here are some rules of thumb:

**Bartenders:** 10% to 15%.

**Bellhops:** at least 50¢ per piece; $2 to $3 for a lot of baggage.
**Cab drivers:** 15% of the fare.
**Cafeterias, fast-food restaurants:** no tip.
**Chambermaids:** $1 a day.
**Checkroom attendants** (restaurants, theaters): $1 per garment.
**Cinemas, movies, theaters:** no tip.
**Doormen** (hotels or restaurants): tipping not obligatory.
**Gas-station attendants:** no tip.
**Hairdressers:** 15% to 20%.
**Parking-lot attendants:** 50¢ ($1 in hotels).
**Redcaps** (airport and railroad station): at least 50¢ per piece, $2 to $3 for a lot of baggage.
**Restaurants, nightclubs:** 15% to 20% of the check.
**Sleeping-car porters:** $2 to $3 per night to your attendant.

**White and Yellow Pages**   There are two basic kinds of telephone directory. The general directory is the so-called **White Pages,** in which private and business subscribers are listed in alphabetical order. The inside front cover lists emergency numbers for police, fire, and ambulance as well as other vital numbers (the Coast Guard, poison-control center, crime-victims hotline, and so on). The first few pages include community service numbers and a guide to long-distance and international calling, complete with country codes and area codes. A thin **Blue Pages** in the back of the White Pages book lists federal, state, and local government offices.

The second basic directory, the **Yellow Pages,** lists local services, businesses, and industries by type of activity, with an index at the back. The listings cover not only obvious items like automobile repairs by make of car and drugstores (pharmacies) by geographical location, but also restaurants by type of cuisine and geographical location, bookstores by special subject and/or language, places of worship by religious denomination, and other information that the tourist might otherwise not readily find.

**See also**   "Fast Facts: Philadelphia," in Chapter 4.

# GETTING TO KNOW PHILADELPHIA

**1. ORIENTATION**
**2. GETTING AROUND**
• **FAST FACTS:**
  **PHILADELPHIA**
**3. NETWORKS &**
  **RESOURCES**

This chapter sets out to answer all your travel questions, furnishing you with all the practical information that you'll need during your stay in Philadelphia to handle any and every experience—from the city layout and transportation to emergencies to business hours.

## 1. ORIENTATION

### ARRIVING
#### BY PLANE

**Philadelphia International Airport** (tel. 215/492-3181), in the southwest part of the city, has become one of the country's busiest in the last 10 years. Under a $315-million improvement plan, the new international Terminal A (Dilworth Terminal) and additional garages have been built; a new runway and general facelift are still in progress.

The airport is laid out with a central corridor connecting the five basic depots. Terminal B is the place to catch taxis, buses, and hotel limousines. The areas with the most amenities are between Terminals B and C and between Terminals D and E.

If you're driving to the airport, long-term parking is available for $14 per day at the Terminals C and D garages or $6 per day for regular long-term parking. The **Guest Quarters/Days Inn** complex on Island Avenue has just instituted in their lot an enclosed, 24-hour security Park-and-Fly with a shuttle bus; parking there costs $6 per day, and the lot is 8 minutes from terminals. You might also try **Flying Carport** (tel. 215/492-2161), an airport valet service where you drop off your car and are taken to the airport by van.

A taxi from the airport to Center City takes about 25 minutes and costs upward of $25 plus tip. If you're interested in airport limousines (actually, some are vans), several connect with area destinations. Expect a rate of $70 for a sedan or $81 for a stretch limo (both include tip) to nonhotel addresses at Center City; $81 and $119, respectively, to Valley Forge; and $115 and $145, respectively, plus tip and tolls, to Atlantic City. Try **Airport-Limelight** (tel. 215/342-5557; fax 215/347-7121), **Carey Limousine** (tel. 215/492-8402), or **Dav-El Livery** (tel. 215/334-7900; fax 215/334-2610).

A high-speed rail link with direct service between the airport and Center City was opened in 1985. The trains run daily every 30 minutes from 6am to midnight. They leave the airport at 10 and 40 minutes past the hour. Trains to the airport depart from Market East (and a Convention Center connection), Suburban Station at 16th Street, and 30th Street Station. The 25-minute trip costs adults $5.75 if they buy their tickets on board, $4.75 if they prepurchase; children's fares are $2.75 and $2.25, respectively, and the family fare is $14.

## BY TRAIN

All Northeast Corridor **Amtrak** trains stop at the 30th Street Station (tel. 215/824-1600, or toll free 800/872-7245), a gloriously clean and well-lit terminal just across the Schuykill River in West Philadelphia. It now handles more than 3.2 million passengers per year, second only to New York City's Penn Station, and more trains are on the way, thanks to the renewed Atlantic City rail link. From 30th Street Station, catch one of the commuter trains for a free shuttle into Suburban Station at 16th Street and John F. Kennedy Boulevard. This station serves Harrisburg and West Chester and connects to the other commuter lines at the Market Street East Station, at 10th and Market streets. Remember, you can also pick up the rail link direct to the airport. If you want to leave a car in the adjoining lots, the rate is $14 per day.

## BY BUS

**Greyhound/Trailways** (tel. 215/931-4000) opened a new 24-hour concrete structure in summer 1987. It's behind the Gallery, an urban mall, at 10th and Filbert streets. Filbert, one block north of Market Street, is a commuter-rail stop and very well situated for the new Convention Center.

## BY CAR

Most of Philadelphia's sights and sounds are in Center City, the band stretching between the Delaware and Schuylkill rivers at the thinnest point. I-95 snakes along the eastern side of Center City, along the Delaware River, while the Schuylkill Expressway, I-76, follows a route along the western side (mostly just over the Schuylkill River). Here are directions to City Hall, in the very center of town, from various directions:

### From the Northeast & Eastern Canada

**NEW JERSEY TURNPIKE SOUTHBOUND EXIT 6** Take the Pennsylvania Turnpike westbound to the first exit, Exit 29, and change to U.S. 13 southbound. Follow the signs a short distance to I-95 southbound and enter at Exit 22, heading south. Exit for Center City at I-676 (Vine Street Expressway) westbound to 15th Street, then turn left and travel southbound two blocks.

**NEW JERSEY TURNPIKE EXIT 4** Take N.J. 73 westbound to N.J. 38 westbound, then change to U.S. 30 westbound and follow it over the Ben Franklin Bridge (90¢) to I-676. Go south on 6th Street to Walnut Street (historic district will be on the left), turn right, and travel westbound to 15th Street.

### From Southeastern Pennsylvania, Delaware & Maryland

**FROM I-95 NORTHBOUND** Just past Philadelphia International Airport, take Penna. 291 toward Center City, Philadelphia. Cross the George C. Platt Memorial Bridge and turn left onto 26th Street, then follow 26th Street directly onto I-76 (Schuylkill Expressway) westbound to exit 39 (30th Street Station). Go one block to Market Street and turn right. Go east on Market Street to City Hall, which will be in front of you.

**FROM THE PENNSYLVANIA TURNPIKE (I-76)**   Take Exit 24 to I-76 (Schuylkill Expressway) eastbound to I-676 (Vine Street Expressway). Take I-676 eastbound to 15th Street, turn right, and proceed southbound two blocks.

## TOURIST INFORMATION

The **Philadelphia Convention and Visitors Bureau,** 1515 John F. Kennedy Blvd., Philadelphia, PA 19102 (tel. 215/636-1666), is one of the very best in America. It looks like a shiny layer cake between Suburban Station and City Hall, and its reception desk is staffed by enthusiastic and knowledgeable volunteers. Between their reference directory and their free information about the city, they can solve almost every puzzle, large or small. You can pick up coupons for reduced admissions to many museums and attractions, too, as well as free aids for the blind and disabled. They parcel out free tickets to the New Year's Day Mummers Parade and to the Mann Music Center for summer concerts in the park and also sell such tickets as the SEPTA DayPass ($4) and "A Gift of Gardens" for 14 regional sites ($7.95). Since the executive offices moved across the street during a 1987 remodeling, some floor space has been devoted to a city giftshop.

The bureau is open daily from 9am to 5pm (except Christmas Day) and until 9pm on summer weekdays. If you miss these hours, call the **Fun Phone** (tel. 215/568-7255)—it's a recording of the day's happenings. If you think ahead, call toll free 800/321-WKND to get material on all the special promotions of the season. In summer, if you show up at noon, there's usually outdoor entertainment on the adjoining plaza, which anchors one end of the Benjamin Franklin Parkway (known simply as "the Parkway").

## CITY LAYOUT

Unlike Boston, Philadelphia has no Colonial cowpaths that were turned into streets. If you can count and remember the names of trees, you'll know exactly where you are in the Center City grid. For the overview, go to (or pretend you're at) the top of **City Hall,** that overiced wedding cake in the very center of things, at the intersection of Broad and Market streets. Admission is free, and it's open daily from 9am to 4:30pm (see Chapter 7). **Broad Street** runs 4 miles south, where the Delaware and Schuylkill flow together, and 8 miles north—all perfectly straight. The other major north-south streets are numbered (the opposite of those in New York City). Except for a few two-way exceptions, traffic on even-numbered streets heads south and on odd-numbered streets, north. **Front Street** (should be 1st Street), once at the Delaware's edge off to the right, and neighboring **2nd Street** were the major thoroughfares in colonial times. In-between streets are named. The major east-west streets in Philadelphia's Center City run from Spring Garden Street to the north and as far south as South Street. You'll spend much of your time between Arch and Pine streets, especially south of Chestnut Street. Addresses on these streets add 100 for every block away from the axis of Market (north-south) or Front Street (east-west); 1534 Chestnut

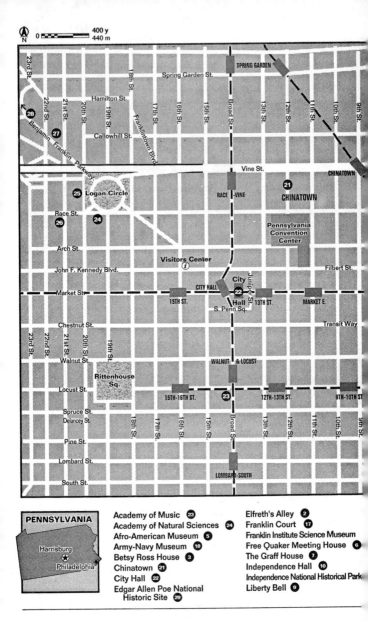

| PENNSYLVANIA | Academy of Music ㉓ | Elfreth's Alley ❷ |
| | Academy of Natural Sciences ㉔ | Franklin Court ⓱ |
| Harrisburg ★ | Afro-American Museum ❺ | Franklin Institute Science Museum |
| Philadelphia ★ | Army-Navy Museum ⓲ | Free Quaker Meeting House ❻ |
| | Betsy Ross House ❸ | The Graff House ❼ |
| | Chinatown ㉑ | Independence Hall ❿ |
| | City Hall ㉒ | Independence National Historical Park |
| | Edgar Allen Poe National Historic Site ㉖ | Liberty Bell ❾ |

Street is between 15th and 16th streets, and 610 S. 5th Street is between six and seven blocks south of Market.

The colonial city, now **Independence National Historical Park** and reconstructed row houses, grew up along the Delaware north and south of **Market Street,** extending west to 6th Street by 1776. The 19th century saw the development of the western quadrants (including most museums and cultural centers) and sub-urbs in every direction. The city blocks planned by William Penn

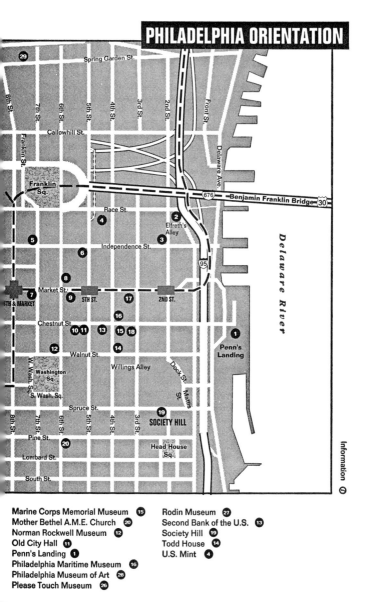

# PHILADELPHIA ORIENTATION

Spring Garden St.
Callowhill St.
Franklin Sq.
Race St.
Elfreth's Alley
Independence St.
Market St.
5TH ST.
2ND ST.
Chestnut St.
Walnut St.
Willings Alley
Washington Sq.
W. Wash. Sq.
S. Wash. Sq.
Spruce St.
SOCIETY HILL
Pine St.
Lombard St.
Head House Sq.
South St.

8th St. 7th St. 6th St. 5th St. 4th St. 3rd St. 2nd St. Front St.

Delaware Ave.
Benjamin Franklin Bridge
Delaware River
Penn's Landing
Dock St.
Martins St.
Information

**Marine Corps Memorial Museum** ⑮
**Mother Bethel A.M.E. Church** ⑳
**Norman Rockwell Museum** ⑫
**Old City Hall** ⑪
**Penn's Landing** ①
**Philadelphia Maritime Museum** ⑯
**Philadelphia Museum of Art** ㉘
**Please Touch Museum** ㉖
**Rodin Museum** ㉗
**Second Bank of the U.S.** ⑬
**Society Hill** ⑲
**Todd House** ⑭
**U.S. Mint** ④

included five parks spaced between the two rivers. Four parks have been named for local notables (including George Washington, who headed the federal government here in the 1790s), and the fifth supports City Hall. A broad northwest boulevard, dividing the grid like a slice of Paris, ends in the majestic arms of the Philadelphia Museum of Art. The entire quadrant west and north of City Hall has been the site of intensive development of hotels, office buildings, and apartment houses.

Just beyond, the Schuylkill separates Philadelphia from West Philadelphia from 24th Street to about 30th Street—if you're looking for an address in this area, ask which side it's on. **Fairmount Park** lines both sides of the Schuylkill for miles above the museum.

For descriptions of Philadelphia neighborhoods, see under "More Attractions" in Chapter 7.

---

# 2. GETTING AROUND

## BY PUBLIC TRANSPORTATION

**SEPTA** (Southeastern Pennsylvania Transportation Authority) operates a complicated and extensive network of trolleys, buses, commuter trains, and subways. In the past 10 years the capital budget for new equipment has increased from $20 million to $120 million; new cars gleam on the Broad Street line, and ridership is up. So, especially in Center City, things are now running quite smoothly.

**Fares** for any SEPTA route are $1.50, with 40¢ more for a transfer, and *exact change or tokens are required.* Anyone can purchase a 10-pack for $10.50. Seniors pay nothing and the disabled pay half-fare during off-peak hours. Certain buses and trolleys run 24 hours a day. The $4 DayPass is good for all buses, subways, and one ride on the Airport loop; a weekly TransPass, good from Monday to the next Sunday, is $16.

An **information center** (open Monday to Friday from 7am to 6pm, also on Saturday in summer) in the underground arcade at 15th and Market streets will give you free timetables and routes for individual lines (take the down escalator across the street from City Hall and turn right). The official street and transit map, which puts the entire picture together, costs $1.50 and is available here or at newsstands. If you have questions about how to reach a specific destination, call SEPTA headquarters at 215/580-7676—but expect to wait.

### SUBWAY-SURFACE LINE

This "local" connects City Hall and 30th Street Station, stopping at 19th and 22nd streets along the way. West of the Amtrak station, it branches out, moving above ground to the north and south.

### RAPID TRANSIT

In Center City, these fast cars speed under Broad Street and Market Street, intersecting under City Hall. The Broad Street line now connects directly to Pattison Avenue and Philadelphia sporting events to the south. The Market Street line stops at 2nd, 5th, 8th, 11th, 13th (Convention Center), 15th, and 30th Street stations and stretches to the west and northeast. Both run all night, but residents suggest caution during late-hour use.

### PATCO

This commuter rail line begins at Walnut and Locust streets around Broad Street, connects with rapid transit at 8th and Market, and crosses the Ben Franklin Bridge to Camden. Transfers connect to the Jersey shore from Lindenwold.

## BUS

Even though there are dozens of routes, you'll often find yourself on the **Chestnut Street Transitway,** a stretch of Chestnut between 17th and 6th streets open only to buses and taxis. Bus no. 42 swoops along Chestnut from West Philadelphia to 2nd at all hours. Route 76, the **Ben FrankLine,** connects Society Hill at 3rd and Chestnut streets to the Parkway all the way to the Museum of Art; it operates every 10 minutes weekdays, every 20 minutes weekends. The first trip from 3rd Street is at 9am, and the last pickup at the Museum of Art is at 6:11pm. Market Street serves several bus routes; the **Mid-City loop** ($1.50, with a 40¢ transfer to another bus) goes up Market and down Chestnut between 5th and 17th streets. Route 32 goes up Broad Street and the Parkway and through Fairmount Park to Andorra; the full trip is 15 miles. New double buses now swivel through many major routes.

## TROLLEY

Tracked trolleys from the 1940s chug up 11th Street and down 12th Street deep into South Philadelphia's Italian-American section. This latter trolley continues up Germantown Avenue to Chestnut Hill, and the entire round trip covers 23 miles and lasts several hours. As with buses, you'll need exact change. A new, privately operated **Penn's Landing Trolley** chugs along Delaware Avenue between the Benjamin Franklin Bridge and Fitzwater Street; you can board at Dock Street or Spruce Street. Fare is $1.50 for adults, 75¢ for children, and the trolley runs Thursday through Sunday from 11am to dusk in the summer.

Replicas of 1930s open-air trolleys operate as 39-seat buses run by **American Trolley Bus,** 4941 Longshore Ave., Philadelphia, PA 19135 (tel. 925-4567), with guides who point out all the high spots. There are four trips daily; admission ranges from $6 to $14, depending on length of tour and family size.

## TRAIN

The Philadelphia area is served by one of the great commuter-rail networks in America. Chestnut Hill, a wealthy enclave of fine shops and restaurants, can be reached from both Suburban Station at 16th Street and John F. Kennedy Boulevard and Reading Terminal at 12th and Market streets, now connected themselves by the new rail link. The famous term "Main Line" refers, in fact, to the old Pennsylvania Railroad line from Suburban (now Penn Center) Station to Harrisburg. In the 1880s executives of the Pennsylvania RR were forced by the firm to establish grand estates along the way in order to make the properties more valuable—and, presto, they became so. What in the suburbs would interest the tourist? Merion is home to the great Barnes Foundation art collection and the Buten Museum of Wedgwood. Bryn Mawr, Haverford, Swarthmore, and Villanova are sites of noted colleges. Devon hosts a great horse and country fair. One-way fares for all destinations are under $5, and you can buy tickets at station counters or vending machines.

# BY OTHER TRANSPORTATION

## TAXI

Philadelphia's notorious shortage of taxis is improving, with about 1,400 currently licensed. Under 1991 legislation, gypsy cabs have been outlawed in return for increasing taxi medallions. Cabbies must pass stringent tests for city knowledge and maintain clean vehicles. Fares are currently $1.50 for the first one-seventh mile and 20¢ for each additional one-seventh of a mile or minute of stasis. Tips are expected, naturally.

If you need to call for a cab while in the city, the three largest outfits are **Yellow Cab** (tel. 922-8400), **United Cab** (tel. 238-9500), and **Quaker City** (tel. 728-8000).

## CAR

Philadelphia's streets were once considered so wide that there was room for market stalls in the divides. Unfortunately, that was 200 years ago, and watching a SEPTA bus turning a corner now is like watching a camel pass through the eye of a needle. So on Center City streets there's little room for parked or moving cars. You might try the streets below Chestnut. Locust, Spruce, and Pine are often the best. Be forewarned that—except for lower Market Street, the Parkway, Vine Street, and Broad Street—*all streets are one way.* Convention and Visitors Bureau at the foot of the Parkway offers a Center City traffic map. Traffic around City Hall follows a counterclockwise pattern, but traffic lights seem to follow none. Try not to get caught vehicle-bound during rush hours.

Since Philadelphia's so walkable, it might be easier to leave your car while you tour. Many hotels offer free or reduced-rate parking to registered guests.

Heaven forbid that you should need an emergency car repair, but if you do, try **Costa's Auto Hospital,** 360 Domino Lane (tel. 483-7525), in the Roxborough neighborhood. **Keystone AAA** is at 2040 Market St., Philadelphia, PA 19103 (tel. 864-5000).

**RENTALS** Philadelphia has no shortage of cars and very good rental rates as a consequence. For example, you can pick up a weekend sedan from **Avis** (tel. toll free 800/331-1212) for $35 per day, with unlimited mileage, at one of their lots: 2000 Arch Street (tel. 563-8976), 30th Street Station (tel. 386-6426), or under Independence Place at 6th and Locust streets (tel. 928-1082). Avis and all other major renters maintain offices at the airport. These include **Budget** (tel. 492-9442 at the airport, 557-0808 at 21st and Market, or toll free 800/527-0700); **Dollar** (tel. 365-1605 at the airport, or toll free 800/421-6868); and **Hertz** (tel. toll free 800/654-3131 to all locations). **Ambassador** now has an office at the Sheraton Society Hill, 2nd and Dock streets (tel. toll free 800/637-8946).

**PARKING** Call the **Philadelphia Parking Authority** (tel. 563-7670 or 977-7275) for current information.

Garage rates are fairly similar: No place exceeds $15 per day, with typical charges $2.50 per hour and $8 for an evening out.

Parking can be found for **Independence Park** at 125 S. 2nd Street (Sansom Street is the cross street); Independence Mall Garage, 41 N. 6th Street; Spruce Street between 5th and 6th streets (private lot); and Head House Square, 2nd and Lombard streets (city meters).

**City Hall Area** parking is at 10th and Ludlow streets (14 S. 10th Street); Hershey Hotel, Broad and Spruce streets (private garage); Kennedy Plaza, 15th Street and John F. Kennedy Boulevard (underground city garage; enter on Arch, one block north of the plaza); and Parkway Garage, 1500 Arch Street.

## BICYCLE

Tourists can rent bicycles at 1 Boat House Row (tel. 236-4359), behind the Museum of Art on the banks of the Schuylkill, in March through November daily from to 8pm. Rate is $6 per hour, plus deposit. Since anyone who enjoys cycling would love the outlying countryside, note that you can also rent bicycles in Lumberville, 8 miles north of New Hope on the Delaware (tel. 215/297-5388), and in Lancaster, the heart of Amish farmland (tel. 717/684-7226).

# FAST FACTS PHILADELPHIA

**Area Code** Philadelphia's telephone area code is **215.**

**Airport** See "Orientation," in this chapter.

**American Express** **AmEx,** 2 Penn Plaza, at 15th Street and John F. Kennedy Boulevard (tel. 587-2342 or 587-2343), can handle currency exchanges, wiring money, and card services such as extension of credit.

**Babysitters** **Rocking Horse Child Care Center** at the Curtis Center, Walnut and 6th streets (tel. 592-8257), can accommodate children almost any age under 6. Hourly care is available for $6 per hour for those under 2, for $5 per hour for ages 3 to 6. Comparable is **Call-A-Granni, Inc.,** 1133 East Barringer Street (tel. 924-8723). Many hotels provide bonded sitters as well.

**Business Hours** **Banks** are generally open Monday through Thursday from 10am to 3pm, Friday until 6pm, with some open on Saturday from 9am to noon as well. Banks charge less commission and offer better exchange rates than hotels or restaurants. Most **bars** and **restaurants** serve food until 10 or 10:30pm (some Chinatown places stay open until 3am), and social bars are open Friday and Saturday until 1 or 2am. **Offices** are open strictly Monday through Friday from 9am to 5pm. **Stores** are open daily from 9am to 5pm, and most Center City locations keep the doors ajar later on Wednesday evening. Olde City, South Street, and Head House Square are the most active late-night districts. Some SEPTA routes run all night, but the frequency of buses and trolleys drops dramatically after 6pm.

**Car Rentals** See "Getting Around," in this chapter.

**Climate** See "When to Go," in Chapter 2.

**Courier Services** During your stay, it might be necessary to send a package from Philadelphia or to other locations in the city. **Federal Express** (tel. 923-3085) and **UPS** (tel. 463-7300), of course, reach almost everywhere in the United States overnight, and they have many drop-off points and offices throughout Center City. For service within the city, try **Heaven Sent,** 60 N. 2nd Street (tel. 923-0929). They will pick up from major hotels and promise same-day service to New York and Washington. For what it's worth, I've gotten cheap and excellent service using **Amtrak Package**

**Express** (30th Street Station; tel. 824-1600) and local pickup. **American Eagle,** 1810 Callowhill Street (tel. 569-3330), goes all around the city with similar dispatch.

**Dentist**   Call 925-6050 in a dental emergency.

**Doctor**   Call the Philadelphia County Medical Society at 563-5343. You can always dial 911 in an emergency. Every hospital in town has an emergency ward.

**Driving Rules**   See "Getting Around," in this chapter.

**Drugstores**   I've searched all over for a 24-hour pharmacy. An alert correspondent tells of a 24-hour **CVS** at 6501 Harbison Avenue (tel. 333-4300), but this is miles from Center City. During regular hours, try **Pickwick Pharmacy,** 1700 Market Street (tel. 563-4860); **Barclay Pharmacy,** 18th and Spruce streets (tel. 735-1410); **Medical Arts Pharmacy,** 128 S. 16th Street (tel. 568-6028); and **Green Drugs,** 5th and South streets (tel. 922-7440).

**Emergencies**   In an extreme emergency, telephone **911.** In case of accidental **poisoning,** call 386-2100. For **police,** call 231-3131; for **fire and rescue,** call 922-6000. Ambulance and emergency transportation can be summoned through **Care & Emergency, Inc.** (tel. 877-5900) or **SEPTA Paratransit** (tel. 574-2780).

**Eyeglasses**   **Snyder Opticians** at 251 S. 17th Street (tel. 735-5656) is not open late, but it does do on-site repairs.

**Hairdressers/Barbers**   Pierre and Carlo, who enjoy a fine reputation with both sexes, are at the **Shops at the Bellevue** (tel. 790-9910). Two other good salons are **Oggi,** 1702 Locust Street (tel. 735-0707), and **Thunder,** 110 S. 19th Street (tel. 563-2665). **Pileggi on the Square,** 717 Walnut Street (tel. 627-0565), has a reputation for great service and competence. Telephone for hours. Many Center City hotels have their own concessions as well.

**Hospitals**   Medical care in Philadelphia is excellent. Major hospitals include **Children's Hospital,** 34th and Civic Center Boulevard (tel. 590-1000); **Graduate Hospital,** 1800 Lombard Street (tel. 893-2000); **Hahnemann,** Broad and Vine streets (tel. 448-7000); **University of Pennsylvania Hospital,** 3400 Spruce Street (tel. 662-4000); **Pennsylvania Hospital,** 8th and Spruce streets (tel. 829-3000); and **Thomas Jefferson,** 11th and Walnut streets (tel. 955-6000).

**Information**   See "Tourist Information," in this chapter.

**Laundry/Dry Cleaning**   Many of the better hotels in town can perform this service for you. Moderate accommodations listed in Chapter 5 often have their own basement washers and dryers. For dry cleaning in a pinch, try **Ye Olde Cleanery,** 23 S. 19th Street (tel. 567-9933) or **J. Brite Cleaners,** at 617 S. 5th Street (tel. 925-6680).

**Libraries**   The jewel of the public system is the **Central Free Library** at 19th and Vine streets (tel. 686-5322; see Chapter 7 for a description). Another central oft-used collection is the **City Institute Branch** at 19th and Locust streets (tel. 735-9137).

**Liquor Laws**   There are some inconvenient things about Philadelphia's Quaker roots. One is the government monopoly on package liquor sales. You, or any tavernkeeper or restaurateur, can buy liquor only in state stores. Usually open Monday through Wednesday from 9am to 5pm, Thursday through Saturday until 9pm, these carry what they carry—period. The selection has improved greatly in the past decade. You cannot get chilled beer or champagne—just what's on the shelf. (Try a delicatessen or licensed supermarket for the bubbles.) See Chapter 9 for some state stores. Minimum drinking age is 18.

**Lost Property**   If you lost something on a SEPTA train or subway, try the stationmaster's office in Suburban Station.

**Mail Information**   The main **post office** at 2970 Market Street (tel. 596-5577), just across the Schuylkill and next to 30th Street station, is always open; the number of its 24-hour window is 895-8989. The post office on the subway concourse at 2 Penn Center, 15th Street and John F. Kennedy Boulevard, is open Monday through Friday from 7am to 6pm, Saturday from 9am to noon. Wanamaker's department store contains a post office that's open Monday through Saturday from 10am to 6pm. The Blue Pages (government offices) of the phone directory contain a complete list.

**Money**   See "Information and Money," in Chapter 2.

**Newspapers/Magazines**   Philadelphia has two main print journals, both now owned by the same firm. The *Inquirer* is the "highbrow" paper, with a string of recent Pulitzer Prizes, and you'll probably want to look at the Friday "Weekend" supplement for listings and prices of entertainment as well as special events and tours. The *Daily News* is more close-to-home Philadelphia material. For the most complete selection of journals and newspapers, try **Avril 50,** 3406 Sansom Street (tel. 222-6108) in University City, with lots of international fripperies such as cigarettes and candies as well. The Society Hill equivalent is **Popi,** 526 S. 4th Street (tel. 922-4119), which recently opened a store at 116 S. 20th Street (tel. 557-8282), near Rittenhouse Square.

**Photographic Needs**   For emergency camera repair, film purchase, or 1-hour processing you might try **Photo Cine Shop,** 129 S. 18th Street (tel. 567-7410), near Rittenhouse Square. **The Camera Shop** and **Jack's Cameras** have branches all over Center City. **Mid-City Camera,** at 1316 Walnut Street (tel. 735-2522) and at the Bourse near the Liberty Bell (tel. 627-3688), offers 24-hour processing of most film.

**Police**   The emergency telephone number is **911.**

**Post Office**   See "Mail Information," above.

**Radio**   There's intense competition among more than 60 stations, so the following programming emphasis is subject to change: all news, KYW (1060 AM); album-oriented rock, WMMR (93.3 FM); oldies, WOGL (98.1 FM) and WFIL (560 AM); soft rock, WIOQ (102.1 FM); country, WCZN (1590 AM) and WXTU (92.5 FM); ethnic urban orientation, WUSL (99.0 FM), WDAS (1480 AM), and WHAT (1340 AM); classical music, WFLN (95.7 FM) and National Public Radio, WHYY (91.0 FM) and WXPN (88.5 FM).

**Religious Services**   The following are some of Philadelphia's places of worship. **Baptist:** 711 S. 12th Street (tel. 922-6691). **Episcopal:** Church of the Holy Trinity, Walnut Street and Rittenhouse Square (founded 1859; tel. 923-7930); St. Clement's, 20th and Cherry streets (1856; tel. 563-1876). **Jewish:** Mikveh Israel, 44 N. 4th Street (1976; tel. 922-5446); Israel, 1610 Spruce Street (tel. 545-3290); Society Hill, 418 Spruce St. (1830; tel. 922-6590). **Lutheran:** 2900 Queen Lane (tel. 438-0600). **Methodist:** St. George's, 324 New Street near Vine (1767; tel. 825-7788). **Presbyterian:** Tenth Presbyterian, 17th and Spruce streets (1854; tel. 735-7688); Old Pine Street, 412 Pine Street (tel. 925-8051). **Roman Catholic:** 936 Market Street (tel. 587-3520); Cathedral of

Saints Peter and Paul, 18th Street at the Parkway (1864; tel. 561-1313). **Society of Friends (Quaker):** Free Meetinghouse, 5th and Arch streets (1783; tel. 923-6777); **Unitarian:** First Unitarian, 2121 Chestnut Street (1886; tel. 563-3980). The Yellow Pages list other places of worship.

**Restrooms**  Public restrooms can be found at 30th Street Station; the Independence National Historical Park Visitors Center; and at major shopping complexes like Liberty Place, the Bourse, the Gallery, and the Shops at the Bellevue. You will virtually never be turned down in requesting use of hotel lobby and restaurant facilities.

**Safety**  Philadelphia exhibits many preconditions of crime: It's large and populous, suffering from overall job losses in the last decade and a widening gap between haves and have-nots. You won't see too much of this underside if you concentrate on major tourist destinations, but stay alert and be aware of your immediate surroundings. Keep a close eye on your possessions. If you are planning to explore Philadelphia in unusual neighborhoods, at unusual hours, or in a style that makes you conspicuous, be especially careful. Center City has recently responded to visible signs of urban distress, including tourist crime, with a combination of police staffing and specially identified "Community Ambassadors," so incidents are rare under normal circumstances.

**Shoe Repairs**  Try **Capa's,** 1015 Chestnut Street (tel. 923-0990), or **Superior Shoe Repair,** 138 S. 15th Street (tel. 972-9680).

**Taxes**  Hotel-room charges incur a 7% state tax and a 5% city surcharge. There is a 7% tax on restaurant meals and on general sales (clothing is tax-free).

**Taxis**  See "Getting Around," in this chapter.

**Television**  Network affiliates include Channel 3 (NBC), KYW; Channel 6 (ABC), WPVI; Channel 10 (CBS), WCAU; and Channel 12 (PBS), WHYY. Most hotels have cable with offerings like Home Box Office, CNN, ESPN, and Disney.

**Time**  Philadelphia is on Eastern Time.

**Tipping**  Aim for 15% in restaurants, 15–20% for taxis, and $1 per bag for porters. See also "Tipping" in "Fast Facts: For the Foreign Traveler," in Chapter 3.

**Transit Info**  If you have questions about how to reach a specific destination, call **SEPTA** headquarters at 215/574-7800—but expect to wait.

# 3. NETWORKS & RESOURCES

## FOR GAY MEN & LESBIANS

Center City is used to, and tolerant of, homosexual populations, and the rectangle bordered by 9th and Broad streets and by Walnut and South streets is filled with gay social services, restaurants, bookstores, and clubs.

**Bookstore**  With a diverse stock, **Giovanni's Room,** 345 S. 12th St., Philadelphia, PA 19107 (tel. 923-2960 or toll free 800/222-6996) is a national resource for publications produced by and for gays and lesbians.

**Counseling**  A national **Gay/Lesbian Crisisline** (tel. toll free 800/767-4297) can provide instant medical or legal counseling and local support listings as well. The **Gay Switchboard** (open daily from 7 to 10pm) is at 546-7100; the **Lesbian Hotline** is at 222-5110.

**Information**    For meetings, classes, gallery exhibitions, and social events, consult **Penguin Place,** 201 S. Camac Street (tel. 723-2220).

**Political/Community    Organizations** To report antigay violence or discrimination, call the **Philadelphia Lesbian and Gay Task Force Hotline** at 563-4581. **ACT UP/ Philadelphia** meets on Monday; call 925-7121.

**Publications**    *Philadelphia Gay News* is widely available, and *Au Courant* is slightly less so. Both are weeklies.

## FOR WOMEN

**Bookstore**    The aforementioned **Giovanni's Room** is also a center for feminist books, recordings, and periodicals.

**Crisis Centers/Clinics**    For serious problems, call **Women Against Abuse** (tel. 386-7777) or **Women Against Rape** (tel. 922-3434). The **Blackwell Center for Women,** 1124 Walnut Street (tel. 923-7577), can direct you to health clinics.

**Information**    The **Women's Switchboard** is at 829-1976.

**Political/Community Organizations**    The **National Organization of Women** local office is at 1218 Chestnut Street (922-6040). **Women's Alliance for Job Equity** is at 1422 Chestnut Street, Suite 1100 (tel. 561-1873). The **Penn Women's Center** (tel. 898-8611), at the University of Pennsylvania, is quite active during the academic year.

**Publication**    *Labyrinth* is available free at Giovanni's Room and some newsstands.

## FOR SENIORS

**Information**    The Philadelphia Corporation for the Aging runs a **Senior Hotline** at 765-9040. Most services are offered for Philadelphians rather than for tourists, however.

**Political/Community Action**    The **Action Alliance of Senior Citizens** is at 1211 Chestnut Street (tel. 564-1622).

# PHILADELPHIA ACCOMMODATIONS

**A** century ago Philadelphia was full of inns, hostelries, and European-style hotels for all pocketbooks and tastes. The names and faces are different today, but the situation is again the same, after decades of less than top quality or quantity in lodgings. As part of a new emphasis on tourism, Philadelphia has begun paying serious attention to the comfort of guests—and it shows.

In 1993 and 1994, Philadelphia hotels will probably be in a position that's good for travelers. There will be more beds and more competition than before but steady or even decreasing demand for downtown rooms. Total hotel beds available in Center City in 1994 will be approximately 6,600 (up from 3,800 around 1990), including the massive Marriott Convention Center Hotel slated for completion that year. Look for abundant discounts and promotions by hotels—especially luxury and near-luxury ones—as they try to maintain occupancy rates. I've already been seeing weekend packages with a 40% discount off standard prices. And check out bed-and-breakfast operations for a cheaper, fresher alternative.

**RATES** Hotel prices in Philadelphia are markedly lower than those in New York City or Washington, D.C. Recommendations are divided here into five categories: **very expensive** ($190 to $290 per night, double occupancy), **expensive** ($140 to $190), **moderate** ($80 to $140), **inexpensive** ($60 to $80), and **budget** (under $60). All rooms have private baths unless otherwise indicated, and you can count on a state tax of 7% plus a city surcharge of 5%. You are strongly advised to bargain for lower rates, because there is keen competition to boost occupancy rates. Also, be sure to inquire about garaging a car or arrangements for children if you are going to bring either with you.

**BED & BREAKFAST AGENCIES** It's natural that the Philadelphia area should have several excellent bed-and-breakfast operations.

**Bed and Breakfast/Center City** (B&B/CC) is run out of 1804 Pine St., Philadelphia, PA 19103 (tel. 215/735-1137), and offers several dozen locations in Center City. Proprietors Stella Pomerantz and Nancy Frenze have attracted hosts in Society Hill, Rittenhouse Square, the Museum of Art area, and West Philadelphia. Houses vary from the clean and comfortable to the luxurious, and most hosts take only one party (single, couple, or family) at a time. Many hosts have other incomes and own their own lodgings. Their occupations include social work, art, interior design, architecture, and teaching—

in short, these are generally people with a sense of style. Guests make individual arrangements with their hosts—some turn over a set of keys, others have a housekeeper, and others stay home. About half the places accept children, and some will make the whole house available for a special occasion. Most of B&B/CC's accommodations range from $45 per night (usually a single with shared bath, often in Society Hill) to $100 (truly sumptuous). It's best to reserve ahead in any season but winter, since the overall occupancy rate is close to 90%. B&B/CC asks for a $25 deposit before your arrival, and there is a slight surcharge for a one-night booking. No credit cards are accepted.

**Bed & Breakfast of Philadelphia,** P.O. Box 252, Gradyville, PA 19039 (tel. 215/358-4747, or toll free 800/733-4747), was started in 1980. One of the owners runs a host home, so they're very close to travelers' needs. B&B of Philadelphia has about 135 homes, 40 in Center City and the remainder in New Jersey, Delaware, and surrounding Pennsylvania counties. The agency has assembled a group of interesting, warm hosts including linguists, gourmet cooks, and therapists; several keep kosher kitchens. Most are not in stay-at-home situations. Philadelphia accommodations include a contemporary loft with a spectacular view of the Delaware River, a converted factory in Society Hill with a three-story winding staircase, and a town house tucked in an alley seconds from Rittenhouse Square. In greener pastures, you could pick from a certified 1810 farmhouse with original fireplaces, a glassed-in former conservatory in Montgomery County, and a nonworking grist mill in Chester County—the bedroom's in the former granary.

B&B of Philadelphia's prices range from $35 to $65 per night for a single person, $35 to $110 for a couple. Many at lower prices have shared baths, and children are a point to discuss. The agency will select a compatible lodging for you or allow you to choose from their directory for $5. American Express, VISA, and MasterCard are accepted for last-minute reservations.

**Bed and Breakfast Traveler** (tel. 215/687-3565) lists more than 35 personally inspected accommodations throughout the area. Rates similar to those above apply, and major credit cards are accepted. **Guesthouses,** R.D. 9, West Chester, PA 19380 (tel. 215/692-4575), has more than 200 host situations lined up, not only in Philadelphia but also throughout the Mid-Atlantic region. Most buildings are architecturally or historically significant. Finally, **All About Town–B&B,** P.O. Box 562, Valley Forge, PA 19481 (tel. 215/783-7838), has town and country choices; singles start at $35 per night, and doubles at $50, with a $5 surcharge for one night's lodging.

# 1. HISTORIC AREA

## VERY EXPENSIVE

**OMNI HOTEL AT INDEPENDENCE PARK, Fourth and Chestnut sts., Philadelphia, PA 19106. Tel. 215/925-0000,** or toll free 800/843-6664. Fax 215/925-1263. 155 rms, 12 suites. A/C MINIBAR TV TEL

**$ Rates:** $190–$255 single or double. Weekend packages available from $125 double per night. Children free in parents' room. AE, CB, DC, MC, V. **Parking:** $11 self-parking, $17.50 valet parking.

This small, polished hotel has a tremendous location in the middle of Independence National Historical Park, three blocks south of Ben Franklin Bridge (Chestnut Street runs one-way east, so approach from 6th Street). All rooms have Independence Park views, and horse-drawn carriages clip-clop past the valet parking drop-off and an elegant glass-and-steel canopy. The $25-million hotel was opened in October 1990, and its prices reflect the new, almost-luxury ambiance. The lobby is classic—with current newspapers, huge vases of flowers, and a bar featuring a piano or a jazz trio nightly.

Each room is cheery—with plants and original pastels of city views—and state-of-the-art—with plastic coded room key, voice mail, VCR, two telephones, and fax- and computer-compatible jacks. All rooms have individual temperature controls, windows that open, and closets with three different kinds of hangers. Rooms for nonsmokers are available. The staff here is noteworthy for its quality and Park knowledge.

**Dining/Entertainment:** The second-floor Azalea is one of Philadelphia's top restaurants; chef Aliza Green has created imaginative treatments of American regional dishes. Typical are cold roast chicken with quince mayonnaise and spicy fried oysters and sirloin with mustard seed and fresh herbs. The restaurant is open for breakfast, lunch (entrées for $8.50–$13.75), brunch, and dinner (entrées for $13.50–$23). Hearty (not English) afternoon tea is served in the lobby lounge, which also features a piano trio most nights.

**Services:** 24-hour room service, concierge, valet parking.

**Facilities:** Indoor lap pool (no lifeguard) available daily 7am–11pm; whirlpool and sauna adjoining, with Stairmaster and exercise area; Ritz 5 movie theater tucked into the back corner.

**SHERATON SOCIETY HILL, 1 Dock St., Philadelphia, PA 19106. Tel. 215/238-6000,** or toll free 800/325-3535. Fax 215/922-2709. 365 rms, 17 suites. A/C MINIBAR TV TEL

**$ Rates:** $165–$185 single, depending on view; double occupancy $25 extra. Weekend packages available from $125–$150 double per night. Children under 18 free in parents' room. AE, DC, MC, V. **Parking:** $11.

Located three blocks from Head House Square and four blocks from Independence Hall, the 1986 Sheraton Society Hill nestles among the tree-lined cobblestone streets of this historic district. Set on a triangular 2½-acre site between Dock and South Front streets, the building was designed in keeping with the area's Flemish Bond architecture. Its skylit, four-story atrium is entered via a circular courtyard with a splashing fountain. To the right waits a sitting/cocktail area with comfortable chintz country sofas.

The guest rooms—on the long, low second, third, and fourth floors (the only Delaware River views are from the latter)—are a bit smaller than you'd expect; half have one king-size bed, and the others have two double beds. The furnishings of each are top-quality Drexel Heritage mahogany, with four lamps, two-post headboards, an upholstered love seat and chair, and glass-and-brass coffee tables. In each bath, dark marble tops the vanity and Martex bathrobes are provided. All rooms have remote-control cable TVs (Spectravision, with pay-per-view movies at $6.35 each). The decor is gender-neutral, with American art prints.

**Dining/Entertainment:** Spectacles, the hotel's video-disco, seats 170 and vies with Flanigans for Philadelphia's nightlife crowds. Americus, the moderately priced restaurant running the length of the hotel, is comfortably furnished with stained wood and blue-and-white-checkerboard–upholstered captain's chairs. A buffet breakfast ($6 to $9), lunch ($8 to $18), and dinner ($20 to $30) are offered.

**Services:** 24-hour room service, free shuttle van to Center City, concierge on duty daily from 6am to 11pm, National Interrent desk in lobby.

**Facilities:** Superior meeting facilities; fourth-floor indoor pool (open daily from 6am to 10pm), whirlpool, and small health club with trainers; third-floor sauna.

## MODERATE

**HOLIDAY INN–INDEPENDENCE MALL, 4th and Arch sts., Philadelphia, PA 19106. Tel. 215/923-8660,** or toll free 800/843-2355. Fax 215/923-4633. 364 rms. A/C TV TEL **Transportation:** Airport limousine stops here.

$ **Rates:** $113 standard with double bed; $130 room with king-size bed. Weekend packages from $98. Extra person $7 (up to four in a room). Children 18 and under free in parents' room. AE, DC, MC, V. **Parking:** $9.

This Holiday Inn, set back from the street, is absolutely the closest you're going to sleep to the Liberty Bell; just turn the corner and you're at the pavilion that houses it. The continued renovation of the bedrooms and public spaces and the addition of a concierge have given it a "superior" rating within the Holiday Inn organization.

**Dining:** You might consider the buffet lunch served in the renovated Benjamin's, done in handsome salmon and blue, or the less expensive Café Plain and Fancy.

**Facilities:** Two washer/dryers per floor; Budget Rent A Car desk in lobby, open weekdays until 7pm, weekends until 2pm.

**INDEPENDENCE PARK INN, 235 Chestnut St., Philadelphia, PA 19106. Tel. 215/922-4443,** or toll free 800/624-2988. Fax 215/922-4487. 36 rms. A/C TV TEL

$ **Rates** (including breakfast and afternoon tea): $115–$130 single; $125–$140 double. Weekend packages from $99. 15% AAA discount. AE, MC, V. **Parking:** $9 at nearby lot.

This top choice for bed-and-breakfast–style accommodations has a great location, two blocks from Independence Hall. It's a handsome 1856 former dry-goods store with renovated rooms, developed by a Philadelphian, Richard Trevlyn—he and his wife designed the front parlor's drapes and the planters out front—and operated by Sterling Hospitality.

The eight floors of guest rooms have four different color schemes; you'll find armoires, lathed bedposts, and lots of illumination, with an overhead light at each entrance foyer and four standing lamps in each room. The baths have big beveled mirrors, dropped ceilings, plush-pile towels, and soap dishes that are at both bath and shower heights. Although all the windows are triple casement and double glazed, specify an interior room if you're sensitive to noise from the

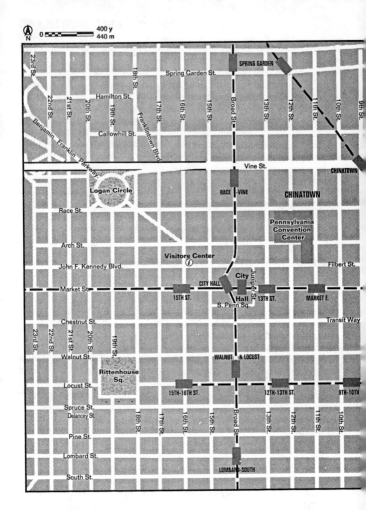

N
0 ━━━ 400 y
440 m

23rd St.
22nd St.
21st St.
20th St.
19th St.
18th St.
17th St.
16th St.
15th St.
Broad St.
13th St.
12th St.
11th St.
10th St.
9th St.

Spring Garden St.
SPRING GARDEN

Hamilton St.
Benjamin Franklin Parkway
Callowhill St.
Franklintown Blvd.

Vine St.

Logan Circle

RACE-VINE

CHINATOWN

Race St.

Pennsylvania Convention Center

Arch St.

Visitors Center
ⓘ

John F. Kennedy Blvd.

Filbert St.

Market St.
CITY HALL
City Hall
S. Penn Sq.
Juniper St.
15TH ST.
13TH ST.
MARKET E.

Chestnut St.

Transit Way

23rd St.
22nd St.
21st St.
20th St.
19th St.

Walnut St.
WALNUT & LOCUST

Rittenhouse Sq.

Locust St.
15TH-16TH ST.
12TH-13TH ST.
9TH-10TH

18th St.
17th St.
16th St.
15th St.
Broad St.
13th St.
12th St.
11th St.
10th St.

Spruce St.
Delancey St.

Pine St.

Lombard St.
LOMBARD-SOUTH

South St.

PENNSYLVANIA

Harrisburg
★
Philadelphia

8th St.
7th St.
6th St.
5th St.
4th St.
3rd St.
2nd St.
Front St.

Callowhill St.

Franklin St.

Franklin Sq.

676

Benjamin Franklin Bridge

30

Race St.

Elfroth's Alley

Independence St.

95

Delaware Ave.

Delaware River

Market St.

9TH & MARKET

5TH ST.

2ND ST.

Chestnut St.

Penn's Landing

Walnut St.

Willings Alley

W. Wash. Sq.

Washington Sq.

S. Wash. Sq.

Dock St.

Mattis St.

Spruce St.

8th St.
7th St.
6th St.
5th St.
4th St.
3rd St.

SOCIETY HILL

Pine St.

Head House Sq.

Lombard St.

South St.

Information ①

traffic on Chestnut Street. A third bed can be wheeled into your room for a child, at no additional charge.

**Dining:** The Independence Park has no restaurant. However, it serves a very passable hot-and-cold complimentary breakfast, with the Dickens Inn (see Chapter 6) supplying a complimentary afternoon tea. Special discount coupons to nearby restaurants are available at the desk.

**PENN'S VIEW INN, Front and Market sts., Philadelphia, PA 19106. Tel. 215/922-7600,** or toll free 800/331-7634. 28 rms. A/C TV TEL
**$ Rates** (including continental breakfast): $120 single or double. Weekend packages from $199 include two nights and Panorama restaurant dinner. AE, DC, MC, V. Guarantee requested on reservation. **Parking:** $8 at adjacent lot.

Tucked behind the Market Street ramp to I-95 in a renovated 1836 shipping warehouse, this inn is small and exquisite, with a European flair. It was developed by the Sena family, who started La Famiglia 150 yards south (see Chapter 6 for details) and have grown a small neighborhood empire. When you enter you'll feel like you're in a private club.

The decor is floral and rich; the basic question is traffic noise, but the rooms are well-insulated, with large framed mirrors, armoires, and efficient bath fixtures. The ceilings have been dropped for modern vents. A third bed can be wheeled into your room for $15.

**Dining:** Ristorante Panorama offers contemporary Italian cuisine at moderate prices. The 120 different wines served by the glass attract a connoisseur clientele.

**THOMAS BOND HOUSE, 129 S. 2nd St., Philadelphia, PA 19106. Tel. 215/923-8523.** 12 rms, 2 suites. A/C TV TEL
**$ Rates** (including breakfast): $80–$150 single or double. MC, V. **Parking:** $10 at adjacent lot.

This 1769 Georgian row house sitting almost directly across from the back of Independence Park is owned by the federal government, which kept the shell and gutted the interior. It's run by John and Peggy Poth, who have turned the guest rooms into cheerful, comfortable colonial-style accommodations. Guests now enter through the former side entrance, encountering a basic cream-and-blue color scheme, with map illustrations and secretary desks. The charming parlor has pink sofas and a replica Chippendale double chair, while the breakfast room has four tables for four. The hotel is named after the first occupant, the doctor who cofounded Pennsylvania Hospital with Benjamin Franklin.

# INEXPENSIVE

**COMFORT INN AT PENN'S LANDING, 100 North Delaware Ave., Philadelphia, PA 19106. Tel. 215/627-7900,** or toll free 800/228-5150. Fax 215/238-0809. 185 rms, 9 suites. A/C MINIBAR TV TEL
**$ Rates** (including continental breakfast): $68 single, $75 double. Weekend packages from $60 per night. AE, DC, MC, V. **Parking:** Free in adjacent lot.

One of Philadelphia's newest hotels, Comfort Inn at Penn's Landing is the area's only waterfront hotel as well, nestled into a corner of Old City between I-95 and the Delaware River, three blocks from the northbound ramp off the expressway. A shuttle van to Center City stops here, and the crosstown subway line is two blocks away.

A basic steel skeleton hung with blue-and-white concrete panels, Comfort Inn has been built to airport-area noise specifications, with insulated windows and other features to lessen the din of traffic. The eastern views of the river are stupendous. Two elevators take you to the guest rooms, which emphasize a contemporary look using light-walnut furnishings. There's a coin laundry on the second floor, and half the rooms are designated for nonsmokers.

Comfort Inn has no restaurant, but a complimentary continental breakfast—cold or microwavable food—is served in the cocktail lounge. Its fitness room stocks weights, treadmills, and bicycle machines.

## BUDGET

**OLD FIRST REFORMED CHURCH, Fourth and Race sts., Philadelphia, PA 19106. Tel. 215/922-4566.** 20 hostel mattresses (shared baths).

**$ Rates** (including continental breakfast): $10 singles aged 18–26 only. Check in between 5–10pm; maximum stay three nights. **Parking:** $8 per day at garage on 5th Street between Market and Chestnut. **Open:** July–Aug.

This church has responded to the major lack of Center City student accommodations by making its basement social hall available. Showers and security for valuables are available. There's a midnight curfew, after which the church doors are locked. Built in 1837, the church is situated one block east and two north of the 5th and Market streets SEPTA station.

# FROMMER'S SMART TRAVELER: HOTELS

1. Relatively few smart hotel patrons end up paying the listed "rack rates." Between corporate rates, AARP memberships, and affiliations with credit cards, frequent-flyer programs, and car-rental clubs, you should be able to find a stated policy for a 5% to 15% discount. The Philadelphia Convention and Visitors Bureau is a clearing house for discount coupons from several hotels (often the Holiday Inns and Comfort Inn) offered seasonally.
2. Ask about summer discounts. All city hotels—even the most expensive in a tourist destination such as Philadelphia—offer dramatic discounts.
3. Most hotels offer big discounts or package rates on weekends (Friday to Sunday night). If you're staying on a weekend, always ask about these.
4. Consider the bed-and-breakfast alternatives.
5. Before selecting a hotel, always ask about parking charges. These can range from complimentary to $15 per night in Center City.

# 2. CENTER CITY

## VERY EXPENSIVE

**HOTEL ATOP THE BELLEVUE, Broad and Walnut sts.** or **1415 Chancellor Court (between Walnut and Locust sts.), Philadelphia, PA 19102. Tel. 215/893-1776,** or toll free 800/222-0939. 170 rms. A/C MINIBAR TV TEL

**$ Rates:** $230 standard, $260 deluxe; $290 executive. Weekend rates as low as $115. AE, DC, MC, V. **Parking:** $13 at connected garage.

The "grande dame of Broad Street" was the most opulent hotel in the country when it opened in 1904. A notch below The Four Seasons, the Rittenhouse, and The Ritz-Carlton, it's still an outstanding experience.

The bottom two sections—the basement and ground floor—have been reshaped for retailers like Ralph Lauren, Gucci, Pierre Deux, and Dunhill. The hotel now occupies parts of floors 12 through 17, its first-class rooms serviced by Cunard Hotels and Resorts.

The rooms, as large as ever, are all slightly different—with a green-and-white decor and wall moldings reproduced from the 1904 designs. The makeover has added to each room extra-large goose-down pillows, three separate two-line phones adaptable for a computer modem, a VCR to supplement the TV/radio, a large bed, a writing desk, a round table, and four upholstered chairs. Closets have built-in tie racks and automatic lighting. The baths are dated but have electronics like hairdryers, TVs, and illuminated closeup mirrors.

**Dining/Entertainment:** Founders, the majestic 19th-floor restaurant, has two spectacular semicircular windows draped with dramatic swags of brown and cream. It is open Monday to Saturday from 7am to 11pm, and serves Sunday brunch from 10:30am to 2:30pm. The 80 seats are split spaciously, with candlelit tables, pink napery, wide armchairs, and modern scrollwork. There are dinner dancing and quiet live music several nights weekly. Service is classic French. The Library Lounge is quiet and a bit precious, with backgammon sets, copies of Gilbert Stuart full-length portraits, and a collection of books by and about Philadelphians. The lounge is open all day but begins serving at 5:30pm; it closes at 1am. The Barrymore Café serves breakfast and tea daily and cocktails from 5:30pm to midnight, with similarly splendid views.

On the 12th floor is the equally impressive Conservatory, at the base of a dramatic 80-foot atrium carved out of the original hotel. It has a wonderful, whimsical café ambiance, with trellises, oval cloud mural, porch swings, and two-story palms. It serves a generous $12 breakfast buffet, a $16 lunch buffet, and a $20 dinner.

**Services:** 24-hour room service, concierge, complimentary glass of champagne or hot drink on arrival, full-day child-care facility at the Sporting Club.

**Facilities:** A fourth-floor skywalk from the hotel at the ballroom level leads directly to the garage on the other side of Chancellor Court. It also goes to the Sporting Club, a Michael Graves–designed facility that boggles the eye with 93,000 square feet of health space, including a full-size NBA basketball court; a half-mile jogging track;

a 4-lane, 25-meter junior Olympic pool; and corridors of squash and racquetball courts. The club is open daily from 6:30am to 10pm and is available only to members and hotel guests (the latter for an additional $15).

**THE FOUR SEASONS HOTEL, One Logan Square, Philadelphia, PA 19103. Tel. 215/963-1500,** or toll free 800/332-3442. Fax 215/963-9562. 363 rms, 8 suites. A/C MINIBAR TV TEL

**$ Rates:** From $225 single, from $235 double, Four Seasons minisuites from $255, suites from $275. Weekend packages from $145 per night. AE, DC, MC, V. **Parking:** $18.50, valet.

The Four Seasons, one of the two best hotels in Philadelphia, is a member of a chain that sets a standard for international luxury lodgings. (Also included are New York's Pierre, the Four Seasons in Dallas and Washington, and London's Inn on the Park.) Its luxury is spare, refined, and understated.

Built in 1983, the Four Seasons is an eight-story curlicue on Logan Square. Its architecture blends into the neoclassical environment beautifully; the only slight drawbacks are the long hallways on the upper floors. It's separated from the "partner" CIGNA headquarters in complementary stone not by a wall but by a fountain and landscaped courtyard that opens as a café in summer. The hotel has landscaped the Logan Circle gardens as well.

As you're waved into the porte-cochere on 18th Street, you'll notice how well everything runs. Don't miss the tongue-in-cheek life-size bronze of a guest rushing to catch a cab! Your first view is of enormous masses of flowers, with stepped-stone levels, water, and honeyed woods stretching far into the distance. The lounge and promenade serve as foyers to the dining and meeting facilities and are paneled in a rare white mahogany; the lighting combines rock-crystal–and–brass chandeliers and silk-shaded lamps.

The guest rooms have distinct Federal-period furniture that's mixed with richer, more Victorian color schemes. Here again there is a very direct American elegance in each room: the desk, settee, armoire, and wing chair/ottoman combinations are top-quality Henredon. All the rooms have large windows or private verandas boasting marvelous views of Logan Circle or the interior courtyard. Many of the unusually large standard rooms have alcoves more likely found in suites. Also featured are free HBO, digital clock-radios, lockable closets, and two telephones. Each suite and the 92 Four Seasons minisuites adds a dining table, a marble-top coffee table, and a sofa. Each room contains a collection of books: the Time/Life series on U.S. history, travel literature, and so forth. The baths have the plushest floormats that you'll ever see plus amenities including hairdryers and all-incandescent lighting.

**Dining:** Of course you'll want to sample the fare in one of the famous Four Seasons restaurants, which have been collecting raves from local reviewers. The Fountain Restaurant, serving all three meals, continues the low-key elegance of the hotel by combining luxury (150 seats in wide, comfortable armchairs) with intimacy. Natural light streams over tapestries, fresh flowers, and walnut paneling. Lunch entrées feature omelets, calves' liver, and simpler fish, while dinner brings out meatier but equally subtle dishes.

The Swann Lounge, closer to the lobby corridor, has marble-top tables and a colorful, civilized look out of a Maurice Prendergast sketch. It's open for an extensive lunch, afternoon tea, early-evening cocktails, and dessert and drinks until midnight. As summer visitors can't help noticing, the Courtyard Café bubbles with light refreshments.

**Services:** Concierge, 24-hour room service, complimentary overnight shoeshine, terry-cloth robes, and town-car service within Center City.

**Facilities:** The Four Seasons has a strong commitment to the health and fitness of its guests, with three full floors reserved for nonsmokers. Besides European spa weekends, there are in-room literature on jogging in Fairmount Park and a basement health center. This complex includes a heated pool (large enough for laps), a superheated whirlpool, Universal machines, exercycles, and exercise mats—all spotlessly maintained. The pool area, in particular, is a beautifully designed setting of greenery, granite, and geraniums. The full-service hair salon right next door to the spa's reception room is open 7:30am–6pm; the small sundries shop off to the left of the lobby is open 7am–7pm.

**RITTENHOUSE HOTEL, 210 W. Rittenhouse Square, Philadelphia, PA 19103. Tel. 215/546-9000,** or toll free 800/635-1042. Fax 215/732-3364. 98 rms. A/C MINIBAR TV TEL

**$** **Rates:** From $190 single; from $215 double. Weekend rates from $155. Packages including health club, dinners, and other amenities are usually available. AE, DC, MC, V. **Parking:** $10.

 Among Philadelphia's luxury hotels, the Rittenhouse has the fewest and largest rooms, the most satisfying views, and the more home grown Philadelphia feel. Built in 1989, it's a jagged concrete-and-glass high-rise off the western edge of Philadelphia's most distinguished public square. The lobby is truly magnificent, with inlaid marble floors and a series of frosted-glass chandeliers and

---

# Ⓕ FROMMER'S COOL FOR KIDS:
## HOTELS

**The Four Seasons Hotel** *(p. 61)* offers the Saturday Lunch Club, a three-course meal for $21.50 designed for and presented to kids; it's featured on the first Saturday of the month.

**Rittenhouse Hotel** *(above)* intermittently offers children's cooking classes taught by Rena Coyle and also features some Saturday theme lunches for kids and their parents.

**Sheraton Inn Northeast** *(p. 80)* makes a special attempt to cater to families with its staffed pool and game room. It offers weekend packages with the nearby Sesame Place.

**Sheraton Society Hill** *(p. 54)* has a special children's check-in to the right of the lobby as well as concierge treatment with free snacks, the use of the game room, and so on.

sconces. This and The Four Seasons (see above) are AAA's only 5 Diamond Award winners in the state.

The Rittenhouse Hotel has 98 guest rooms on floors 5 through 9; the other floors contain coop residences. The rooms have bay windows, reinforced walls between rooms, and solid-wood doors. All have great views: The park is wonderfully green nine months of the year, but the western view of the Schuylkill and the Parkway is even more dramatic. (Be sure to specify a city or park view when making your reservation.) The regular rooms have one bay window; the luxury rooms have two; and all but five rooms have king-size beds. The decor in some rooms is primarily dark woods set against greens and purples, with wing chairs. Other rooms have peony-patterned moldings, squares of white pine, and canopy beds. Armoires contain the TVs and VCRs, with spirited renderings of city scenes by local artists on the walls. Note that power surges tend to throw off the digital clocks, though. The bathrooms are sumptuous, with brown marble, three-sided mirrors, TVs, telephones, and patron-sized shampoos and toiletries.

**Dining:** Executive Chef Gary Coyle, formerly of New York's La Côte Basque, oversees the cuisine in the hotel's two restaurants and two lounges. The restaurants occupy the second floor and overlook the park. The "star" is 210, serving lunch and dinner (closed Sunday). Physically, it's a stunning contemporary study in black and white, with a daily menu including such appetizers as beggars' purses (exotic dumplings) and fish carpaccio and such entrées as filet of mallard duck and chateaubriand of lotte fish. TreeTops is a sun-filled café that has surprisingly moderate prices for midday sandwiches and superb dinners. Breakfast is also served. The Boathouse Row Bar is the nicest imaginable Ralph Lauren–type re-creation of an authentic boathouse, with an entire rowing scull mounted overhead; however, it does get rowdy in the evening.

Completing the picture is the ground-floor Cassatt Tea Room and Lounge. The site was the original town house of the painter Mary Cassatt's brother, and the Rittenhouse has adorned an ingenious trellised private garden triangle with three drypoints by this American master.

**Services:** 24-hour room service, 2 Clef d'Or concierges, turndown service with written weather report for the morrow and radio tuned to soft classical music, twice-daily room cleaning. Many cooking classes and/or lunch events are held for children.

**Facilities:** The third floor is split between Nan Duskin (the city's toniest retailer) and Toppers Spa, a fitness club with a five-lane indoor pool, a sundeck, and an exercise-machine and aerobics room. The floor above is devoted to an executive business center, with fax machines and typists on call. Philadelphia National Bank maintains a personal service branch and ATM in the building.

**THE RITZ-CARLTON PHILADELPHIA, 17th and Chestnut sts. at Liberty Place, Philadelphia, PA 19103. Tel. 215/563-1600,** or toll free 800/241-3333. Fax 215/564-9559. 290 rms, 17 suites. A/C MINIBAR TV TEL

**$ Rates:** $205–$245 single or double; $285 Ritz-Carlton Club. Weekend rates from $139. Packages include valet parking and fitness center. AE, DC, MC, V. **Parking:** $15.75 self-parking, $18 valet.

✪ If The Four Seasons is luxury with a 20th-century slant and the Rittenhouse captures the 19th century, then The Ritz-Carlton claims the 18th century. Opened in 1990 as part of Liberty Place, the past decade's most exciting effort to reclaim the preeminence of "downtown," the hotel is a superb blend of luxury amenities and service, steps away from the best in urban life.

The Ritz-Carltons have been on a boom during the last decade; their exteriors fit into the terrain from Boston to Laguna Niguel, but their interiors feature valuable Georgian antiques, china, and paintings, set among top-of-the-line reproduction furniture. The Liberty Place development was designed around this hotel. A small porte-cochere and a ground-floor lobby on 17th Street lead to a series of smaller, almost residential rooms that contain the front and concierge desks, the dining areas, and the elevators on the second floor.

The guest rooms feature bedside walnut tables, desks, beds with spindle-top headboards (with four pillows!), and Wedgwood or Sandwich glass lamps. Large walnut armoires house the TVs, clothing drawers, and minibars. The color schemes are muted, and all rooms are provided with two phone lines and fax- or computer-capable lines. The modern baths are outfitted with black and white tiles, silverplate fixtures, Miroir Brot (magnifying mirrors), and lots of toiletries. The service is simply impeccable, as a result of fanatical training. The Club accommodations on floors 14 and 15 (an extra $40 per day) add private-key access, a separate concierge, a wonderfully relaxing lounge with newspapers and magazines, and a rotating feast of five light buffet servings daily. These floors are wonderful for families.

**Dining/Entertainment:** Three distinctive locations combine uncompromising cuisine with gracious service and ambiance. (See also Chapter 6.) The Dining Room is decorated in American Federal and concentrates on contemporary French dishes under the hand of chef Francesco Martorella, late of award-winning Ciboulette a few blocks away. On the other side of the lounge fireplace, the mahogany-paneled and period-furnished Grill and Grill Bar have quickly become "Best of Philly" winners, with daily lunches and dinners of steaks, chops, and fish specialties. The Lobby Lounge has expanded its offerings to a continental breakfast, a formal tea, and hors d'oeuvres and desserts, with a constantly crackling fireplace. Classical and pop music accompanies afternoon and evening service.

**Services:** 24-hour room service, 24-hour concierge, turndown service, complimentary morning newspapers, transport to and from airport, car-rental arrangements, very frequent weekend or month-long festivals in connection with museum exhibitions or city theme events.

**Facilities:** There are a small exercise and sauna facility, superb business meeting rooms, and the like, but the most impressive extra is the internal connection to the 70 Shops at Liberty Place (see Chapter 9), a very successful urban mall built around a Crystal Palace–like rotunda. The shops include The Coach Store, J. Crew, Godiva, Handblock, and Brentano's.

# EXPENSIVE

**THE BARCLAY, 237 S. 18th St., Philadelphia, PA 19103. Tel. 215/545-0300,** or toll free 800/421-6662. Fax 215/545-2896. 240 rms. A/C TV TEL

**$ Rates:** $135–$175 single; $145–$175 double; minisuites from $200. Weekend packages from $75 double per night on Fri–Sat. AE, DC, MC, V. **Parking:** $15.75 in nearby lot.

The Barclay, a quiet hostelry on Rittenhouse Square East since 1929, used to be the host of such diverse celebrities as Katharine Hepburn and the Grateful Dead and the residence of such local luminaries as Eugene Ormandy. From the lobby, a long, thin arcade of glass and ivory, to the fine amenities of the French provincial guest rooms with their high four-poster beds and antique armoires, it's always been a sentimental favorite.

However, The Barclay is having a tough time since the opening of the Rittenhouse across the square; it was put up for sale in 1989 but still has no takers. So look for deep discounts, especially on weekends—the $75 basic is the lowest in this category—but also don't expect the best.

**Dining/Entertainment:** There's one restaurant, Le Beau Lieu. A jazz pianist entertains in the hotel lounge.

**Services:** Concierge, room service.

**KORMANSUITES HOTEL AND CONFERENCE CENTER, 2001 Hamilton St. (just off the Parkway), Philadelphia, PA 19130. Tel. 215/569-7300.** Fax 215/569-0584. 250 rms, 12 Grand Club suites. A/C MINIBAR TV TEL

**$ Rates** (including continental breakfast): $129–$139 single; $149–$159 double; one-bedroom suite $169; two-bedroom suite $179. Weekend packages from $79 double per night. Children free in parents' room. AE, DC, MC, V. **Parking:** Free.

The amenities and the location of this hotel make it an excellent value at rack rates; the weekend packages make it outstanding. You'll recognize it by the bright neon scribble near its roof north of Logan Circle, visible from anywhere south.

KormanSuites is really a grand hotel, but it's in separate pieces. Two 28-story towers are joined by a marble-and-mahogany lobby and a glass-enclosed corridor that looks out onto KormanSuites' lush Japanese sculpture garden and pool.

The standard rooms are unbelievably spacious, and a corridor contains a microwave, a minibar, and a coffeemaker. The suites add full kitchens with dishwashers, stoves, coffeemakers, and telephones. Each "living" area has a full dining table for four, a TV, a full couch, and three double closets. Each bedroom features a queen-size bed and another TV (in suites, with built-in VCR), and the adjoining bath has a stacked washer/dryer. The views are great: to the north, highlights of 19th-century manufacturing and churches; to the south, 20th-century Center City, and these are the only hotel rooms in town with doorbells. In short, you could live here with a family very happily for the price of a single room.

**Dining:** Catalina is not the hotel restaurant; it's a freestanding operation within the complex that is succeeding as a neighborhood favorite for moderate California-style mixtures of East Coast and West Coast. Hotel guests are offered complimentary continental breakfasts, served from the bar from 6 to 10am.

**Services:** Complimentary shuttle van running hourly through Center City to Independence Park, concierge, 24-hour message center and garage attendants.

**Facilities:** Outdoor pool, Jacuzzi, two tennis and platform tennis courts, high-tech spa and fitness center, full-service hair salon, ATM on-site.

**THE LATHAM, 135 S. 17th St. at Walnut St., Philadelphia, PA 19103. Tel. 215/563-7474,** or toll free 800/528-4261. Fax 215/563-4034. 140 rms, 3 suites. A/C MINIBAR TV TEL

**$ Rates:** $130 standard single; $150 double; $160–$180 superior with king-size bed; $325+ suite. Basic weekend package $89 double per night (breakfast and parking included); other packages $129+ double per night (with more amenities). One or two children free in parents' room. AE, DC, MC, V. **Parking:** $14 in nearby lot.

The Latham brings to mind a small, superbly run Swiss hostelry, with its charm, congeniality, and small attentions. The Latham was an apartment house until about 20 years ago; now it's a Lincoln Hotel, but nothing has gone the chain route.

On weekday mornings the lobby, a high-ceilinged salon with terrazzo highlights, is filled with refreshed executives who look as though the Latham truly is their home away from home. Dealings with the reception area are quick and professional, and newsstand and lobby phones discreetly nestle in one corner. The Latham does no convention business.

The guest rooms, renovated from 1988 to 1990, are exquisite — not huge or lavish but perfectly proportioned and done in burgundy or light green. About half come with one double bed, the others with two singles. Each minibar combines a digital drink dispenser (with totals registered automatically at the cashier's) with space for storing your own supplies. Louis XIV–style writing tables, modern upholstered armchairs, and contemporary prints mix the taste of different eras harmoniously. The bathrooms feature Princess phones, embossed soaps, and Bic disposable razors. Full-wall mirrors, large marblelike basins, and oversize towels accentuate the white-toned interiors. *Note:* The weekend packages are great bargains.

**Dining:** The Latham is located near Philadelphia's most vaunted restaurants—nevertheless, its own kitchen, at Bogart's, is extremely well regarded, as is the bar at Allegra. Bogart's prepares modern American fare like roast duckling and braised salmon; it's open for breakfast, lunch, and dinner.

**Services:** Concierge, turndown service with Godiva chocolate mints, valet parking.

**Facilities:** Free access to nearby fitness club with indoor pool; complimentary HBO, CNN, and ESPN.

**PHILADELPHIA HILTON AND TOWERS, Broad St. at Locust St., Philadelphia, PA 19107. Tel. 215/893-1600,** or toll free 800/445-8667. 439 rms. A/C MINIBAR TV TEL

**$ Rates:** $130–$160 single; $145–$175 double; $185–$200 deluxe. Weekend package $79+ per night available for up to four family members staying in one room. AE, DC, MC, V. **Parking:** $11 in adjoining garage.

In 1991, Hilton took over the Philadelphia Hershey (built in 1983), a very solid anchor on South Broad Street. Although the location is no longer ideal for business travelers, it is prime for tourists, and the weekend packages are quite affordable.

You'll probably enter through the corridor connecting the lobby to the garage on the block's southern side. The motor entrances ingeniously keep traffic flows separate for three floors of meeting facilities. During registration, take a good look at the four-story atrium: A web of steel struts finished in black enamel supports a diagonal sheet of glass panes, sloping down to a glass wall at street level. Down here, small patches of salmon brick in herringbone patterns alternate with patches of green carpeting by the love seats. The human scale is somewhat affirmed by greenery and nooks on the overhanging balconies.

The guest rooms, all completely renovated in the last two years, each have two views of town because of the sawtooth design. Obviously, the higher floors afford the better views; the views of the Delaware River (eastern) or City Hall (northeast corner) are the most popular. The amenities include a color TV with built-in AM/FM radio and alarm clock, two upholstered barrel chairs, a wide antechamber with a writing table and telephone, and sliding-door closets. The bathrooms have travel emergency supplies, safety-grip bars in the shower, and well-placed soap dishes. Ten rooms, next to the elevators on certain floors, are designed for the disabled.

**Dining:** The Café Académie, an informal 220-seat restaurant and lounge, continues the glossy atrium connection. If you dine here (breakfast, lunch, and dinner served), ask for one of the tables overlooking the action outside. The decor is Colonial-meets-California. Thirty wines are available for tasting at your table or the Wine Bar, a 120-seat lounge open 4pm to 2am.

**Services:** A guest services desk is staffed 16 hours daily. Avis will deliver rental cars to the hotel door.

**Facilities:** The Spinning Wheel is a well-stocked sundries shop. The fifth-floor Racquet and Health Club is free to all guests. You can tan, steam, swim in an indoor pool, sun, whirlpool, or work out on a CAM II exercise machine, a sort of dial-your-weight Nautilus. Two racquetball courts can be reserved for $8 per hour, with no equipment charge. A small jogging track circles a huge oak-planked deck, and summer brings many hotel parties and parade views.

**PHILADELPHIA MARRIOTT, 12th and Market sts., Philadelphia, PA 19107. Tel. 215/972-6700,** or toll free 800/228-9290. Fax 215/972-6704. 1103 rms. A/C MINIBAR TV TEL
**$ Rates:** Not set at press time; anticipate $165 single or double. Weekend specials $110+ per night. AE, DC, MC, V. **Parking:** $10.

The Convention Center's Marriott has been more than a decade in the planning; no hotel could commit until city and state funding for the center itself was assured. This is finally the case, and the Marriott in May 1992 broke ground for the biggest hotel in Pennsylvania. Opening is anticipated in September 1994. The major entrance to the hotel itself will be on Filbert Street, between Market and Arch streets, with an elevated covered bridge to Reading Terminal to the east. Setbacks and terraces will provide plenty of natural light and views.

**Dining:** Three restaurants are planned: one gourmet, one casual, and a continental sidewalk café. Three lounges also are planned.

**Services:** All possible corporate and some luxury services.

**Facilities:** Health club with indoor lap pool, whirlpool, aerobics room, and saunas.

**WYNDHAM FRANKLIN PLAZA HOTEL, 16th and Vine sts., Philadelphia, PA 19103. Tel. 215/448-2000,** or toll free 800/822-4200. Fax 215/448-2864. 758 rms, 38 suites. A/C MINIBAR TV TEL

**$ Rates:** $145 single; $165 double; $185–$205 deluxe. Weekend package $69 for one night; upgraded $119 package includes virtually all meals at hotel restaurants. Group rates negotiable. Children 18 and under free in parents' room. AE, DC, MC, V. **Parking:** $13, self; $17, valet.

The Wyndham is a convention hotel in a city that's soon to have a real convention center seven blocks away. Nevertheless, it's been functioning as a convenient meeting center and urban resort just off I-676 (two blocks north of Suburban Station) since the late 1970s, with four restaurants, a health club, a swimming pool, a clever and breathtaking lobby, and rooftop dancing.

The complex uses a full city block, splitting it between two towers (one's the headquarters of SmithKline Beecham) and a massive convention facility/health club/restaurant area. The lobby, lounge, and three restaurants are beautifully integrated under a dramatic 70-foot glass roof sloping down to a small public park off Vine Street—in fact, the design won the 1978 hotel architecture award. Free-standing escalators and stairs wind their way up to the mezzanine and ballroom levels.

Two thirds of the guest rooms have a pair of double beds. All are done in pleasant pastel shades and have such near-deluxe features as floor-to-ceiling mirrors, TVs with AM/FM radios, and upholstered chrome chairs. Request a west view above the 19th floor to get an unobstructed peek at the Parkway, although be forewarned that the cathedral bells below ring hourly from 7am. You'll also find a complimentary sewing kit, fine-washables detergent, and a shower cap.

**Dining:** Horizons—open Monday to Friday from 5pm to 11pm, Saturday and Sunday until 1am—is a swanky rooftop affair, with pinlights and mirrors. The Terrace is a coffee shop with a difference: Separated informally from the lobby by textiles and planters, it seats 190 on two levels and serves excellent fare daily from 7am to 11pm. Between Friends, the flagship, features French tableside service in opulent surroundings of oil portraits, banks of flowers, and mirrored angle piers. Dinner will cost about $40 per person; lunch is also served. A small atrium with an enclosed sidewalk café connects to the SmithKline building; the café is open daily from 7am to 3pm.

**Services:** Room service, travel service.

**Facilities:** The third-floor Clark's Uptown offers an indoor swimming pool (21 by 45 feet), a sauna, and a track—all free to hotel guests. An all-day fee of $10 gets you racquetball (three courts), squash (three courts), outdoor handball (three courts), and tennis (two courts). Around the latter is a one-eighth-mile jogging track. A sundeck, a whirlpool, a Nautilus machine, a snackbar, and superb locker and exercise facilities round out the picture.

# MODERATE

**HOLIDAY INN–CENTER CITY, 18th and Market sts., Philadelphia, PA 19103. Tel. 215/561-7500** or toll free 800/465-4329. Fax 215/561-4484. 445 rms, 54 suites. A/C TV TEL

**$ Rates:** $105 single; $120 double; $132 suite. Children under 18 free in parents' room. AE, DC, MC, V. **Parking:** $11.

Believe it or not, the Holiday Inn was the only hotel to open in

Philadelphia in the 1970s, and it underwent a 1986 top-to-bottom refurbishment. It's very popular with conventioneers and relocating executives, but hotel policy is to leave at least 40% of the 445 rooms free for tourists. For solid accommodations with no real surprises, slightly above normal Holiday Inn criteria, this is an excellent choice.

The lobby, which is a people-watchers' bar in the evening, combines lush greenery, plush armchairs, and entrances from both 18th Street and the garage. Above lobby level, a parking garage and meeting halls occupy the next 6 floors, and rooms and several suites fill the next 17.

By Philadelphia standards, the inn's guest rooms are large, each holding two firm double beds, brown vinyl furniture, a Formica desk or table, and cheerful quilted bedspreads. The redone furnishings include color TVs, digital clock-radios, deep carpeting, drapes, and mauve patterns in the wallpaper. Two floors are devoted to Executive Level suites, offering upgraded decor and complimentary breakfast.

**Dining:** You've a choice of three hotel restaurants. The formal restaurant, Reflections (open Monday to Friday from 11:30am to 1am, Saturday and Sunday from 4pm to 1am) serves largely continental cuisine. Dinner runs about $18 per person.

**Facilities:** The outdoor pool perched atop the garage extension's roof (open daily from 10am to 9pm in summer) is free to guests, who can use a weight room with rowing and Nautilus machines for a nominal charge.

**THE WARWICK,** 17th and Locust sts., Philadelphia, PA 19103. Tel. 215/735-6000, or toll free 800/523-4210. Fax 215/790-7766. 187 rms, 3 suites. A/C MINIBAR TV TEL

**$ Rates:** $125 single with one queen-size bed; $140 double with two beds; suites from $175. Package rates available from $95. AE, DC, MC, V. **Parking:** $12 in adjacent lot.

If you wanted to live in a luxurious older apartment building in the most cosmopolitan section of Philadelphia, you'd head for The Warwick. Most recently renovated in 1988, 210 rooms are rented or belong to condo owners, while 190 rooms and suites are the hotel's.

The Warwick's lobby stunningly mixes the old and the new: Many of the 1926 friezes and mantels have been reworked and repainted, while gleaming contemporary ensembles stretch themselves on Persian carpets. The mirrored pilasters may edge toward garishness, but the wall braziers and broad-leafed plants ensure a warm, splendid atmosphere. A double security system guards all floors, with locking doors in the halls between suites and the elevator. Hall phones are provided for visitors.

The guest rooms are basically done in English country, with hand-milled sandalwood soap, bedside clock-radios, and complimentary HBO on the armoire-mounted TVs. The Warwick remains one of the few hotels with different, original art in every bedroom and bath.

The Theater Package, $290 per couple, includes Friday and Saturday accommodations, valet parking, a $40 credit at the 1701 Café on Friday evening, a breakfast in the 1701 Café on Saturday, Saturday evening at a dinner theater, and a Sunday champagne brunch in the Polo Bay.

**Dining:** The 1701 Café, with white tablecloths and dark wood paneling, offers continental cuisine at moderate prices. It's open for breakfast, lunch, and dinner.

**Services:** Concierge (Betty George is one of the best in town), room service, complimentary admission to Polo Bay nightclub, overnight complimentary shoeshine.

# INEXPENSIVE

**QUALITY INN HISTORIC DOWNTOWN SUITES, 1010 Race St., Philadelphia, PA 19107. Tel. 215/922-1730,** or toll free 800/228-5151. Fax 215/922-1730. 96 suites. A/C MINIBAR TV TEL

**$ Rates** (including continental breakfast): $75 king; $79 two double beds. Each additional person $10. AE, DC, MC, V. **Parking:** Free in garage next door, discount at nearby lot.

You'll find spacious and reasonable accommodations at the new Quality Inn Historic Downtown Suites in the heart of Philadelphia's Chinatown—and around the corner from the new Convention Center. It's a property purchased at a low price and then properly renovated for high hotel occupancy.

The building itself, from the 1880s, is handsome dark-red brick with lots of terra-cotta tiling and wide arches. For many years a bentwood furniture factory, it retains 13-foot ceilings, solid floors, and wood crossbeams. You'll enter the inn through large double Chinese doors flanked by Ming lions. The reception desk is to the right, while the Lotus Inn—the somewhat incongruous spot for breakfast—can be reached on the left or from the street. Check-in is set a bit late, at 3pm, but your bags can be left with reception.

Quality Inn Downtown offers a couple special advantages for families. There's a very clean and well-stocked Chinese market directly across the street, and Reading Terminal Market is within two blocks. (No hotel restaurant, however.) The Gallery, the Rouse Corporation's urban family-oriented mall, is also only two blocks away. If you're considering late-night explorations of Philadelphia, though, try to avoid the Reading Terminal train underpass at Race and 13th streets.

**Facilities:** Health club, sauna.

**RAMADA INN–CENTER CITY, 501 N. 22nd St., Philadelphia, PA 19130. Tel. 215/568-8300,** or toll free 800/272-6232. Fax 557-0259. 278 rms, 4 suites. A/C TV TEL

**$ Rates:** $56–$72 single; $78–$82 double. Children under 18 free in parents' room. Weekend packages from $49. AE, CD, MC, V. **Parking:** Free.

This hotel joined the Ramada system in late 1991, after previous stints as a Quality Inn. Renovations completed in early 1992 were long overdue. It's now the single best hotel buy for families in Center City, just off the Parkway.

The Ramada Inn–Center City is an easy 10-block distance from all three major train stations and a short loop off the Schuylkill Expressway. Under the porte-cochere you'll find three wings of rooms off a central hub. They face the Parkway and the gardens of the Rodin Museum. There are a swimming pool and parking around and even under the facility, since part of the Ramada Inn is raised on concrete piers. California lodge patterns prevail—blond oak and brass and a lot of beige and burgundy, with wicker barrel chairs.

**Dining:** Situated where the three room-wings converge, the glassed-in 150-seat City Lights Café takes advantage of the southern exposure. The café serves an opulent $8.95 breakfast buffet. Logan's Tavern is a sports bar.

**Facilities:** Swimming pool, free parking, convenience store across Hamilton Street.

---

# 3. UNIVERSITY CITY

## MODERATE

**PENN TOWER HOTEL, Civic Center Blvd. at 34th St., Philadelphia, PA 19104. Tel. 215/387-8333,** or toll free 800/356-7366. Fax 215/386-8306. 231 rms, 10 suites. A/C TV TEL **Transportation:** Limo service to and from the airport.

**$ Rates:** $85–$115 single; $85–$125 double. A 25% discount for relatives of patients in University and Children's hospitals. Weekend packages start at $85 per couple per night. AE, DC, MC, V. **Parking:** $9.

**⑤** Penn Tower is a greatly improved version of a former Hilton, built with a direct skywalk to University Hospital and within steps of the University of Pennsylvania, 30th Street Station, the Civic Center, and Drexel University. The University of Pennsylvania bought it in 1986. The hotel part of the tower comprises floors 11 through 20 (lower floors are used by the university as medical offices), as well as an enclosed garage and ground-floor restaurants and shops.

You'll have to get used to spirited displays of red and blue, the Penn colors, and a long lobby corridor of rough-textured concrete that leads to the reception desk. Florist and sundries shops are on the right, and I.D.E.A.S., a lounge, is on the left. Also on the left is an escalator that leads to second-floor meeting areas. Those handsome chairs and rugs were picked up for a song from the Bellevue Hotel in 1986.

**Dining:** I.D.E.A.S. is the lobby cocktail lounge. P.T.'s, a casual restaurant-coffee shop, serves breakfast, lunch, and dinner.

**Facilities:** Penn Tower is fully accessible to the disabled. It offers complimentary guest passes to Penn's nearby Hutchinson Health Complex for its track and rowing machines and makes tennis reservations at courts one block away.

**SHERATON UNIVERSITY CITY, 36th and Chestnut sts., Philadelphia, PA 19103. Tel. 215/387-8000,** or toll free 800/325-3535. Fax 215/387-7920. 377 rms. A/C TV TEL

**$ Rates:** $112–$124 single; $122–$134 double; $195+ suites. Extra person $10. Children under 12 free in parents' room. Weekend and package rates from $77 to $89 per night. AE, DC, MC, V. **Parking:** Free.

A favorite with business and academic visitors, located west of the Schuylkill River, this cheerful, moderately priced hotel is close to Center City via public transport or car. Though privately owned, this Sheraton offers the same comfort standard of any Sheraton—a little nicer, in fact, because the building (14 years old) is totally renovated. Also, there's a fine view of the university and the Philadelphia skyline (the Civic Center is only four blocks away).

You'll enter the inn through a spacious Spanish-tiled lobby with

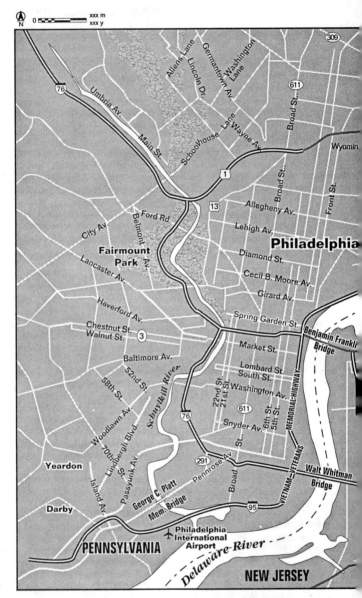

access to the parking garage, located on the first five floors. The remaining 15 floors hold guest rooms with the same basic decor of floral-print bedspreads and curtains, dark-blue or gold carpeting, and beige wallpaper. The accoutrements include white molded-plastic chairs, octagonal coffee tables, and low-slung Mediterranean dressers with TVs and AM/FM radio consoles built in. The beds are extremely firm.

**Dining:** In the hotel are Smart Alex restaurant, a deli, and a cocktail lounge.

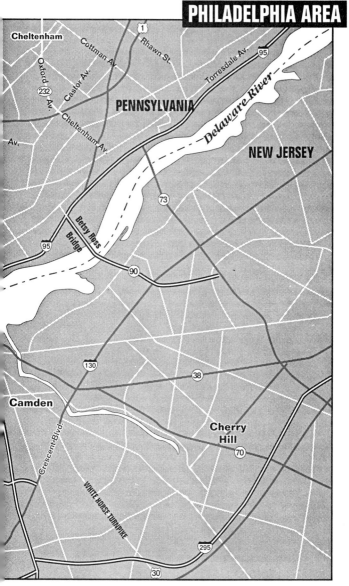

**PHILADELPHIA AREA**

**Facilities:** Small outdoor pool open in summer, ice and soft drinks available on every other floor.

## BUDGET

**INTERNATIONAL HOUSE, 3701 Chestnut St., Philadelphia, PA 19104. Tel. 215/387-5125.** Fax 215/895-6562. 379 rms (none with bath). A/C
**$ Rates:** $49 single; $57 double. Deposit fee equal to one night's

stay required on registration. No children allowed. MC, V. **Parking:** Many lots are nearby.

This is a tremendous value, but it depends on who you are, since International House is not a formal hotel but a residence for non-U.S. students and academics during the school year. About 200 rooms for academically affiliated transients are open year round, more in summer. Related facilities and programs include a low-cost International Bazaar shop; many coffee hours, concerts, and films, all at nominal costs; and a cafeteria, Eden, a favorite dining spot in University City. To get here, you can take bus D on Walnut Street from Center City.

Most guest rooms will resemble your college single; doubles are rarely available. Tough tan carpeting covers all floors, and the lighting is adequate, with two lamps and a vanity lamp above the mirror. The walls are solid and acoustically dead. Linen and towels are in the rooms, but soap and cups are your own responsibility. There are plenty of sparkling-clean showers, sinks, and bathrooms on each floor.

**Facilities:** Lounges with pay phones on each floor, stream of cultural and social events, laundry.

**DIVINE TRACY HOTEL, 20 S. 36th St., Philadelphia, PA 19104. Tel. 215/382-4310.** Fax 215/387-0157. 100 rms (95 with bath). A/C in 50% of rooms.
**$ Rates:** $20 single with shared bath; $23–$26 single with bath; $34–$40 double. Traveler's checks accepted but no credit cards.
**Parking:** Garage nearby.

**S** Divine Tracy was a major African-American evangelical based in Philadelphia, and this very proper and dignified residence for weekend religious retreats has 100 rooms available for weekday tourists. Except for the doubles, the floors are single-gender, with no smoking, indecorous clothing, or loud behavior. The front desk is open daily from 7am to 11pm only. The guest rooms are spotless and a step back in time. The Keyflower Restaurant is a low-priced vegetarian cafeteria open for lunch and dinner. To get here, you can take bus D on Walnut Street from Center City.

**UNIVERSITY CITY GUEST HOUSES, P.O. Box 28612, 2933 Morris Rd., Philadelphia, PA 19151. Tel. 215/387-3731.** A/C TEL
**$ Rates:** $25–$75 single or double. Children allowed in some situations. Traveler's checks accepted but no credit cards.

This is basically a neighborhood collection of bed-and-breakfasts, most within walking distance of the University of Pennsylvania and University Hospital. Most hosts are academically affiliated. Parking is provided at most places.

# 4. AIRPORT

## EXPENSIVE

**GUEST QUARTERS SUITE HOTEL, 4101 Island Ave., Philadelphia, PA 19153. Tel. 215/365-6600,** or toll free 800/

424-2900. Fax 215/492-9858. 251 units. A/C MINIBAR TV TEL
**Transportation:** Free shuttle from the airport.
**$ Rates** (including buffet breakfast): $155 single; $175 double.
Eighth-floor club-style Top of the Quarters $15 extra. Weekend
package $69 Friday, $89 Saturday. Children under 12 free in
parents' room. AE, DC, MC, V. **Parking:** Free.

For first-class prices you get deluxe suites of beautifully furnished
bedrooms and living rooms, which ring dramatic multistory atriums
containing restaurant and lounge seating. The occupancy rates here
are among the highest in town.

The developer, Beacon Hospitality Group, has been working on
the Gateway Center complex between I-95 and Penna. 291 on Island
Avenue—so far, it includes the Guest Quarters Hotel and an
excellent-value Days Inn (see below). Near the entrance is a modern
version of Independence Hall's "Rising Sun" chair. You'll be struck
by the expanse of the atrium area, with its dramatic glass skylights,
wicker armchairs, and several terraced pavilions. A credit card–type
key works for your door only during the length of your stay.

A glass elevator hugs the interior wall of the atrium. The hall
walkways line the atrium, giving light and security that are particularly appreciated by families and women business travelers. The standard rooms have recently been done in deep green and mauve, with
king-sized beds, round dining room tables for four, armoires conceal-
ing remote-control TVs, convertible sofabeds, and telephones with
speakers. There's minimal airport noise. Individual climate controls
are located near the wet bar, small refrigerator, and marble-top vanity
and bath. The small patterns on the upholstery, white oak inlay, and
Chinese vase lamps continue into the bedrooms, with king-size beds,
digital clock-radios, and yet more telephones and TVs. Mirrored
closets will contribute to your impression of occupying a furnished
apartment.

**Dining/Entertainment:** The Terrace Lounge offers fairly lavish
complimentary hors d'oeuvres and low drink prices daily from 5 to
7pm. Pianists and vocalists perform Friday and Saturday. At the
Atrium Lounge and Café underneath palms and ficus trees, the
favorites include a delicious shellfish-and-mushroom bisque and
samplings from the mesquite grill, served with stir-fried vegetables.
It's open evenings.

**Services:** *USA Today* delivered to door, complimentary coffee
machines, Ambassador car-rental desk in lobby.

**Facilities:** Complimentary indoor pool, whirlpool, sauna,
steambath.

**PHILADELPHIA AIRPORT MARRIOTT HOTEL, at Philadel-
phia International Airport, Philadelphia, PA 19153. Tel.
215/365-4150,** or toll free 800/228-9290. Fax 215/365-3875.
331 rms. A/C MINIBAR TV TEL
**$ Rates:** $139 single; $149 double. Weekend rate $94 single or
double. AE, DC, MC, V. **Parking:** Free.

The Philadelphia Airport Marriott ranks with the Hyatt Regency
O'Hare in Chicago as one of the nicest airport hotels in America. It's
removed from flight patterns, features a lobby and cocktail lounge
built around a lushly planted indoor pool, and offers serious dining
possibilities. As in all airport hostelries, business travelers predominate during the week and reservations would be desirable. For drivers
from the airport, exit on Route 291 and travel 1⅓ miles. The hotel is

on the left. From I-95, exit at Enterprise Avenue, go to Island Avenue, and turn right. The hotel is ½ mile on the right. There's also a free shuttle service to and from the airport.

The guest rooms are classically American—spacious, comfortable, and anonymously elegant. The headboards of the queen-size beds are cane framed in chrome, which match the sprightly quilted spreads. All TV controls can be handled from the night tables. The barrel chairs and sofa beds, in tan and deep brown, show an unusual understanding of human contours.

**Dining/Entertainment:** Harper's, a turn-of-the-century bistro, offers a salad bar and prime ribs plus an $8 lunch buffet. Sigi's fits the bill as a cocktail lounge with a disc jockey. There's a "Hungry Hour" buffet (5–6pm). Pride of place belongs to Chardonnay's, one of Philadelphia's best wine-by-the-glass restaurants (open for dinner Monday to Saturday from 6 to 10pm).

**Services:** Free cable with HBO, ESPN, and CNN; complimentary daily newspaper.

**Facilities:** Indoor pool, whirlpool, health club (open daily 6am–11pm), sauna.

**RADISSON HOTEL PHILADELPHIA AIRPORT, 500 Stevens Dr., Philadelphia, PA 19113. Tel. 215/521-5900,** or toll free 800/333-3333. Fax 215/521-4362. 353 rms. A/C TV TEL

**$ Rates:** $139 single; $149 double. Lower weekend packages available. AE, DC, MC, V. **Parking:** Free.

Opened in March 1991, the Radisson is trading on its spanking-new looks, sleek 12-story glass atrium, and corporate clout to support its rates. The design is ingenious, with northward balcony views of Center City expanded by a second enclosed atrium, overlooking a pool and health club. The guest rooms have two phones (one a speakerphone), and the materials are mostly veneers and hollow core. To get here, drivers should take Rt. 291, 1 mile west of the airport, and follow the signs over a winding road. There's also free van transport to and from the airport.

**Dining:** The Atrium Lounge (open to 1am) has a triangle of bar seats around postmodern pyramids. Trophies sports bar (open to 2am) is a 1960s-style room with jukeboxes and the like. Hampton Grille, a trendy coffee shop, serves breakfast, lunch, and dinner.

**Services:** Room service.

**Facilities:** Indoor pool, health club, game rooms.

## MODERATE

**AIRPORT HILTON INN, 10th St. and Packer Ave., Philadelphia, PA 19148. Tel. 215/755-9500,** or toll free 800/445-8667. Fax 215/462-6947. 238 rms. A/C TV TEL

**$ Rates:** $79–$120 single; $89–$130 double. AE, DC, MC, V. **Parking:** Free.

Philadelphia is one of the few eastern cities with a vast sports complex within its city limits. On the former marshes where the Delaware meets the Schuylkill, the Airport Hilton Inn sits across the street from the Spectrum's hockey and basketball and pop concerts and Veterans Stadium, home of the Phillies and Eagles. It's the closest major hotel to the Navy Yard as well and a convenient midpoint between Center City and the airport. To get here, drivers on I-76 East should take the last exit before the bridge to New Jersey. From the airport, take I-95 North to the bridge exit and stay on Packer Avenue. There's also free van transport to and from airport.

All the bedrooms were renovated in 1991, with Bombay Company–style furnishings, Sony clock-radios, and solid-core doors. Baths have new 9-inch Italian tiles but otherwise are slightly dated. The city-side views are great.

**Dining:** The nearby sports facilities are woefully bereft of watering holes, and Cahoots, the Hilton's club/bar, and Cinnamon's restaurant, downstairs, are packed after games.

**Services:** The Hilton organizes night trips down to Atlantic City, only 60 minutes away via the Walt Whitman Bridge. (Call 389-3004 for information. The chartered bus leaves Friday and Saturday at 7:45pm and returns at 2am with rates as low as $13 round trip.)

**Facilities:** Outdoor pool.

**AIRPORT RAMADA INN, 76 Industrial Hwy., Essington, PA 19029. Tel. 215/521-9600,** or toll free 800/228-2828. Fax 215/521-9388. 290 rms and suites. A/C TV TEL
**$ Rates:** $89 single; $94 double. Weekend packages from $67 per couple. Children under 18 free in parents' room. AAA and AARP discounts. AE, DC, MC, V. **Parking:** Free.

South of Philadelphia International Airport on Penna. 291, airport hotels cram the town of Essington. The Airport Ramada Inn, 3 miles from the airport and more than 10 miles from downtown, is considered distant because other, closer hotels have sprung up—so the rates and packages here are a steal. There's free 24-hour shuttle service to and from the airport.

The carpeted two-story foyer sparkles under that characteristic sunburst Ramada chandelier. The guest-room decor is slightly loud: The carpets of thick acrylic pile mix a dozen autumnal colors.

**Dining:** There are a coffee shop, a lounge, and a dining room.
**Facilities:** Outdoor pool, tennis courts, game rooms.

**DAYS INN, 4101 Island Ave., between I-95 and Penna. 291, Philadelphia, PA 19153. Tel. 215/492-0400,** or toll free 800/325-2525. Fax 215/365-0635. 177 rms. A/C TV TEL
**$ Rates:** $89 single; $99 double. Children under 18 free in parents' room. Weekend flat rate of $65 may be available. AE, DC, MC, V. **Parking:** Free.

Most people know that Days Inn was founded by a Mormon with very stringent standards for budget roadside havens. The chain was sold in 1985 to Prudential, which licensed the Gateway Center developers to follow the guidelines. Because these people built to their own operating requirements, they were able to stretch the $56,000-per-room investment pretty far.

You can choose between a pair of guest-room configurations: two double beds or a king or double bed and a convertible couch. Most traveling couples prefer a sink outside the bathroom to allow for joint use, and Days Inn has obliged. The sink and counter material is Corian. Each burgundy-toned room has a Zenith color TV and, for a real change, good illumination. Rooms are designated for smokers and nonsmokers, and those near elevators are equipped for the handicapped.

**Dining:** Food is available at Seasons Café.
**Facilities:** Free use of all common areas at the splendid Embassy Suites, right across the driveway; coin laundry; outdoor pool.

## INEXPENSIVE

**COMFORT INN AIRPORT, 53 Industrial Hwy., Essington, PA 19029. Tel. 215/521-9800,** or toll free 800/228-5150. Fax 215/521-4847. 150 rms. A/C TV TEL

**$ Rates** (including continental breakfast): $66 single; $72 double. Children under 18 free in parents' room. Weekend special $49 for two. AE, DC, MC, V. **Parking:** Free.

This Comfort Inn opened in April 1990, 3 miles from the airport (just west of the junction of routes 291 and 420). The look is identical to all the others: red brick with homey lettered signs. The lobby has a hearth and lounge seating, near the microwaves and toasters that heat up the continental breakfast. The elevators are slightly concealed. The guest rooms are clean and comfortable, each with two double beds or a single king-size bed.

**Dining:** A freestanding Shoney's shares the lot.

**Services:** Complimentary breakfast; free 24-hour airport shuttle service; cable TV with free HBO, ESPN, and CNN or pay-per-view movies; same-day laundry service.

**Facilities:** Fitness center.

## BUDGET

**RED ROOF INN, 49 Industrial Hwy., Essington, PA 19029. Tel. 215/521-5090,** or toll free 800/843-7663. Fax 215/521-5090, ext. 444. 50 rms. A/C TV TEL

**$ Rates:** $40–$44 single; $50–$54 double. Children under 18 free in parents' room. AE, DC, MC, V. **Parking:** Free.

There are 209 Red Roof Inns 5 to 10 miles outside metropolitan areas from Texas to New England. Each is a basic two-story motel, with outdoor corridors on the second level and a basic lobby. The look of gray carpeting, three lamps, and tan-and-wood tones is surprisingly cheery, and the baths work well. Given the large windows and doors, it can get cold in winter.

**Services/Facilities:** Free morning coffee and *USA Today* in lobby; ice and snack machines; free local calls, in-room movies, and ESPN.

# 5. CITY LINE & NORTHEAST

## EXPENSIVE

**ADAM'S MARK PHILADELPHIA, City Line Ave. and Monument Rd., Philadelphia, PA 19131. Tel. 215/581-5000,** or toll free 800/231-5858. Fax 215/581-6509. 449 rms, 66 suites. A/C TV TEL

**$ Rates:** $142 single or double; from $157 executive room. Getaway weekend package $89+ per night. AE, DC, MC, V. **Parking:** Free.

City Line Avenue (U.S. 1) just off the Schuylkill Expressway has become a vital part of the Philadelphia scene, with such major retail stores as Saks Fifth Avenue and Lord & Taylor anchoring booming malls. The Adam's Mark looks like an airport control tower, but now there's also an extensive brick complex of connected restaurants and function rooms.

After you park, a doorman will guide you into the lobby, with its parquet floors and Erté paintings (Fred Kummer, Adam's Mark's president, has a welcome penchant for placing original art in his hotels). From there, four elevators ascend to 22 floors in which the previous Holiday Inn affiliation is still somewhat evident. Things have been spruced up substantially, of course—each guest room has solid-core doors; two barrel chairs with a round wood table; quality fabrics and wallpaper; and an RCA TV with an AM/FM radio, carrying movie and sports cable channels. All hallway vents have been removed for the new climate-control system. The bathrooms are small, but the Adam's Mark touch is evident in the classier-than-average bath provisions.

**Dining/Entertainment:** The Adam's Mark's food-and-beverage operation really shines. The gardenlike Appleby's is several notches above your average all-day coffee shop, with 30-foot ziggurat skylights and local antiques. Lines start forming early at the Marker, an improbable re-creation of a French château's orangerie, a paneled English library, and a western ranch that's somehow relaxing. Open for lunch and dinner, it seats 150 on three levels; evenings bring French tableside service. Quincy's, with some of the city's best hors d'oeuvres, is the area's hotspot, offering backgammon, dancing to live bands, and so forth to 2am in a decor of old copper and wood. There's no cover Monday through Thursday, $10 on Friday and Saturday (open from 8pm to 2am). Pierre's, next to the Marker, is a more private, smaller evening home for jazz combos; the seating is all love seats scattered around marble coffee tables.

**Services:** Budget car-rental desk in lobby.

**Facilities:** The Adam's Mark is extremely proud of its health-club operation (open daily from 7am to 10pm), which includes indoor and outdoor pools with a sunken whirlpool in a comfortable, high-ceilinged room. Two racquetball courts rent for $10 for a 45-minute session, and an eight-station Nautilus machine and a sauna round out the area. There's also a hair salon.

## MODERATE

**HOLIDAY INN CITY LINE, 4100 Presidential Blvd. (City Line Avenue at I-76), Philadelphia, PA 19131. Tel. 215/477-0200,** or toll free 800/465-4329. Fax 215/473-2709. 350 rms. A/C TV TEL

**$ Rates:** $98–$108 double with king-size bed. Special family packages. AE, DC, MC, V. **Parking:** Free.

At City Line Avenue, just across the parking lot from the Adam's Mark (see above), this hotel was reopened as a Holiday Inn franchise in May 1986. The exterior is a bit cold, with vertical bands of white stucco and smoked glass, but the cheerful guest rooms extend over eight L-shaped floors. You can expect a cherry-red wall behind the bed, a drawerless counter/desk, two gray rough-textured barrel chairs, and new deep-pile carpeting. The bedside lights are remarkably functional, and each room is equipped with a city guide and (naturally) Holiday Inn material. The bathrooms are absolutely predictable. You have a choice of three bed configurations: two doubles, a single and a double, or a king-size. As usual, try for an upper floor with a Philadelphia skyline view.

**Dining:** There the Glass Tree restaurant. The Holiday Inn shares a parking lot with T.G.I. Friday's.

**Services:** Individualized Cor-Key.

**Facilities:** Kidney-shaped pool (sorry, no lanes) in gazebo.

**RADNOR HOTEL, 591 East Lancaster Rd., St. Davids, PA 19087. Tel. 215/688-5800,** or toll free 800/537-3000 outside Pennsylvania. Fax 215/341-3299. 174 rms. A/C TV TEL

**Directions:** 14 miles west of Center City on U.S. 30, reached by City Line Avenue in the northwest.

**$ Rates:** $89–$120 regular with one king or two double beds. Children under 18 free in parents' room. Third bed free. AE, MC, V. **Parking:** Free.

This is an unassuming but high-quality family hotel under new ownership. (It was known as St. David's Inn until 1991.) The rooms, done with Victorian dark-wood touches, feature cable TV, and the summer months are enlivened by the Olympic-side swimming pool.

**Dining:** The Windsor Room, with lots of modern wood, serves breakfast, lunch, and a fairly formal dinner. The Abbey Bar and Grille is open to midnight.

**Services:** 24-hour room service.

**Facilities:** Pool, exercise room.

## INEXPENSIVE

**SHERATON INN NORTHEAST, 9461 Roosevelt Blvd. (U.S. 1 at Grand Ave.), Philadelphia, PA 19114. Tel. 215/671-9600,** or toll free 800/325-3535. Fax 215/464-7759. 194 rms. A/C TV TEL

**$ Rates:** $70 single; $79 double. Weekend rates sometimes available at $60 per night double ($90 with tickets to Sesame Place). AE, CD, MC, V. **Parking:** Free.

The Sheraton Inn, beyond question the nicest hotel in Northeast Philadelphia, is one of the most attractive properties outside Center City. It's 5 minutes off I-95 or 5 miles south of Exit 28 of the Pennsylvania Turnpike. The lobby is somewhat cramped, with less room for registration than for electronic games and lounge chairs, but the elevators are swift and have floor indicators in braille.

All guest rooms are identical. Everything about them shows an attention to comfort that's unusual in a motor inn, although the free amenities have decreased since Dunfey's operated this property. Each room is equipped with a color TV with night-table controls, climate controls, and original contemporary art. The counters are topped with Italian marble, and all the bathrooms have clotheslines. The weekend packages and the quality accommodations—not to mention nearby Sesame Place—make this an excellent choice for families. The newly renovated Winthrop Café and Lounge are right next to the pool.

## BUDGET

**BEST WESTERN PHILADELPHIA NORTHEAST, 11580 Roosevelt Blvd., Philadelphia, PA 19116. Tel. 215/464-9500,** or toll free 800/528-1234. Fax 215/638-7085. 87 rms. A/C TV TEL

**$ Rates:** From $55 single; from $60 double. Children under 18 free in parents' room. Discount for AARP members. Weekend discount; special $79 package includes admission to Sesame Place. AE, DC, MC, V. **Parking:** Free.

This basic motor court, a recent franchisee of Best Western, is built around an office with the familiar Howard Johnson's orange roof and blue spire. By car, the motor lodge is 20 minutes from Center City and less to Sesame Place in Langhorne. (To get on Roosevelt Boulevard [U.S. 1] by car, take Exit 28 south from I-276 or U.S. 1 north from U.S. 611.) The guest rooms each contain either two queen-size beds or one queen-size and a convertible sofa, with red-and-green decor downstairs and gold upstairs. Special nosmoking and handicapped-accessible rooms are available.

The outdoor pool, set in a grassy knoll, is open during the summer, along with a separate children's wading pool. The old HoJo's Restaurant alongside has been turned into Andrew's. There's free ice-skating next door at the Liberty Bell Ice Palace.

## A YOUTH HOSTEL

**CHAMOUNIX MANSION, West Fairmount Park, Philadelphia, PA 19131. Tel. 215/878-3676.** About 70 beds. **Directions:** Take I-76 (Schuylkill Expressway) to Exit 33, City Line Avenue, turn left (south) on City Avenue to Monument, left onto Monument, left again at Ford Road, then a left onto Chamounix Drive and follow to the end. **Bus:** Take SEPTA route 38 from the Convention and Visitors Bureau to Ford and Cranston streets (a 20-minute ride), then walk under the overpass and left onto Chamounix Drive to the end.

**$ Rates:** $9.50 AYH members; $12.50 nonmembers; $2 sheet charge. Maximum three-day stay. Traveler's checks accepted but no credit cards. **Closed:** Dec 15–Jan 15.

The oldest building offering accommodations in town, this renovated 1802 Quaker farmhouse is also the cheapest. Chamounix Mansion is a Federal-style edifice constructed as a country retreat at what is now the upper end of Fairmount Park. About 20 years ago the only thing about to cross the threshold was the wrecker's ball, but then it was converted into a youth hostel. It has 6 dormitory rooms for 48 people, with limited family arrangements, and another 26 spots in an adjoining carriage house during the summer. Write or call ahead for reservations, since the hostel is often 90% booked in summer by groups of boat crews or foreign students.

You can check in daily between 4:30 and 8pm and show an American Youth Hostel card or IYHF card for member rates. Check out is from 8 to 9:30am. Call AYH directly at 215/925-6004 for information on hostel trips in the area.

# PHILADELPHIA DINING

**A** restaurant renaissance captured Philadelphia's imagination in the 1970s and 80s. New ones opened constantly, with distinctive menus, superb service, and cozy surroundings. No one is sure why so many young entrepreneurs here got turned on to gourmet fare, although Jay Guben, who formerly operated the Restaurant School in University City (see below), made a career of training young enthusiasts to own and manage their own spots.

Unfortunately, this chapter cannot include many of the more renowned Main Line and other suburban restaurants. If you're heading that way, volunteers staffing the desk at the **Convention and Visitors Bureau,** 16th Street and John F. Kennedy Boulevard (tel. 568-1666), often hail from those parts and have crackerjack knowledge.

## DINING NOTES

Dining in Philadelphia is an excellent value! Compared to places in New York, the average quality and attention in Philadelphia restaurants set a higher standard, and the prices fall between one-third and one-half less, particularly in the upper reaches. This chapter will categorize **very expensive** restaurants as those charging $40 or more per person for dinner without wine; **expensive** as $30 to $40 per person; **moderate** as $20 to $30; **inexpensive** as $10 to $20; and **budget** as under $10. These are only rough guidelines, however, since many luxury restaurants also include lower-priced choices. The cost of wine can be a considerable expense—restaurants usually double the state store prices. You might call ahead to ask about bringing your own.

Meal tax is 7%, and standard tipping is 15% (the latter is occasionally included on the tab). For most restaurants I have given only summer hours; you can expect plenty of 9pm (as opposed to 10pm) closings in other seasons.

It's always a good idea to make reservations—they're a necessity for the posher spots, especially on the weekend. Ask about validated parking nearby, too.

What do Philadelphians wear to dine? Pants (not jeans) on women are accepted everywhere, and a man with a jacket but without tie has almost universal success. A sweater could substitute for the sports jacket in most budget and moderate restaurants.

# 1. HISTORIC AREA

## VERY EXPENSIVE

### OLD ORIGINAL BOOKBINDER'S, 125 Walnut St. Tel. 925-7027.

**Cuisine:** SEAFOOD/AMERICAN. **Reservations:** Recommended.

**$ Prices:** Appetizers $4.95–$12.95; main courses $17.95–$40.95; lunch $5.95–$24.95. AE, DC, MC, V.

**Open:** Lunch, Mon–Fri noon–2:45pm. Dinner, Mon–Fri 2:45–10pm, Sat noon–10pm; Sept–June, Sun 1–9pm; July–Aug, Sun 1–3pm.

If dining at an institution is your predilection, head for this place. Sam Bookbinder opened this seafood restaurant in 1865; his wife announced lunch by ringing a bell. The restaurant acquired status as the *only* place to dine in town for decades. The family sold to the Taxins in the 1930s and moved to 15th Street (see "Bookbinder's Seafood House" in "Center City," below).

Over the years this Bookbinder's has expanded to encompass almost the entire block across from the Sheraton Society Hill. Just past two cigar-store Indian sentries, to the left of the ship's wheel, Bookbinder's Gift Shop sells city memorabilia along with pies; recipe books, including one with drink recipes; and cans of the most popular soups—snapper with sherry, New England clam chowder, and Manhattan clam chowder. To the right the rooms stretch on and on—three bars and seven dining rooms that are served by 185 dedicated staff. (I've had some feedback about long waits, but I've been assured that these are unusual.) The main dining areas parade framed photographs of visiting celebrities, along with valuable old maps and prints. You'll never have to worry about close quarters—there's room to lean back from the plain starched tablecloths.

Bookbinder's is most renowned for lobsters, which it transports live from Maine in tanks. The less-expensive baked imperial crabmeat with pimientos, a touch of Worcestershire, and green peppers is beyond reproach. The dinner menu is huge: all sizes and kinds of shellfish and fish, steaks, and veal. The hot seafood platter combines fresh fish with seven or eight varieties of shellfish, along with a baked potato and coleslaw. The daily catches are prepared simply with butter and lemon. Their shortcake, strawberry cheesecake, and apple-walnut pie have all won gastronomic awards. The wine list, fairly standard, offers plenty of domestic vintages for under $15. If you loved the meal, you'll surely like the gift shop on the way out.

## EXPENSIVE

### THE CHART HOUSE, 555 S. Delaware Ave. at Penn's Landing. Tel. 625-8383.

## FROMMER'S SMART TRAVELER: RESTAURANTS

1. By eating the same fare for luncheon that you would eat for dinner—and if you're on vacation, why not?—you'll save from 20% to 30%. Put another way, you can sample the best restaurants in town at lunch but pay a fraction of the dinner prices.
2. Philadelphia has some great inexpensive ethnic restaurants, particularly Greek, Italian, and Chinese.
3. To save time and money, picnic or grab a sandwich at a takeout spot or a food court like Liberty Place or the Bourse.
4. Watch your liquor intake with meals: Individual drinks can add a lot to the tab.
5. Some Philadelphia restaurants have adopted the pleasant French custom of a prix-fixe menu, which usually includes three courses for 30% less than à la carte prices. The portions are generally a bit smaller, however.
6. Many smaller hotels and bed-and-breakfasts have discount arrangements with fine neighboring restaurants. Don't accept or reject these without checking a little first, however.

**Cuisine:** SEAFOOD. **Reservations:** Not accepted (be prepared for a wait).

**$ Prices:** Appetizers $4.95–$8.95; main courses $12.95–$27.95. Sun brunch $16.95. AE, DC, MC, V.

**Open:** Dinner, Mon–Thurs 4–11pm; Fri 5pm–midnight; Sat 4pm–midnight; Sun 4–10pm. Brunch, Sun 10:30am–2pm.

The busiest restaurant in all Philadelphia has to be The Chart House, a convention center right on the Delaware River. You may not love everything about it—expect a spirited crowd and frequent birthday celebrations—but the Chart House chain has a track record for reasonably priced dinners, with soup, fresh molasses or sourdough bread, and an unlimited salad bar included. All seats have spectacular views, and the service will make you wish you had had camp counselors that enthusiastic.

Start with New England clam chowder, of course, or raw oysters. The unlimited salad bar is $10.95 by itself—with plenty of extras, such as beets, cherry tomatoes, bean sprouts, and hearts of palm—or free with an entrée such as prime rib or a steak of halibut, tuna, and other fish. The desserts are very sweet: mudpie, turtlepie, or an ice-cream sundae built on a crust of chocolate cookies.

## LA FAMIGLIA, 8 S. Front St. Tel. 922-2803.

**Cuisine:** ITALIAN. **Reservations:** Required.

**$ Prices:** Appetizers $5.95–$8.95; main courses $16–$26. AE, CB, DC, MC, V.

**Open:** Lunch, Tues–Fri noon–2pm. Dinner, Tues–Fri and Sun 5:30–9:30pm; Sat 5:30–10pm. **Closed:** Mon.

The name La Famiglia should tip you off that this place is a refined Italian restaurant—and in this case it refers to both the proprietors and the clientele. In the 1980s La Famiglia was chosen one of the 25 best Italian restaurants in the country by *Bon Appetit* magazine. The Neapolitan Sena family (parents and three children) aim for elegant dining, service, and presentation; their success here has spawned Penn's View Inn and its Ristorante Panorama (see below).

This restaurant seats 60 in a private, warm setting of hand-hammered Venetian chandeliers, majolica tiles, and an antique balance by the bar ("So far, it's on our side," say the owners). Recordings of arias give some of the best aural accompaniment in the city. Downstairs by the restrooms, you can see the privy excavations and 1680s foundations; they're more interesting than Franklin Court and hold some of the best Italian wines anywhere.

The chefs at La Famiglia make most of their own pasta, so you might concentrate on such dishes as gnocchi al pesto, which adds walnuts and pecorino cheese to the noodles. You might also explore a prize-winning calamari appetizer. The very popular Milanese appetizer for two includes mozzarella cheese and Italian ham breaded in cornbread and eggs. There's a choice of five or six vegetables with meals, and the marinated string beans and zucchini with pepper have never failed to please. For dessert, try a mille foglie, the Italian version of the napoleon, or the profiteroles in chocolate sauce. People often remain here well after the closing hour, lingering over Sambuca.

## MODERATE

**CHEF THEODORE,** Delaware and Washington aves. Tel. 271-6800.

**Cuisine:** GREEK. **Reservations:** Recommended.

**$ Prices:** Appetizers $4.25–$8.95; main courses $8.95–$16.95. AE, CB, DC, MC, V.

**Open:** Tues–Sat 4–11pm; Sun 1–10pm.

The best Greek restaurant along South Street migrated to the waterfront in 1989, to a Delaware Avenue shopping center near the multiplex Riverfront cinemas (it's not practical to get there unless you have a car). While the decor is unassumingly white and the ambiance is casual, the quality of the food is unusually good. Start with the enormous mezze (a combination platter of standards like baba, tarama, and octopus) or with the sausage or dry goat's milk cheese; both are flamed at your table. You can sample from more combination platters for an entree or stick with the salmon with roasted potatoes or the shrimp casserole. The service is unobtrusive.

**CITY TAVERN,** 2nd and Walnut sts. Tel. 923-6059.

**Cuisine:** AMERICAN. **Reservations:** Recommended.

**$ Prices:** Appetizers $4.50–$7.50; main courses $12.50–$22; lunch $5.50–$9.50. AE, MC, V.

**Open:** Lunch, daily 11:30am–3:30pm. Dinner, Sun–Thurs 5–9pm; Fri–Sat 5–10pm.

If the hunger to relive those good old 1780s overcomes you in Independence Park, there's at least one authentic restaurant that will let you use that newfangled credit card to pay for colonial fare: City Tavern—the same tavern that members of the Constitutional Convention used as coffee shop, ballroom, and club some 200 years ago. The U.S. government now owns the building, which is operated by a concessionaire.

The first floor has four square rooms off a broad hallway: two dining areas on the left and two lounges on the right for those content with drinks and a platter of cheese and fruit. All have wide-bottomed captain's chairs facing tables laid with linen and pistol-grip flatware.

The meals at City Tavern have improved (after a long hiatus), and a cheery winter start might be the hot cider with rum or brandy. Crumbly whipped butter and small rolls soon follow. All dishes are authentic but not necessarily exotic; the "Beef Pye," for example, is a brioche hollowed out and filled with a beef stew, and the onion soup hasn't really been altered. After the help clean your table with bone scrapers, sample the English trifle or the apple crisp for dessert, along with coffee served in a metal pitcher.

## THE DICKENS INN, 421 S. 2nd St. Tel. 928-9307.

**Cuisine:** BRITISH. **Reservations:** Recommended.

**$ Prices:** Appetizers $5.25–$7.25; main courses $16.50–$24.95; lunch $4.95–$7.95. AE, CD, DC, MC, V.

**Open:** Lunch, daily 11:30am–3pm. Dinner, Mon–Sat 5:30–10pm; Sun 4:30–9pm. Brunch, Sun 11:30am–3pm.

This three-story Federal town house on Head House Square has proved to have real staying power since it has survived with NewMarket behind it. The key elements here are atmosphere and friendly service. Opened in 1980 by the owners of the famous Dickens Inn near the Tower of London, the American version re-creates an English pub and restaurant (19th-century London is all over the walls and tables) that serves fine country-house cuisine.

The decor is neither Tudor nor Pickwickian, but neither is it disconcertingly fabricated. Paneling lines the walls, and wooden tables, exposed beams, and frosted-glass lamps mix with lithographs of scenes from Dickens novels and framed Dickensiana. Don't miss the cupboard of Blue Willow.

The appetizers include Highland country pâté with apple-and-onion chutney; filet of chicken with pesto dressing; and radicchio, spinach, and crab salad. The main courses are extremely generous, tasty, and attractive, served on large speckled crockery. Traditional beef Wellington and prime rib with Yorkshire pudding are offered along with lighter dishes. The sauce for the large portion of roast duckling with honey and herbs doesn't solidify as it cools—a mark of painstaking clarification. The seafood choices include bay scallops poached with basil, tomatoes, and muscadet as well as red snapper bouillabaisse with mussels and shrimp. All entrees are served with a platter of steamed fresh vegetables. The house red and white wines are fine. To finish, select a dessert from the Dickens Inn's own bakery, rolled in on a trilevel wooden cart, or sample the English Stilton cheese with fresh fruit.

Lunch at Dickens Inn is a less ambitious affair, but it still offers a satisfying range of dishes—Cornish pasty (traditional pastry filled with lamb, carrots, and potatoes and flavored with fresh herbs), shepherd's pie, trout filet, and a wild-mushroom–and–vegetable crêpe—all at about 40% of the cost of dinner. A traditional homemade soup is offered daily.

The skylit tavern room, with one of the best happy hours in town, was chosen by *Esquire* magazine to be one of the top 100 bars in America. Draft British ales such as John Courage, Bass, Whitbread, and Guinness flow into traditional pint pots; other British beers are served by the bottle. Snacks such as shepherd's pie, sausage rolls, and fish and chips are served, along with over 20 single-malt whiskies.

### DINARDO'S FAMOUS CRABS, 312 Race St. Tel. 925-5115.

**Cuisine:** SEAFOOD. **Reservations:** Required for six or more.

**$ Prices:** Appetizers $2.95–$6.95; crabs $2 each; other main courses $8.95–$17.95; lunch $3.95–$7.95. AE, CB, DC, MC, V.

**Open:** Mon–Thurs 11am–11pm; Fri–Sat 11am–midnight; Sun 4–9pm.

Dinardo's Famous Crabs springs to mind as the best moderately priced spot in the area around the Betsy Ross House and Elfreth's Alley. The door nearest 3rd Street is the real entrance.

Dinardo's expanded to the City of Brotherly Love only because too many Philadelphians were trekking to the original Wilmington locale. It's still a tight family operation: Only William Dinardo and his son mix the crab seasonings, and they, along with managing partner Tony D'Lauro, care about offering the absolute best in seafood—at reasonable prices.

Dinardo's has two unique factors—the site and the prices. The building at 312 Race Street was an inn for Tory soldiers in 1776, in the oldest part of town, and later it served as a prison for Confederate soldiers. Three ground-floor dining rooms were recently reclaimed from mid-20th-century disrepair. The well-lighted chambers have subtly striped wallpaper, huge crab specimens, various net buoys, and simple Formica tables.

Prime live catches from Texas and Louisiana are flown up north daily. After culling and chilling them in ice water, experienced hands dredge the crabs with the house seasoning of 24 spices and pack heavy-gauge steel hampers with them. Then the crabs are steamed, not boiled (this keeps the seasoning on), for 25 minutes. Uniquely at Dinardo's, the crustaceans are graded down according to weight—which is to your advantage, since crabs shed their skins four times a year. Elsewhere, right after shedding, a small crab rattling around in a larger shell is often sold as a large crab. All crabs are served on plastic platters, with nutcrackers and red sauce. If you're not in a crabby mood, there are at least 30 other succulent items, from raw-bar oysters to seafood platters.

### DOWNEY'S PUB, northwest corner of Front and South sts. Tel. 629-0526.

**Cuisine:** IRISH. **Reservations:** Recommended.

**$ Prices:** Appetizers $3.25–$5.75; main courses $6–$19; lunch $8–$11. AE, DC, MC, V.

**Open:** Lunch, Mon–Fri 11:30am–3pm. Dinner Mon–Fri 4:30–10:45pm; Sat 4:30pm–12:30am; Sun 4:30–9:45pm. Brunch, Sat–Sun 11am–3pm.

About 250 years ago Front Street from Race to Fitzwater streets was a jumble of docks, shops, and public houses that reminded English and Irish seamen of home. Downey's Pub has succumbed to such modern blandishments as electricity and daily quiche, but it's still a place any Irishman or -woman would be proud to frequent. Much of the ground floor was lifted from a Dublin bank built in 1903; the upstairs is from a pub in Cork City.

Downey's obviously started off less "lace curtain" than it is now, since the downstairs walls are covered by yellowing shellacked newspapers. The current urbane, comfortable layer throws in brass rails, coat stands, and framed Victorian prints. In summer, café tables grace both the South Street and the river patios. Upstairs, which opened in 1982, is tonier still, with Beerbohm caricatures, skylights, and beveled mirrors on beautiful wood paneling. Don't miss the details here, such as the Irish coins nailed to the portal and the tin-sheet-plate ceiling. The staff, in white shirts and Limerick-green bow ties, is gracious and lively.

Lunch and dinner both offer Irish dishes with American fillips, and vice versa. The soups are strong here—the potato soup and the lobster bisque use thick milk and have plenty of body. Corned beef and cabbage, which tops the lunch menu, comes with a boiled potato but retains plenty of flavor itself. The fish of the day is broiled and served with a fresh vegetable. The dinner portions, substantially larger, add filet mignon and sirloin to the above.

Live music is a staple of Downey's, both at the weekend brunches and in the upstairs Piano Bar on Friday and Saturday from 9:30pm to 2am.

## JEANNINE'S BISTRO, 10 S. Front St. Tel. 925-2928.

**Cuisine:** FRENCH BISTRO. **Reservations:** Recommended.
**$ Prices:** Appetizers $3.95–$6.95; main courses $8.95–$16.95. AE, MC, V.
**Open:** Tues–Fri noon–2pm; Mon–Sat 5:30–11pm. **Closed:** Sun.

In 1991, the popular classic French restaurant downstairs decided to open a bistro, with cut-down dishes. Lunch is served downstairs, with dinner and entertainment upstairs. Owner Jeanne Mermet herself makes a vocal appearance on Fridays to augment the guitar-and-violin duo that plays most nights. The chef, Todd Davies, has cooked at Aureole and the River Café in Manhattan.

The dining room is charming, with floral-print wallpaper and tablecloths, burgundy pillows, and candlelight. Watch the climb, though. The menu selections include braised pork, grilled fish, and poultry. The desserts are most like what restaurant diners get downstairs, with white-chocolate mousse and the like.

## JUDY'S CAFE, 3rd and Bainbridge sts. Tel. 928-1968.

**Cuisine:** AMERICAN. **Reservations:** Recommended.
**$ Prices:** Appetizers $2.95–$6.95; main courses $13–$22. AE, DC, MC, V.
**Open:** Dinner only, Mon–Thurs 6–10pm; Fri–Sat 6–11pm; Sun 5–9:30pm.

An agreeable bistro outgrowing its countercultural beginnings, Judy's is one of the finest examples of the South Street renaissance. The place opened in 1976, with Judy and Eileen as co-owners. Judy left soon after (a reward goes to anyone who can learn why it's not called Eileen's), but the locale retains a neighborhood feeling, though it's not really a family place. The regulars banter with the waiters, who dine here on their nights off, and the service at the well-stocked bar may depend on how you strike the person behind it.

Judy's two rooms are simply furnished: Photorealist canvases coexist with a quizzical neon strip embracing the wall behind the bar. There's nothing quizzical about the cuisine, however. The limited menu changes with the season, but the quality is high. The hors d'oeuvres include an absolutely enormous neighborhood salad topped with grated cheese and sliced cherry tomatoes. For a more continental flavor, try a pâté or terrine, a usual special.

The entrées are eclectic. The prices are moderate but vary not only with the dish but also with the level of expertise needed. A Monday through Thursday special includes your choice of stir-fried duck, lamb stew, or the catch of the day with soup and coffee. The honey-glazed roast duckling has added stylish touches—port mixed with the honey and hot pear slices as a garnish. If you've never tried sweetbreads, a platter graced with a wonderful mushroom-and-cream reduction will make you a believer. Whatever seafood's on the menu will undoubtedly be fresh. The very, very chocolate cake could deserve a third *very;* for those not hooked on fudge, the carrot cake's moist and scrumptious. *Note:* Local papers often advertise 2-for-1 weeknight specials.

## LA GROLLA BAR AND TRATTORIA, 782 S. 2nd St. Tel. 627-7701.

**Cuisine:** ITALIAN. **Reservations:** Required for Sun lunch.

**$ Prices:** Appetizers $4.95–$8.95; main courses $11.95–$24.95. AE, DC, MC, V.

**Open:** Dinner only, Mon–Thurs 5–10pm; Fri–Sat 5pm–midnight.

Just when you think the gentrified area south of South Street is about to run into South Philadelphia's corner stores and artificial stone facades, La Grolla spreads its bright-orange awning amid an enticing fragrance of garlic, spices, and stock. As of 1991, a relaxed Piedmontese restaurant was turned into a bar and trattoria, but rotund and expansive Giovanni Massaglia and Mamma Bertina still preside over casalinga pasta and unusual dishes. There's plenty of on-street parking nearby.

La Grolla (Italian for "cup of friendship") is narrow and fairly small, and you'll probably want to head straight to the intimate back room, with its salmon stucco, wood railings, and inlaid wood tabletops. There's no sense of hurrying, so your meal may take upward of two hours from soup to espresso. Waiters in white shirts and black bow ties will not let you order before explaining all the dishes—you should listen, because the more Piedmontese ones are quite unusual.

You might start with the cannelloni stuffed with veal sausage and topped with a tomato bechamel or a tarragon seasoning. The salads are on the small side but fresh. No pasta is offered as an entrée, but there are always several venison dishes, for which the place is especially known. One venison special comes with melted fontina and gorgonzola cheeses and Italian mushrooms, with asparagus and green beans on the side. The choice of a pizzaiola sauce for many dishes is a bit salty with capers, but the seafood is very fresh and the helpings are large—try the butterfly filet of trout. The side helpings of vegetables are seasonal, and winter brings braised fennel bulbs and a sweet fried polenta cake. The wine list is on the expensive side, with few choices under $20.

The desserts are especially good and unusual. The torta di mele is actually not a tart but a cold custard pie with apples, cocoa, and cinnamon. If pastry's what you want, try the sfogliatelle, a custard underneath a napoleon that's beribboned with fresh whipped cream.

## MEIJI-EN, upstairs at Pier 19, on the Delaware River at Callowhill St. Tel. 592-7100.

**Cuisine:** JAPANESE. **Reservations:** Recommended.

**$ Prices:** Appetizers $4–$8; main courses $12–$18. AE, CB, DC, MC, V.

**Open:** Lunch, Mon–Fri 11:30am–2:30pm. Dinner, Mon–Thurs 5–10pm; Fri–Sat 5–11pm; Sun 5–9pm. Brunch, Sun 10:30am–3pm.

Meiji-en opened in 1988 as a huge harbinger of the waterfront development needed to support a 600-seat restaurant. The restaurant now enjoys high volume and offers consistent quality. Meiji-en falls somewhere between an indoor tennis court and a Japanese theme park; everyone from a romantic couple to a huge family can take pleasure in a visit.

Be sure to call ahead to request a water view and don't be deterred by the slightly forbidding Delaware Avenue approach, four blocks north of the Benjamin Franklin Bridge. Parking nearby is $4; then walk along the Marine Center downstairs and take the elevator to the second-floor foyer, a terrarium that also includes live birds.

You'll almost need a floor plan to plot your course because there are separate areas for sushi, tempura, teppanyaki (or stovetop at table), and regular table seating (the latter two are river views to the east), as well as a bar with live jazz on Friday and Saturday. Everything is scrupulously clean, and the service is impeccable. The decor features lots of hanging rice-paper globes, blond-wood screens and seats, and comfortable black-and-red cushions. In summer, a large decked-over patio with sliding walls extends to the west, back toward town. Banks of plants, Japanese bridges, and a waterfall garden separate these areas.

Many of Meiji-en's dishes have the same basic ingredients—filets of fish and chicken—done with different preparations, from being boiled to being quick grilled to being diced in gyoza dumplings. Many dishes are marked as especially health conscious. Among the appetizers I recommend the shrimp shumai (light rice dumplings served in a bamboo steaming tray, with dipping sauce) and the fried eggplant boats with chicken. The teppanyaki entrées are cheapest and most fun; your group will sit around horseshoe-shaped tables of granite-and-steel stovetops while you're served seared meat and greens. If you're ordering regular service, expect fish steaks or marbled beef that are beautifully presented. The Sunday brunch has an opulent $15.95 buffet.

## PHILADELPHIA FISH & COMPANY, 207 Chestnut St. Tel. 625-8605.

**Cuisine:** SEAFOOD/AMERICAN. **Reservations:** Recommended.

**$ Prices:** Appetizers $2.95–$6.95; main courses $10.95–$24.95. AE, MC, V.

**Open:** Lunch, Mon–Fri 11:30am–4pm; Sat noon–3pm. Dinner, Mon–Thurs 4–10pm; Fri–Sat 4pm–midnight; Sun 3–10pm.

It's inevitable that you'll pass Philadelphia Fish & Company, given its location next to Independence National Historical Park sites. I can confirm that it's okay to enter, since the restaurant offers a quite modern selection of fish and preparations new to Philadelphia, with premium freshness. For example, you'll encounter lots of grilling over mesquite: yellow-fin tuna, salmon, and rock cod. Try the conch chowder as an appetizer; it's got a healthy helping of small bits of meat amid a tomato-based stock. The wine list, skewed toward white wines, is very reasonable for Philadelphia, with good quality. Late night here can get noisy amid the windsor chairs and soft lighting.

## RISTORANTE PANORAMA, Front and Market sts. Tel. 922-7600.

**Cuisine:** ITALIAN. **Reservations:** Recommended.

**$ Prices:** Appetizers $4.95–$7.95; main courses $8.95–$15.95. AE, CB, DC, MC, V.

**Open:** Daily noon–midnight. Dinner service 5:30–10pm.

Although the Ristorante Panorama is on the waterfront, its view is a colorful mural of the Italian countryside. The cuisine is a wonderful, choice list of lighter Italian dishes. Pasta, salads, and fish predominate, with a few veal and beef favorites. The bread is served without butter but with a tiny bowl of pesto.

Favorite appetizers are the fantasy platter of grilled vegetables, beautifully arranged, and the croquettes of shrimp and lamb served on a bed of arugula. The fish are usually grilled and lightly seasoned with garlic and tomatoes. The tiramisu, with its triple-creme mascarpone cheese drizzled with chocolate, needs either an espresso or a dessert wine as an accompaniment.

Panorama is also one of the city's best new wine bars, with 120 (not all Italian) wines served in 3- or 5-ounce glasses from a Cruvinet system to a sophisticated, lively crowd. In fact, diners can take a "map" of their selections, with space for notes and ratings.

## SIVA'S, 34 S. Front St. Tel. 925-2700.

**Cuisine:** INDIAN. **Reservations:** Recommended. Jacket and tie required.

**$ Prices:** Appetizers $3.95–$8.95; main courses $13.95–$19.95. AE, MC, V.

**Open:** Lunch, Tues–Fri noon–2pm. Dinner, Tues–Fri and Sun 5:30–10:30pm; Sat 5:30–11:30pm. **Closed:** Mon.

Tandoori, which composes about 50% of the menu here, will introduce you to North Indian–style barbecue—with no curry but 40 herbs and spices. The place went through a slump in the late 1980s, but it seems to have fully recovered.

Owner Amar Bhalla has stinted on nothing in the food, decor, and service. The enormous brass-on-teakwood doors would suit a temple (much less a restaurant), and the interior is a subtle, beautiful mix of East and West. Natural-finish wicker chairs and plush banquettes populate the two-level dining area, which is accented with gold-and-tan linen, Indian tapestries, and wicker-shaded lighting. At the rear you can see the distinctive tandoori ovens, plain imported clay kilns, through the glass booth.

A feast at Siva's should begin with an appetizer of samosa (patties with peas and potatoes) or pakora (a type of spiced fritter)—these come in chicken, vegetable, and fish varieties. The superb biryani, here a puréed stew of mutton, chicken, and long-grain rice, makes other restaurants' biryanis seem anemic. The classic kiln-baked chicken is made with spices, yogurt, and herbs. Be sure to order one of the breads—Siva's is one of the few places in America where bread is baked strictly to order. Try the round roti, crisp at the edges, or the puffy naan. The Sunday brunch (12–2pm) for $16 is an on-and-off proposition.

# INEXPENSIVE

## BANGKOK HOUSE, 117 South St. Tel. 925-0655.

**Cuisine:** THAI. **Reservations:** Recommended.

**$ Prices:** Appetizers $4–$6; main courses $7–$13. AE, DC, MC, V.

**Open:** Dinner only, daily 5:30–10pm.

One of the best-established restaurants in town, Bangkok House boasts all the sweet and hot pastes and spices you'd expect. It isn't much to look at—white, clean, and spare—so start right in on the satay, a highly spiced and marinated meat kebab. For something hot that doesn't sear the taste buds, try the chicken ka prow (chicken with fried hot pepper) done in an unusual basil-and-lemongrass sauce. The desserts here are not their strong points; perhaps dessert doesn't flourish in cultures accustomed to single-pot communal meals.

## LOS AMIGOS, 50 S. 2nd St. Tel. 922-7061.

**Cuisine:** MEXICAN. **Reservations:** Not accepted.

**$ Prices:** Appetizers $2.95–$5.50; main courses $8–$13; combination plates $8–$11. Dinner minimum $5 per person. AE, DC, MC, V.

**Open:** Mon–Thurs 11:30am–11:30pm; Fri–Sat 11:30am–1am; Sun 1–10pm. Bar open Mon–Sat until 2am.

Unassuming, piquant touches encourage your eye to wander around Los Amigos's arcade of brick and stucco. You might expect sombreros and silver-plate photographs, but not the clay wall niches, the inset bricks, and the inactive bell.

One of the combination plates makes a satisfying light meal and a sampler in Mexican cooking as well. Chile rellenos, one of Los Amigos's best items, are chile peppers stuffed with a cheese mixture, thoroughly cooked in batter (not just dipped in it for a quick fry), then served with tomato sauce and a dollop of sour cream. The chile taste never overwhelms. I also like the chicken budin azteca, a chicken and sausage casserole with tortilla layers. One or two nontortilla dishes, such as arroz con pollo (chicken with rice), sneak onto the menu. The refried pinto beans have a finely puréed smokiness, although the rice seems overbaked. For dessert, the flan is smooth in a light caramel sauce and the sopapillas come with honey and powdered sugar on their fried dough. Exotic coffees and Mexican beer are available, as is a limited selection of wines and pitchers of margaritas.

## WALT'S KING OF THE CRABS, 804–806 S. 2nd St. Tel. 339-9124.

**Cuisine:** SEAFOOD. **Reservations:** Not accepted.

**$ Prices:** Appetizers $2.95–$4.95; main courses $7.95–$12.95. No credit cards.

**Open:** Mon–Sat 11am–12:30am; Sun 2–10pm.

Walt's makes no bones (or shells?) about the house specialty, and this little, unpretentious storefront hangout has acquired a fanatical following. Walt's, explains owner Ted Zalewski, is simply one of the few city restaurants in America where a family can eat as much great seafood as they can hold and yet walk out not even close to broke. Ted is an extremely nice, beefy Queen Villager who cares about serving lots of people well. Unless your taste includes both bizarre ocean-scene murals and Patti Page records, ignore the decor and dig in.

The platters include truly tasty coleslaw and french-fried potatoes. The deviled crab comes in a great minced patty, fried but never greasy. At last hearing, chicken lobsters were offered for $8.75 each. The house specialty features two jumbo shrimp stuffed with crabmeat. Draft beer costs $1 a glass or $6 a pitcher. Take-out costs 25¢ extra. You'd be advised to call ahead to find out about waiting time, because the lines in summer and on weekends are fierce. To get here, you can take bus no. 5 on 2nd Street to the Catherine Street stop.

## BUDGET

### JIM'S STEAKS, 400 South St. Tel. 928-1911.

**Cuisine:** AMERICAN. **Reservations:** Not accepted.
**$ Prices:** Lunch and main courses $3.50–$4.95. No credit cards.
**Open:** Mon–Thurs 10am–1am; Fri–Sat 10am–3am; Sun noon–10pm.

Philadelphia cheesesteak is nationally known. The best practitioner of the fine art of hoagie-dom in this area is Jim's Steaks in Queen Village; they also do the mightiest steak sandwiches in town.

Jim's has a certain art deco charm, with a black-and-white enamel exterior and tile interior, plus omnipresent chrome. But most of the ground floor is taken up by the counters, containers, and ovens, although there is a counter with bar stools along the opposite wall. Take-out is highly recommended in clement weather.

Proper hoagie construction can be debated endlessly, but Jim's treatment of the Italian hoagie with prosciutto ($3.95) is a benchmark. A fresh Italian roll is slit before your eyes and layers of sliced salami, provolone, and prosciutto (Italian ham) are laid over the open faces. You choose your condiment: mayonnaise or oil and vinegar. Salad fixings—lettuce, tomatoes, and green peppers, with options on onion and hot peppers—come next, with more seasoning at the end. Nimble fingers close the hoagie, slice it in half, and wrap it. The result is not subtle but pungent, filling, and delicious. The steak submarines (or heros, as we Yankee transplants know them) are less succulent than in the past but also cheaper at $3.25 (melted cheese additional). Beer and soft drinks are sold in cans and bottles.

### OLD ORIGINAL LEVIS', 507 S. 6th St. Tel. 627-2354.

**Cuisine:** AMERICAN. **Reservations:** Not accepted.
**$ Prices:** Hot dogs $1.50; other items $1.75–$4. No credit cards.
**Open:** Winter, daily 10am–9pm. Summer, daily 10am–11pm.

Old Original Levis' has turned 90, but there wasn't too much fanfare. (It's been franchised, however, and a replica recently opened in Atlantic City.) After all, it's surrounded by Colonial Philadelphia. It's still the same old hot-dog–and–fishcake diner, though, under the neon hot dog opposite Starr Gardens Playground. In 1890 the "champ" cherry cost a penny a glass, and three hot dogs went for a nickel. Each hot dog now fetches $1.50—still a bargain for an all-beef dog. The fishcakes, formed by hand, make a great eat-and-run combination with the cheese fries. As for "champ" cherry, this drink was developed in the same way as Coca-Cola and at about the same time. *Champ* is short for *champagne,* since carbonation tickled every Gibson Girl's fancy. Chocolate cherry, egg creams, and a few upstarts continue to be drawn from the oldest soda fountain in America. For a splurge, go for the double shake or the one-pound serving of hot waffles and ice cream. There are 36 new seats inside, for rainy days, and even parking.

# 2. CENTER CITY

## VERY EXPENSIVE

**LE BEC-FIN, 1523 Walnut St. Tel. 567-1000.**

**Cuisine:** FRENCH. **Reservations:** Required—a week ahead for weeknights, months ahead for Fri–Sat.

**$ Prices:** Prix-fixe lunch $31; prix-fixe dinner $89. AE, DC, MC, V.

**Open:** Lunch, Mon–Fri seatings at 11:30am and 1:30pm. Dinner, Mon–Sat seatings at 6 and 9pm. Bar Lyonnais downstairs serves food and drink until midnight.

There's no doubt that Le Bec-Fin is the best in Philadelphia and certainly one of the top 10 in the country. Patron Georges Perrier hails from Lyon, France's gastronomic capital, and commands the respect of restaurateurs on two continents for his culinary accomplishments.

Le Bec-Fin looks exactly as it's supposed to—elegant and comfortable, with apricot silk covering acoustic panels. A portrait of one of Perrier's ancestors, a Russian émigré, peers benignly from the 18th century. Mirrors in back of wall brackets and candlelight add to the warm lighting—seeing your food can only enhance your meal. The table settings include bountiful bouquets; Christofle silver; and the same china—an 18th-century Limoges pattern—Paul Bocuse uses in his Lyon restaurant. In addition to the main dining room, the Blue Room (seating 25) may be reserved for private parties. As review after review has noted, it is virtually impossible not to enjoy yourself here, even before your meal begins.

With leisurely timing, an evening at Le Bec-Fin waltzes through hors d'oeuvres, a first course, an entrée, a salad, cheese, a dessert, and coffee with petits-fours. As an hors d'oeuvre, the terrine of three fish contains a layer of turbot mousse, then a layer of salmon mousse, then one of sole mousse, each with its own dressing; the total effect, with shallots, couldn't be more subtle. The escargots au champagne are renowned as a first course, as the garlic butter also includes a touch of chartreuse and hazelnuts.

The entrées give you the opportunity to try some rarities—pheasant, venison, and pigeon. The last (stuffed with goose liver, leeks, and mushrooms) comes in a truffle sauce. So does the mouthwatering dish of four filets of venison, covered by a thick milk-mustard sauce—the best single dish I have ever ordered. The desserts become grand opera, with trays, tables, and ice cream and sherbets (in the little aluminum canisters they were churned in) zooming from guest to guest. The dessert tray looks like Dante's Paradiso, especially the 18-inch-high Mont Blanc with sides of sheet chocolate. The finest coffee in the city, served in Villeroy & Boch flowered china, makes those petit-fours you really don't need easier to take. Cigars, cordials, liqueurs, and marcs and other fortified spirits gild the lily.

The wine list starts at around $35 per bottle and rises astronomically.

In 1991 M. Perrier opened the basement **✪ Le Bar Lyonnais** for more affordable snacking and champagne toasts. Open until midnight, it has only four tables and bar stools, but trompe l'oeil pilasters and paisley wallpaper expand its effect. Expect to spend about $10 a nibble and $7 for a glass of house wine. The later it gets, the more likely dishes from upstairs are to arrive—and M. Perrier himself, for that matter.

## EXPENSIVE

### BOOKBINDER'S SEAFOOD HOUSE, 215 S. 15th St. Tel. 545-1137.

**Cuisine:** SEAFOOD. **Reservations:** Recommended for Fri lunch and for dinner.

**$ Prices:** Appetizers $3.95–$10.95; main course $14.95–$28.95; lunch $3.95–$12.95. AE, CB, DC, MC, V.

**Open:** Mon–Fri 11:30am–11pm; Sat 11:30am–midnight; Sun noon–10pm. Dinner served from 3pm.

A trip to Philadelphia once automatically meant a seafood meal at Old Original Bookbinder's (see "Historic Area," above). But even before the 1970s restaurant renaissance, the third generation of Bookbinders moved downtown and set up shop at Bookbinder's Seafood House. Now Sam presides over 400 seats spread over two floors.

The two Bookbinder's are now quite friendly. The Old Original trades off its worldwide fame, age, and location near the Delaware; the 15th Street Booky's is less self-congratulatory and has its own solid clientele. Especially now that its facade has been cleaned down to the original brick, Booky's 15th Street is a traditional seafood house, as enshrined as places like Anthony's in Boston and DiMaggio's on Fisherman's Wharf in San Francisco. The high ceilings give plenty of room for the mounted fish, nautical chandeliers, oak paneling, and captain's chairs. The heavy wood tables hold goblets of croutons for chowder. The place is vast, and sometimes the harried help is apt to be brisk, although not perfunctory.

You might start with the famous snapper soup laced with sherry. All the seafood but the smoked fish comes from Chesapeake Bay trawling—the smelts get especially high marks for freshness. You can get that basket of clams you've been pining for, a large box of Chincoteague oysters, or lobsters from $19.95. The mussels in red sauce are probably the best known among Philadelphians. To adapt to modern tastes, more sauces are being served on the side and new imports, such as mako shark, have been added.

### CIBOULETTE, 1312 Spruce St. Tel. 790-1210.

**Cuisine:** FRENCH. **Reservations:** Strongly recommended.

**$ Prices:** Appetizers $5.95–$8.95; main courses at lunch $9–$12; main courses at dinner $17.95–$25.95; pretheater menu $29; four-course prix-fixe menu $45; five-course prix-fixe tasting menu $60. AE, DC, MC, V.

**Open:** Lunch, Mon–Fri 11:30am–2:30pm. Dinner, Mon–Thurs 6–9:30pm, Fri–Sat seatings at 6 and 9pm. **Closed:** Sun.

⭐ This site has housed some of Philadelphia's finest restaurants over the past 20 years, and Ciboulette has been a worthy successor since its November 1988 opening. *Esquire* called it one of the 100 best new restaurants in the country in 1990. *Ciboulette* is French for "chives," and the staff of chef Bruce Lim earned their herbs at The Four Seasons Hotel. The decor in the 40-seat dining room is a severe dream of upturned Italian lighting and art deco chairs and cream walls, although the look has recently been softened to include touches of lace and tableside bouquets. Clearly, the patron is meant to participate in a predesigned experience rather than help shape it; this is partially due to the table space that is too small to foster spontaneity.

The food on the selective menu is wonderful, from peak to peak of southern France. This hearty, rustic cuisine makes extravagant use of duck, goose, vegetables, and herbs, and in the past decade it has been lightened for American tastes by the sophisticated chefs. If you're feeling explorative, by all means order one of the prix-fixe meals: the three-course menu or the five-course dégustation—with both you'll usually go off the regular menu, with such items as a vegetarian Wellington with truffles. On the à la carte menu, lobster salad with fried leeks could precede beef tournedos with shallot sauce and other entrées. The desserts are exemplary, from crème brûlee to a hot banana tart.

## DILULLO CENTRO, 1407 Locust St. Tel. 546-2000.

**Cuisine:** ITALIAN. **Reservations:** Strongly recommended.

$ **Prices:** Antipasto $4–$10; main courses $14.50–$25.50; lunch $10–$16. AE, CB, DC, MC, V.

**Open:** Lunch, Mon–Fri 11:45am–1:45pm. Dinner, Mon–Sat 5:30–10:30pm. Dilullo's Fox Chase: Dinner, Mon–Thurs 5:30–10pm; Fri–Sat 5:30–11pm; Sun 4:30–9pm.

⭐ Philadelphia residents know that the best choice in town for sophisticated, exquisite Italian cuisine is Dilullo's, either right across from the Bellevue in a renovated theater or in the original Fox Chase suburban location. Dilullo Centro lacks the original's booth with grandmothers making fresh filled pastas, but it is even more spectacular, with at least $750,000 invested in such opulent and slightly decadent items as a huge copper antipasto cart, enlarged copies of impressionist and expressionist works, a series of booths separated by etched glass, ebonied wood, and wrought-metal armchairs. In fact, this kind of product is especially threatened by the curtailment of business expense accounts, but go while you can.

Begin a meal with an antipasto—sautéed buffalo-milk mozzarella slices, marinated pepperoni, sun-dried tomatoes, and the like on a single plate or a single seafood terrine or mousse. Italian meals of this quality demand a small first course of pasta; followed by a second of fish, meat, or poultry with vegetables; then a complimentary radicchio salad; and finally optional fruit, sweets, and coffee. The spinach pasta with wild mushrooms and smoked pork could make you emigrate, but make your companions order the cappelletti and the very creamy fettuccine Alfredo as well. For a real splurge, the tagliatelle with black mushrooms is smoky and wild yet smooth. Entrées include thin-sliced fresh monkfish in lemon sauce and three slices of veal loin sautéed, then baked after a slow marinade in rosemary and garlic. If you order a grilled dish, be aware that many Americans perceive the Italian style as underdone. The vegetables are strictly seasonal, and the all-Italian wine list ranges from $17 (Orvieto, Corvo) to $48 (Gattinara).

Naturally, you'll want to finish with an espresso, which comes in a silver pot, and some dessert. Dilullo's produces its own gelato, with ground fruits or beans and a splash of spirits.

## FRIDAY SATURDAY SUNDAY, 261 S. 21st St. (between Locust and Spruce sts.). Tel. 546-4232.

**Cuisine:** CONTINENTAL. **Reservations:** Accepted only for parties of five or more.

**$ Prices:** Appetizers $5–$9; main courses $14–$22. AE, CB, DC, MC, V.

**Open:** Lunch, Mon–Fri 11:30am–2:30pm. Dinner, Mon–Sat 5:30–10:30pm; Sun 5–10pm.

There's a lot to be said for a restaurant that installed a window on Manning Street for the kitchen staff. Friday Saturday Sunday is a romantic survivor of the early restaurant renaissance that has adapted to the times, offering informality, abundant personal attention, and a relaxed confidence in cuisine. Chef Aliza Green of Azalea recently upgraded ingredients and found better suppliers for the 1990s.

Friday Saturday Sunday is classy but unostentatious: The cutlery and china don't match, flowers are rare, and the menu is a wall-mounted slate board with inscriptions in several Day-Glo colors. But these touches of bohemia are eclectic or vestigial, since the interiors are darkly handsome. Pinlights frame a row of rectangular mirrors set in wood paneling, and fabric flecked with gold swathes the upstairs ceiling (downstairs, it's striped). The sound system, tuned to Mozart and the like, is one of the city's best, and an aquarium bubbles behind a cosmopolitan holding bar. Dress is anywhere from jeans to suits, and the service is vigilant but hands-off.

Try the fairly spicy Yum-Yum scallops served with carrots on a bed of romaine lettuce, pungent and clean tasting. Or sample the colorful Szechuan salad with sweet red peppers and wok-fried beef slivers. The portions (both first and second courses) are well laden, so you're advised to split an appetizer and even a dessert between two. If you have any taste at all for duck, the double-baked and mildly curried half duck is excellent, closely followed by the stuffed Cornish game hen Normandy. The fish of the day is sure to be delicate and unusual, and the tender veal roast is done with fresh tomatoes rather than a sauce. The wine card lists about 30 vintages. The desserts change often.

## THE GARDEN, 1617 Spruce St., near Rittenhouse Square. Tel. 546-4455.

**Cuisine:** CONTINENTAL. **Reservations:** Recommended.

**$ Prices:** Appetizers $5–$10; main courses $14.95–$24.95; lunch $10.95–$19.95. AE, CB, DC, MC, V.

**Open:** Lunch, Mon–Fri 11:30am–1:45pm. Appetizers, Mon–Fri 2:30–5:30pm. Dinner, Mon–Sat 5:30–10pm. **Closed:** Sat–Sun in July–Aug.

The Garden keeps sprouting up. Although it's only 17 years old, Kathleen Mulhern's place captures the city's sense of style—taste without ornateness—better than any other spot I know. The tables and bar are antiques, set off by the many 19th-century prints of fruit and animals. In this former music academy, the oyster bar on the left is being renovated in 1993, but it will keep the liquor. The three softly lit dining areas—Swan Room, with wooden decoys; Print Room, a floral back parlor; and the Main Room, a former concert hall with practice rooms—can become noisy when crowded; fortunately, the great outdoors is only paces away, weather permitting. Thanks to 5 tons of soil and gravel brought in each spring, the gaily bedecked back garden is a fragrant and spectacularly quiet enclave, making it the preferable dining locale, either for candlelit evenings or for sun-shaded luncheons. Potted flowers vie with the yellow umbrellas for brightness. *Note:* The Garden now picks up the entire tab for garage parking nearby.

The house's favorite appetizer, a raw filet of beef (carpaccio) sliced very thinly and laid in a chutney sauce, is more typical of dinner than lunch, which leans more toward seafood, poultry, quiche, and salads. Spinach gnocchi made by "Aunt Nitty" is featherlight with a sweet gorgonzola sauce. All main courses include salad and vegetables. Four or five dishes—featuring baked salmon, oysters, and delicate Dover sole—can be ordered as delicious light entrees. The French chocolate cake has been called the best dessert in Philadelphia by *Food & Wine* magazine, and the chocolate sampler plate is frighteningly good.

## HARRY'S BAR AND GRILL, 22 S. 18th St. Tel. 561-5757.

**Cuisine:** AMERICAN. **Reservations:** Recommended.

**$ Prices:** Appetizers $3.95–$8.95; main courses $10.95–$24.95.
**Open:** Lunch, Mon–Fri 11:30am–2pm. Dinner, Mon–Fri 5:30–9:30pm.

Described by *Esquire* as one of the city's most sophisticated bars, Harry's exudes a clubby, comfortable atmosphere—soft lighting on terra-cotta walls with blue and gold accents, hunting prints, mirrors, and handmade Italian brass lamps on the tables. Because Harry's has loyal regulars among Philadelphia's business world, lots of deals are closed here.

A steakhouse with an Italian flair, its generous servings meet the demands of its heavy-eating clientele: Such pasta appetizers as gnocchi and tagliatelle are popular. Other appetizers range from melon and prosciutto to smoked salmon to shrimp salad. Steaks are the entrée menu's centerpiece, but Harry's offers a fish of the day (the Dover sole is often asked for), as well as veal, lobster, and Italian seafood dishes. But, after all, you'll go to Harry's for steak, and these are among the best: aged USDA prime beef, grilled to order, served with potatoes and a ramekin of your choice of marchand de vin, béarnaise, or roquefort (smaller portions are available at lunch). Filet mignon, chateaubriand, and rack of lamb are on hand for the meat-loving gourmet.

Harry's offers an excellent selection of imported wines, starting at $22 a bottle, as well as a full selection of California wines, priced slightly lower. Wine by the glass is sold by the Cruvinet system. A full line of fine American and imported beers, ales, and stouts is also available. At lunch you'll find Harry's service is paced to accord with businesspeople's time constraints; for a more leisurely meal, come for dinner.

## JACK'S FIREHOUSE, 2130 Fairmount Ave. Tel. 232-9000.

**Cuisine:** CONTEMPORARY AMERICAN. **Reservations:** Recommended.

**$ Prices:** Appetizers $4.95–$11.95; main courses $16.95–

$22.95; prix-fixe menus $45 and $52. Bar service available; sandwiches from $6.95. AE, DC, MC, V.
**Open:** Mon–Sat 11:30am–10:30pm; Sun brunch 11am–3pm. Bar open nightly until 2am.

In many ways this is one of the most imaginative, and one of the most hotly debated, restaurants now operating in Philadelphia. Chef Jack McDavid has taken a turn-of-the-century firehouse and incorporated contemporary (and rotating) art by Philadelphia artists, a beautiful rowing shell, and a glass-and-walnut island bar. It's warm and homey, but the cuisine features dramatic juxtapositions of American ingredients and flavors, with special emphasis on the rare, the nearly lost varietal, and the inheritances of immigrant cultures. The game is outstanding, and McDavid's dressing and preparation of gopher, bear, bison, and beavertail (to name a few) make this a national pilgrimage of sorts. The historical steeping in many dishes, such as Pennsylvania shad and bacon, is impeccable.

A typical menu starts with a basket of buttermilk muffins. It then presents main courses like suckling pig with a thin and slightly sweet sauce, garnished with lettuce and Granny Smith tempura; shrimp with fennel in a lime-pepper sauce; and three thick medallions of venison in a succulent berry-and-meat stock, served with haricots and baby carrots and a red-bean–and–wild-rice mélange. The desserts could be a smooth peanut-butter–and–chocolate cake or sweet pecan pie.

The same stretching goes for the extensive all-American wine list, ranging from $16 to $90 per bottle. Several microbreweries, such as Stoudt's of Pennsylvania, are represented with quality beer, on tap and in bottles.

To save a bundle, try a simple meal of the black-eyed pea soup, the cornmeal crêpe, or a hearty sandwich for under $20 with your drink.

**MORTON'S OF CHICAGO, One Logan Square (19th and Cherry sts.) Tel. 557-0724.**
**Cuisine:** STEAK. **Reservations:** Accepted for 5:30–7pm only.
**$ Prices:** Appetizers $6.95–$9.95; main courses $18–$29. AE, CB, DC, MC, V.
**Open:** Lunch, Mon–Sat 11:30am–2:30pm. Dinner, Mon–Sat 5:30pm–midnight.

Looking for sirloin? Morton's of Chicago has become a staple both for business lunches near Logan Square and for celebratory evenings. Don't kid yourself about the specialty—the double-cut filets, sirloins, and T-bones come in aged, well-marbled tender masses. The house porterhouse weighs in at 24 ounces; if you wish, the waiter will bring your cut of meat or fish raw to your table for precooking inspection. The cauliflower soup also is touted, and the Sicilian veal chop with garlic bread crumbs is a "hometown" hit. If you must branch out farther, sample the crab cocktail or the smoked salmon served on dark bread with horseradish cream, capers, and onions.

Morton's looks as sedate as you'd expect, with glass panels between the tables and booths and dim lighting that makes the brass glow. The art deco bar has a wall lined with wine bottles. Expect to pay $25 for lunch, at least $35 for dinner. *Note:* Jacket and tie required.

## MODERATE

**CAROLINA'S, 261 S. 20th St. Tel. 545-1000.**

**Cuisine:** AMERICAN. **Reservations:** Required.
$ **Prices:** Appetizers $2.95–$7.95; main courses $8.95–$17.95; lunch $4.95–$8.95. AE, CB, DC, MC, V.
**Open:** Lunch, Mon–Fri 11:45am–2:30pm. Dinner, Sun–Thurs 5:30–10pm; Fri–Sat 5:30–11pm. Brunch, Sun 11am–2:30pm.

Carolina's has found the right place at the right time. The old 20th Street Café has gotten younger, less pricey, and more accessible, although it still gets neighborhood residents of all ages—the bar area is extremely popular, and on summer evenings there are lines outside. Even though you must contend with the din, fairly weak drinks, close seating, overworked service, and long waits for the restrooms, try Carolina's for some fairly adventuresome standard American cuisine with odd touches—not gourmet, but good and solid.

The neon that once decorated the restaurant has been removed and replaced with light-maroon stenciled walls and dark-maroon trim and fresh flowers and candles enlivening the plain vinyl tablecloths. The large computerized menu reflects daily changes prompted by what's available in market. There are plenty of appetizers, reflecting the Benetton "one world" approach to nibbled food: Chinese steamed dumplings, Mexican quesadillas, and Middle Eastern grilled vegetables with a sesame-and-chickpea dip. What has everyone excited, though, is the veal loaf—it's undoubtedly better than what you remember as home-cooking and even comes with great mashed potatoes and gravy. If you're already used to meatloaf, you can move up all the way through back ribs with mustard-and-bourbon sauce to duck à l'orange, which gets mixed reviews. Half the entrées are under $12. The bread is good peasant fare. Although the wine list is fairly small, it's well priced. The desserts range from apple brown betty to blueberry pie.

**CUTTER'S GRAND CAFE AND BAR, in the Commerce Square building on Market St. at 20th St. Tel. 851-6262.**
**Cuisine:** AMERICAN. **Reservations:** Recommended.
$ **Prices:** Appetizers $5–$9; main courses $12–$20. AE, DC, MC, V.
**Open:** Lunch, Mon–Fri 11am–2:30pm. Dinner, Mon–Thurs 5–10pm; Fri–Sat 5–11pm.

This place has all the things you'd expect of a restaurant in a big, spanking-new, impressive skyscraper—modern, cool lighting and a huge bar (120 seats) for singles. There aren't too many competitors for this type of urban bistro. But it's also an impeccable, convenient, 180-seat restaurant that's surprisingly warm for a romantic dinner, given that you're in white-collar clothes and paying white-collar prices.

The bar has become noted for its huge selection, with the bottles stacked vertically so that bartenders scamper up and down like gymnasts. Look for highly polished surfaces in wood and stone, glass lampshades, and floor-to-ceiling murals in leafy hues. Fortunately the high ceilings soak up much of the din.

Seafood (the corporate owner is based in Seattle) and pasta—from yakisoba buckwheat noodles to fettucini—are what's notable here. The biggest single item is the filet of salmon (flown in fresh daily) grilled over mesquite wood. Pasta comes with seafood also—the fettucine with scallops, for example—and such touches as toasted hazelnuts. Pizza, lamb chops, game, and steaks fill out the extensive menu, with delicious flat bread to nibble while you wait. The desserts are as good as you'd expect: lots of chocolate and a wonderful crème brûlee and bread pudding. The validated parking is complimentary after 5pm.

## IL GALLO NERO, 254 S. 15th St. Tel. 546-8065.

**Cuisine:** ITALIAN. **Reservations:** Required.

**$ Prices:** Appetizers $4.95–$7.95; main courses $13.95–$18.95. AE, MC, V.

**Open:** Lunch, Tues–Thurs 11:30am–2:30pm. Dinner, Tues–Thurs 5:30–10pm; Fri–Sat 5:30–11pm. **Closed:** Sun–Mon.

Il Gallo Nero has the look and taste of a truly authentic Tuscan ristorante, which will make it an experience to crow about for lovers of Italian restaurants this side of the Arno. Clever Carla and Enzo Fusaro transformed the interior into a gorgeous ebony-and-brass-rail bar that serves one of Philadelphia's best martinis. Steps lead up to four "balcony" tables overlooking this. Curtain walls of peony patterns accent the Modena cream-and-gray tiles and unusual postmodern Windsor chairs. Next door, the rustic room keeps the original beamed ceiling. The highlight is a tempered glass panel revealing the back of a peasant spit oven that's perfect for bistecca ai ferri. The Medici Room beyond has retained old town-house mantels and ceiling moldings. Finally, the "giardino" uses exposed brick and textured latex stucco to re-create a Boboli Garden nook.

With the wine glasses replete with Gallo Nero label (it means "black rooster" and refers to the quality mark on the best chianti riserva) and rustic crockery vases, it's all very beautiful. Carla Fusaro pushes herself to develop new dishes each season and hosts many special dinners that celebrate Florentine holidays, such as May 1 (the Feast of Love, not Labor!) and Carnevale in February. The bilingual dinner menu (plan on $37 per person, without wine) starts with antipasti—a variety of such traditional appetizers as stuffed peppers and Parma ham with melon. A favorite pasta dish (all are homemade) is paglia e fieno, "hay and straw," a platter of spinach and egg noodles. If you know what you want and it isn't on the menu—saltimbocca, for example—the kitchen will prepare it on the spot. All tomato sauces vary with the dish. The fruit tarts or liqueur-based desserts with espresso round off a meal of impeccable quality. The wines are Italian, of course, and reasonably priced for Philadelphia. The small lunch menu, in Italian only, concentrates on simple, more countrified preparations.

## THE MAGNOLIA CAFE, 1602 Locust St. Tel. 546-4180.

**Cuisine:** CAJUN. **Reservations:** Accepted only for parties of eight or more.

**$ Prices:** Appetizers $5–$9; main courses $11–$15. AE, MC, V.

**Open:** Mon 11:30am–9pm; Tues–Thurs 11:30am–10pm; Fri 11:30am–11pm; Sat 11am–11pm; Sun 11am–9pm. Bar open daily until midnight.

The Magnolia Café, on the site of the old La Panetière (an 1853 house built for Benjamin Franklin's grandson-in-law), is quite a different kettle of catfish. The increasing drive of restaurants to serve more casual and reasonable fare, as well as the widespread interest in regional American cooking, has led to the skyrocketing popularity of Cajun and Creole dishes.

Under Sam Talucci, the café has kept the formal French chandeliers and ornate wall treatments, but the complimentary plastic beads for the ladies, the wooden tables, and the major bottles of Tabasco sauce give it a cheerful incongruence. You might start with a cup of the spicy jambalaya gumbo or the shrimp-and-artichoke soup. Cajun popcorn (deep-fried crayfish tails) is often made with bits of fish smothered in spice; they're authentic here—hot and tasty.

An entrée usually on the menu is crayfish étouffée—not stuffed, as the French would imply, but basically a crayfish stew. The salt level varies, but one of the best sauces is the cream-and-tomato bisque with flecks of carrot and zucchini; it's served over seafood or pasta, or both, in various guises. And, of course, traditional New Orleans red beans and rice (seasoned with andouille, a spicy sausage) makes an appearance. The French silk pie for dessert is really a delicious chocolate cream pie.

### RUTH'S CHRIS STEAK HOUSE, 260 S. Broad St. Tel. 790-1515.

**Cuisine:** STEAK. **Reservations:** Recommended.

**$ Prices:** Appetizers $3.50–$8.95; main courses $13.95–$22.95; lunch $8.50–$13.95. AE, MC, V.

**Open:** Mon–Fri 11:30am–11:30pm; Sat 5–11:30pm; Sun 5–10:30pm.

The newest addition to the steak scene, Ruth's Chris Steak House, just south of the Academy of Music, has gotten rave reviews since 1989. Ruth's Chris serves only U.S. prime beef that's custom aged, never frozen and rushed to Philadelphia by the New Orleans distributor for the chain. The rib-eye steak in particular is presented lovingly, almost ritually, in a quiet and respectful setting, and garnishes are almost nonexistent. The portions are so large that you might want to skip the side dishes, although Ruth's Chris touts potatoes done nine ways. Several fish and chicken choices also are available. The desserts, mostly Southern recipes with lots of sugar and nuts, average $5.

### SANSOM STREET OYSTER HOUSE, 1516 Sansom St. Tel. 567-7683.

**Cuisine:** SEAFOOD. **Reservations:** Not accepted.

**$ Prices:** Appetizers $2.95–$6.95; main courses $8.95–$16.95; lunch $3.95–$13.95. AE, DC, MC, V.

**Open:** Lunch, Mon–Sat 11am–3pm. Dinner, Mon–Sat 3–10pm.

Chef David Mink knows oysters from every angle—where they come from, how their flavors differ, and how to prepare them. The Sansom Street Oyster House, located on one of Philadelphia's most colorful shopping blocks, is where David puts his acumen into action. In 1989, he added the Samuel Adams Brew House upstairs, the first brew pub in town, with two ales and porter on tap.

The ambiance is that of a traditional seafood parlor, with such 20th-century concessions as a tiled floor (instead of sawdust) and plywood paneling. Recently installed wooden tables are welcome replacements for the previous Formica-topped furniture. The blackboards listing the daily specials perch beside an endless collection of antique oyster plates and nautical lithographs.

You'll probably want an appetizer of several different types of oysters: metallic belons; cooler, meatier Long Island half-shells; and larger, fishier box oysters. You can judge a similar rivalry between cherrystone and little-neck clams for yourself. All are opened right at the raw bar. For dinner, most people choose one of the specials—sea bass or tile fish, for instance. The homemade bread pudding is the most reliable dessert. The liquor prices are high, except for the draft beer.

**SUSANNA FOO, 1512 Walnut St. Tel. 545-2666.**
 **Cuisine:** CHINESE. **Reservations:** Recommended for dinner.
$ **Prices:** Appetizers $3–$9; main courses $15–$24; lunch $9–$16. AE, MC, V.
 **Open:** Lunch, Mon–Fri 11:30am–2:30pm. Dinner, Mon–Thurs 5–10pm; Fri–Sat 5–11pm.

Susanna Foo has been touted in *Gourmet* and *Esquire* magazines and just about everywhere else as one of the best blends of Asian and Western cuisines in this country. In previous editions of this book I declared myself a fan of their more overtly Chinese restaurant, Hunan's, and feel that Susanna Foo's isn't quite up to its press but is still a creditable effort. However, bear in mind a fortune that I've gotten during several excursions there: "A woman's guess is much more certain than a man's certainty."

The restaurant's decor has retained the carriage upholstery, wall banquettes, and dim lighting from its previous incarnation as a steak house and has brought over the cutlery and glass from Hunan. The cuisine is the main thing, so expect to pay first-class prices. Appetizers feature such delicacies as curried chicken ravioli with grilled eggplant, slightly crispy but not oily. Noodle dishes, salads, and entrées similarly combine East and West: water chestnuts and radicchio, smoked duck and endive, grilled chicken with Thai lemongrass sauce, and spicy shrimp and pear curry. Ms. Foo does include French caramelizing of certain dishes but not any butter-based sauces, or roux; the Asian technique is to sear small amounts of ingredients, combining them just before service. The wine list, designed to complement these dishes, specializes in French and Californian white wines. Desserts such as the ginger creme with strawberries and the hazelnut meringue are light and delicate.

*Note:* Late diners may encounter a zealous cleanup at surrounding tables, including use of liquid cleansers.

## INEXPENSIVE

**CATALINA'S, KormanSuites Hotel and Conference Center, 2001 Hamilton St. (20th St. between Parkway and Spring Garden sts.). Tel. 659-7500.**
 **Cuisine:** AMERICAN REGIONAL. **Reservations:** Recommended.
$ **Prices:** Salads and pastas $3.95–$9.95; sandwiches $5.95–$14.95; lunch $4.95–$9.95. AE, CB, DC, MC, V.
 **Open:** Hotel breakfast Mon–Fri from 6:30am; Sat–Sun from 7:30. Lunch and dinner, daily 11am–2am.

Bill Hoffman, who founded Carolina's in 1986 (see above), has set up shop at this attractive California-style, health-conscious section of the new KormanSuites Hotel, four blocks north of the Parkway at Logan Circle. The Korman family was willing to stint on nothing to integrate Catalina's into the hotel and yet also give it a distinguished, fun identity. Since it's off the street, they added a few hooks, such as one of the best single-malt whiskey selections around, and offer discounts through chits available at Parkway cultural institutions.

The menu goes from the subtle—for example, the chicken and angel-hair pasta combination garnished with broccoli—to steamed mussels and grilled vegetables with mozzarella. Look for grilled fish and boneless chicken as well, with interesting sauces and garnishes.

## DOCK STREET BREWING COMPANY, Two Logan Square (corner of 18th and Cherry sts.). Tel. 496-0413.

**Cuisine:** INTERNATIONAL. **Reservations:** Recommended at lunch.

**$ Prices:** Appetizers $4–$8; main courses $7–$10; lunch $4–$9. Fresh-brewed tap beer $2.50–$3.50 per glass. AE, CB, DC, DISC, MC, V.

**Open:** Mon–Thurs and Sun 11am–10pm; Fri–Sat 11am–midnight.

This brew-pub is just right for the 1990s: relaxed, with a definite hook in the spotless on-premises microbrewery. Jeffrey Ware saw a market niche for a brewery that could operate in combination with a popular restaurant, since other "normal" microbrewery costs wouldn't apply. You can take a tour, but at any time six or more fresh beers, ales, stouts, and porters will be on tap; sample the subtle distinctions in hops, yeast, temperature and length of fermentation, and filtration. The 200-seat restaurant features a 40-foot bar, a paneled billiard room to the rear, spacious banquettes, and high ceilings (it's ironic that this place is located in a brand-new corporate granite skyscraper!). *Note:* Dock Street brewery products are served only at the bar.

Almost all the entrees are under $10. The lunch menu offers soups, pub-style sandwiches, and burgers with two-potato fries. Dinner entrées include many of these, along with Welsh rarebit, Alsatian choucroûte, and jerked pork. The summer menu brings gazpacho, seafood sausage, and Caribbean classics.

## FRATELLI, 1701 Spruce St. Tel. 546-0513.

**Cuisine:** ITALIAN. **Reservations:** Not required.

**$ Prices:** Appetizers $5–$8; main courses $8–$16. AE, CB, DC, MC, V.

**Open:** Lunch, Mon–Fri 11am–3pm. Dinner, Mon–Thurs 5–11pm; Fri–Sat 5pm–midnight; Sun 4–10pm.

Despite its spic-and-span chic, Fratelli is a solid neighborhood type of restaurant. The "brothers" are right in the Rittenhouse Square boutique area: Mama Rago cooks, and Papa runs a florist shop and pizza parlor on 20th Street.

Fratelli's three levels of seating are enlivened by contemporary flower arrangements, squiggles of neon, pink walls, and bright-green carpets. The upstairs dining room overlooks the more "designed" ground floor and has a few more intimate touches—about 150 places in all. Stick to the basics: pasta, meatballs, and even sausage and spaghetti. The tomato sauces and grated cheeses are fresh and clean tasting, the pasta newly made and not overcooked, and the sausages and salamis spicy and complex. Of course, Fratelli's cuisine goes well beyond luncheonette food—witness the fettuccine Alfredo and the mussels in red sauce. More and more restaurants are pushing enormous, three-dimensional wedges of what used to be called pizza, and Fratelli is on the bandwagon. The quality is good, if you like the idea. The salads and desserts are recommended; don't miss the white-chocolate gelato.

**MARABELLA'S, 1420 Locust St. Tel. 545-1845.**
  **Cuisine:** INTERNATIONAL. **Reservations:** Not accepted for dinner.
**$ Prices:** Appetizers $2.95; main courses $7.95–$14.95; lunch $3–$6. AE, DC, MC, V.
  **Open:** Mon–Thurs 11:30am–11:30pm; Fri–Sat 11:30am–12:30am; Sun 11:30am–11pm.

Are you looking for a trendy trattoria that offers pastas, pizza, sandwiches, and grilled seafood, all with contemporary flair? That's Marabella's, a restaurant that is not only fun and chic but also reasonably priced. Marabella's offers the same menu at lunch and dinner, with almost every item under $12. This place is especially convenient for families and post-theater dining; the multilevel interior is contemporary and cheerful, decorated with fabric hangings and abstract art, colorful enameled jukeboxes, metal chairs, and vinyl tablecloths.

Before you order, your waiter will bring you bread and roasted peppers—hard to resist. The appetizers range from such old favorites as mussels in red or white sauce, fried mozzarella, and antipasto to a more unusual platter of fish and shellfish in sauce, something like a seafood stew. The roasted garlic cloves to be spread on the delicious bread are another pleasure, even though you may later regret overdoing. The wine list boasts a good selection of inexpensive California and Italian wines.

For an entrée, try a contemporary dish such as tortellini with goat cheese, sun-dried tomatoes, and olives. The old standards, spaghetti and meatballs and lasagne with meat sauce, are very well done here; the pasta is homemade, and the sauces are carefully seasoned. If you want to go with pizza instead, the version with goat cheese, sun-dried tomatoes, and black olives is very popular. When neither pasta nor pizza appeals, turn to the mesquite-grilled seafood instead. Deep-frying is something Marabella's does unusually well—the deep-fried eggplant, zucchini, or potatoes are welcome side dishes. The desserts are gelati, ricotta cheesecake, burned-sugar custard, and a chocolate concoction called "original sin" (don't ask). If you must stop here, then choose cappuccino or espresso to finish off your evening smoothly.

**MEZZANOTTE, 1701 Green St. Tel. 765-2777.**
  **Cuisine:** ITALIAN. **Reservations:** Recommended.
**$ Prices:** Appetizers $3.95–$5.95; main courses $7–$14. AE, DC, MC, V.
  **Open:** Daily 11:30am–midnight; bar open until 2am.

Mezzanotte, six blocks north of the Wyndham Plaza and north of Logan Circle, features a quirky combination of contemporary Italian-American food at moderate prices. The interior is the ground floor of three adjoining row houses, and it's quite a change from their sober red-brick exterior, with splashes of Day-Glo color against black and a suspended lattice ceiling. The bar at the entrance leads back to two levels of about 75 seats, with black marble tables, skylights, and chrome detailing. In summer, you can eat outdoors.

Mezzanotte is most known for its individualized pizzas: a thin crust (a combination of white and whole wheat) topped with various combinations, including caramelized onions, walnuts, and gorgonzola. Many of the recipes are taken from Spago's in Los Angeles or Greens in San Francisco—you get the idea. Other recipes include frittatas—thicker Italian versions of omelets—special pastas, and fish with herbs. The wine list is short and affordable.

### RIB-IT, 1709 Walnut St. Tel. 568-1555.

**Cuisine:** AMERICAN/RIBS. **Reservations:** Not accepted.
$ **Prices:** Appetizers $2.95–$5.95; main courses $6.95–$14.95. AE, DC, MC, V.
**Open:** Lunch, Mon–Sat 11:30am–3pm. Dinner, daily 4:30–10pm. Early Bird Special, Mon–Fri 3:30–5:30pm; Sun noon–4pm. Bar Mon–Sat until 2am, Sun 12:30–10pm.

If there's any type of cooking a Northeast city lacks, it's usually ribs with all the trimmings. This gap is filled in Philadelphia with Rib-It, which does a lot of casual, off-the-street trade and gives wonderful value. If you lived nearby, you'd bring visiting friends in for ribs, an onion loaf, or a quick drink at every opportunity.

Rib-It has a relaxed sense of comfort, featuring an old tin ceiling with cone moldings and soft lighting that sets a subdued, but not unpleasant, tone. Swirling stained glass, much from the old Waldorf-Astoria in New York, fits the bar and all the windows. The enormous braziers along exposed-brick walls are fit for dinner, as country-and-western tapes croon.

Vernon Hill, Rib-It's young entrepreneur, won't reveal exactly what's in the western barbecue, but it's brushed on the baby-back ribs ($14 at dinner, $8 at lunch) for a lean, smoky taste. The portions are statuesque, to say the least. An appetizer called Wonder Wings dishes up over a pound of barbecued chicken wings, and it's known to make a meal for two. Whatever you order, don't leave without trying the onion-ring loaf, which consists of true onion rings pressed into a bread mold. Recently, Rib-It has explored the exciting world of international cuisine, with "Northern Italian" specialties and Cajun lamb ribs. The drinks average $3, with draft beer $1.50 per mug. If you get hungry between lunch and dinner, try the Early Bird Special, a full dinner for $6.

### SAMUEL ADAMS BREW HOUSE, 1516 Sansom St., 2nd floor. Tel. 563-2326.

**Cuisine:** PUB. **Reservations:** Not required.
$ **Prices:** Appetizers $3.95; main courses $5–$12. AE, DC, MC, V.
**Open:** Lunch, Mon–Sat 11am–4pm. Dinner, Mon–Thurs 4–11pm; Sat–Sun 4pm–midnight.

The Samuel Adams is a traditional, no-smoking English-style brew pub with an American twist—a microbrewery. While you sit at the handsome hand-carved English bar, you can watch as three varieties of beer are made. The menu features such English favorites as fish and chips and grilled sausage, plus such Americanisms as burgers and grilled salmon. The beer is still better than the food, but the gap is steadily narrowing.

## BUDGET

### CHARLIE'S WATER WHEEL, downstairs at 1526 Sansom St. Tel. 563-4155.

**Cuisine:** DELI/ROMANIAN. **Reservations:** Not accepted.
$ **Prices:** Sandwiches/main courses $5–$7. No credit cards.

**Open:** Lunch only, Mon–Sat 11am–4pm.
Charlie is a Romanian circus all in himself, and the Water Wheel is best known for the massive quantity of freebies—pickles, fried mushrooms, and meatballs—available with any order. The steaks, sandwiches, and cheesesteaks here have pinstriped adherents.

### DINER ON THE SQUARE, 19th and Spruce sts. Tel. 735-5787.
**Cuisine:** AMERICAN. **Reservations:** Not necessary.
**$ Prices:** Appetizers $2.50–$4.50; main courses $5–$10.
**Open:** 24 hrs.
Say that you're strolling around Rittenhouse Square and have an urge for the type of square meal you'd associate with a roadside restaurant. A dressed-up place like that is waiting for you at Diner on the Square. Don't let its pink neon fool you; it has booths at which burgers, hash browns, and the best milkshakes in Philadelphia make their cheerful appearances—for about $5 per person. The Diner also branches out as a deli, with a whitefish platter and delicious omelets, and offers some fancier cuisine, such as a chicken-breast sandwich. The lunch and Sunday-brunch crowds can be fierce, so try to beat the rush.

### REX PIZZA, 20 S. 18th St. Tel. 564-2374.
**Cuisine:** ITALIAN. **Reservations:** Not accepted.
**$ Prices:** Pizza $3.75–$7.25; hoagies from $3.55. No credit cards.
**Open:** Mon–Sat 11am–1am.
For those self-indulgent moments when you need a large pepperoni pizza or a tuna hero, one of the most convenient—and surprisingly good—spots is Rex Pizza. They do a fine, nongreasy, thick-crust whole pizza for about $5 and a full-scale submarine sandwich for $3.55. Even when they're busy, your wait will rarely exceed 10 minutes.

# 3. SOUTH PHILADELPHIA

## EXPENSIVE

### OSTERIA ROMANA, 935 Ellsworth St. Tel. 271-9191.
**Cuisine:** ITALIAN. **Reservations:** Recommended.
**$ Prices:** Appetizers $7–$12; main courses $12–$25. AE, DC, MC, V.
**Open:** Dinner only, Tues–Thurs 5:30–10:30pm; Fri–Sat 5:30–11pm; Sun 5–9:30. **Closed:** Mon.
Fine Italian (as opposed to Italian-American) trattorie and ristoranti have been cropping up almost everywhere in Philadelphia, except for—you guessed it—near the Italian Market. Finally one opened in 1981: Osteria Romana. The DiMarcos (Ivana is Roman-born and will run the kitchen until she finds satisfactory help—which, by her standards, may take forever) get rave reviews for such simple, unpretentious specialties as pasta, osso buco, and saltimbocca.

You start off with a basket of coarse, crusty peasant bread and plates of hot peppers waiting on your table. A white-jacketed waiter is sure to follow; slow service has been cited by several diners, but this seems to be due to the shortage of kitchen help. If you've never had an honest minestrone, this might be the place and the time to try it.

The tomato stock is light and sweet, and the vegetables retain body and flavor. As a first course, the pastas are uniformly excellent—thick, tubular, and gently resilient. The arrabiata sauce is fairly spicy and tomato-based; for the hottest thing around, sample the puttanesca, which the menu chastely translates as pasta "harlot-style." Note that if you're used to American pasta sauces, these may seem a bit dry and meager but startlingly fresh.

The best meat entrée (and the most expensive) is a grilled steak that tastes just off a charcoal fire: While crispy outside, it retains tenderness within. The veal stew with green peppers and onions also features unusually tender meat. All the entrees come with a seasonal vegetable, such as asparagus with crushed garlic and lemon. If the limited dessert tray has a sort of custard torte covered with fresh fruit, jump at it.

**THE SALOON, 750 S. 7th St. Tel. 627-1811.**
   **Cuisine:** CONTINENTAL. **Reservations:** Virtually required.
$ **Prices:** Appetizers $5–$16; main courses $12–$32. AE.
   **Open:** Lunch, Tues–Fri 11:30am–2pm. Dinner, Mon–Thurs 5–11:30pm; Fri–Sat 5pm–12:30am.

The Santore family has tended here since the late 1960s, and the tastes of the time have again rolled around to the freshness and quality of their cuisine, which deserves its rare four-star rating from *Philadelphia Magazine*. The decor is solid wood paneling, soft uplit sconces, and etched and beveled glass on the second floor, above one excellent bar and surrounding a second with its old National cash register.

The Saloon has a long menu, and many specials add to it. The Santores like such standards as clams casino and crabmeat salads, but also sautéed radicchio with shiitake mushrooms and superb salads. The heavy artillery is the 25-ounce porterhouse steak with greens and roasted potatoes and the lightly breaded veal slices with sweet and hot peppers. The wines are expensive, and the desserts high-cholesterol and exquisite, thanks to the pastry chef on board.

# MODERATE

**VICTOR'S CAFE, 1303 Dickinson St. Tel. 468-3040.**
   **Cuisine:** ITALIAN. **Reservations:** Recommended.
$ **Prices:** Antipasti and appetizers $4.25–$6.95; main courses $12.75–$19.75. AE, CB, DC.
   **Open:** Dinner only, Tues–Thurs 5–11pm; Fri–Sat 4:30pm–12:30am; Sun 4–9:30pm.

Victor's is a South Philly shrine to opera, with waiters who deliver arias along with hearty Italian classics. Started in the 1930s by John Di Stefano, who covered the walls with photos of Toscanini, local Mario Lanza, and the like, the restaurant is run by a family that still plays over 70,000 78s and engages the best voices they can find. To get here, follow Broad Street south (take SEPTA bus C) to Dickinson, then walk two blocks east.

The Italian bread in baskets is bouncy and airy; the deep-fried mozzarella comes with a wonderful anchovy bagna cauda. Ten pasta dishes are named after operatic roles, but feel free to challenge the chef. The cannelloni Don Carlos has two enormous shells with beef and veal, covered in marinara. Vitello fiorentino uses fresh spinach for the bechamel. The Chianti classico as the house wine rings in around $20.

# INEXPENSIVE

### RALPH'S, 760 9th St. Tel. 627-6011.
**Cuisine:** ITALIAN. **Reservations:** Recommended.
**$ Prices:** Antipasti and appetizers $5.50–$7.50; pasta $8; main courses $9–$15. No credit cards.
**Open:** Dinner only, Sun–Thurs noon–10pm, Fri–Sat noon–11pm.

This two-story no-smoking restaurant a few blocks above the Italian Market is the epitome of the "red-gravy" style: unpretentious, comfortable, reasonable, and owned by the same family for decades. The baked lasagne has fans all over the city, and the extensive menu features veal and chicken. The service is friendly and attentive.

### STROLLI'S, 1528 Dickinson St. Tel. 336-3390.
**Cuisine:** ITALIAN. **Reservations:** Required.
**$ Prices:** Antipasti and appetizers $1.50–$3; pasta $3; main courses $5–$8. No credit cards.
**Open:** Lunch, Mon–Sat 11:30am–1:30pm. Dinner, Mon–Sat 5–10pm; Sun 4–9pm.

With all those Italians in South Philly, you'd figure there would be an extremely inexpensive, wholesome, family restaurant in the middle of the neighborhood, right? That place is Strolli's. It used to look like a burned-out storefront at the corner of Mole Street—now there's a sign and an identifiable side door. Implacable, pipe-puffing John Strolli presides (get him to divulge the secrets behind his bountiful platters, if you can). To get here, follow Broad Street south (take SEPTA bus C) to Dickinson, then walk two blocks west.

Strolli's consists of two plain rooms, with plywood paneling and bare plaster enlivened by an ancient cigarette machine and a life preserver dedicated to Strolli's wife, Carmela. Music emanates from a corner radio. You'll make your own atmosphere, and any description of the size, taste, or pricing of the dishes won't be believed without corroborating evidence.

You'll want to start with an antipasto; a medium-size one is fully 10 inches long and 4 inches high, so the large would suit three fine. All seafood platters come with tomato, lettuce, and coleslaw—would you believe a scallop-crammed plate for $5.50? The veal-cutlet platter offers an extraordinary piece of sautéed red veal. While you're making reservations, you might ask for the special stuffed shells—they're legendary. The regular items will take you back 15 years: homemade gnocchi with sausage and veal scaloppine with spaghetti.

### THE TRIANGLE TAVERN, intersection of Passyunk Ave. and 10th and Reed sts. Tel. 467-8683.
**Cuisine:** ITALIAN. **Reservations:** Recommended.
**$ Prices:** Main courses about $6–$10. No credit cards.
**Open:** Dinner only, Mon–Sat 4pm–midnight; Sun 3pm–midnight.

Inexpensive, heaping dishes of homemade pasta and bowls of mussels are served here amid a steamy atmosphere of stained tablecloths and good humor. You'll enter through the neighborhood bar, complete with a large-screen TV; keep pushing toward the back. Nothing costs more than $10, and most items are closer to $6: chicken cacciatore, gnocchi, and

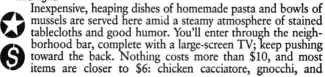

spaghetti in white clam sauce. The mussels in red sauce are famous. On Friday and Saturday night, look for plenty of audience participation in helping the steady guitar trio along with old favorites. Be prepared to wait for a table.

**MARRA'S, 1734 E. Passyunk Ave. (between Morris and Moore sts.) Tel. 463-9249.**
   **Cuisine:** ITALIAN. **Reservations:** Not required.
**$ Prices:** Pizza $8.50–$12. No credit cards.
   **Open:** Lunch, Tues–Sat 11:30am–4pm. Dinner, Mon–Fri 4–11:30pm; Sat 4pm–1am; Sun 2–11:30pm.

**⑤** No list of eateries would be complete without a pizzeria, and Marra's wins the "Best Pizza" award hands down. It's in the heart of South Philadelphia, and the brick ovens give these thin-crust versions a real Italian smokiness. Marra's is noted for its homemade lasagne, tomato sauce, and squid on Friday.

# 4. UNIVERSITY CITY

## MODERATE

**PALLADIUM, 3601 Locust Walk. Tel. 387-3463.**
   **Cuisine:** CONTINENTAL. **Reservations:** Recommended.
**$ Prices:** Appetizers $5–$9; main courses $12–$22; pretheater dinner $25. AE, DC, MC, V.
   **Open:** Lunch, Mon–Fri 11:30am–2:30pm. Dinner, Tues–Sat 5–11pm; Sun 5–9pm.

In the heart of the University of Pennsylvania campus is Palladium, the latest enterprise of co-owners Roger Harman and Duane Ball. Strictly speaking, Palladium is an elegantly appointed full-service restaurant and bar overlooking the heart of the Penn campus; it's reminiscent of an old-time faculty club—Chesterfields and wing chairs with footstools face an old stone fireplace, while leaded-glass windows, oak wainscoting, and an ornate ceiling add the final touches. In the spacious dining room the atmosphere is similar, if slightly less cozy. The prices here are a little high to make the Palladium a student hangout, but they're quite reasonable given this restaurant's quality. You can choose à la carte dishes, a fixed-price menu, or a pretheater special.

The appetizers might include lasagne verde, creole crab cakes, and leek-and-onion tart. The entrées at Palladium are particularly good, especially the pechugas de polla con rajas (a chicken breast cooked with chile peppers, prepared hot or mild according to your tastes), which is a refreshingly different approach to chicken. The leg of lamb is delicately seasoned, if a somewhat small portion. The cold poached Norway salmon is served with a cream sauce flavored with cucumber and dill. All entrées are accompanied by potatoes au gratin (good enough to be a meal in themselves) and a mélange of fresh vegetables.

The desserts do not quite live up to the standard set by the entrées, although the cold lime mousse is quite pleasantly tart. Pastries, homemade ice cream, and ices also are offered. Watch the (largely student) service, which is at best uneven, and sometimes downright slow.

Downstairs is The Gold Standard, a cafeteria that heats up with comedy, dinner theater and the like.

## WHITE DOG CAFE, 3420 Sansom St. Tel. 386-9224.

**Cuisine:** AMERICAN. **Reservations:** Recommended.

**$ Prices:** Appetizers $3.50–$6; main courses $12–$18.50; desserts $5; lunch $8–$15. AE, DC, MC, V.

**Open:** Breakfast, Mon–Fri 7:30–9:30am. Lunch, Mon–Fri 11:30am–2:30pm. Dinner, Mon–Thurs 5:30–10pm; Fri–Sat 5:30–11pm; Sun 5–10pm. Brunch, Sat–Sun 11:30am–2:30pm. Frequent theme dinners and parties.

Judy Wicks is one of Philadelphia's great citizens: She led the fight against the University of Pennsylvania to save this block of Sansom Street and has evolved into a smart, tough, and fun-loving entrepreneur. All this comes through in the White Dog Café. The name is indebted to the mystic and theosophist Madame Blavatsky, who resided here a century ago. Blavatsky was about to have an infected leg amputated, when a white dog in the house slept across the leg and cured all. It's still got cure-all food.

You'll enter two row houses with the dividing wall knocked out and with the most sophisticated kitchen equipment and electronics concealed behind an eclectic mélange of checkered tablecloths, antique furniture and lights, and white dogs, dogs, and dogs. The friendly pups are everywhere—on the menu, holding matchbooks, pouring milk, and in family photographs. There's an unusual vivacity, even intimacy, about the place.

From Sansom Street, you'll first see the three-counter bar with its own small grill menu. The bar specializes in such all-American beers as McSorley's Ale, New Amsterdam, and Anchor Steam, as well as inexpensive American wines by the glass or bottle. Dining areas lie to the rear and right—there are several, and the White Dog has completed an ambitious glassed-in porch across the rear.

The staff offers frequently changing menus as well as "theme" dinners based on the season or a particular American region. Two delicious constants are the fresh rolls and muffins, vestiges of Judy's original bakery concept for the White Dog. The appetizers include Yucatán chicken soup with coriander and lime and brook trout with apple horseradish. The grilled vegetables served with hummus dip are light and delicious.

The White Dog attracts everyone, from Penn students to the mayor. Judy pulls in American musicians—banjoists, swing trios, Dixieland bands—on most nights. Just next door at 3424 Sansom Street, **The Black Cat** (tel. 386-6664) offers more of Judy's antiques and crafts; living-room articles are sold in the living room and so on. It's open Monday and Tuesday from 11am to 9pm, Wednesday and Thursday from 11am to 11pm, and Friday and Saturday from 11am to midnight; closed Sunday.

# INEXPENSIVE

## BOCCIE BAR AND RESTAURANT, The Warehouse, 4040 Locust St. Tel. 386-5500.

**Cuisine:** ITALIAN. **Reservations:** Not accepted.

**$ Prices:** Pizzas $7–$13. AE, DC, MC, V.

**Open:** Sun–Thurs 4–10:30pm; Fri–Sat 4pm–12:30am.

The Warehouse was built as a multilevel retail-and-restaurant space. This relatively new and very popular hangout near campus has a boccie court in the middle of the floor, providing a great way to pass the time while your pizza is cooking in their stone, wood-fired ovens. You can choose your own from the presliced ingredients or select one of their more exotic toppings. Their English beers are priced low.

**EDEN, International House, 3701 Chestnut St. Tel. 387-2471.**
 **Cuisine:** INTERNATIONAL. **Reservations:** Not required.
$ **Prices:** Appetizers $3–$5.50; main courses $6–$11. AE, MC, V.
 **Open:** Mon–Fri 7:30am–9pm; Sat 11:30am–8pm.

Segmented off the southwest corner and outdoor café area of International House, Eden features imaginative cafeteria cuisine that includes pan-sautéed pastas, chili, and over 20 soups and desserts. Eden aims to provide quality salads, burgers, fish, and chicken using Asian, Latin, and African influences. The interior has those wonderful earthen tiles, wooden tables, and a central island and small waterfall. Even though it's packed—International House students have the option of taking all meals at Eden—the sound level is comfortable, and the student staff is enthusiastic and well trained. The desserts here are reflective of the sweet-toothed students. You get unlimited refills of the freshly ground coffee, a blend of French roast and mocha java. On Thursday, Friday, and Saturday nights Eden features live jazz.

**MANUS PLACE, 4251 Walnut St. Tel. 386-4404.**
 **Cuisine:** THAI. **Reservations:** Not required.
$ **Prices:** Appetizers $3–$7; main courses $6–$13. AE, MC, V.
 **Open:** Lunch, daily noon–3pm. Dinner, Mon–Thurs 5–10:30pm; Fri–Sun 5–11pm.

It's in University City, and Manus Place is the kind of place you can drop into on a whim. The decor consists of the sprightly pastels and spotlighting onto exotic bud vases that seem to be a staple of Thai restaurants, along with attractive posters of a breathtaking homeland; recent reports are that it's getting somewhat faded. If sweet soups beguile you, don't pass up the large bowl of chicken soup with coconut extract and coriander (a standard at Thai places); its opposite is the clear, vegetable broth with mushrooms. A staple entrée is pad thai, a Thai assortment of broad rice noodles, bean sprouts, and shrimp with a blended peanut sauce; the comforting version here comes crunchy. As in all other Thai restaurants, the beverage of choice is Singha beer, usually $3 a bottle.

**NEW DECK TAVERN, 3408 Sansom St. Tel. 386-4600.**
 **Cuisine:** AMERICAN. **Reservations:** Recommended.
$ **Prices:** Main courses $6–$11.
 **Open:** Lunch, dinner, and late supper, daily 10am–2am.

Virtually next door to the White Dog (see above), the New Deck Tavern is less of a restaurant than a relaxed watering hole, with truly Irish beers and barmaids and a 37-foot solid cherrywood bar. Try to catch Dottie Ford, a secretary to Penn's physics department, on the piano nightly between 7 and 9pm; she has an amazing range of thousands of show and other tunes, built up over the past 50 years.

**THE RESTAURANT, 4207 Walnut St. Tel. 561-3649.**

**Cuisine:** ECLECTIC. **Reservations:** Required on weekends, accepted after 3pm.

**$ Prices:** $13.50 prix fixe for appetizer and main course; extra $3 for desserts. AE, CB, DC, MC, V.

**Open:** Dinner only, Tues–Sat 5:30–10pm.

The Restaurant is simply the final project for students at the Restaurant School, a cooking school central to Philadelphia dining and restaurateurs that emphasizes business and management. After eight months of instruction, teams plan a menu and kitchen protocol, then take over the ground floor for eight weeks at a time.

So why eat here? There are several reasons, so Philadelphians say. The food is never downright bad and is often quite good. A month of Texan turkey recipes once left most people cold, but the following month a New Orleans menu was worth three times the price. In fact, it's popular to check out the month's crop, and it's not unusual for a good team to attract sufficient financial backing to set up elsewhere in town. Since the students are paying for the right to cook your meal, the prices are extremely low. The restaurant has acquired a liquor license and offers a fine selection of apéritifs, wines, and cocktails. You can count on at least one soup, one salad, and five entrées.

## ZOCALO, 36th St. and Lancaster Ave. (one block north of Market St.). Tel. 895-0139.

**Cuisine:** MEXICAN. **Reservations:** Recommended.

**$ Prices:** Appetizers $4–$6.50; main courses $9–$15; three-course prix-fixe dinner $12.95 Mon–Thurs. AE, DC, MC, V.

**Open:** Lunch, Mon–Fri noon–2:30pm. Dinner, Sun–Thurs 5–11:30pm; Fri–Sat 5pm–12:30am.

This sparely decorated restaurant presents contemporary Mexican cuisine, from all the provinces, using fresh ingredients. It's undoubtedly the best Mexican place around, and its food is priced accordingly—from such traditional dishes as carne asada to such modern classics as fresh shrimp in adobo. There's lively Latin music on most nights, with a pleasant deck in back for use in summer.

# BUDGET

## LE BUS, 3402 Sansom St. Tel. 387-3800.

**Cuisine:** AMERICAN. **Reservations:** Recommended.

**$ Prices:** Main courses $5–$9. No credit cards.

**Open:** Mon–Fri 7:30am–11pm; Sat 8:30am–11pm; Sun 9:30am–11pm.

Le Bus actually used to be one; stationary, it dispensed simple fare from four wheels in the funkier days of Sansom Street. It has since moved indoors to a simple row house, with the expected contemporary art on the walls, an uncluttered decor and bar, and even a neon sign. You'll still learn about the homemade breads, baked goods, vegetarian lasagne, chili, soups, and salads from a blackboard over the counter, though, and you must bus them yourself to your table. Expect the entrées to be under $9, with unusual spices. The apple pie with sour cream is a wonderful dessert.

## NEW DELHI, 4004 Chestnut St. Tel. 386-1941.

**Cuisine:** INDIAN. **Reservations:** Not required.

**$ Prices:** Main courses $4.50–$9; all-you-can-eat lunch buffet $5.95 daily; dinner buffet $8.95 Mon–Thurs only. AE, MC, V.

**Open:** Mon–Thurs noon–10pm; Fri–Sat noon–11pm.

New Delhi is a fairly good Indian restaurant near the University of Pennsylvania campus with an all-you-can-eat, 26-item buffet. It boasts quality ingredients, a tandoor clay oven, and friendly service.

# 5. CHINATOWN

## MODERATE

**GOLDEN POND, 1006 Race St. Tel. 923-0303.**
    **Cuisine:** CHINESE. **Reservations:** Recommended.
**$ Prices:** Appetizers $3.95–$7.95; main courses $6.50–$16. Lunch special $5.95. Prix-fixe dinner $15. MC, V.
    **Open:** Mon–Fri 11:30am–10pm, Sat–Sun noon–11pm.

This very stylish Hong Kong–style place costs a bit more than others in the neighborhood, but the impeccable service and the obviously fresh preparation are worth it. Wing Ming Tang, the chef, is a survivor of the Tiananmen Square riot in 1989 and has years of Hong Kong training. This Chinese cuisine features some potato dishes, chicken, duck, and seafood, but no pork or beef. It's one of the few places that serves brown rice.

## INEXPENSIVE

**HARMONY VEGETARIAN RESTAURANT, 135 N. 9th St. Tel. 627-4520.**
    **Cuisine:** CHINESE. **Reservations:** Recommended.
**$ Prices:** Appetizers $3.95–$5.95; main courses $6.95–$12.95. MC, V.
    **Open:** Lunch, daily 11:30am–3pm. Dinner, Sun–Thurs 3–10pm, Fri–Sat 3–11pm.

This winner of the 1991 *Travel/Holiday* Good Value dining award is intimate and candlelit and prohibits smoking. Despite the menu listings for meat and fish, absolutely everything is made with vegetables (that also means no eggs or dairy). George Tang makes his own gluten by washing the starch out of flour; this miracle fiber is then deep-fried and marinated as appropriate to simulate "beef" or "chicken" or even "fish." Raves go to the hot-and-sour soup and the various mushroom dishes. You must bring your own bottle of liquor or wine.

**IMPERIAL INN, 142 N. 10th St. Tel. 627-5588.**
    **Cuisine:** CHINESE. **Reservations:** Recommended.
**$ Prices:** Appetizers $2.95–$6.95; main courses $7.95–$12.95. AE, CB, DC, MC, V.
    **Open:** Lunch, daily 11:30am–3pm. Dinner, Mon–Thurs 3pm–1am, Fri–Sun 3pm–2am.

The Imperial Inn, with another location at 942 Race Street (tel. 627-2299), has shown its true staying power in Chinatown under proprietor Luis Sust. The North 10th Street location, opened in 1980, serves an enormous variety of Szechuan, Mandarin, and Cantonese dishes. Many recent immigrant chefs, in fact, have passed through the kitchen to learn other regional cuisines before setting up on their own restaurants.

Lunch here features dim sum, appetizer-size dishes that are

trundled around on carts for diners to take as the fancy strikes them, with $1.50 the average cost per dish. It's a great form of instant gratification for samples, and Imperial Inn has the best in town, with 30 varieties served daily from 11am to 3pm. Among the most tantalizing selections are the steamed flat noodles with soy, spare ribs with currants and scallions, steamed pork-and-shrimp dumplings, and crispy shrimp toast. For dinner, the lemon chicken features a sautéed boneless breast in egg batter, laced with a mild lemon sauce. Sumptuous banquets for eight or more can be arranged by reservation. On a smaller scale, you can order a full-course dinner, which includes a choice of soup, rice, a main course, and a dessert for about $3 more than the entree itself.

The setting for all this is a standard arrangement of booths and round tables, with green bamboo wallpaper, octagonal paneled windows and mirrors, wood trim, stylized dragons, and the like. The full bar (unusual in Chinatown) stocks standard and exotic drinks. The tea is perfumed jasmine.

## BUDGET

**CAPITAL,** 1008 Race St. Tel. 925-2477.
   **Cuisine:** VIETNAMESE. **Reservations:** Recommended.
**$ Prices:** Main courses $2.75–$6.75. MC, V.
   **Open:** Daily 11am–10pm.

The positive restaurant reviews placed at every table are not merely a major part of the decor: Capital is one of the best spots in town for Vietnamese cuisine, which needs some explanation. Look for ground pork, sweet or pungent herbs and greens, and slight French touches. Bun thit nuong is a small, savory serving of pork with garlic flavor over rice noodles. You must bring your own bottle of liquor or wine.

**JOE'S PEKING DUCK HOUSE,** 925 Race St. Tel. 922-3277.
   **Cuisine:** CHINESE. **Reservations:** Recommended.
**$ Prices:** Appetizers $2.50–$4.95; main courses $5.95–$10.95. No credit cards.
   **Open:** Daily 10:30am–11:30pm.
Chef Joe Poon, a graduate of the Culinary Institute of America, churns out Chinatown's best Peking duck, Szechuan duck, and barbecued pork with consistent quality. The decor is unassuming.

**RAY'S COFFEE SHOP,** 141 N. 9th St. Tel. 922-5122.
   **Cuisine:** CHINESE. **Reservations:** Not required.
**$ Prices:** Main courses $5–$12; coffee $2.50–$5. MC, V.
   **Open:** Breakfast, Fri–Wed 10–11:30am. Lunch, Fri–Wed 11:30am–5pm. Dinner, Fri–Wed 5–10pm. **Closed:** Thurs.
I predict that the popularity of this place will skyrocket after the Convention Center opens, since it features an unusual combination of subtle Taiwanese cuisine (dumplings are especially touted) and a selection of dozens of exotic coffees, each brewed to order in smart little glass siphons. The iced coffee here is great.

**SANG YEAN SEAFOOD HOUSE,** 1004 Race St. Tel. 625-9898.
   **Cuisine:** CHINESE. **Reservations:** Not required.
**$ Prices:** Appetizers $2.95–$4.95; main courses $5–$10.50. CB, DC, MC, V.

**Open:** Lunch, daily noon–3pm. Dinner, daily 3–2am.

A recent change in management hasn't altered the quality of this tiny Hong Kong–style place. The decor is fairly drab, but the steamed dumplings—eight to an order for $4—are freshly made and the size of huge oysters. The large salmon or other filets wor ba with a light bean sauce are smothered in a bed of onions and green and red peppers. The rice is freshly made all night.

# 6. SPECIALTY DINING

## LOCAL FAVORITES

**READING TERMINAL MARKET, 12th and Arch sts. Tel. 922-2317.**
**Cuisine:** INTERNATIONAL/AMERICAN. **Reservations:** Not accepted.
**$ Prices:** Depend on vendor. Cash only at most vendors.
**Open:** Mon–Sat 8am–6pm. Many vendors close at 5pm.

The Reading Terminal Market has been a greengrocer, a snack shop, a butcher, a fish market, and a sundries store for smart Philadelphians since the turn of the century. The idea was to use the space beneath the terminal's tracks for the food business so that commuters and businesses could stock up easily and cheaply. By the late 1970s only 27 vendors remained from the original 190, set in rows of stalls crammed with meats, fish, produce, and pudding. After renovation, the Market is half English covered market—with cool brick floors and faint smells of fresh provender and baked bread—and half gourmet grocer/charcuterie. Again a wonderful place to snack and browse, it's fighting to remain so even with the tidal wave of the new Convention Center around it.

What's at Reading Terminal exactly? Scrapple, mangoes, clam chowder, and pretzels—you name it, it's here if it's fresh and unpackaged. This is where most of the "retail," as opposed to restaurant or institutional, Amish farm products come to market. You can still see the Amish in the big city on their market days of Wednesday and Saturday, and you can buy individual egg custards (75¢), liver pudding, or chicken pot pie with those rich egg noodles. If you're in the market for meat, **William Notis, Harry Ochs,** and **Pierce Schorr** have most extensive selections. **Stella's** and **Dorothy Herman's** offer gourmet cheeses and tinned goods, while **Margerum's,** now in its fourth generation, sells flours, spices, and coffee beans from barrels and kegs.

If your stomach is rumbling uncontrollably, **Terminal Bakery** will still it with terrific bagels (40¢) or egg challah ($2.25 a loaf), as well as danish and other pastries. **Edible Adventures** has more ethnic hearty breads. For more protein, **Pearl's Oyster Bar** practically gives away six cherrystone clams for $2 and a shrimp platter with french fries, bread, and coleslaw for $3. Or try **Coastal Cave Trading Co.,** which has a great clam chowder ($2.50), oyster crackers, and smoked fish. Next door, just inside 12th Street, **Bassett's** purveys Philadelphia's entry in the best American ice cream contest at $1.25 a cone. The shakes ($2.50) are no less enticing, and the turkey sandwiches ($4.50) are simply the best anywhere. And a new contender, **Old Post Road Farm,** has a cherry pie that tastes just like it should.

The renovation of the Market has left it with many more stools and counters. **Vorspeise** has a great selection of hearty soups, for starters. A lunch at **Primarily Pasta,** such as linguine with clam sauce, will cost $3; **Spataro's,** an oldtime favorite, vends fresh buttermilk, cottage cheese, and huge slabs of fresh pies. The **12th Street Cantina** sells not only tasty enchiladas and burritos but also authentic ingredients, such as blue cornmeal. Oriental stir-fry and upscale chocolate-chip cookies are available near a central ice-cream parlor, which can also serve as a rest stop.

# HOAGIES & STEAK SANDWICHES

I've already mentioned **Jim's Steaks** at 400 South Street (tel. 928-1911).

## BUDGET

### LEE'S HOAGIES, 44 S. 17th St. Tel. 564-1264.
> **Cuisine:** AMERICAN. **Reservations:** Not accepted.
>
> **$ Prices:** $4–$10. No credit cards.
>
> **Open:** Mon–Fri 10:30am–8pm; Sat 10:30am–6pm.

For more than 30 years Lee's hoagies have captured the hearts and mouths of many native Philadelphians, at a low-slung complex between Market and Chestnut streets and also on Chestnut itself between 13th and 14th streets. The regular hoagie (basically an elongated spicy cold-cuts sandwich) measures about 8 inches long, the giant about twice as long. They will create various combinations, such as the Italian (four meats and provolone) and the turkey (with provolone and mayonnaise)—order these a day in advance. Lee's minors in steak sandwiches, served with fried onions and sauce.

### PAT'S KING OF THE STEAKS, 1237 E. Passyunk Ave. (between 9th and Wharton sts). Tel. 468-1546.
> **Cuisine:** AMERICAN. **Reservations:** Not accepted.
>
> **$ Prices:** $3.50–$10. No credit cards.
>
> **Open:** 24 hrs.

Pat's, so its adherents claim, serves the best steak sandwiches this side of the equator. The location and hours make for an interesting mix at the take-out counter.

### TACCONELLI'S, Somerset St. at Aramingo Ave. Tel. 425-4983.
> **Cuisine:** ITALIAN. **Reservations:** Required; place pizza orders in advance.
>
> **$ Prices:** Pizzas $5.50–$12. MC, V.
>
> **Open:** Dinner only, Wed–Sun 4–9pm.

A real insider recommendation for pizza is Tacconelli's—not, as you'd think, in South Philly, but north of the new discos along Delaware Avenue. Tacconelli's is open until whenever the crusts run out (about 9pm). It's imperative to call ahead to reserve the type of pizza you want, which is prepared in a brick oven. The place has been redone recently, with booths and Tiffany-style lights; the brisk, friendly "Can I help you, hon?" style of service prevails. The white pizza with garlic oil and the spinach and tomato pies are particularly recommended. To get here, take the Frankfort subway line from Market Street to Somerset Street, then walk eight blocks east. If you drive from Society Hill, take Front Street north, make a right onto Kensington Avenue, then make another right onto Somerset.

# HOTEL DINING

Almost every hotel in Philadelphia has at least one restaurant, and before 1980 these were virtually all superannuated, fussy establishments with overboiled and tasteless cuisine. Things couldn't be more different now.

## HISTORIC AREA
### Moderate

**AZALEA, Omni Hotel, 4th and Chestnut sts. Tel. 931-4260.**
  **Cuisine:** AMERICAN. **Reservations:** Recommended.
  **$ Prices:** Appetizers $4.75–$12.75; main courses $13.50–$22.25; breakfast $6.25–$13.75; lunch $8.50–$13.75; prix-fixe dinner $19.50. AE, CB, DC, MC, V.
  **Open:** Breakfast, Mon–Fri 6:30–10:30am; Sat–Sun 7–11am. Lunch, daily 11am–2pm. Dinner, Sun–Thurs 5:30–10pm; Fri–Sat 5:30–11pm.

For imaginative interpretations of American produce, including local dishes, this is one of the two best spots in town, with a treetop view of Independence National Historical Park. Azalea features arched windows, chandeliers, and comfortable armchairs.

The menu selections include such traditional Pennsylvania Dutch specialties as chicken-corn soup with saffron and apple fritters, shad in sorrel sauce (what saved the troops at Valley Forge), and pheasant pot pie. The menus change seasonally, and Kennett Square mushrooms, Lancaster County persimmons and quince, and elderberry preserve make an appearance. The local brook trout is sealed in cornmeal, then topped with smoky bacon. The desserts offer a choice of five freshly made sorbets or an old-fashioned apple–and–sour-cherry pie.

### Inexpensive

**SOCIETY HILL HOTEL, 301 Chestnut St. Tel. 925-1919.**
  **Cuisine:** AMERICAN. **Reservations:** Not required.
  **$ Prices:** Appetizers $2.50–$4.95; main courses $4.95–$12.95. AE, CB, DC, MC, V.
  **Open:** Daily 11am–1am; Sun brunch 11am–2:30pm.
This is a very pleasant, lively spot opposite Independence National Historical Park, with outdoor bar service during the summer. The light menu includes burgers and club sandwiches, written up in *The Wall Street Journal,* along with omelets and salads. Ted Gerike makes this one of the city's top piano bars.

## CENTER CITY
### Very Expensive

**THE DINING ROOM, The Ritz-Carlton Philadelphia, Liberty Place (between Chestnut and Market sts. at 17th St.). Tel. 563-1600.**

**Cuisine:** CONTEMPORARY FRENCH/INTERNATIONAL. **Reservations:** Required.

**$ Prices:** Dinner $50; Lunch $35.

**Open:** Breakfast, Mon–Sat 6:30–11am. Lunch and Sun brunch, 11:30am–2:30pm. Dinner, Tues–Sat 6–10pm. **Closed:** Sun and Mon dinner.

After a shakedown period, The Dining Room made the steal of the year in luring chef Francesco Martorella away from Ciboulette (see above) in late 1991 and adding maître d'hôtel Danny Fleischmann and sommelier David Fischer in early 1992. The room itself is stunning, with large crystal chandeliers, royal carpets, dark cabinets, and hand-blown cobalt-blue goblets. If you have reason to leave your seat, you'll find that your napkin is refolded when you return.

Try the soups to start: The cream of broccoli sounds parochial but comes with a tureen and aged cheddar ready to melt. The salads combine various tender greens with chevre and walnuts. Martorella has enlivened a very formal, elegant atmosphere and French service with festive interpretations of such classic dishes as pheasant in fruit reductions, grilled or baked fish, veal, and lamb. The crème brûlée is one of the finest in the country.

**THE FOUNTAIN, The Four Seasons Hotel, One Logan Square (between 18th St. and the Franklin Parkway). Tel. 963-1500.**

**Cuisine:** INTERNATIONAL. **Reservations:** Required.

**$ Prices:** Appetizers $6–$13; main courses $18–$28; lunch $8–$17; prix-fixe four-course menu $42. AE, CB, DC, MC, V.

**Open:** Breakfast, Mon–Fri 6:30–11:30am; Sat–Sun 7–11am. Lunch, daily 11:30am–2:30pm; Dinner, daily 6–11pm. Brunch, Sun 11:30am–2:30pm. Fri and Sat dessert and dancing in Swann Lounge.

The Zagat Restaurant Survey's 1992 edition ranked this Philadelphia's second most popular restaurant (behind Le Bec-Fin). The views partially explain why: unparalleled plumes from the Swann Fountain in Logan Circle on one side, and the hotel's own courtyard cascade on the other. The chief reason is the wonderful cuisine, expertly prepared and quietly served in expansive surroundings.

The menu is complicated and understated, and my recommendation is to accept the $42 prix-fixe menu rather than go à la carte for 35% more. After a complimentary canapé or two, you might have filet of skate with capers, a mesclun salad with pear and purple potato, sautéed lamb tenderloin and veal kidneys with mustard-seed sauce, a cheese tray, and fresh fruit pastry. A favorite à la carte starter is the pierogi of foie gras in Savoy cabbage with truffles. The entrees include salmon filet and pheasant with bacon and more Savoy cabbage.

Similar care is taken with the breakfasts, which offer buttered grits, warm brioche, cereal with crème fraiche, and compote.

**GRILL ROOM, The Ritz-Carlton Philadelphia, Liberty Place (between Market and Chestnut sts. at 17th St.). Tel. 563-1600.**

**Cuisine:** AMERICAN/ENGLISH. **Reservations:** Required.

**$ Prices:** $41 average for dinner; $30 for lunch.

**Open:** Breakfast, daily 6:30–11am. Lunch, Mon–Fri 11:30am–2:30pm. Dinner, daily 5:30–10pm.

The Ritz-Carlton's Grill Room has become one of the city's chief spots for business lunches, and at least in the Ritz's early days it has outstripped its formal Dining Room. The entrance bar features a marble bar and an antique wood-burning fireplace and opens into a clublike atmosphere for 85 with mahogany paneling and period furnishings and paintings. Under executive chef Ian Orr (a veteran of other Ritz restaurants), the Grill serves steaks, chops, and fish for lunch and dinner. Specific entrées include pappardelle with smoked duck and radicchio and the traditional prime aged beef, creamed spinach, and scalloped potatoes. The breads and house wines are superb.

## Expensive

**210, Rittenhouse Hotel, 210 W. Rittenhouse Square. Tel. 546-9000.**
**Cuisine:** CONTEMPORARY FRENCH. **Reservations:** Required.
**$ Prices:** Appetizers $8–$11; main courses $18.50–$31.50; breakfast $5.75–$9.50; pretheater three-course prix fixe menu $29.75.
**Open:** Breakfast, Mon–Sat 6:30–11am. Lunch, Mon–Fri 11:30am–2:30pm. Dinner, Mon–Sat 6–10:30pm.

There are many New Yorkers who think that Gary Coyle is the chef who got away; a graduate of the Culinary Institute of America, he was at La Côte Basque and the Rainbow Room until the Rittenhouse lured him in 1989. Cited in *Food & Wine's* "What's Hot for 1990" column, 210 is the flagship of this luxury hotel's dining rooms (TreeTops and Cassatt Lounge round out the picture). The sweeping windows look out over Rittenhouse Square, with contemporary art and cherry floors around. Tiny spotlights dramatize the floral table centerpieces.

The $29.75 prix-fixe menu is a bargain, given that desserts will run an additional $5 to $7 à la carte. The menu changes constantly; typical appetizers include beggars' purses of exotic mushrooms and a mosiac of seafood carpaccios, while entrées include a roasted chateaubriand of lotte with fennel purée and a fan of medallions of mallard duck. Tiny pots of exotically flavored crèmes brûlée come in a basket of spun sugar. Even the breakfasts veer into fantasyland, with savory blintzes and sour-cream waffles.

# DINING WITH A VIEW

I've already mentioned **210,** with a view of Rittenhouse Square; **The Fountain** at The Four Seasons, overlooking Logan Circle's fountains; **Meiji-En,** on the Delaware waterfront; and the **Chart House,** also on the Delaware River.

## Moderate

**FOUNDERS ATOP THE BELLEVUE, Broad and Walnut sts. Tel. 790-2814.**
**Cuisine:** CONTINENTAL. **Reservations:** Recommended.
**$ Prices:** Appetizers $4.95–$11.95; main courses $14.95–$26.95. AE, CB, DC, MC, V.
**Open:** Dinner only, daily 6–10:45pm.
Founders is actually the keystone of the Bellevue Hotel's restaurants, but a shaky period makes it attractive primarily for fans of views and

elegant dining rooms, given its arched windows, flourishes and swags of draperies, and plush armchairs. The "founders" are the statues of Philadelphia luminaries that surround you. There's also live entertainment.

**TOP OF CENTRE SQUARE, 1500 Market St. Tel. 563-9494.**
> **Cuisine:** INTERNATIONAL. **Reservations:** Recommended.
> **$ Prices:** Appetizers $3.95–$6.95; main courses $12.95–$21.95; lunch $5.95–$11.95. AE, CB, DC, MC, V.
> **Open:** Lunch, Mon–Fri 11:30am–3pm. Dinner, Mon–Thurs 5:30–10pm; Fri–Sat 5:30pm–midnight; Sun 4:30–9pm.

Situated on the 41st floor of an office building directly west of City Hall, this modern restaurant with bilevel seating wraps around the city, from the two rivers to surrounding states. The lunch menu focuses on sandwiches, pastas, and quickes; the dinner menu features salmon, fish, ribs, and steaks. It's not the best food for the price, but the views are wonderful.

# DINING COMPLEXES

I've already described the outstanding **Reading Terminal Market.**
✪ ⑤ The top new choice in town is the **Food Court at Liberty Place** on the second level (accessible by escalator or elevator) of Liberty Place between Chestnut and Market streets and 16th and 17th streets, in the heart of Center City. Reading Terminal alumni like **Bain's Deli, Bassett's Original Turkey,** and **Original Philly Steaks** are joined by **Mandarin Express, Mentesini Pizza, Sbarro,** and **Chick-fil-A.** Best of all, the food court is spotless, large, and reasonable, with full lunches from $3.50. You'll find it easy to keep your eyes on the kids as they wander. The Food Court is open Monday to Saturday from 9:30am to 7pm, Sunday from noon to 6pm.

Another good collection of snacks is at **Market Fair** at the Gallery, on Market at 9th Street. The Gallery parades ropes of people up and down four floors of shops under a massive glass roof, and the lowest level near Gimbels houses an enclave of oyster bars; ice-cream stands; and stalls with baked potatoes, Greek snacks, and eggrolls. Seats and counters abound.

The third level of the **Bourse,** 21 N. 5th Street (just east of the Liberty Bell), has 14 snack/restaurant operations, all moderately priced and designed for take-out to the benches that ring this cool and stunning restoration of the 1895 merchant exchange. The Indian tandoor at **Nandi's,** a branch of Siva's on Front Street, has been especially touted; there's also yet another Bain's Delicatessen and sandwiches from the International Sausage Shop. The Bourse is open from late morning to early evening.

# LIGHT, CASUAL & FAST FOOD

**AU BON PAIN, 2 Penn Plaza and other locations. Tel. 854-9926.**
> **Cuisine:** FRENCH CAFE. **Reservations:** Not required.
> **$ Prices:** Croissants $1.25; sandwiches $4–$5. No credit cards.
> **Open:** Mon–Sat 7am–6pm.

This national chain of French breadstuffs features fresh croissants and delicious soups and sandwiches, and you're even sheltered from sun and traffic in this shaded square. The tables go fast, but if you do take out there's alternative makeshift seating close by. Wine and beer are served.

### BROADWAY AT THE BELLEVUE, Broad and Walnut sts. Tel. 732-3737.

**Cuisine:** DELI. **Reservations:** Recommended.

**$ Prices:** Club sandwiches $8.95 and up. AE, DC, MC, V.
**Open:** Mon–Thurs 7:30am–11:30pm; Fri–Sat 7:30am–midnight; Sun 10am–9pm.

The dinner menu consists of hearty New York–style deli sandwiches named after prominent Philadelphians.

### CATALINA'S, KormanSuites Hotel, 2001 Hamilton St. (20th St. between Parkway and Spring Garden sts.). Tel. 659-7500.

**Cuisine:** AMERICAN REGIONAL. **Reservations:** Recommended.

**$ Prices:** Salads and pastas $3.95–$9.95; sandwiches $5.95–$14.95; lunch $4.95–$9.95. AE, CB, DC, MC, V.
**Open:** Hotel breakfast, Mon–Fri from 6:30am. Lunch Sat–Sun from 7:30, and dinner, daily 11am–2am.

The continental and California-style menu here is designed for grazers. You can choose a stew, sandwich, and dessert, or reverse the order of courses.

### GIRASOLE, 1305 Locust St. Tel. 985-4659.

**Cuisine:** ITALIAN. **Reservations:** Recommended.

**$ Prices:** Appetizers $3.95–$6.95; main courses $8.95–$15.95. AE, CB, DC, MC, V.
**Open:** Lunch, Mon–Fri noon–2:30pm. Dinner, Mon–Thurs 5–10:30pm; Fri–Sat 5–11pm.

Although it's a handsome restaurant, Girasole is prime grazing ground for its antipasto salad of tiny shrimp and white beans and for its terrific pizzas with irregular crusts and fresh ingredients, cooked in a wood-burning oven.

### MARABELLA'S, 1420 Locust St. Tel. 545-1845.

**Cuisine:** INTERNATIONAL. **Reservations:** Not accepted for dinner.

**$ Prices:** Appetizers $2.95; main courses $7.95–$14.95; lunch $3–$6. AE, DC, MC, V.
**Open:** Mon–Thurs 11:30am–11:30pm; Fri–Sat 11:30am–12:30am; Sun 11:30am–11pm.

A colorful and upbeat setting that's great for families, Marabella's offers a menu and a noise level to match. Pizzas, simple Italian grazing breads and salads, and mesquite-grilled fish are available without the pretense of a meal in several courses. (See also page 105.)

### SFUZZI, 1650 Market St. (One Liberty Place). Tel. 851-8888.

**Cuisine:** ITALIAN. **Reservations:** Recommended.

**$ Prices:** Appetizers $4–$6; main courses $9–$15. AE, CB, DC, MC, V.
**Open:** Lunch, daily 11am–3pm. Dinner, Sun–Thurs 5:30–10pm; Fri–Sat 5:30–midnight.

Clean, bright, modern, Sfuzzi has a silent *S*. The service at the bar or at the tables concentrates on pastas, pizzas, desserts, and such Italian specialties as sausage-and-pepper stromboli, fried artichokes with aioli, and crispy chicken strips with romano cheese dustings.

**16TH STREET BAR & GRILL, 264 S. 16th St. Tel. 735-3316.**
   **Cuisine:** CONTINENTAL. **Reservations:** Not required.
**$ Prices:** Appetizers $2.95–$6.95; main courses $6.95–$13.95. AE, CB, DC, MC, V.
   **Open:** Mon–Sat 11:30am–midnight; Sun 11:30am–11pm.
Originally a "back-home" adjunct to the restaurant renaissance, the Bar & Grill is a very comfortable neighborhood gathering place for those wanting traditional Mediterranean cooking and jukebox music. Tapas are a specialty.

**ZANZIBAR BLUE, 305 S. 11th St. Tel. 829-0300.**
   **Cuisine:** CONTINENTAL. **Reservations:** Not required.
**$ Prices:** Appetizers $3.95–$8.95; main courses $7.95–$15.95.
   **Open:** Dinner, Sun–Thurs 5:30–10pm, Fri–Sat 5:30–11pm; late supper, daily to 1am; Sun brunch, 11am–2:30pm.
This new café and restaurant between Pine and Spruce streets is in a renovated building, with nightly jazz and roomy, sophisticated seating. The menu features bouillabaisse, crab cannelloni, Caesar salad, and bruschetta.

## SUNDAY BRUNCH

Nearly every restaurant in Philadelphia offers Sunday brunch, ranging from standard bagels with spreads to full English breakfasts. The entries above provide full descriptions of **Carolina's, Chart House, Commissary, Downey's, Famous Deli, Magnolia Café, Swann Lounge** and **The Fountain** at The Four Seasons (generally voted the best in town), and **White Dog Café** (the funkier favorite).

## AFTERNOON TEA

The advent of true luxury hotels in Philadelphia has brought exquisite afternoon teas to the first-floor lounge at the **Omni Hotel,** the **Cassatt Lounge at the Rittenhouse Hotel** (the most cheery, with a beautiful outdoor garden), the **Swann Lounge at The Four Seasons Hotel,** and **The Ritz-Carlton.** The **Dickens Inn** in Head House Square does a more solid, English burgher version. See the above listings for fuller descriptions.

## ICE CREAM & DESSERTS

**Bassett's Ice Cream** (tel. 925-4315) at Reading Terminal has long claimed supremacy for its rich and smooth flavors. The king of the hill may have been dethroned by **Hillary's** (tel. 922-4931), a relative newcomer at South and 5th streets, at Front and Chestnut streets, and at Chestnut and 21st streets. All three open at noon and stay open late. The **Rocking Horse,** 1218 Spruce Street, features Bassett's and Häagen-Dazs as bases for splendid creations.

# LATE-NIGHT/24-HOUR

Philadelphia is not the most vivacious of cities late at night, and you're most likely to find late-night or all-night food either at bars known to close at 2am, or on South Street. I have already mentioned Cutters, Downey's, Dock Street Brewing Company, Los Amigos, Pat's King of the Steaks, and the Sam Adams Brew House.

### COPABANANA, 4th and South sts. Tel. 923-6180.

**Cuisine:** AMERICAN. **Reservations:** Not required.

**$ Prices:** Burgers $4.95–$7.50; Tex-Mex main courses $6.95–$10.95. AE, MC, V.

**Open:** Daily noon–1am.

People-watching is a favorite pastime at this tropical neon fantasy bar and grill overlooking South Street. It features Tex-Mex food and gourmet burgers, with upbeat tapes providing atmosphere.

### MELROSE DINER, Broad and Snyder sts. Tel. 467-6644.

**Cuisine:** DINER. **Reservations:** Not accepted.

**$ Prices:** Main courses $2.95–$8.95. No credit cards.

**Open:** 24 hrs.

Somewhere between kitsch and postmodern, the Melrose's logo of a coffee cup with a clock face and knife-and-fork hands is eternal. Scrapple and eggs and the like are dished out near the sporting stadiums in South Philly.

### PIZZERIA UNO, 509 S. 2nd St. Tel. 592-0400; and 18th and Locust sts. Tel. 790-9669.

**Cuisine:** ITALIAN. **Reservations:** Not required.

**$ Prices:** Pizzas $6.95 and up. AE, CB, DC, MC, V.

**Open:** Sun–Thurs 11:30am–midnight; Fri–Sat 11:30am–1:30am.

This string of dark-green bar/cafés, festooned with signs and brass rails, serves a reliable deep-dish Chicago pizza that's more like a meal-on-bread than a traditional pizza.

# PICNIC FARE

### THE COMMISSARY, 1710 Sansom St. Tel. 569-2240.

**Cuisine:** CHARCUTERIE.

**Open:** Mon–Thurs 11:30am–10pm, Fri–Sat 11:30am–11pm, Sun 9:30am–10pm. AE, MC, V.

The soups here run the gamut from gingered cream of carrot to cold avocado. As for the entrées, would you believe Sicilian scallops with pasta and broccoli and chicken Kiev with pistachio butter? Don't neglect the charcuterie, with its hefty slabs of unusual pâtés.

### FAMOUS DELI, 4th and Bainbridge sts. Tel. 922-3274.

**Cuisine:** DELI.

**Open:** Mon–Sat 7am–6pm; Sun 7am–4pm. AE.

Before South Street turned funky, it was a mostly Jewish neighborhood, and Famous has weathered the demographics in fine style. The deli does a lot of carry-out of lox, whitefish, pastrami, and corned beef, but it seats about 30 around Formica-and-aluminum kitchen tables. It stocks all the Sunday papers, too.

### FOODTEK, 26 S. 2nd St. Tel. 238-1115; and 308 South St. Tel. 592-7377.

**Cuisine:** CHARCUTERIE.

**Open:** Sun–Thurs 7:30am–12:30am; Fri–Sat 7:30am–2am.
These unassuming storefronts on two of the historic area's busiest blocks open up in back to a wonderful deli/breakfast seating area, with provisions ranging from sliced meats to stuffed quail. There is a bakery and a small greenmarket, too.

 **FROMMER'S COOL FOR KIDS:**
### RESTAURANTS

**Ben's Restaurant** (tel. 448-1200) in the Franklin Institute at Logan Circle *(p. 137)* is a Steve Poses operation, and it is well set up for kids with cafeteria food, hamburgers, and hotdogs. You can enter with or without museum admission, and it's open daily from 11am to 8pm. No credit cards are accepted.

**Chinatown** between 9th and 11th streets and Race and Vine streets, is full of family-oriented places.

**Cutter's Grand Café and Bar** *(p. 100)* has lunch and dinner menus for children, with a $2.95 peanut butter and jelly sandwich, $5 fettucini Alfredo, grilled cheese sandwiches, and fish and chips. Try for a window banquette.

**Food Court at Liberty Place,** between Market and Chestnut streets at 17th Street *(p. 121)*, is great—clean, comfortable, and anonymous. Kids have their choice of cuisines from among 25 stalls, and they can wander without going out of sight.

**Marabella's** *(p. 105)*, is a natural in Center City; its pizzas, burgers, and grilled chicken come quickly and as you order them, and the noise and the color are cheerful. You'll have plenty of family company.

**White Dog Café** *(p. 111)*, in the heart of University City, has special kid's breakfasts and lunches at reduced prices.

# CHAPTER 7

# WHAT TO SEE & DO IN PHILADELPHIA

onsider the sightseeing possibilities—the most historic square mile in America; over 90 museums; innumerable Colonial churches, row houses, and mansions; an Ivy League campus; more Impressionist art than you'd find in any place outside of Paris; and leafy, distinguished parks, including the largest one within city limits in the United States. Philadelphia has come a long way from what it was in 1876, when a guidebook recommended seeing the new Public Buildings at Broad and Market streets, the Naval Yards, the old YMCA, and the fortresslike prison.

Most of what you'll want to see within the city falls inside the original grid plan, between the Delaware and Schuylkill rivers and South and Spring Garden streets. In fact, it's possible to organize your days into walking tours relatively easily—see Chapter 8, "Strolling Around Philadelphia," for suggestions. Even if you ramble on your own, nothing is that far away. A stroll from City Hall to the Philadelphia Museum of Art takes about 25 minutes, although you'll undoubtedly be sidetracked by the flags and flowers along the Parkway. A walk down Market or one of the "tree" streets (Chestnut, Spruce, Pine, Locust) to Independence National Historical Park and Society Hill should take a little less time—but it probably won't, since there's so much to entice you on the way.

## SUGGESTED ITINERARIES

### IF YOU HAVE 1 DAY

Start at the Liberty Bell in Independence National Historical Park, then move south through Independence Hall and on to residential Society Hill, which is interwoven with U.S. history. In the evening, see

**DID YOU KNOW . . . ?**

- The "hex" signs that adorn barns and houses in Pennsylvania Dutch Country were a sign to travelers that German was spoken within.
- It is still against the law in Philadelphia to sleep in a barber shop and to take a cow to Logan Circle.
- The first public protest in America against slavery was held at the Germantown Friends (Quaker) Meeting House in 1688.
- The Benjamin Franklin Parkway is one of the widest streets (250 feet) in the world.
- Early fire-insurance companies offered rewards for stopping fires. This led to street battles between rival volunteer brigades racing to arrive at a blaze first, often while buildings burned down!
- It was in Philadelphia that Charles Goodyear superheated sulfur to harden India rubber, at the same time preserving its pliancy.

what's on at the Academy of Music, the Annenberg Center at the University of Pennsylvania, or the Spectrum for sports.

## IF YOU HAVE 2 DAYS

**Day 1**   Follow the itinerary given above.

**Day 2**   Starting at City Hall, walk up the Benjamin Franklin Parkway to Logan Circle and spend the afternoon at Franklin Institute or the Philadelphia Museum of Art. Try to circle back to Rittenhouse Square and the Liberty Place complex before closing.

## IF YOU HAVE 3 DAYS

**Days 1–2**   Follow the itinerary given above.

**Day 3**   Spend the morning in Old City viewing its Christ Church and Elfreth's Alley, then explore the Delaware River waterfront at Penn's Landing. Finally, either visit the New Jersey State Aquarium by ferry to Camden or continue shoreward to eclectic South Street.

## IF YOU HAVE 5 DAYS OR MORE

**Days 1–3**   Follow the itinerary given above.

**Day 4**   Explore the Rittenhouse Square/South Broad Street area, with a visit to the Academy of Fine Arts, winding up with a stroll through Reading Terminal Market and Chinatown.

**Day 5**   Fairmount Park's Zoo and many restored Colonial mansions beckon. If you hunger for more Georgian, make a trip to Germantown for the afternoon.

# 1. THE TOP ATTRACTIONS

Of course, the attractions below only scratch the surface. Depending on your interests, the Philadelphia Zoo, Fairmount Park, South Philadelphia's Italian Market, the Rosenbach Museum, the Afro-American Historical and Cultural Museum, the University of Pennsylvania campus, or the Museum of American Jewish History might be tops. They'll be covered either later in this chapter or mentioned in Chapter 8, "Strolling Around Philadelphia."

## INDEPENDENCE NATIONAL HISTORICAL PARK, "America's most historic square mile." Visitor Center at 3rd and Walnut sts. Tel. 597-8787, 627-1776 for 24-hour recording.

Is there anyone who doesn't know about the Liberty Bell in Independence Hall? It may not be there anymore, but you get the point: The United States was conceived on this ground in 1776, and the future of the young nation was assured by the Constitutional Convention held here in 1787. The choice of Philadelphia as a site was natural because of its centrality, wealth, and gentility. The delegates argued at Independence Hall (then known as the State House), ate and drank at such places as Man Full of Trouble Inn, and boarded and dined at City Tavern. Philadelphia was the nation's capital during Washington's second term, so the U.S. Congress and Supreme Court met here for 10 years while awaiting the construction of the new capital at Washington, D.C. The title of the "most historic square mile in America" may sound debatable—but it's true. From the first penny to the First Amendment, Philadelphia led the nation.

The National Historical Park comprises 40 buildings on 37 acres of Center City real estate (see Walking Tour 1 in Chapter 8 for more information). Independence Hall and the Liberty Bell in its glass pavilion lie between 6th and 5th streets. The Visitor Center, at the corner of 3rd and Walnut streets, is well equipped to illustrate the early history of this country, in a neighborhood that ranks as a superb example of successful revitalization. Fifty years ago, this area had become overgrown with warehouses, office buildings, and roominghouses; many fine colonial buildings were in danger of demolition, and tours of the area started—and ended—at Independence Square. The National Park Service stepped in, soon followed by the Washington Square East urban-renewal project now known as Society Hill. Buildings were bought and then torn down to create Independence Mall, a wide swath of greenery opposite Independence Hall. To the east, gardens replaced edifices as far as the Dock Street food market, which was replaced by Society Hill Towers in 1959. Graff House, City Tavern, Pemberton House, and Library Hall all were reconstructed on the original sites; Liberty Bell Pavilion, Franklin Court, and the Visitor Center are contemporary structures that were erected for the Bicentennial of the Declaration of Independence celebrations.

A park ranger must lead you through Independence Hall, and you must reserve a place for the frequent guided tours of the Bishop White House and the Todd House. This can be done at the **Visitor Center,** 3rd and Chestnut streets (tel. 597-8974, voice or TDD), which should be your first encounter with the park. Here you can pick up a map of the area and information in any of 10 languages. The modern bell tower houses a 5-ton bell given by Queen Elizabeth II of England to this country in 1976, and it rings at 11am and 3pm. The displays in the center give you an idea what life in 1776 Philadelphia was like (before you get too nostalgic, don't forget about the dust, grime, insects, nonexistent plumbing, and unlit streets). The gift shop sells mementos and park publications, and every 30 minutes the center shows a John Huston feature, *Independence,* without charge.

**Admission:** Free. Some of the park's building interiors require reservations. Other adjacent historic buildings have separate admissions.

**Open:** Daily 9am–5pm, often later in summer. **Subway:** SEPTA Market-Frankford Line to 5th and Market streets or 2nd and Market streets. **Bus:** No. 76 or any Chestnut Street Transitway bus from Center City. **Car:** From I-76, take I-676 east to 6th Street (last exit before the Ben Franklin Bridge), then turn south (right) along Independence Mall. From the Ben Franklin Bridge, make a left onto 6th Street and follow the same directions as above. From I-95 southbound, take the Center City exit to 2nd Street. From I-95 northbound, use the exit marked "Historic Area." Continue straight ahead to Reed Street; turn right on Reed and follow it to Delaware Avenue. Turn left on Delaware and follow it to the exit for Market Street (on right). **Parking:** Meters are along most streets; parking facilities (all $9 per day) are at 2nd and Sansom streets, at Independence Mall between Arch and Market streets, and at the corner of Dock and 2nd streets.

## INDEPENDENCE HALL, Chestnut St. between 5th and 6th sts.

Even if you knew nothing about Independence Hall, flanked by Old City Hall to the left and Congress Hall to the right, you could tell that noble and important works took place here. From an architectural standpoint, the ensemble is graceful and functional; from the standpoint of history and American myth, it's unforgettable. Along with the Mall in Washington, D.C., Independence Square sets you thinking about the boldness of forming an entirely sovereign state from a set of disparate colonies and about the strength and intelligence of the representatives who gathered here to do it. Although these buildings are best known for their national role, remember that city, county, and state governments used them at various times too.

The French and Indian War (1754–63) required troops who, in turn, required money, and King George III saw no reason why the colonists shouldn't pay for their own defense through taxes. The colonists disagreed, and the idea that the king harbored tyrannical thoughts swept through the colonies but was felt most strongly in Virginia and Massachusetts. Philadelphia, as the wealthiest and most culturally anglophile of the seacoast cities, was leery of radical proposals of independence, as Franklin was in his role as American agent in London. But the news that British troops had fired on citizens defending their own property in Concord pushed most moderates to reconsider what they owed to England and what they deserved as free people endowed with natural rights.

The Second Continental Congress convened in May 1776 in the Pennsylvania Assembly Hall, to the left of the Independence Hall entrance. Each colony had its own green baize–covered table, but not much of the original room's furnishings escaped use as firewood when British troops occupied the city the following December. The Congress acted quickly, appointing a tall Virginia delegate named George Washington as commander of the Continental Army. After the failure of a last "olive branch" petition, the Congress, through John Adams, instructed each colony's government to reorganize itself as a state. Thomas Jefferson worked on a summary of why the colonists felt that independence was necessary. The resulting

## ? DID YOU KNOW . . . ?

- Ben Franklin's kite-flying experiment in 1752 took place at what is now the corner of 10th and Ludlow streets.
- Thirty-two bridges span the Schuylkill River within the city limits.
- George Washington lived in a mansion at the corner of 5th and Chestnut streets for his entire two terms as president.
- Philadelphian Robert Green's chance decision to combine ice cream and soda water has refreshed millions since 1861.
- W. C. Fields's epitaph does *not* read, "On the whole, I'd rather be in Philadelphia."
- The U.S. Congress held a rare session outside the capital for the special July 4, 1976, Bicentennial celebration at Independence Mall.
- The first law school (1790) and medical school (1765) in America were established at the University of Pennsylvania.
- The oldest U.S. fire-insurance company, the Philadelphia Contributionship (1752), still offers a standing toast to George Washington at its monthly board meetings.

Declaration of Independence, wrote noted historian Richard Morris, "lifted the struggle from self-interested arguments over taxation to the exalted plane of human rights." Most of the signatories used Dr. Philip Syng Physick's silver inkstand, which is still in the room. The country first heard the news on July 8 in Independence Square.

Before and after the British occupied the city, Independence Hall was the scene of the U.S. national government. Here the Congress approved ambassadors, pored over budgets, and adopted the Articles of Confederation, a loose structure for a country composed of states. However, it had problems: Under the Articles, taxation power was minimal, and the power of the smaller states disproportionate; and, like the Pennsylvania state government, the United States lacked a sufficient executive power. The Congress moved to New York after the war's end, and it grudgingly allowed delegates to recommend changes.

The delegates who met in the Assembly Room in Philadelphia in 1787 did more than that—they created a new Constitution that has guided the country for more than 200 years. Jefferson's cane rests here, as does a book of Franklin's. Washington, as president of the convention, kept order from the famous "Rising Sun Chair." Delegates were mature, urbane (24 of the 42 had lived or worked abroad), and trained to reason, and many had experience drafting state constitutions and laws. They decided on approaches to governance that are familiar today: a bicameral Congress, a single executive, an independent judiciary, and a philosophical belief in government by the people and for the people. No wonder John Adams called the convention "the greatest single effort of national deliberation that the world has ever seen."

Across the entrance hall from the Assembly Room, the courtroom served as Pennsylvania's Supreme Court chamber. Like the court at Williamsburg, Virginia, this room exemplifies pre–Bill of Rights justice—for example, your ranger guide will probably point out the tipstaff, a wooden pole with a brass tip that was used to keep onlookers subdued. Other period details include little coalboxes to keep feet warm on chilly days and manacles for rambunctious defendants. This is one of the first courtrooms in America to hear the argument that disagreement with a political leader isn't sedition, one of the great concepts in modern Anglo-American law.

The stairwell of Independence Hall held the Liberty Bell until 1976 (you can still see the traces). The ranger will conduct you upstairs to the Long Gallery, the largest Pennsylvania room of its time. Now it's set up as a banquet hall with a harpsichord (some of the guides even play) and a rare set of maps of the individual 13 colonies. During the British occupation, though, it housed American prisoners of war, and later it held C. W. Peale's museum of art and natural history. Its view of Independence Mall is superb.

Two smaller rooms adjoin the Long Gallery. To the southwest (toward City Hall), the royal governors of Pennsylvania met in council in a setting of opulent blue curtains, silver candlesticks, and a grandfather clock. Beneath a portrait of William Penn, governors met with foreign and Native American delegations, in addition to conducting normal business. On the southeast side, the Committee Room fit the whole Pennsylvania Assembly while the Second Continental Congress was meeting downstairs. More often, it stored the assembly's reference library or arms for the city militia.

---

 **FROMMER'S FAVORITE**
**PHILADELPHIA EXPERIENCES**

**Afternoon Tea at the Swann Lounge** The quintessential luxury tea is held at The Four Seasons, overlooking one of the city's finest squares with its fountains on both sides.

**A Nighttime Stroll Through Independence Square** The combination of history, elegance, and proportion among the three basic buildings that contained America's first government always induce a sense of wonder at this country's good fortune in its founding citizens.

**Barnes Foundation** Admission to this private Merion art collection is restricted, and the collection itself is overwhelming in its Impressionist coverage and thematic groupings.

**Regattas Along the Schuylkill** On all spring weekends along Boathouse Row just north of the Philadelphia Museum of Art, crews race each other every 5 minutes or so, with cheering friends along the riverbanks.

**Reading Terminal Market** From Amish custards and Bassett's ice cream to Bain's turkey sandwiches and the food of the 12th Street Cantina, this is the motherlode of unpackaged, fresh, honest-to-goodness provisions. It celebrates its centennial in 1993.

**Open-House Tours** If you're in the city at the right times, don't miss tours of restored mansions in Society Hill, Rittenhouse Square, or Fairmount Park for some true connoisseurship in interior design and Americana.

As you descend the stairs, look at calm **Independence Square,** with its elm trees and statue of Com. John Barry. The clerk of the Second Congress, John Nixon, first read the Declaration of Independence here, to a mostly radical and lower-strata crowd (Philadelphia merchants didn't much like the news at first, since it meant a disruption of trade, to say the least).

**Tours:** A park ranger must lead you through Independence Hall; free tours leave every 15 minutes. Avoid waits by arriving early.

**Open:** Summer, daily 9am–8pm. Winter, daily 9am–5pm. **Bus:** 76.

## LIBERTY BELL, Chestnut St. between 5th and 6th sts.

You can't leave Philadelphia without seeing the Liberty Bell. In fact, during the first minute of 1976 it was taken out of Independence Hall and put in its own glass Liberty Bell Pavilion across the street, once the site of the Executive Mansion.

The Liberty Bell, America's symbol of independence, was commissioned in 1751 to mark the 50th anniversary of another noble event: William Penn, who governed Pennsylvania by himself under Crown charter terms, was forced into declaring that free Colonials had a right to govern themselves, so he established the Philadelphia Assembly under a new Charter of Privileges. The bell, cast in England, cracked as it was tested, and the Philadelphia firm of Pass and Stow repaired it by 1753. It hung in Independence Hall to "proclaim liberty throughout the land" as the Declaration of Independence was announced and survived a bumpy trip to an Allentown church in 1777 so that the British wouldn't melt it down for ammunition. The last time it tolled was in 1835, for the funeral of Chief Justice John Marshall, who was treated unsuccessfully by Dr. Philip Syng Physick.

You can touch the bell during open hours. You can photograph it. You can even see it through the glass walls at night. The brick arcades with terrazzo floors and marble benches one block north of the bell were built for the 1976 Bicentennial, but they have been considered white elephants more recently.

**Admission:** Free.

**Open:** Summer, daily 9am–8pm. Rest of year, daily 9am–5pm. **Bus:** 76.

## FRANKLIN COURT, Chestnut St. between 3rd and 4th sts., with another entrance at 314 Market St.

⭐ Franklin Court may just be the most imaginative, informative, and downright fun museum run in America by the National Park Service. Designed by noted architect Robert Venturi, it was very much a sleeper when it opened in April 1976, because the Market and Chestnut streets' arched passages give little hint of the court within and the exhibit below.

Franklin Court once held the home of Benjamin Franklin, who'd resided with his family in smaller row houses in the neighborhood. Like Jefferson at Monticello, he planned many of the timesavers and interior decorations of the house; but unlike Jefferson, Franklin spent the building period as Colonial emissary first to England, then to France. His wife, Deborah, oversaw the construction, as the engraved flagstones show, while Ben sent back continental goods and a constant stream of advice. Unfortunately, they were reunited only in the family plot at Christ Church Burial Ground, since Deborah died weeks before the end of Ben's 10-year absence. Under the steward-ship of his daughter, Sarah, and her husband, printer Richard Bache, Franklin Court provided a gentle home for Ben until his 1790 death.

Since archeologists have no exact plans of the house, a simple frame in girders indicates the dimensions of the house and the smaller printshop. Excavations have uncovered wall foundations, bits of walls, and outdoor privy wells, and these have been left as protected cutaway pits. This is all very interesting—but enter the exhibition entrance for the fun. After a portrait and furniture gallery, a mirrored room reflects Franklin's almost limitless interests as a scientist, an inventor, a statesman, a printer, and so on. The Franklin Exchange will make you feel like a kid—pick up a phone and dial various American and European luminaries to hear what they thought of Franklin. And they're not all positive (just ask Mark Twain!).

The middle part of the same hall has a 15-minute series of three climactic scenes in Franklin's career as a diplomat. On a sunken stage, costumed doll figures brief you, and each other, on the English Parliament in 1765 and its Stamp Act; the Court at Versailles when its members were wondering whether to aid America in its bid for independence; and the debates of the Constitution's framers in 1787, right around the corner at Independence Hall. Needless to say, Ben's pithy sagacity wins every time.

On your way in or out on the Market Street side, stop in the 1786 houses that Ben rented out. One is the Printing Office and Bindery, where you can see Colonial methods of printing and bookmaking in action. Next door, get a letter postmarked at the Benjamin Franklin Post Office (remember that Ben was postmaster-general, too!). The Colonial-costumed employees still hand-stamp the marks. Upstairs, a postal museum is open in summer.

**Admission:** Free.

**Open:** Daily 9am–5pm, including the post office and postal museum (summer). **Bus:** 76.

# THE TOP MUSEUMS

## PHILADELPHIA MUSEUM OF ART [PMA], 26th St. and Benjamin Franklin Pkwy. Tel. 763-8100, 787-5488 for 24-hour information.

Even on a hazy day you can see America's third-largest art museum from City Hall: Resplendent and huge, it's a beauti-fully proportioned Greco-Roman temple set on a hill. Because the museum, established in the 1870s, has relied on donors of great wealth and idiosyncratic taste, its collection does not aim to present a comprehensive picture of Western or Eastern art. But its strengths are dazzling—it's undoubtedly one of the finest groupings of art objects in America, and no visit to Philadelphia would be complete without at least a walk-through. The exhibits are clearly labeled, and a free map is available at the information desk, recently redesigned with bright benches by the architectural firm of Venturi, Rauch, and Scott Brown.

The museum is designed simply, with L-shaped wings off the central court on two stories. The first-floor John G. Johnson Collection, a Renaissance treasure trove, displays Italian (Lorenzetti, Veronese) and northern masters. The rest of the wing contains some superb 20th-century art, including the Arensberg Collection assem-bled from the 1910s onward. The highlight here, Marcel Duchamp's

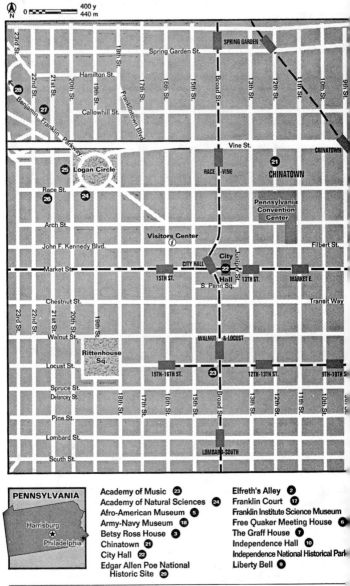

*Nude Descending a Staircase,* doesn't seem nearly as revolutionary as it did in 1913. The other first-floor wing specializes in American crafts, furniture, glass, and painting. The 19th-century gallery has many works of Philadelphia's Thomas Eakins, who evoked the spirit of the city in watercolors and oil portraits.

Upstairs takes you far abroad—to medieval Europe, 17th-century battlefields, Enlightenment salons, and Eastern temples. A 13th-century cloister from the Pyrenees, with a cool fountain and an arcade, shows Moorish influence. A Hindu temple hall from South

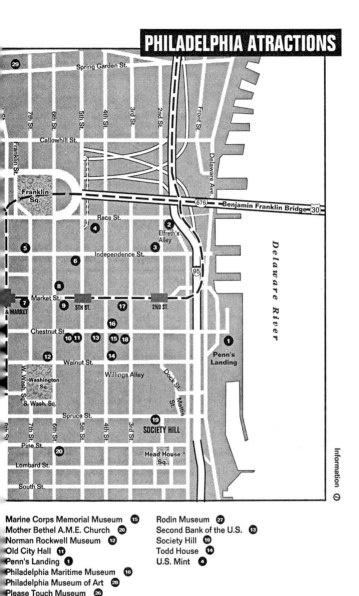

Spring Garden St.

7th St.
6th St.
5th St.
4th St.
3rd St.
2nd St.
Front St.

Callowhill St.

Franklin St.

Franklin Sq.

676 Benjamin Franklin Bridge 30

Race St.

Elfreth's Alley

Independence St.

Delaware Ave.

Delaware River

Market St.
5TH ST.
2ND ST.

Chestnut St

Walnut St.

Willings Alley

W. Wash. St.
Washington Sq.
S. Wash. Sq.

Penn's Landing

Dock St.

Spruce St.

7th St.
6th St.
5th St.
4th St.
3rd St.

SOCIETY HILL

Pine St.

Lombard St.

Head House Sq.

South St.

Information

India, brought over and reassembled, is the only such example in an American museum; it's covered with fanciful gods and relief panels. A ceremonial teahouse from Japan and a Chinese reception hall are galleries of wondrous artifacts. Opposite the Great Stair Hall, the museum's European masterpieces are exhibited. There's so much here that it may take you two visits to see everything, even if you make only a walk-through. And don't miss the Alfred Stieglitz photography galleries.

The museum has excellent dining facilities as well. A cafeteria, open Monday to Saturday from 10am to 3:30pm and Sunday from 11am to 3:30pm, dispenses simple hot lunches and salad plates for about $4. The restaurant across the way, open Monday to Friday from 11:45am to 2:15pm and Sunday from 11am to 2pm (brunch), has a $4 minimum and take-your-own service.

**Admission:** $6 adults; $3 students; children under 5 free. Free Sun 10am–1pm. Parking is free and plentiful.

**Open:** Tues–Sun 10am–5pm. A recently instituted series of Wednesday evening hours until 8:45pm with music, talks, and socializing has proved enormously popular. However, recent city funding cuts may require closings of separate galleries within these hours. **Bus:** 76.

## PENNSYLVANIA ACADEMY OF FINE ARTS (PAFA), Broad and Cherry sts. Tel. 972-7600.

Located three blocks north of City Hall, the Pennsylvania Academy of Fine Arts (PAFA), the oldest in the country (1805) and at one time the unquestioned leader of American beaux arts, in 1976 got a healthy dose of Cinderella treatment as its headquarters celebrated its centennial at the same as the U.S. Bicentennial. At the end of all the scrubbing, repainting, and stuccoing, Philadelphians were amazed again at the imagination of the Frank Furness masterpiece built in 1876. Go for the American paintings and sculpture or for the building itself—but go.

None of the permanent galleries is located on the ground floor, which houses an excellent bookstore and card shop, new exhibitions (often of Philadelphia artists), and the academy's classrooms. A splendid staircase, designed from archways to light fixtures by Furness, shines with red, gold, and blue walls. The bottom-left corner of the mezzanine wall was left unrestored—you can see how dingy the entire building was. The arcaded space in front of the galleries holds some of the larger sculptures and paintings. The middle gallery space exhibits student works or paintings from PAFA's vast storage vaults, while the permanent gallery rooms house products of this country's finest 19th- and 20th-century artists. Each May, half the museum is devoted to the annual academy school exhibition.

As is evident from the PAFA galleries, such early American painters as Gilbert Stuart, the Peale family, and Washington Allston congregated in Philadelphia, because it was America's capital and wealthiest city. Their idea of great painting, imported from Europe, was either large, moralistic historical canvases or portraits of the great. Both types are represented here: Washington Allston's *Dead Man Revived by Touching the Bones of Elisha,* for which the academy mortgaged the building, and Gilbert Stuart's famous full-length Lansdowne portrait of George Washington.

The four rooms of rotating exhibitions come from the museum's stores of over 6,000 canvases. Faculty members of PAFA discuss aspects of the exhibitions each Wednesday at noon, and the rotunda has been the scene of occasional Sunday concerts since Walt Whitman sat spellbound to listen. The adjoining rooms display works from the illustrious years of the mid-19th century, when PAFA probably enjoyed its most innovative period.

**Tours:** Leave from the Grand Stairhall Mon–Fri at 11am and 2pm (only at 2pm during summer weekends).

**Admission:** $5 adults; $3 seniors; $2 students. Free Sat 10am–1pm.

**Open:** Tues–Sat 10am–5pm; Sun 11am–5pm. **Bus:** C, 48.

## FRANKLIN INSTITUTE SCIENCE MUSEUM, 20th Street and Benjamin Franklin Pkwy. Tel. 448-1200, or 564-3375 for a taped message.

The Franklin Institute Science Museum isn't just kid stuff—everyone loves it because it's a thoroughly imaginative trip through the worlds of science that shows their influence on our lives. The complex covers four floors of a handsome neoclassical building, with large recent additions. The museum actually has three parts. The first is the home of the Franklin National Memorial, with a 30-ton statue of its namesake and a collection of authentic Franklin artifacts and possessions.

The second part is a collection of 1940s through 1970s science- and technology-oriented exhibition areas that were pioneers in hands-on displays, from a gigantic walk-through heart—actually, the passageway leads to the lungs and back so you can get a breath of fresh air—with heartbeat recordings and explanations, to ship models and Hall of Aviation, with its small planes and a chance to sit in a cockpit of a Wright brothers' biplane. For a hair-raising experience, plug into a Van de Graaff generator at the lightning gallery. On the third floor, an energy hall bursts with Rube Goldberg contraptions, noisemakers, and light shows. Everything exhibits a principle, but that doesn't get in the way of pure enjoyment: For example, a toddler can move a 500-pound block with enough pulleys. Over in the physics room, whisper into one corner—your voice will sound clearly in the other. The nearby Discovery Theater gives afternoon shows featuring liquid air and other oddities. The fourth floor specializes in astronomy and mathematical puzzles. The basement Fels Planetarium (tel. 563-1363) rounds out the picture.

The third part of the Franklin Institute is the result of an ambitious 1991 campaign to construct a Futures Center addition—with $22 million from city and state, $36 million from private sources. Just past the Franklin National Memorial on the second floor, you'll enter an energy-charged atrium with cafés, ticket counters, and ramps and stairs leading to the new exhibits. Just beyond is a separate-admission Omnimax arena, showing films ranging from undersea explorations to the Rolling Stones in spectacular 70mm format. Besides the two-level atrium are eight permanent, interactive exhibits taking you into the 21st century with Disney World–style pizzazz, including ones on space, earth, computers, chemistry, and health. My personal favorites are the video driving exercise in "Future Vision," "The Jamming Room" of musical synthesizers, and the "See Yourself Age" computer program in "Future and You." The Musser Choices Forums and public lectures will be daily features for all visitors; special keypads built into the auditorium chairs let you vote on, and see analyses of, issues that come up during presentations. The texts throughout are witty and disarming.

Of course, you'll eventually get hungry—with a family, the institute's a full afternoon. Your choices are excellent: a vending-machine space in the **Wawa Lunchroom** on the first floor, open only to museum-goers; the new all-American with a nutritional twist **Ben's Restaurant** on the second floor, accessible without museum admission and open Monday to Friday from 8:30am to 2:30pm, Saturday and Sunday from 9am to 3:30pm; and the **Omni Café** in the Futures Center lobby, open daily from 11am to shortly before museum closing and serving beer and wine. For dessert, vendors outside sell Philadelphia soft pretzels with plenty of mustard.

**Admission:** This is confusing and depends on what you want. Basic to exhibitions and Futures Center: $8.50 adults; $7.50 children. Planetarium, Omniverse, and laser shows: $6 adults; $5 children. Combinations of the two: $13.50 adults; $11.50 children.

**Open:** Science Center, daily 9:30am–5pm. Futures Center, Mon–Wed 9:30am–5pm; Thurs–Sun 9:30am–9pm. **Bus:** 33, 76.

# 2. MORE ATTRACTIONS

## ARCHITECTURAL HIGHLIGHTS

### BENJAMIN FRANKLIN BRIDGE, entrance at 5th and Vine sts.

An old fixture on the Olde City landscape has jumped into the 21st century—the Benjamin Franklin Bridge, designed by Paul Cret, one of the architects of the Parkway across town. The largest single-span suspension bridge in the world (1.8 miles) when it was finished in 1926, it carries cars and commuter trains and also has a foot/bicycle path along its south side. For the bicentennial of the U.S. Constitution, a Philadelphia team, including Steven Izenour (of Venturi, Rauch, and Scott Brown), a leading American architect and planner, created a computer-driven system for illuminating each and every cable. At night Philadelphians are treated to the largest lighting effects short of Ben Franklin's lightning itself.

**Admission:** Free.

**Open:** Daily 6am–dusk. **Bus:** 50.

### CITY HALL, Broad and Market sts. Tel. 569-3187.

When construction of City Hall began in 1871, it was planned to be the tallest structure in the world. But that elaborate 1901 wedding cake by John McArthur, Jr., with an inner courtyard straight out of a French château was dated in more ways than one, and it still arouses wildly differing reactions. Also, gracing City Hall is the largest piece of sculpture in the world: Calder's 37-foot-tall statue of William Penn.

You may wish to wander inside its vast floors, which range from breathtaking to bureaucratically forlorn; both inside and out, City Hall boasts the richest sculptural decoration of any American building and is a major showcase of architectural sculpture by A. M. Calder. The Mayor's Reception Room (Room 202) and the City Council Chamber (Room 400) are especially rich.

The highlight of City Hall is the **tower view.** The Juniper Street entrance is most convenient, but you can take any corner elevator to the seventh floor and follow the red signs (always indicative of city government). In this case, it leads to two escalators and a waiting area for the tower elevator. The elevator up to Penn's recently renovated shoestrings at 480 feet can hold only eight people, and the outdoor cupola cannot hold many more. On the way, notice how thick the walls are—City Hall is the tallest building ever constructed without a skeleton of steel girders, so that white stone stretches 6 feet thick at the top and 22 feet at ground level. (The need for repair increases as the building approaches its centenary. There's a 1990 bolster of hand-riveted wrought iron now, which you can see around the clock mechanism.) The simply stupefying view from the top encompasses not only the city but also the upper and lower Delaware Valley and port, western New Jersey, and suburban Philadelphia. It's windy up there, though. If you look straight down, you can see more of the hundreds of sculptures designed by Calder, the works of whose descendants—Alexander Sterling Calder (1870–1945) and Alexander Calder (1898–1976)—beautify Logan Circle and the Philadelphia Museum of Art.

**Admission:** Free.

**Open:** Daily 10am–3pm. During school year, Mon–Fri 10am–noon reserved for school groups. Last tour at 2:45pm. **Bus/Subway:** Most lines converge beside or underneath the building.

### FURNESS LIBRARY, Locust Walk and 34th St. on the University of Pennsylvania campus. Tel. 898-8358.

Like the Pennsylvania Academy of Fine Arts building (see above), this citadel of learning has the characteristic chiseled thistle of Frank Furness, although it was built a decade later from 1888 to 1890. The use of stained glass here is even richer. The library now houses, appropriately, the fine arts library of the University of Pennsylvania.

**Admission:** Free.

**Open:** During academic year only, Mon–Fri 9am–9pm; Sat–Sun noon–6pm. **Bus:** 44.

### PHILADELPHIA MERCHANTS EXCHANGE, Walnut and 3rd sts. Tel. 597-8974.

This sloped site, alongside one of the city's original creeks emptying into a Delaware cove, was used by hometown architect William Strickland from 1832 to 1834 as a forerunner of a stock-and-trading market. It's a pity that this building, once obviously central to city life, isn't open to the public, because the exterior is fascinating—a Greek semicircular front end on the river side and a strong coffer of a building with a portico facing the city. Note the entrances on two levels. The tower was built to provide instant information on arriving ships.

**Admission:** Free. **Bus:** D, 42.

## CEMETERIES

### CHRIST CHURCH BURIAL GROUND, 5th and Arch sts. (enter on 5th St.).

This expansion of the original graveyard of Christ Church (see below) contains the graves of Benjamin Franklin and his wife, Deborah, along with those of four other signers of the Declaration of Independence. It's a remarkably simple and peaceful place. There are always pennies on Ben's grave; tossing them there is a local tradition of wishes for good luck.

**Admission:** Free.

**Open:** Apr–Sept only, daily 9:30am–4:30pm. **Bus:** 48, 50.

### LAUREL HILL CEMETERY, 3822 Ridge Ave., East Fairmount Park. Tel. 228-8200.

How come you find Benjamin Franklin buried in a small, flat plot next to a church (see above) but Civil War Gen. George Meade buried in a bucolic meadow? Basically, the views of death and the contemplation of nature got more romantic in the 19th century, and Laurel

Hill was a result of that romanticism. Laurel Hill (1836), the first American cemetery designed by an architect, was the second (after Mount Auburn in Cambridge) to develop funerary monuments— even small Victorian palaces—amid the rolling, landscaped hills overlooking the Schuylkill. Its 100 acres also house plenty of tomb sculpture, pre-Raphaelite stained glass, and art nouveau sarcophagi. People picnicked here a century ago, but there's nothing but walking allowed now.

**Admission:** Free, although restrictions may apply, since it's still in use as a private institution. The Friends of Laurel Hill arrange tours (tel. 242-9437).

**Open:** Mon–Fri 8am–4pm; Sat 9am–1pm. **Directions:** Go north on East River Drive; make a right on Ferry Road, go one block to Ridge Avenue, and turn right. The entrance is ½ mile along on the right. **Bus:** 61.

### MIKVEH ISRAEL CEMETERY, Spruce St. between 8th and 9th sts. Tel. 922-5446 (synagogue number).

Philadelphia was an early center of American Jewish life, with the second-oldest synagogue (1740) organized by English and Sephardic Jews. While this congregation shifted location and is now adjacent to the Liberty Bell, the original cemetery—well outside the city at the time—was bought from the Penn family by Nathan Levy and later filled with the likes of Haym Solomon, a Polish immigrant who helped finance the Revolutionary government, and the daughter of a fine local family, Rebecca Gratz, who provided the model for Sir Walter Scott's Rebecca in his *Ivanhoe*.

**Admission:** Free.

**Open:** Summer, Mon–Fri 10am–4pm. Off-season, contact synagogue or park service. **Bus:** 47, 90.

## CHURCHES & SYNAGOGUES

### ARCH STREET MEETING HOUSE, 4th and Arch sts. Tel. 627-2667.

The current, simple brick building dates from 1804, but William Penn gave the land to his Society of Friends in 1693. In this capital city of Quakers, the Yearly Meeting in March still brings 13,000 here to pray. They use a spartan chamber, with hand-hewn benches facing one another. Other areas of the meeting house display Bibles, clothing and implements of Quaker life past and present, along with a simple history of the growth of the religion and the life of William Penn.

**Admission:** Free. Guided tours Apr 15–Oct 30.

**Open:** Mon–Sat 10am–4pm. Services Thurs 10am and Sun 10:30am. **Bus:** 17, 33, 48, 50.

### CHRIST CHURCH, 2nd St., a half block north of Market St. Tel. 922-1695.

The most beautiful Colonial building north of Market Street has to be Christ Church (1724–54). Its spire gleams white from anywhere in the neighborhood, now that the north-side market buildings have been replaced by a grassy park and a subway stop. The churchyard also has benches, tucked under trees or beside brick walls.

Christ Church, dating from the apex of English Palladianism, follows the proud and graceful tradition of Christopher Wren's churches in London. As in many of them, the interior spans one large arch, with galleries above the sides as demanded by the Anglican Church. Behind the altar, the massive Palladian window—a central columned arch flanked by proportional rectangles of pane—was the wonder of worshipers and probably the model for the one in Independence Hall. The main chandelier was brought over from England in 1744, and banners of English peers often drape the upper galleries. As in King's Chapel in Boston, seating is by pew— Washington's is marked with a plaque. So is Betsy Ross's, although she worshiped mainly at Free Quaker Meeting House at 5th and Arch streets.

With all the stones, memorials, and plates, it's impossible to avoid history—although you wouldn't suspect that riots occurred in 1726 over the numerous affairs of Rector Francis Phillips. William Penn was baptized at the font, which All Hallows' Church in London sent over. Penn was no Anglican (he spent most of his 20s in English jails because of it), but his charter included a clause that an Anglican church could be founded if 20 residents requested it, which they did. The socially conscious Philadelphians of the next generations chose Anglicanism as the "proper" religion, and Episcopalianism after the Revolution required disowning the religion of George III.

There's also a small gift shop.

**Admission:** Free, although donations are welcome.

**Open:** Mon–Sat 9am–5pm; Sun 1–5pm. Sun services at 9 and 11am. **Closed:** Mon–Tues Jan 1–Mar 10 and major holidays. **Bus:** 5, 17, 33, 48.

## GLORIA DEI, 916 Swanson St., near Christian and Delaware aves. Tel. 389-1513.

Take Swanson Street under I-95 at Christian Street in Queen Village and then a turn onto Water Street to reach Gloria Dei, or Old Swedes' Church. The National Park Service administers this oldest church in Pennsylvania (1700). At its dedication, the self-styled "Hermits of the Wissahickon" performed a public concert on viola, trumpets, and kettledrums. Inside the enclosing walls, you'll think yourself back in the 1700s, with a miniature parish hall, a rectory, and a graveyard amid the greenery. The one-room museum directly across from the church has a map of the good old days, and the graves of tubby Gov. Johan Printz and President of the Confederate States John Hanson lie nearby.

The thin, simple church interior has plenty of wonderful details— the two Chippendale chairs by the altar, the brass candelabra, and the very Swedish carving of the angel Gabriel. Everybody loves the ship models suspended from the ceiling: The *Key of Kalmar* and *Flying Griffin* carried the first Swedish settlers to these shores in 1638. And catch the silver crown in the vestry—any woman married here wears it during the ceremony.

**Admission:** Free.

**Open:** Apr–Oct, daily 9am–5pm. By appointment in the off-season. **Bus:** 5, 64, 79.

## MOTHER BETHEL AFRICAN METHODIST EPISCOPAL CHURCH, 419 S. 6th St. Tel. 925-0616.

This National Historic Landmark site is the oldest piece of land continuously owned by blacks in the United States. Richard Allen, born in 1760, was a slave in Germantown and bought his freedom in 1782, eventually walking out of St. George's down the street to found the African Methodist Episcopal order, today numbering some

5,000,000. This handsome, varnished-wood–and–stained-glass 1890 building is their mother church.

**Admission:** Free (donations welcome).

**Open:** Tues–Wed, Fri–Sat, 10am–3pm; Sun 2–4pm. Sunday service, 10:45am.

### OLD ST. JOSEPH'S CHURCH, Willings Alley near 4th and Walnut sts. Tel. 923-1733.

At its 1733 founding, St. Joseph's was the only place in the English-speaking world where Roman Catholics could celebrate mass publicly. The story goes that Benjamin Franklin advised Father Greaton to protect the church physically, since religious bigotry wasn't unknown even in the Quaker city. That's why the building is so unassuming from the street, a fact that didn't save it from damage during the anti-Catholic riots of the 1830s. Such French allies as Lafayette worshiped here. The present building (1838) is Greek Revival merging into Victorian, with wooden pews and such unusual colors as mustard and pale yellow, but the interior has preserved a Colonial style unusual in a Catholic church. Filigreed wainscoting rings a classically inspired altar backdrop that's supported by fluted columns. The graceful gallery contains a small pipe organ and wooden pews.

**Admission:** Free.

**Open:** Daily 6:30am–6pm. Five masses on Mon–Sat, 7 on Sun. **Bus:** D, 42, 50.

### ST. PETER'S EPISCOPAL, 3rd and Pine sts. Tel. 925-5968.

St. Peter's (1761) was originally established through the Bishop of London and has remained continuously open since. So like all pre-Revolutionary Episcopal churches, St. Peter's started out as an Anglican shrine. But why was this so, with Christ Church at 2nd and Market? In one word—mud. In the words of a local historian, "the long tramp from Society Hill . . . was more and more distasteful to these fine gentlemen and beautiful belles in damasks and brocades, velvet breeches and silk stockings, powdered hair and periwigs." A petition to build St. Peter's was approved in 1753.

Robert Smith, the builder of Carpenters' Hall, continued his penchant for red brick, pediments on the ends, and keystoned arches for gallery windows. Not much has ever changed inside, with its white square pews. Unlike in most churches, the hourglass pulpit is set into the west end, but the chancel is at the east, so the minister had to do some walking during the service. George Washington and Mayor Samuel Powel sat in pew 41. The 1789 organ blocks the upper east windows. Unfortunately, the steeple outside doesn't fit, since it was constructed in 1842.

The graveyard contains seven Native American chiefs, victims of the 1793 smallpox epidemic. Painter C. W. Peale, Stephen Decatur of naval fame, Nicholas Biddle of the Second Bank of the United States, and other notables also are interred here.

**Admission:** Free.

**Open:** Tues–Sat 9am–4pm; Sun 1–4pm. **Bus:** 5, 50, 90.

# UNIVERSITY

### UNIVERSITY OF PENNSYLVANIA, 34th and Walnut sts. Tel. 898-5000.

This private, now coeducational, Ivy League institution was founded by Benjamin Franklin and others in 1740; it boasts America's first medical (1765), law (1790), and business (1881) schools. Penn's liberal arts curriculum, dating to 1756, was the first to combine classical and practical subjects.

The university now has 4 undergraduate and 12 graduate schools, spanning over 100 academic departments. Its progress and excellence have been revitalized in the last two decades, thanks to extremely successful alumni and fundraising drives. The total campus entolls 22,000 students, and the 260-acre campus includes the **University Museum of Archaeology and Anthropology,** the **Annenberg Center for the Performing Arts,** and **the Institute for Contemporary Art.**

# HISTORIC BUILDINGS & MONUMENTS

## BETSY ROSS HOUSE, 239 Arch St. Tel. 627-5343.

One Colonial home everybody knows about is this one, restored in 1937 and distinguished by the Stars and Stripes outside. Elizabeth (Betsy) Ross was a Quaker needlewoman, married in Gloria Dei Church and newly widowed in 1776. So she worked as a seamstress and upholsterer out of her home on Arch Street (nobody is quite sure if No. 239 was hers, though). In any case, the Revolutionary forces needed flags, and congressional delegate George Ross that knew his niece needed work, so he dragged George Washington and Robert Morris along to request her services. Nobody knows if she did the original American flag of 13 stars set in a field of 13 red and white stripes, but she was commissioned to sew for the American fleet ship's flags that replaced the earlier Continental banners.

The house takes only a minute or two to walk through, and the wooden stairwell was designed for shorter colonial frames—certainly not Washington's! Since the house is set back from the street, the city maintains the Atwater Kent Park in front, where Ross and her last husband are buried. The upholstery shop, now a gift shop, opens into the period parlor. Other rooms include the cellar kitchen (standard placement for this room), tiny bedrooms, and model working areas for upholstering, making musket balls, and the like. Note such little touches as reusable note tablets made of ivory; pine cones, used to help start hearth fires; and the prominent kitchen hourglass.

**Admission:** Free.

**Open:** Summer, daily 9am–6pm. Rest of year, daily 9am–5pm. **Bus:** 5, 17, 33, 48.

## CARPENTERS' HALL, 320 Chestnut St. Tel. 925-0167.

Carpenters' Hall (1773) was the guild hall for—guess who?—carpenters; at the time the city could use plenty, for 18th-century Philadelphia was the fastest-growing urban area in all the colonies and perhaps in the Empire outside of London. Robert Smith, a Scottish member of the Carpenters' Company, designed the building (like most carpenters, he did architecture and contracting as well). He also designed the steeple of Christ Church, with the same calm Georgian lines. It's made of Flemish Bond brick in a checkerboard pattern, with stone window sills, superb woodwork, and a cupola that resembles a salt shaker.

You'll be surprised at how small Carpenters' Hall is because such great events transpired here. In 1774 the normal governmental channels to convey Colonial complaints to the Crown were felt inadequate, and a popular Committee of Correspondence invited delegates from each of the 13 colonies to attend—a bold move, since England much preferred the colonies not to talk or trade with one another. Yet only Georgia declined the invitation.

The committee was offered the State House (now Independence Hall) for this First Continental Congress but turned it down, since this site had always represented the royalist point of view. Instead, the Congress debated in Carpenters' Hall. The more radical delegates, led by Patrick Henry, had already expressed treasonous wishes for independence, but most wanted to exhaust possibilities of bettering their relationship with the Crown. They voted to reconvene in May 1775; by the time they did, the shooting at Concord and Lexington had roused the colonies to contemplate forming a United States.

What's in there now isn't much—an exhibit of colonial building methods; some portraits, including a Gilbert Stuart; and Windsor chairs, which seated the First Continental Congress. If some details look as if they're from a later period, you're right: The fanlights above the north and south doors date from the 1790s, and the gilding dates from 1857.

**Admission:** Free.

**Open:** Tues–Sun 10am–4pm (hours are curtailed because the Carpenters' Company still maintains it). **Bus:** D, 42, 76.

## DECLARATION HOUSE (GRAFF HOUSE), 7th and Market sts. Tel. 597-2505.

Bricklayer Jacob Graff constructed a modest three-story home in the 1760s, figuring on renting out the second floor for added income. The Second Continental Congress soon brought to the house a thin, red-haired tenant—Thomas Jefferson—who was in search of a quiet room away from city noise. If the Declaration of Independence is any indication, he found it, because he drafted it here between June 10 and June 18, 1776.

The reconstruction uses the same Flemish Bond checkerboard pattern (only on visible walls; it was too expensive for party walls) for brick, windows with paneled shutters, and implements that the house exhibited in 1775. If you compare it with Society Hill homes, it's tiny and asymmetrical, with an off-center front door. You'll enter through a small garden and see a short film about Jefferson and a copy of Jefferson's draft (which would have forbidden slavery in the United States, had the clause survived debate). The upstairs rooms are furnished as Jefferson would have seen them.

**Admission:** Free (part of Independence National Historical Park).

**Open:** Daily 9am–5pm. **Bus:** 17, 33, 48, 76.

## ELFRETH'S ALLEY, 2nd St. between Arch and Race sts. Tel. 574-0560.

✪ The modern Benjamin Franklin Bridge shadows Elfreth's Alley, the oldest continuously inhabited street in America. Most of Colonial Philadelphia looked much like this: cobblestone lanes between the major thoroughfares; small two-story homes; and pent-eaves over doors and windows, a local trademark. Note the busybody mirrors that let residents see who is at the door (or someone else's) from the second-story bedroom. In 1700 the resident artisans and tradesmen worked with shipping, but 50 years later haberdashers, bakers, printers, and house carpenters set up shop. Families moved in and out rapidly, for noisy, dusty 2nd Street was the major north-south route in Philadelphia. Jews, blacks, Welsh, and Germans made it a miniature melting pot. Because of luck and the vigilant Elfreth's Alley Association, the destruction of the street was averted in 1937. Ironically, houses that were then redeemed for $1,500 are selling today for $150,000, although I-95 vibrations and fumes cause unprecedented cracking and pitting of the foundations. The minuscule, sober facades hide some ultramodern interiors, and there are some restful shady benches on Bladen Court, off the north side of the street.

Number 126, the **Mantua Maker's House** (that's a cape maker), now serves as a museum and is the only house open to the public. An 18th-century garden in back has been restored, and plans include refurbishing the upper floor, now a plaster nightmare. But you can still buy Colonial candy and gifts and peek in some of the open windows on the street. On the first Saturday in June all the houses are thrown open for inspection—don't miss this.

**Admission:** Museum is free.
**Open:** Daily 10am–4pm. **Bus:** 5, 48, 76.

## MASONIC TEMPLE, 1 N. Broad St. Tel. 988-1917.

Quite apart from its Masonic lore, the Temple—one of the world's largest—is one of America's best on-site illustrations of the use of post–Civil War architecture and design, because the halls are more or less frozen in time and because no expense was spared. There are seven lodge halls, designed to capture the seven "ideal" architectures—Renaissance,Ionic,Oriental,Corinthian,Gothic,Egyptian, and Norman (notice that Renaissance was the most contemporary architect James Windrim could come up with!). Many of the Founding Fathers, including Washington, were Masons (this is actually the "mother church" of American Masonry), and the museum has preserved their letters and emblems. Lafayette and Andrew Jackson also were Masons. The more you like looking at memorabilia connected with ritual, such as china, gavels, and aprons, the more you'll love the tour. Don't miss William Rush's wood sculptures; he was the finest plastic artist of Federal America.

**Admission:** Free.
**Open:** Tours Mon–Fri at 10 and 11am and 1, 2, and 3pm; Sat at 10 and 11am only. **Bus:** 17, 33, 44, 48, 76.

## PENNSYLVANIA HOSPITAL, 8th and Spruce sts. Tel. 829-3971.

Pennsylvania Hospital, like so much in civic Philadelphia, owes its presence to Benjamin Franklin, who devised a rudimentary matching-grant scheme so that the Assembly wouldn't feel it was subsidizing something that private citizens didn't want. This was the first hospital in the colonies, and it seemed like a strange venture into social welfare at the time. Samuel Rhoads, a fine architect in the Carpenters' Company, designed the Georgian headquarters; the east wing, nearest 8th Street, was completed in 1755, and a west wing matched it in 1776. The grand central hall by David Evans completed the ensemble in 1804. The marble pilasters and arched doorway of the middle structure add curving grace to the anchorlike wings. Instead of a dome, the hospital decided on a surgical amphitheater's skylight. In spring, the garden's azaleas brighten the neighborhood, and the beautifully designed herb garden is equally popular.

The hospital was the workplace of Philadelphia's many brilliant doctors, among them Philip Syng Physick, Benjamin Rush, and Caspar Wistar. The entrance on 8th Street, between Spruce and Pine, highlights Benjamin Rush's other occupation, that of painter, with his famous *Christ Healing the Sick*. The tour includes a look at the paneled and portraited historical library, with its chair of William Penn's and a Rittenhouse clock. If you're interested in old medical instruments, be sure to get a glimpse of the surgical amphitheater with its skylight and three tiers, the first in the country. The first gall bladder operation was performed here. The tour includes a look at the history of nursing and medical care.

**Admission:** Free.

**Open:** Mon–Fri 9am–5pm. Guided tours are no longer obligatory; copies of a walking tour itinerary are available from the Marketing Department on the second floor of the Pine Street building. **Bus:** 47, 90.

## POWEL HOUSE, 244 S. 3rd St. Tel. 627-0364 or 925-2251.

If Elfreth's Alley (see above) leaves you wondering about how someone really well-to-do lived in Colonial Philadelphia, head for the Powel House. Samuel Powel was mayor, and he and his wife, Elizabeth, hosted every Founding Father and foreign dignitary around. (John Adams called these feasts "sinful dinners," which shows how far Samuel had come from a Quaker background.) He spent most of his 20s gallivanting in Europe thanks to the family's wealth, collecting wares for this 1765 mansion.

Unbelievably, this most Georgian house was slated for demolition in 1930 because it had become a decrepit slum dwelling. Period rooms were removed to the Philadelphia Museum of Art and the Metropolitan Museum of Art in New York. But the Society for the Preservation of Landmarks saved it and has gradually refurnished the entire mansion as it was. (Because of inventories done for Ben Franklin's fire-insurance companies, they knew exactly what each room contained.) The yellow satin Reception Room, off the entrance hall, has some gorgeous details, such as a wide-grain mahogany secretary. Notice that since Georgian design demanded balanced doors, the right one opens into a blank wall. Under the sideboard in the neighboring dining room, the tea caddy held pure Chinese tea, which the Powels would blend. Upstairs, the magnificent ballroom features red damask drapes whose design is copied from a bolt of cloth found untouched in a Colonial attic. There is also a 1790 Irish crystal chandelier and a letter from Benjamin Franklin's daughter referring to the lively dances held here. In the winter, the Powels lived in the smaller rear portion of the house: It still has the family bed (both Powels were obviously large-boned), as well as a rocking cradle and a Martha Washington sewing table. An 18th-century garden lies below.

**Admission:** $3 adults; $2 students; children under 6 free.

**Open:** Guided tours only, Tues–Sat 10am–4pm; Sun 1–4pm. Tours are given whenever a group of six or more congregates; be sure to arrive at least 30 minutes before closing. **Bus:** 50, 76, 90.

# LIBRARIES & LITERARY ATTRACTIONS

**ATHENAEUM OF PHILADELPHIA, 219 S. 6th St. (Washington Square East). Tel. 925-2688.**

The age when a group of private subscribers could fund the dissemination of useful knowledge—or even keep tabs on it in diverse fields—has long since passed, but a 15-minute peek into the Athenaeum will show you one of America's finest collections of Victorian-period architectural design and also give you the flavor of private 19th-century life for the proper Philadelphian. In particular, don't miss the second-floor main reading room, with its original gas-lighting fixtures, creamy faux-marble piers, leaded-glass bookcases, and period carpets. There's a surprisingly good collection of 19th-century American art, too, and such curios as an 1867 globe and an antique water filter. The building, beautifully restored in 1975, houses almost 1 million library items for the serious researcher in American architecture.

**Admission:** Free.

**Open:** Mon–Fri 9am–5pm. Permission to enter and guided tours are given on request. **Bus:** D, 42, 90.

**FREE LIBRARY OF PHILADELPHIA, Central Library, 19th and Vine sts. Tel. 686-5322.**

Across Logan Circle from the Academy of Natural Sciences (see below), the Free Library of Philadelphia rivals the public libraries of Boston and New York for magnificence and diversity. The library and its twin, the Municipal Court, are plagiarisms of buildings in the Place de la Concorde in Paris (the library's the one on the left). If you're hungry, the rooftop cafeteria is one of the nicest locations for a snack and one of the only Parkway dining areas.

The main lobby and the gallery always have some of the institution's riches on display—from medieval manuscripts to modern bookbinding. Greeting cards and stationery are sold for reasonable prices, too. The second floor houses the best local history, travel, and resource collection in the city. The third-floor rare-book room hosts visitors on Monday to Saturday from 9am to 5pm. If you're interested in manuscripts from the 19th century, children's literature, incunabula, and early American hornbooks, this is the place. Down the corridor, peek at a chamber taken lock, stock, and barrel from William Elkin's mansion, Whitemarsh. It also has two Paul Revere prints and plenty of Dickensiana.

There's also an active concert and film series.

**Admission:** Free.

**Open:** Mon–Wed 9am–9pm; Thurs–Fri 9am–6pm; Sat 9am–5pm; Sun 1–5pm. **Bus:** 76.

**EDGAR ALLAN POE NATIONAL HISTORICAL SITE, 532 N. 7th St. Tel. 597-8780.**

The acclaimed American author lived here from 1833 to 1834. "The Black Cat," "The Gold Bug," and "The Tell-Tale Heart" were published while he was a resident. It's a simple place—after all, Poe was badly off most of his life—and the National Park Service keeps it unfurnished. An adjoining building contains basic information on Poe's life and work, along with a reading room and slide show. The Park Service also runs intermittent discussions and candlelight tours on Saturday afternoons.

**Admission:** Free.
**Open:** Tues–Sat 9am–5pm. **Bus:** 47.

### ROSENBACH MUSEUM AND LIBRARY, 2010 Delancey Place (between Spruce and Pine sts). Tel. 732-1600.

In Philadelphia there are certain families of such understated wealth and influence that you could be in town for years before learning of their position. The Rosenbach Museum and Library has some similar characteristics—but with one big difference. The Rosenbach specializes in books: illuminated manuscripts, parchment, rough drafts, and first editions. If you love the variations and beauty of the printed word, they'll love your presence. And their collection, a lifetime labor of love for two brothers, will be a revelation.

You're not allowed absolute freedom in the opulent town-house galleries, nor free rein among the 30,000 rare books and 270,000 documents. But the admission fee allows you a 75-minute tour with one of the genteel volunteer guides. Some rooms preserve the Rosenbachs' elegant living quarters, with Hepplewhite furniture and Sully paintings. Others are devoted to authors and illustrators: Marianne Moore's Greenwich Village study is reproduced in its entirety, and the Maurice Sendak drawings represent only the tip of the iceberg—or the forest. The second-floor foyer holds the original manuscript of Joyce's *Ulysses* and first editions of Melville, in Melville's own bookcase. And the third-floor special exhibitions explore anything from the colors used in illuminated manuscripts to children's books. Don't miss the shop, tucked behind the entrance, for bargains in greeting cards and a superb collection of Sendak.

**Admission:** $2.50 adults; $1.50 children under 18 and seniors.
**Open:** Tues–Sun 11am–4pm. **Closed:** Aug. If you have a special scholarly interest, contact the library before you visit. **Bus:** 17, 90.

# MARKETS

### ITALIAN MARKET, 9th St. between Christian and Federal sts.

While touring South Philadelphia, be sure to visit the Italian Market, where you can buy the freshest produce, pasta, seafood, and other culinary delights—this is what shopping used to be like before supermarkets and malls. It's increasingly safe and interesting to head for the market from South Street, which has been gentrified from Front to Ninth streets. Only a couple of blocks filled with notable Italian restaurants—Ralph's, Felicia's, and Palumbo's—separate South Street from the market proper. Fast-talking vendors, opera-singing butchers, and try-it-before-you-buy-it cheese merchants hawk their wares here.

**Open:** Daily, dawn to dusk. **Bus:** 47, 64.

### READING TERMINAL MARKET, 12th and Arch sts. Tel. 922-2317.

The Reading Terminal Market has been a greengrocer, snack shop, butcher, fish market, and sundries store for smart Philadelphians since the turn of the century. The idea was to use the space beneath the terminal's tracks for the food business so that commuters and businesses could stock up easily and cheaply.

What's at Reading Terminal exactly? You'll find scrapple, mangoes, clam chowder, and pretzels—you name it, if it's fresh and unpackaged, it'll be there. This is where most of the "retail," as opposed to restaurant or institutional, Amish farm products come to market. Chapter 6, "Philadelphia Dining," provides a fuller description of the individual vendors and local specialties, but there is a pleasant central café with seating as well as many bar-stool and café-table setups by individual vendors.

**Open:** Mon–Sat 8am–6pm. Many vendors close at 5pm. **Bus:** 17, 33, 44, 48.

# MORE MUSEUMS & EXHIBITIONS

### ACADEMY OF NATURAL SCIENCES, 19th St. and Benjamin Franklin Pkwy. Tel. 299-1000.

This is another of Philadelphia's "oldest" attractions—it's been exhibiting natural history continuously since 1812. The academy has been sprucing up many of the public spaces, including the downstairs cafeteria (food from machines only, though), the small gift shop, and most of the first floor. Kids love the big diorama halls, with cases of several species mounted and posed in authentic settings. A new $2.5-million permanent display, "Discovering Dinosaurs," features more than a dozen specimens, including a huge Tyrannosaurus rex with jaws agape, and this was joined in late 1991 by "What on Earth!" on geology; many of the displays are hands-on or interactive. The North American Hall, on the first floor, has enormous moose, buffalo, and bears. A small marine exhibit shows how some fish look different in ultraviolet light and how the bed of the Delaware has changed since Penn landed in 1682.

The second floor features groupings of Asian and African flora and fauna—not only the lions and tigers you'd expect but delicate goats and antelopes as well. Many of the cases have nearby headphones that tell you more about what you're seeing. Five or six live demonstrations are given here every day; the handlers are expert in conducting these sessions with rocks, birds, plants, and animals. Several daily Eco Shows are given in the auditorium downstairs, too. The Egyptian mummy, a priest of a late dynasty, seems a bit out of place, but this is about the only museum in America with a translation of the coffin inscriptions and explanations of all the burial formulas.

Upstairs, "Outside In" is a touchable museum designed for children under 12, with a model campsite, fossils, minerals, shells, and other unbreakables. It stimulates almost every sense: Children can see, feel, hear, and smell live turtles, mice, and snakes (all caged) and wander around mock forests and deserts. "Outside In" is open Monday to Friday from 1 to 4pm, Saturday and Sunday and holidays from 10am to 5pm. Admission here is part of the general admission. A large bird hall and a hall of endangered species round out the picture, along with frequent films.

**Admission:** $5.50 adults; seniors $5; children 3–12 $4.50; under 3 free.

**Open:** Mon–Fri 10am–4:30pm; Sat–Sun and holidays 10am–5pm. **Bus:** 33, 76.

### AFRO-AMERICAN HISTORICAL AND CULTURAL MUSEUM, 7th and Arch sts. Tel. 574-0380.

Three blocks northwest of the Liberty Bell is the only building in America specifically constructed to display the history of African-Americans. It's built in five split levels of ridged concrete, meant to evoke African mud housing, off a central atrium and ramp. As you ascend, you follow the path from African roots through to the role blacks have played in U.S. development. The specific exhibitions do change.

The ground floor contains the admissions office, the gift shop, and the African Heritage Gallery (here's your chance to see photographs of original cornrow hairstyles and customs). The second level, concentrating on slavery and captivity, is undoubtedly the most dramatic and informed section. It emphasizes that the slave trade was hardly exclusive to, or even predominant in, North America, and that it persisted in South America until 1870. In fact, semi-African communities of descendants of runaway slaves still exist today in Suriname and Jamaica.

The upper three levels, dealing with black history and culture after Emancipation, lose some focus since blacks slowly gained acceptance and/or visibility in so many areas of American life. Black cowboys, inventors, athletes, spokespeople, businesspeople—all are presented, along with such organizations as the NAACP and CORE and the civil rights movements of the 1960s. Culturally, the Harlem Renaissance and the development of jazz and soul music also have their space.

**Admission:** $3.50 adults; $1.75 children and seniors.
**Open:** Tues–Sat 10am–5pm. **Bus:** 47, 48.

### AMERICAN-SWEDISH HISTORICAL MUSEUM, 1900 Pattison Ave. Tel. 389-1776.

Modeled after a 17th-century Swedish manor house, this small museum chronicles 350 years of the life and accomplishments of Swedish Americans. Specific rooms highlight John Ericsson, inventor of the Civil War ironclads, and 19th-century opera singer Jenny Lind. Seasonal festivals are part of the mix here: In April, the museum hosts *Valborgsmassoafton* (Spring Festival), with folk dancing, singing, and refreshments; and St. Lucia's Day in December is a softly lit Christmas precursor.

**Admission:** $1.50 adults; $1 students and seniors; children under 12 free.
**Open:** Tues–Fri 10am–4pm; Sat noon–4pm. **Bus:** C.

### ATWATER KENT MUSEUM, THE HISTORY MUSEUM OF PHILADELPHIA, 15 S. 7th St. Tel. 922-3031.

Across the street from the Balch Institute (see below), the small Atwater Kent Museum occupies the former home of the Franklin Institute. Using more artifacts than the Visitor Center, the Atwater Kent shows you what Philadelphia was like from 1680 to 1880. The founder, you may remember, built most of America's early radios, and much of this fortune benefited Philadelphia gardens and societies. Nothing was too trivial to ignore—the collection jumps from dolls to dioramas, from cigar-store Indians to period toy shops. One favorite is the Michelet grandfather clock, which parades six dragons to the tune of a French march at every hour. Sunbonnets, train tickets, rocking horses, ship models, dioramas of famous events, and military uniforms are all part of the display.

**Admission:** Free.
**Open:** Tues–Sat 9:30am–4:45pm. **Bus:** 17, 33, 42, 76.

### BALCH INSTITUTE FOR ETHNIC STUDIES, 18 S. 7th St. Tel. 925-8090.

Everyone comes from someplace—and the United States is

virtually the only country where everyone (except the Native Americans) comes from someplace else and knows it and is proud of it. The Continental Congress had a new vision of the basic human rights of these newcomers, and that's why it's fitting that the Balch Institute lies next door to the site where Jefferson composed the phrases of the Declaration of Independence. The institute has a terrific library that covers everything you've always wanted to know about your roots, if you're one of more than 100 ethnicities. The exhibition "Freedom's Doors" makes the point that one-third of all immigrants disembarked not at New York but at Boston, Miami, New Orleans, Los Angeles, and so forth. To the left, the exhibits change every couple of months; they range from ethnic images in World War I posters to African crafts.

**Admission:** Free, although donation requested.
**Open:** Mon–Sat 10am–5pm. **Bus:** 17, 33, 42, 76.

**BARNES FOUNDATION, 300 N. Latches Lane, Merion Station, PA 19066. Tel. 215/667-0290.**

Take a train, a taxi, a bus, or a car, or even walk if you have to—if you're interested in art, the Barnes Foundation will stun you with its magnificence. Albert Barnes crammed his French Provincial mansion with over 1,000 masterpieces—180 Renoirs, 80 Cézannes, innumerable Impressionists and Postimpressionists, and a generous sampling of European art from the Italian Primitives onward.

The central gallery alone contains Cézanne's *Card Players;* several large Renoirs; a Matisse mural, *The Dancers;* and more. Most of the old masters—a Giorgione, a Titian, and an El Greco—peek out of small rooms to the left, while Impressionists splash light and color on the right. Barnes believed that art has a quality that can be studied scientifically—for example, one curve will be beautiful and hence art, and another that's slightly different will not be art. That's why the galleries display antique door latches, keyholes, keys, and household tools with strong geometric lines right next to the paintings. And the connections beg to be drawn between neighboring objects—an unusual van Gogh nude, an Amish chest, and New Mexico rural icons. Certain Postimpressionists, such as Soutine, solid or joyous Picasso, and Modigliani, also are displayed, both here and upstairs. In fact, virtually every first-rank European artist is included: Degas, Seurat, Bosch, Tintoretto, Lorrain, Chardin, Daumier, Delacroix, Corot, and so forth. The second floor functions more as a study collection and repository for non-European objets d'art, but it's no less impressive. This is not a bad use of a fortune derived from selling patent medicine!

At press time, the Barnes is changing from archaic rigidity that used to govern its policies, since the first generation of trustees has passed on. Until now, the foundation admitted only 200 visitors on Friday, 200 on Saturday, and 100 on Sunday. No cameras and no children were allowed, no postcards were sold, and security checks were made at the gate. The Barnes paintings inhabit a gilded cage and are never loaned to other museums.

**Admission:** $1; children under 12 not admitted.
**Open:** Fri 9:30am–4:30pm; Sat 9:30am–4:30pm; Sun 1–4:30pm. Reservations were mandatory for 50% of admittees, but this restriction seems to be going. **Closed:** July–Aug; because of budget constraints the east and west wings are each open only half of daily

hours. **SEPTA:** Take Paoli local train to Merion; walk up Merion Avenue and turn left onto Latches Lane. **Bus:** 44 to Old Lancaster Road and Latches Lane. **Car:** I-76 (Schuylkill Expressway) north to City Line Avenue, then south on City Line 1.5 miles to Old Lancaster Road. Turn right onto Old Lancaster, continue 4 blocks and turn left onto Latches Lane.

### HILL-PHYSICK-KEITH HOUSE, 321 S. 4th St. Tel. 925-7866 or 925-2251.

As with the Powel (p.146) and Bishop White (p.179) homes, the Hill-Physick-Keith House combines attractiveness through design and interest through history on Society Hill. This home is, if anything, the area's most impressive—it's free-standing but not boxy, gracious but solid. Built during the 1780s boom, it soon wound up housing the father of American surgery, Philip Syng Physick, a very professional name for a physician. The usual pattern of descendants, neglect, and renovation has applied here, on an even grander scale.

All the cloths and wallpapers were fashioned expressly for use here, and the mansion as restored is a landmark of the Federal style about 1815. The drawing room opens onto a lovely 19th-century walled garden and shows the excitement caused by the discovery of the buried city of Pompeii by including a Roman stool and 18th-century Italian art. Many of the furnishings in the upstairs parlor were lent by the Society of Cincinnatus, among them an inkstand tarnished by Ben Franklin's fingerprints. Dr. Physick treated Chief Justice Marshall, and Marshall's portrait and gift of a wine stand testify to his powers.

**Admission:** $3 adults; $2 students and seniors; children under 6 free.

**Open:** Tues–Sat 10am–4pm; Sun 1–4pm. Guided tours are for six or more only; last tours are given 30 minutes before closing. As with other houses on Society Hill, it's occasionally rented for parties and receptions, so call beforehand. **Bus:** 50, 90.

### HISTORICAL SOCIETY OF PENNSYLVANIA, 1300 Locust St. Tel. 732-6200.

This museum houses the finest collection of Colonial furniture and art in Center City. Only members and scholars are admitted to the archives, but the museum exhibits sprawl over the first floor of this solid 19th-century building. It helps if you have a basic background of local history, since almost every notable of the city (and some famous out-of-towners such as Napoleon's brother, Joseph, and George Washington, both of whom lived here) has a portrait or chair represented.

**Admission:** $2.50 gallery; $5 library.

**Open:** Tues and Thurs–Sat 10am–5pm; Wed 10am–9pm. **Closed:** All major holidays. **Bus:** A, C, 38, 90.

### NATIONAL MUSEUM OF AMERICAN JEWISH HISTORY, 55 N. 5th St. Tel. 923-8811.

This is the only museum that's specifically dedicated to preserving and presenting Jewish participation in the development of the United States. Don't expect to walk into another Colonial structure. The complex was built in the aftermath of the 1950s clearance that allowed for Independence Mall, although the congregation connected to it, Mikveh Israel, was established in Philadelphia in 1740 (see the "Cemetery" listing, above). The walkway between 4th and

3rd streets displays an 1876 statue by Sir Moses Ezeliel, an English lord born in America, symbolizing religious freedom. It was fittingly given by the Jewish congregation in Philadelphia, and you can see how much lower the street level was a century ago. You'll enter close to 4th Street (passing Christ Church Cemetery, with Ben Franklin's grave the major attraction here) into a dark-brick lobby that serves both the museum and the adjoining Mikveh Israel Synagogue. The museum starts with a permanent exhibition, "The American Jewish Experience: From 1654 to the Present," combining dry-mounted reproductions of portraits and documents, actual books and letters, and utensils and religious articles to attest to the diversity and vitality of American Jews. It's a fascinating show, and the museum should be proud of sponsoring its recent tour. Smaller rotating exhibitions supplement this presentation. Official annual attendance clocks in at more than 40,000, but it's usually cool and restful and makes a good break from a hot Independence Park tour. A small gift shop is attached.

**Admission:** $1.75 adults; $1.50 students and seniors; $11.25 children; children under 5 free.

**Open:** Mon–Thurs 10am–5pm; Fri 10am–3pm; Sun noon–5pm. **Bus:** 17, 33, 48, 50.

### NORMAN ROCKWELL MUSEUM, 6th and Sansom sts. (lower level). Tel. 922-4345.

The Norman Rockwell Museum in the corner of the old headquarters of the Curtis Publishing Company on Washington Square exhibits about 60 of his famous covers for the *Saturday Evening Post*. Only a couple of these are the original paintings and sketches, although a re-creation of Rockwell's studio has an unfinished one on the easel. You can see the classic Four Freedoms posters, which stimulated war-bond sales in World War II. The gift shop has more Rockwelliana than you could imagine.

**Admission:** $1.50 adults; children under 12 free.

**Open:** Daily 10am–4pm. **Bus:** D, 42, 90.

### PLEASE TOUCH MUSEUM, 210 N. 21st St. Tel. 963-0667.

This is deliberately not merely a children's museum—adults have been known to linger at the play/exhibit modular spaces while those of the younger generation pull impatiently toward the pint-sized (and crowded) coat racks. The name conveys the converted factory's tugs at the creative, exuberant, and receptive in us all. The location is great—just off the Parkway, two blocks south of Franklin Institute—and it's one of the best indoor activities for a young family, Philadelphian or tourist.

The museum's thoughtful design is evident in its lobby: You can enter the separate gift shop, with plenty of cute and challenging items, without paying admission. Once you're in the lobby, you can park strollers, check coats, and buy tickets at counters that cater to kids. From the entrance, check out the Performance Center in the rear of the first floor. You may be able to catch a mime, painter, or puppeteer right away or at least make note of the next scheduled act. Otherwise, walk up the ramp under a huge cloth Chinese New Year's dragon to the second-floor Resource Center (ages five or older are requested). Children will love identifying the utensils and toys that fit together to form unconventional life-size animals. From here, wander throughout the selection of hearths where children can try on native costumes or shop for goods. It's a terrific idea for introducing them to other cultures in a tangible, meaningful way. Mirrors are amply provided.

The theme of a wider world continues in the museum's Cultural Corridor, full of indestructible furniture, toys, and implements from West Africa, Native American settlements, and an Indian market. Other sections include a small menagerie, a module full of simple machines for busy minds and fingers (watch the weights on the pulley system!), and clothes from earlier eras in American life. The roundabout route finishes up with a tour of the working environments of many parents—stores, businesses, and a health-care center.

The Please Touch Museum is not a day-care center; you cannot simply drop the kids off, and you won't want to. It's a great place to celebrate a child's birthday, if you plan ahead.

**Admission:** $5 adults and children; maximum of three kids per adult. Free admission Sun 10–11am.

**Open:** Daily 10am–4:30pm. **Bus:** 76.

### RODIN MUSEUM, Benjamin Franklin Pkwy. between 21st and 22nd sts. Tel. 763-8100.

The Rodin Museum exhibits the largest collection of the master's work—129 sculptures, 72 drawings, and several sketch books—outside the Musée Rodin in Paris. It has inherited a little of its sibling museum's outer facelessness, making a very French use of space within and boasting much greenery without. Entering from the Parkway, virtually across the street from the Franklin Institute (see above), you'll contemplate *The Thinker* contemplating other things, then pass through an imposing arch to a front garden of hardy shrubs and trees surrounding a fish pond. Before going into the museum, study the *Gates of Hell.* These gigantic doors, once intended for the Musée des Arts Décoratif in Paris, reveal an awesome power to mold metal by the force of passionate imagination. Damned souls lunge and leap halfway out of the bronze, while contorted groups clamber over one another in the searing recognition of their fate. If you look closely, you can see that many of the figures reappear as sculptures in their own right—*The Thinker* and *The Three Graces,* for example.

The galleries were restored to their original sparkle in 1989. The main hall holds authorized casts of *John the Baptist, The Cathedral,* and *The Burghers of Calais.* Several of the side chambers and the library hold powerful erotic plaster models, along with Steichen photographic portraits of Rodin.

**Admission:** Donation of 50¢ adults, 25¢ children requested. Free with same-day admission ticket from the Philadelphia Museum of Art (see above).

**Open:** Tues–Sun 10am–5pm. **Bus:** 76.

### U.S. MINT, 5th and Arch sts. Tel. 597-7350.

The U.S. Mint building was the first authorized by the government during Washington's first term. Fortunately for us, the present edifice, diagonally across from Liberty Bell Pavilion (see above), turns out enough cash to keep us all solvent, about 1,500,000 coins every hour. This is one factory tour that's quite stingy with free samples, but a self-guided walk through the process has its own rewards.

The coinage process involves melting raw metal, rolling it to coin thinness, punching out blanks from these sheets, and pressing designs on them. The metal slabs and coils look cherry red from the heating they undergo, and after the coins are done a counting machine automatically sews lots of 5,000 into bags, headed for Federal

Reserve Banks. Points along the route have prerecorded explanations, if you wish to listen (ever wonder how the layers in composite coins stick together?). Afterward, view the small exhibition of various coins, presses, and memorabilia.

**Admission:** Free.

**Open:** Oct–Dec and Apr, Mon–Sat 9am–4:30pm. Jan–Mar, Mon–Fri 9am–4:30pm. May–Sept, Mon–Sun 9am–4:30pm. **Closed:** New Year's Day, Christmas. **Bus:** 5, 48, 76.

## THE UNIVERSITY MUSEUM OF ARCHAEOLOGY AND AN-THROPOLOGY, 33rd and Spruce sts. Tel. 898-4026.

Higher buildings have left this museum's Romanesque brickwork more secluded, but when you consider its contents, it's seen quite a bit of the world. The University of Pennsylvania, which celebrated the museum's centennial in 1986 and 1987, got into archeology and anthropology on the ground floor, and hundreds of excavations have endowed it with Benin bronzes, biblical inscriptions, Mesopotamian masterpieces, Incan gold, and artifacts from every continent.

The museum is intelligently explained. Individual objects are left unlabeled in their cases, which is useful because you tend to study them and not the words. Probably the most famous excavation display, located on the third floor, is a spectacular Sumerian trove of jewelry and household objects from the royal tombs of the ancient city of Ur. Adjoining this, huge cloisonné lions from Peking's (now Beijing's) Imperial Palace guard Chinese court treasures and tomb figures. In the classical world collection, study some of the fine red-figure pottery—a flower of the Greek civilization—and an unusual lead sarcophagus from Tyre that looks like a miniature house. The first floor, closer to home, displays Native American culture, Mideast site explorations, and a small but excellent West African collection of bronze plaques and statues.

The glass-enclosed Museum Café, overlooking the museum's inner gardens, serves cafeteria-style snacks and light meals daily from 10am to 4pm. The Museum Shop has cards and objects brought back by world-hopping graduate archeologists, and The Pyramid Shop has children's items. Stimulating films and concerts—many geared to families—are held virtually every Sunday at the University Museum.

**Admission:** $4 donation adults; $2 students and seniors; free for children under 6.

**Open:** Tues–Sat 10am–4:30pm; Sun 1–5pm. **Closed:** Mon, holidays, and Memorial Day through Labor Day. **Bus:** No. 21, 30, 40, 42, or 90 (from 30th Street Station).

# NEIGHBORHOODS

Philadelphia is a collection of neighborhoods more than it is a unified metropolis. Many neighborhoods have special interest for the visitor because of their history, ethnicity, architecture, or attractions. Below are short descriptions designed to alert you to the possibilities of several neighborhoods. Many individual attractions are discussed elsewhere in this chapter.

## CHINATOWN

Philadelphia has enjoyed a healthy relationship with East Asia since 1784, when a group of merchants sent the *Empress of China* sailing for the China trade. The Chinese themselves arrived later. Emigrating from the West Coast and from western Pennsylvania, where they had been brought as strike breakers, by 1885 several hundred Chinese lived in the area centered around Race Street between 8th and 11th streets, which today is known as Chinatown.

Nowadays it's largely a commercial neighborhood, with Chinese restaurants, groceries, and gift shops abounding. (Also of interest to tourists is the fact that many of the city's largest and cheapest parking facilities are located here.) Strolling through Chinatown, you'll pass under the **Chinese Friendship Gate** at 10th and Arch streets, the largest authentic Chinese gate outside China. Built by mainland artists and dedicated in 1984, it symbolizes the bond between "friendship cities" Tianjin and Philadelphia.

Erected in 1831, the **Chinese Cultural and Community Center,** 125 N. 10th Street (tel. 923-6767), is a rare example of the Peking Mandarin Palace style. At the Chinese New Year many festivities take place here. It's open weekdays from 11am to 3pm, with scheduled tours in July and August.

When you shop in Chinatown, you'll discover many unusual imported gifts, and the delicious smells drifting from the area's numerous restaurants will surely tempt you inside for a post-shopping meal.

**Bus:** 17, 23, 33, 44, 48.

## GERMANTOWN

On the original route west to Reading, Germantown is one of the most ancient settlements in Philadelphia, and it was founded by German émigrés attracted by Penn's religious tolerance. In the 1700s, Germantown Avenue was the location of many citizens of means as well as a busy site of early factories and shops. The 3-mile stretch from Loudoun to Cliveden remains particularly historic today, although now discount stores share the avenue until it slopes through Mount Airy and rises west toward Chestnut Hill's suburban affluence. See Chapter 11, "Easy Excursions from Philadelphia," for more details.

**Transportation:** SEPTA commuter rail or bus 23 from Center City.

## MANAYUNK

The name may sound tacky—but this neighborhood, 4 miles up the Schuylkill River from Center City, has rocketed to gentility in the last 5 years, with many of the city's hottest boutiques, galleries, and café/restaurants on Main Street, overlooking a 19th-century canal adjoining the Schuylkill. Emerging from 19th-century textile mills and abandoned store fronts, Manayunk now celebrates a June-long renaissance, replete with pro cycling races, open houses, and street fairs. It's not much in the way of highbrow history, but the neighborhood is a picturesque and vital place for an afternoon stroll. Favored restaurants here include **Jake's,** 4305 Main Street (tel. 483-0444), and **Jamey's,** 4417 Main Street (tel. 483-5354).

**Bus:** 27, 32, 61.

## OLDE CITY

⭐ Olde City, a rough rectangle overshadowed by the Benjamin Franklin Bridge just north of Independence National Historical Park, is an eclectic blend of row houses dating from William Penn's time, 19th-century commercial warehouses, and 20th-century rehabs à la SoHo in New York City. In Colonial and 19th-century Philadelphia, Market Street separated the social strata—and the northern district, now called Olde City, was the wrong side of the cart tracks. It's not that the inhabitants weren't good-hearted Irish, Scottish, and English, but they worked with their hands and lived where they worked. Highlights from this era include **Christ Church, Elfreth's Alley** (the oldest continuously inhabited street in the country), and **Loxley Court,** between 321 and 323 Arch Street. Many of these 17th- and 18th-century row houses crumbled as loft warehouses accommodated Victorian port activity. The neighborhood gentrified very rapidly from the 1960s until the late 1980s, with lots of crafts and art galleries and their artists. If you're interested in either the very old or the very new, this is the place to spend a few hours, and the odd alleyways between the city grid streets provide nooks for quaint and quiet cafés and shops. The first Friday night of every month is like a giant block party, with all the shops and stores open until 8pm. See Walking Tour 2 in Chapter 8.

**Transportation:** SEPTA bus or subway line to 2nd Street. Bus 5 goes north on 3rd Street, south on 2nd Street.

## QUEEN VILLAGE & SOUTH STREET

**QUEEN VILLAGE**   On a pleasant day you'll want to walk south from Society Hill along the Delaware or 2nd Street (known as "Two Street" among old Philadelphians). The Swedish originally settled this area, along with river islands below the confluence with the Schuylkill. The National Park Service administers **Gloria Dei** (1700), the Swedes' oldest church in the state, and the **American-Swedish Historical Museum** is nearby. The English quickly made this area their own, naming it Southwark after the London district. Now it's called Queen Village, where rehabilitation of the old row houses by the young and affluent mixes with the edges of the Italian district.

**Bus:** 64.

**SOUTH STREET**   Located below Society Hill and above Queen Village, South Street was the city limit in the plan Thomas Holmes drew up for William Penn. Philadelphians still like to think of it as far out, even though it isn't—but a lot of artists, free spirits, and late-night activity do make it the most bohemian area of Center City. At any hour of the day or night, you'll find something happening on South Street.

Don't look for history here. Most of the colonial structures on South and Bainbridge streets succumbed years ago to drab storefronts, and the properties host a mixture of Jewish traditionalists (try **Famous Delicatessen** at 4th and Bainbridge), black Philadelphians (the **Mother Bethel African Methodist Episcopal Church** at 6th and Addison, founded in 1787, has the oldest land title owned continuously by black Americans), aging hippies, punkish teenyboppers, and new entrepreneurs and restaurateurs. With many bookstores, hoagie shops, handcrafted contemporary furniture stores, natural-food stores, European cafés, and art galleries, the South Street renaissance spreads from 2nd to 9th streets, with offshoots into Bainbridge.

**Bus:** 40.

## SOCIETY HILL

✪ This neighborhood, loosely bounded by Walnut and Lombard streets and Front and 7th streets, takes its name from a group of businessmen, the Free Society of Traders, who William Penn persuaded to settle here. Today it's a fashionable section of the old city, just south of Independence National Historical Park, where you can stroll among restored Federal, Colonial, and Georgian homes. Two of Philadelphia's finest houses, the **Hill-Physick-Keith House,** 321 S. 4th Street, and the **Powel House,** 244 S. 3rd Street, are open for guided tours (see the full descriptions, above). For further coverage, see Walking Tour 1 in Chapter 8.

**Bus:** D, 5, 40, 42, 76.

## SOUTH PHILADELPHIA

The rest of the nation first heard of South Philadelphia when Sylvester Stallone brought his Rocky character to silver-screen fame, but this community was one of the earliest settlements along the Delaware. Dutch and Swedish settlers arrived here in the early 17th century and since then have been joined by people of many nations. Successive waves of Jewish and Italian immigrants arrived at Pier 53 in the 19th and 20th centuries. In the 1940s Southern blacks moved north and joined the black community that has resided here since Colonial times. Since the 1950s many Lebanese, Koreans, and Southeast Asians have made South Philly their home. Today it is Philadelphia's most colorful and ethnically diverse neighborhood, although the stereotypes and most of the restaurants and bars are Italian.

Year-round festivities reflect the contributions of South Philadelphia's many ethnic groups. The New Year begins with the famous Mummers' Parade along Broad Street. You can learn more about the history and tradition of Philadelphia mummery at the **New Year's Shooters and Mummers Museum,** 2nd Street and Washington Avenue (tel. 336-3050); it's open Tuesday to Saturday from 9:30am to 6pm, Sunday noon to 5pm. In July, **bocce,** traditional Italian lawn bowling, takes place at Bardascino Park, 10th and Carpenter streets, and in October homage is paid to **St. Mary Magdalena dei Pazzi** on her feast day with a traditional procession carrying the saint's statue through the streets of the neighborhood. The **Sports Complex** along Broad Street south of Packer Avenue contains **Veterans Stadium,** home of the Phillies and the Eagles; the **Spectrum;** and the new **Spectrum II,** home of the 76ers and Flyers. Don't forget the **Italian Market,** described above.

A neighborhood center for free art instruction under the administration of the Philadelphia Museum of Art, the **Samuel S. Fleisher Art Memorial,** 709–721 Catharine Street (tel. 922-3456), houses a choice collection of 13th-, 14th-, and 15th-century art in the Sanctuary, a small Italian-Romanesque church. The memorial also features exhibitions of contemporary Philadelphia artists. It's open Monday to Thursday from noon to 5pm and 6:30 to 9:30pm, Friday from noon to 5pm, and Saturday from 1 to 3pm; it's closed holidays and June to mid-September.

**Transportation:** The Broad Street subway line runs through South Philadelphia with stops at Ellsworth-Federal, Tasker-Morris, Snyder, Oregon, and Pattison streets. Buses through the neighborhood are 5, 23, 47, 50.

## UNIVERSITY CITY

West Philadelphia was farmland that didn't begin to be settled until the first permanent bridge across the Schuylkill in the 1810s. Things didn't really pick up until the **University of Pennsylvania** moved here from 9th and Chestnut streets in the 1870s, though. You ought to wander through the main campus, both for the architecture and for the suitably preppie students. Locust Street has been converted into a walk, and if you stroll west you'll come to an intersection with mobile fruit and refreshment vendors; they're out daily, with student-size prices. On the way back, enter the original college quadrangle, built in 1895 but based on Oxford and Cambridge models, with just a touch of Dutch gables. When classes are in session, the *Daily Pennsylvanian* lists cultural events, such as **Annenberg Theater** productions. This area is also home to **Drexel University; Children's Hospital** and **University Hospital;** and the **Civic Center,** host of many quality shows from boats to horticulture and antiques.

**Bus:** D, 42.

# OUTDOOR ART & PLAZAS

Since the late 1950s, Philadelphia has required that all new developments dedicate 1% of the total cost of the project toward public art. As a result, a burst of modern art has joined the inevitable war memorials, Alexander M. Calder's massive program for City Hall, and the early sculpture placed in Fairmount Park. Of the dozens of pieces, the most notable seem to be Claes Oldenburg's 1976 *Clothespin,* an enigmatic symbol of union opposite City Hall at 15th and Market streets; Robert Indiana's 1978 *LOVE,* a slickly ironic statement opposite the Visitors Center at 16th Street and John F. Kennedy Boulevard; Isamu Noguchi's 1984 *Bolt of Lightning—Franklin Memorial,* at the entrance to the Franklin Bridge at 5th and Vine streets; and, of course, the replica of Rocky Balboa in victory, at the entrance to the Sports Complex in South Philadelphia.

# PARKS & GARDENS

**BENJAMIN FRANKLIN PARKWAY**

The Parkway, a broad diagonal swath linking City Hall to Fairmount Park, wasn't included in Penn's original plan. As the national sesquicentennial year (150th anniversary) rolled around, Philadelphians thought that a grand boulevard in the style of the Champs Elysées was appropriate. In fact, the city's architectural darlings, Cret and Greber, hailed from Paris, and they found an ally in Eli Price, who later headed the Philadelphia Museum of Art, the massive wings of which embrace the Parkway. In summer, a walk from the Visitors Center to the "Museum on the Hill" becomes a flower-bedecked and leafy stroll; but all year round, institutions, public art, and museums enrich the avenue with their handsome facades. Most of the city's parades and festivals pass this way too. The **Frankline Express,** bus route 76, goes both ways every 20 minutes.

   **Logan Circle,** outside the Academy of Natural Sciences (see above), used to be Logan Square before the Parkway was built, and it was a burying ground before becoming a park. The designers of the avenue cleverly made it into a low-landscaped fountain, with graceful figures cast by Alexander Sterling Calder. From this point, you can see how the rows of trees make sense of the diagonal thoroughfare, although all the buildings along the Parkway are aligned with the grid plan. Under the terms of the city permit, The Four Seasons Hotel now landscapes and tends Logan Circle, to magnificent effect.

## FAIRMOUNT PARK

The northern end of the Benjamin Franklin Parkway leads into Fairmount Park, the world's largest landscaped city park, with 8,700 acres of winding creeks, rustic trails, and green meadows, plus 100 miles of jogging, bike, and bridle paths. In addition, this park features more than a dozen historical and cultural attractions, including some of America's finest colonial mansions, as well as gardens, boathouses, America's first zoo, and a Japanese teahouse. See the map on the facing page and the description (p.163) of Philadelphia Zoological Gardens.

   **Bus:** 76 to the Museum of Art entrance; 38 to the upper end.

## PENN'S LANDING

Philadelphia started out as a major freshwater port, and its tourism and services are slowly nudging it back to the water after 50 years of neglect. You can always see freighters moving along the Delaware, but in the 20th century Philadelphia turned its back on the urban waterfront, building I-95 between the city and its port. In 1945, 155 "finger" piers jutted out into the river; today, only 14 remain. Since 1976 the city has bitten off parts of a complete waterfront park at Penn's Landing, on Delaware Avenue between Market and Lombard streets, with an assembly of historic ships, performance and park areas, cruise facilities, and a marina. The city's quincentennial celebration of Columbus's first voyage to America, "Neighbors in the New World," gave this area added impetus in 1992, when tall ships from many lands paid their respects. The lack of private development in response, however, gives Penn's landing a piecemeal but pleasantly spacious feeling.

**ATTRACTIONS IN AND NEAR THE WATER**   Several ships and museums are berthed around a long jetty at Spruce Street. Queen Elizabeth "parked" her yacht *Britannia* here in 1976. From the north down, these attractions are the Philadelphia Maritime Museum's **Workshop on the Water** (tel. 925-7589), a wood boatbuilding shop and classroom housed in a 1939 lighter barge (open from May through October only, Wednesday to Sunday from 9:30am to 4:30pm); the **U.S.S. *Becuna*** (tel. 922-1898), a guppy-class submarine, commissioned in 1944 to serve in Admiral Halsey's South Pacific fleet; the **U.S.S. *Olympia*** (tel. 922-1848), Admiral Dewey's own flagship in the Spanish-American War (tel. 922-1898), with a self-guided three-deck tour taking you past one of the steam engines, the hammocks and mess tables for a crew of 440, Dewey's cabin and stateroom, the battery of eight-inch guns, and the conning tower (admission to both the *Olympia* and the *Becuna* is $3 for adults,

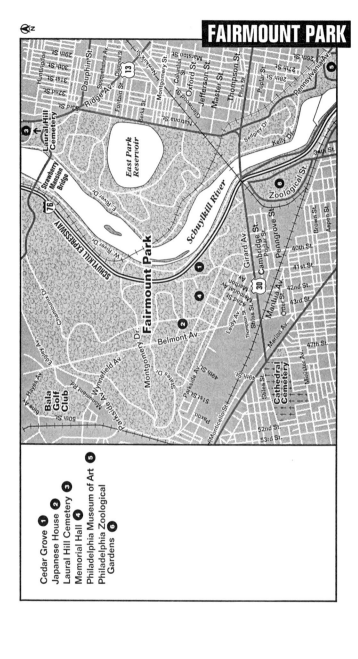

# FAIRMOUNT PARK

Cedar Grove **1**
Japanese House **2**
Laural Hill Cemetery **3**
Memorial Hall **4**
Philadelphia Museum of Art **5**
Philadelphia Zoological
Gardens **6**

$1.50 for children under 12; both are open daily from 10am to 5pm); a **water taxi** (tel. 351-4170) that serves the restaurants and clubs on the piers north of the Benjamin Franklin Bridge as well as the New Jersey State Aquarium in Camden; and the **Liberty Belle II** (tel. 629-1131), a harbor cruise boat. Anchoring the southern end is the **Chart House** restaurant (see Chapter 6 for details).

Another group of boats occupies the landfill directly on the Delaware between Market and Walnut streets. In front of the Port of History and Maritime museums at Walnut Street, the **Delawhale Riverbus** (tel. toll free, 800/634-4027) plies a round-trip route to the New Jersey State Aquarium in Camden every half hour ($2 adults, $1.50 children). The **Gazela Primiero,** a working three-masted, square-rigged wooden ship launched from Portugal in 1883, has visiting hours on Saturday and Sunday from 12:30 to 5:30pm when it's in port. Adjoining are the **Barnegat Lightship** and **Jupiter** a tugboat; all the above are operated by the Philadelphia Ship Preservation Guild (tel. 923-9030); admission $2.50 adults, $2 students. From April to October, the **Spirit of Philadelphia** cruises the dock area on the Delaware, going as far south as the site of Fort Mifflin. Lunch, dinner, and moonlight dance cruises offer a meal prepared in the ship's own gallery, along with drinks and live entertainment. Lunch cruises cost $14 per person; dinner costs $22 on weekdays, $25 on weekends; and moonlight dancing begins at $12. Reservations are required for all cruises (tel. 923-1419).

**MUSEUMS** Opposite Walnut Street, between the two dock areas, the contemporary poured-concrete structure north of the Olympia jetty is the **Port of History Museum.** The museum was opened by the city in December 1981 as a center for international exhibitions of the fine arts, crafts, and design. The good news is that John Carter, the dynamic director of the **Philadelphia Maritime Museum** now at 321 Chestnut Street, will be moving the Maritime to this much-underused site, if $2.7 million needed for renovations comes through. It's open Wednesday to Sunday from 10am to 4:30pm; admission is $2 for adults, $1 for children. Even if you don't go in, take in the great views from the upper terraces.

**PLAZA & PARK AREAS** On a walk north along the river, charts help you identify the Camden shoreline opposite and the funnels of passing freighters. The hill that connects the shoreline with the current Front Street level has been enhanced with the festive **Great Plaza,** a multitiered, treelined amphitheater that hosts many Visitors and Convention Bureau festivals, such as Jambalaya Jam. The terrace itself is a wonderfully landscaped and informative view of quirky facts about the site and city, with plenty of benches. At Delaware Avenue and Spruce Street, the sober 1987 **Philadelphia Vietnam Veteran Memorial** lists 641 local casualties.

**Admission:** Free.

**Open:** 24 hrs. **Bus:** 21 on Chestnut Street to Front Street. No. 42 east on Chestnut Street to 2nd Street, down 2nd Street to Dock Street, and then down to Walnut Street. **On Foot:** Pedestrian walkways across Front Street on Market, Chestnut, or Walnut street; Front Street connects directly at Spruce Street. **Car:** Take I-95 northbound or southbound. Take Exit 16 and make a left onto Columbus Boulevard. From I-76, take 676 to I-95 south. Ample parking is available on site.

# ZOO & AQUARIUM

**PHILADELPHIA ZOOLOGICAL GARDENS, 34st St. and Girard Ave. Tel. 243-1100.**

⭐ The Philadelphia Zoo was the nation's first, opened in 1874, but by the late 1970s the 42 acres tucked into West Fairmount Park were run-down and had few financial resources. That's when Bill Donaldson, Cincinnati's former hotshot city manager, who died tragically in the winter of 1992, stepped in. Donaldson turned things around at the zoo, aiming to make it not only an excellent regional zoo but also one on a par with the nation's reigning animal kingdoms, such as the San Diego Zoo and Washington's National Zoo. Some visitors think that he's come pretty close. Donaldson, who kept a 300-animal menagerie in his backyard when he was a kid, built a new "World of Primates" exhibit that gives the visitor the illusion that he or she is actually in the forest. The monkeys themselves now have a new home on four naturally planted islands, where a variety of primate species live together naturally, much as they would in the wild. (This area is open in summer only; the monkeys are segregated in the Primate Pavilion during the rest of the year.) Visitors walking through the exhibit are separated from the animals only by moats, so they can see families of lemurs, gorillas, and other primates interacting with one another in a setting as close to natural as possible.

The old Bird House also has been changed to the new Jungle Bird Walk, where you can walk among free-flying birds. The glass enclosures have been replaced with wire mesh so that the birdsong can now be heard from both sides. More than 100 plant species have been imported for the Bird Walk, with lighting that gives them 12-hour days.

As part of the zoo's concern to educate visitors about animal life, a spectacular children's exhibit, The Treehouse ($1), was opened in 1985. It contains six larger-than-life habitats for kids of all ages to explore—oversize eggs to hatch from, an oversize honeycomb to crawl through, and a four-story ficus tree to climb through and see life from a bird's-eye view. The very popular Camel Rides ($1.50) start next to The Treehouse. A Children's Zoo (50¢) portion of the gardens lets your kids pet and feed some baby zoo and farm animals; this area closes 30 minutes before the zoo proper. Pony rides ($1) also are given here.

Don't miss the Reptile House, which bathes its snakes and tortoises with simulated tropical thunderstorms on the hour on weekends and three times a day on weekdays. Cavorting antelopes, zebras, and giraffes coexist on the African Plains exhibit, and the bears look extremely pleased with their new watering hole. For a quick survey, consider the Monorail Safari (operated April to November, costing $2 for adults, $1.50 for children on Monday to Friday, 50¢ more on Saturday and Sunday). It circumnavigates the zoo in 18 minutes with a prerecorded narrative. Many of the outside exhibits have these, too, and if you buy a storybook key (75¢) you can trigger the tapes.

Finally, in April 1992 the zoo opened a $6-million Carnivore Kingdom, featuring snow leopards, jaguars, river otters, and other animals in native environments. Feeding time is around 11am for the smaller carnivores, at 3pm for the tigers and lions.

The zoo has several snack areas, and the Picnic Grove has been recently refurbished with new landscaping and Victorian benches and tables. A cafeteria-style restaurant with an airy, sky-lit dining room and outdoor tables stands next to the Rare Mammal House. Look for a new education hall and an animal health-care facility by 1993.

**Admission:** $5.75 adults; $4.75 seniors and children 2–11; under 2 free. A family membership for $35 might be worth it.

**Open:** Most of year, Mon–Fri 10am–4:15pm. Winter, Sat–Sun 10am–4:45pm. Summer, Mon–Fri 10am–4:45pm; Sat–Sun 10am–5:45pm. **Closed:** Some holidays. Parking is available. **Bus:** 38, 76.

### THOMAS H. KEAN NEW JERSEY STATE AQUARIUM, 1 South Riverside Dr., P.O. Box 95004, Camden, NJ 08101. Tel. 609/365-3300.

This aquarium opened in February 1992 with state funding of $52 million, as the first step in reclaiming the once-vital (and now denuded) Camden waterfront with a hotel and marina, a trade center, and an office-and-commercial development. As an aquarium, it fills a true niche in the Delaware Valley, only minutes away from Philadelphia.

Up to 3,000 fish live here. The main attraction is a 760,000-gallon tank, the second largest (next to Epcot Center's) in the country, with stepped seat/benches arranged in a Greek amphitheater on the first floor. Three times a day, a diver answers questions through a "scuba phone." This window wall is by far the best; parents of younger children will find few other flat edges for them to stand on for views. This tank also contains sharks, rockfish, a shipwreck, and a mock-up of underwater Hudson canyon off the Jersey coast. Also on the first floor is an open-air New Jersey beach setting, complete with shore birds; a pine barrens stream; and a salt marsh. The second floor has more didactic explorations of ocean life, fish senses, and water babies. Touch tanks are on both floors.

Between the ticket pavilion and the building is a reproduction of a Delaware Water Gap brook stocked with trout and a 170,000-gallon outdoor tank with recuperating Atlantic seals. The Riverview Café serves basic fast food; the outdoor seating is frequently windswept.

**Admission:** $8.50 adults; $7 students and seniors; $5.50 children 2–11; children under 2 free. You can reserve admission (recommended) through TicketMaster, toll free 800/922-6572 (handling charge).

**Open:** Daily 9:30am–5:30pm. **Closed:** New Year's Day, Easter, Thanksgiving, and Christmas. **Car:** From I-676 eastbound (Vine Street Expressway/Benjamin Franklin Bridge [90¢]) or from I-295/New Jersey Turnpike westbound, take the Mickle Boulevard exit and follow the signs to the aquarium. The **Delawhale Riverbus** ferry from the Port of History Museum at Penn's Landing directly to the aquarium is $2 for adults and $1.50 for children each way.

# 3. COOL FOR KIDS

Philadelphia is one of the country's great family destinations: It has a great many attractions for different types of kids, and because it's so walkable and neighborhoodlike, a respite or an amenity is never far away. Since so many of the family attractions are explained in more detail elsewhere in this or other chapters, I'll restrict myself to a list of the basics. See "Fast Facts: Philadelphia" in Chapter 4 for babysitting options.

A monthly publication on what to do with kids in Philadelphia, *Metrokids,* is available at the Visitors Center, 16th Street and John F. Kennedy Boulevard.

**MUSEUMS & SIGHTS**　In Center City, there are the **Please Touch Museum,** 210 N. 21st Street; **Franklin Institute,** Benjamin Franklin Parkway and 20th Street; and the **Academy of Natural Sciences,** the Parkway and 19th Street. The **Free Library of Philadelphia Children's Department** across Logan Circle at Vine and 19th streets is a joy, with a separate entrance, 100,000 books and microcomputers in a playgroundlike space, and weekend hours. Around Independence Hall are the **Liberty Bell** at Market and 5th streets; **Franklin Court,** between Market and Chestnut streets at 4th Street; the waterfront at **Penn's Landing,** off Front Street; and, of course, the guided tour of **Independence Hall.** You can also take the ferry from Penn's Landing to the new **aquarium** in Camden. In Fairmount Park are the **bicycle rentals** along Kelly (East River) Drive and the **zoo** in West Fairmount Park.

**SHOPPING AREAS**　These include **Liberty Place** on Chestnut Street between 16th and 17th streets, with a wonderful food court and distinguished rotunda and escalators; **The Gallery** at Market East, at Market and 8th streets; the **Bourse** at Chestnut and 5th streets; and the outdoor **Head House Square** at Spruce and 2nd streets. Also, see the children's fashions and toys sections of Chapter 9.

**PLAYGROUNDS**　**Rittenhouse Square** at 18th and Walnut streets has a small playground and space to eat and relax. Other imaginative urban playgrounds on this side of Center City are **Schuylkill River Park** at Pine and 26th streets and at 26th Street and the Benjamin Franklin Parkway, opposite the art museum. From Society Hill, try the **Delancey Park** at Delancey between 3rd and 4th streets (with lots of fountains and animal sculptures to climb on) or **Starr Garden** at 6th and Lombard streets. The best in Fairmount Park is the **Smith Memorial** (head north on 33rd Street, then take a left into the park at Oxford Avenue).

**EXCURSIONS**　There are **Sesame Place,** based on public TV's *Sesame Street,* in Langhorne, and the working and participatory **Quarry Valley Farm** in Lahaska—both in Bucks County; plus there's **Ridley Creek State Park** and its 17th-century working farm in Montgomery County.

**ENTERTAINMENT**　The **Philadelphia Marionette Theater** has heavily reserved programs in Belmont Mansion in West Fairmount Park; call 879-1213 for details.

**Bill Cosby,** fresh from 8 years on "The Cosby Show," has signed a contract to produce his new syndicated show, "You Bet Your Life," at the WHYY-TV studios at 150 N. 6th St., Philadelphia, PA 19106. At press time, he was scheduled to videotape 196 episodes through March 1993, with more in the works should the show prove a hit. Tickets may be reserved in advance by calling 215/574-3300 or toll free 800/942-9295 on Monday to Friday from 10am to 5pm.

The **Philadelphia Museum of Art** has dedicated itself to producing Sunday-morning and early-afternoon programs for children, without fail and at minimal or no charge. Your kids could wind up drawing pictures of armor or watching a puppet theater about dragons, visiting a Chinese court, or playing with Picasso-style cubism. Call 763-8100, or 787-5488 for 24-hour information.

# 4. ORGANIZED TOURS

**BUS TOURS** **Grayline Tours,** P.O. Box 5985, Philadelphia, PA 19103 (tel. 215/569-3666), offers three different sightseeing tours of the Philadelphia area, ranging from a 3-hour historic tour to a short cultural tour to a combination of both lasting 4½ hours. Tours, scheduled from late spring through October, range from $16 to $32 for adults and from $10 to $14 for children under 12. All tours depart from the Visitors Center at 16th Street and John F. Kennedy Boulevard, many Center City hotels, and the Holiday Inn–Independence Mall.

Those double-decker buses decked out like trolleys, clanging along the city streets, are from **American Trolley Tours** (tel. 333-2119). Tours of historic areas, conducted by guides in the climate-controlled vehicles, leave mornings and afternoons from the Visitors Center and from the Independence National Park Visitor Center at 3rd and Walnut streets. A similar venture, with guides in colonial dress, is **Tracey Tours** (tel. 457-8660).

**WALKING TOURS** To explore the four-block historic district at your own pace with the benefit of a prerecorded commentary, you can rent an AudioWalk and Tour cassette player and tape. The narration describes each attraction as you walk from site to site. An illustrated souvenir map comes with the tape. Players and cassettes are available daily from **AudioWalk and Tour,** Norman Rockwell Museum, 6th and Sansom streets (tel. 925-1234), on Washington Square. It's open from 10am to 6pm on Monday to Saturday, 11am to 5pm on Sunday. The charge is $8 for one person, $18 from two to six people. If you prefer to purchase the cassette and use your own recorder, the cost is $10.95.

If you wish to stroll through this area or one of the other neighborhoods without the benefit of prerecorded commentary, consult the walking tours described in Chapter 8.

**CANDLELIGHT STROLLS** From May through October, evening tours of the historic area, led by costumed guides, leave from the City Tavern at 6:30pm. Tours of Olde City (Friday) and Society Hill (Thursday and Saturday) take 90 minutes and end at NewMarket; the cost is $5 for adults, $4 for seniors and children. Call 735-3123 for reservations with **Centipede Tours, Inc.,** 1315 Walnut Street.

**HORSE & CARRIAGE TOURS** To get the feel of Philadelphia as it was (well, almost—asphalt's a lot smoother than cobblestones!), try a narrated horse-drawn carriage ride. Operated daily by the **76 Carriage Co.,** (tel. 923-8516), tours begin at 5th and Chestnut streets in front of Independence Hall from 10am to 5pm, with later hours in summer. Fares range from $10 for 15 minutes to $20 for 30 minutes, with a maximum of four per carriage. Reservations are not necessary.

**BOATING TOURS**   Two choices are available at Penn's Landing. The *Spirit of Philadelphia* (tel. 923-1419) at the Great Plaza combines lunch, brunch, or dinner with a cruise on a 600-person passenger ship, fully climate-controlled, with two enclosed decks and two open-air decks. Trips, which require reservations, are for the noon to 2pm lunch buffet ($17.95 for adults, $8.75 for children) or the Sunday brunch ($19.95 for adults, $10.95 for children); evening dinner cruises are daily from 7 to 10pm ($30.95 per person on Monday to Friday, $34.95 per person on Saturday and Sunday); and moonlight party cruises are on Friday and Saturday from 11:30pm to 2am ($15 per person, with a cash bar).

The *Liberty Belle II* (tel. 629-1131) boards from the Chart House restaurant at the southern end of Penn's Landing and can accommodate up to 475 passengers on three decks. It offers the following sailings: lunch daily from noon to 2pm, with banjo entertainment ($17.95 per person); dinner and dancing with DJ onboard from 7 to 10pm Monday to Saturday and from 4 to 7pm on Sunday ($27.95 per person Sunday through Thursday, $29.95 per person Friday and Saturday); Sunday brunch 12:30 to 2:30pm ($19.95 per person); and moonlight cruises 11:30pm to 2am on Friday and Saturday nights ($19.95 per person).

With the opening of the new New Jersey State Aquarium, the new *Delawhale Riverbus* (tel. toll free 800/634-4027) provides a 10-minute crossing from a landing just outside the Port of History (and soon-to-be Maritime) Museum at Penn's Landing. There's a large interior to the ferry, and the views of the Philadelphia skyline are great, although the Aquarium is the only possible destination in New Jersey. Departures from Penn's Landing are on the quarter hour and every half hour thereafter; from Camden, on the hour and half hour. Summer hours are Monday to Friday from 7am to 6:45pm, Saturday from 9am to 11:45pm, and Sunday from 9am to 7:45pm; from mid-September through mid-May, the weekend hours are curtailed at 6:45pm. One-way fares are $2 for adults, $1.50 for children and seniors.

# 5. SPORTS & RECREATION

## SPECTATOR SPORTS

Philadelphia fields teams in every major sport and boasts a splendid complex at the end of South Broad Street to house them all. **Veterans Stadium** (tel. 686-1776) is a graceful bowl with undulating ramps that can seat 58,000 for the Phillies in baseball and 68,000 for the Eagles in football. **The Spectrum II,** being built at press time, will house the pro hockey and basketball teams; until it does, these teams will continue to rely on **The Spectrum** (tel. 336-3600), which also functions as one of the best rock-concert forums around. It also hosts the U.S. Pro Indoor Tennis Championships.

All these are next to one another and can be reached via a 10-minute subway ride straight down South Broad Street to Pattison Avenue ($1.50). The same fare will put you on the SEPTA bus C, which goes down Broad Street slower but with a bit more safety late at night.

Professional sports aren't the only game in town, though. Philadelphia has a lot of colleges, and **Franklin Field** and the **Palestra** dominate West Philadelphia on 33rd below Walnut Street. The Penn Relays, the first intercollegiate and amateur track event in the nation, books Franklin Field on the last weekend in April. Regattas pull along the Schuylkill all spring, summer, and fall, within sight of Fairmount Park's mansions.

A call to Teletron (tel. toll free 800/233-4050) or TicketMaster (tel. 212/507-7171 in New York, 215/336-2000 in Philadelphia) can get you tickets in many cases before you hit town.

**BASEBALL** The **Philadelphia Phillies,** Box 7575, Philadelphia, PA 19101 (tel. 463-1000 for ticket information, 463-5300 for daily game information), play at Veterans Stadium, Broad Street and Pattison Avenue. Day games usually begin at 1:35pm, regular night games at 8:05pm on Friday, at 7:35pm on other days. When there's a twi-night double-header, it begins at 5:35pm. The huge computerized scoreboard and the antics that follow a Phillies home run will leave you laughing and amazed.

Tickets for the Phillies have been increasing rapidly in cost; box seats overlooking the field are around $15, and the cheapest bleacher seats are $6, if you're over 14. For a steady draw like the Phillies, though, they have an awful lot of special nights, so you could cash in on either reduced rates or some baseball-related paraphernalia.

**BASKETBALL** The **Philadelphia 76ers,** Box 25050, Philadelphia, PA 19147, play about 40 games at the Spectrum. Call 339-7676 for ticket information; tickets range from $8 to $18. There's always a good half-time show, and the promotion department works overtime with special nights, especially involving 76ers T-shirts.

There are five major college basketball teams in the Philadelphia area, and the newspapers print schedules of their games. If you can name any more than 1985 NCAA champion **Villanova,** you probably don't need to look at the newspaper. (The other four are the **University of Pennsylvania, LaSalle, St. Joseph's,** and **Temple.**) Most games are at the Palestra, with tickets going for $4 to $6. Call 898-4747 to find out about ticket availability.

**BICYCLING** The CoreStates Pro Cycling Championship, held each June, is actually a top world event in the cycling world. The 156-mile races starts and finishes along the Benjamin Franklin Parkway.

**BOATING** From April to September, you can watch regattas on the Schuylkill River, which have been held since the earliest days of "the Schuylkill Navy" a century ago. The **National Association of Amateur Oarsmen** (tel. 769-2068) and the **Boathouse Association** (tel. 686-0052) have a complete schedules of races. The Dad Vail Regatta is one of the best known.

**FOOTBALL** Football, without a doubt, is Philadelphia's favorite sport, even though football days in Philadelphia resemble Hobbes's state of nature: cold, nasty, brutish, and short. It will take all your ingenuity to come up with tickets for a game, since all **Philadelphia Eagles** games (at Veterans Stadium, Philadelphia, PA 19148) are popular, especially now that their young, talented team is getting on track. Call 463-5500 for ticket advice; there are over 70 ticket agencies in town that can help you track down ducats. The games start at 1 or 4pm, and tickets cost up to $40.

**HORSE RACING**   The racing closest to Philadelphia is at **Garden State Park,** N.J. 70 and Haddonfield Road in Cherry Hill, New Jersey (tel. 609/488-8400), which runs thoroughbred races in the spring. Call for exact schedules, but the first post time is usually on Monday to Friday at 7:30pm and on Saturday at 1pm. Clubhouse admission is $4, and grandstand admission is $2.50.

For more thoroughbred horse racing, **Philadelphia Park** (the old Keystone Track) has races every day except Monday from January 1 to February 13 (post time is 12:30pm) and from June 15 to December 31 (post time is 1pm). The $2.50 admission includes parking and a program; the park is on Street Road in Bensalem, half a mile from Exit 28 on the Pennsylvania Turnpike. Call 639-9000 for information.

The **Turf Club Parlor and Dining,** 7 Penn Center, 1635 Market Street, on the concourse and lower mezzanine levels (tel. 245-1556), features 270 color video monitors and an ersatz art deco design; it brings the wagering to you in the comfort of Center City.

**ICE HOCKEY**   The Spectrum rocks to the **Philadelphia Flyers** from fall to spring, and their tickets are even harder to get than the Eagles'. Call 755-9700 for ticket information; if you can find some, they'll cost between $12 and $23.

**TENNIS**   Philadelphia has several world-class tournaments annually. February brings the **Ebel U.S. Professional Indoor Championships** at the Spectrum, with $600,000 in prize money; call 947-2530 for information. The women's invitational held at Haverford College (tel. 896-1000) in late September has attracted top players, including Martina Navratilova, and the late-summer **USTA Senior Men's Grass Court Championships** at Germantown Cricket Club (tel. 438-9900) can bring you face-to-face with former greats.

**TRACK & FIELD**   The city hosts the **Penn Relays,** the oldest and still the largest amateur track meet in the country, in late April at Franklin Field. There's a November annual **Marathon** and a September **Philadelphia Distance Run,** a half-marathon; the latter is becoming a world-class event. Call 686-0053 for more details.

## RECREATION

I can't begin to make a complete list of the number of leisure sports and recreations in which you can indulge while in Philadelphia, so contact the Department of Recreation (tel. 686-3600). The following is merely a sample:

**BICYCLING**   From March through November, you can rent 10-speeds or mountain bikes at **Fairmount Park Bike Rental** (tel. 236-4359), just north of the Museum of Art on 1 Boathouse Row, Kelly (East Fairmount) Drive. The biking is flat near the Schuylkill on either side but loops up sharply near Laurel Hill Cemetery or Manayunk. Rental rates are $6 per hour (deposit and ID are required). It's open Monday to Friday from 10:30am to 8pm, Saturday and Sunday from 9am to 8pm.

**BOATING**   You can rent rowboats, canoes, and sailboats (sorry, no sculls) at the Schuylkill **Public Canoe House** (tel. 225-3560), Kelly Drive south of Strawberry Mansion Bridge. The charge is $10 per hour, with a $10 deposit required. It's open March through November, daily from 10am to one hour before dusk. Outside of the city, try **Northbrook Canoe Co.,** north of Rt. 842 in Northbrook on Brandywine Creek (tel. 793-2279) or **Point Pleasant,** on Rt. 32, 7 miles north of the New Hope exit on I-95, with canoeing, inner-tubing, and rafting on the Delaware River (tel. 297-8823).

**FISHING**   It's true that **Pennypack Creek** and **Wissahickon Creek** are stocked from mid-April through December with trout and muskie and provide good, even rustic, conditions. A required license of $12.25 for Pennsylvania residents or $20.25 for out-of-staters is available at such sporting-goods stores as I. Goldberg or at the Municipal Services Building near the Visitors Center. Out of the city, **Ridley Creek** and its **state park** (tel. 566-4800) and **Brandywine Creek** at Hibernia Park (tel. 384-0290) are stocked with several kinds of trout.

**GOLF**   The city of Philadelphia operates 5 municipal courses out of the more than 100 in the region. All have 18 holes, and the current fees are $14 on Monday to Friday and $16 on Saturday and Sunday. Call 877-8813 or the numbers below for more information on **Cobbs Creek and Karakung** (two adjacent courses), 7800 Lansdowne Avenue (tel. 877-8707); **Franklin D. Roosevelt,** 20th Street and Pattison Avenue (tel. 462-8997); **J. F. Byrne,** Frankford Avenue and Eden Street (tel. 632-8666); **Juniata,** M and Cayuga streets (tel. 743-4060); and **Walnut Lane,** Walnut Lane and Henry Avenue (tel. 482-3370).

Among the better county-operated courses outside the city are **Montgomeryville Golf Club,** Route 202 (tel. 855-6112); **Paxon Hollow Golf Club,** Paxon Hollow Road in Marple Township (tel. 353-0220); and **Valley Forge Golf Club,** 401 North Gulph Road, King of Prussia (tel. 337-1776).

**HEALTH CLUBS**   Many people regard a visit to the health club as part of their normal routine, when traveling or not. Those staying at The Four Seasons, the Rittenhouse, Sheraton Society Hill, or The Hotel Atop the Bellevue can count on in-house facilities at an additional charge. Most other moderately priced hotels have at least a few exercycles and an aerobics space; the KormanSuites, 4 blocks from Logan Circle, has a full gym room, pool, and tennis court. Near Society Hill, the top health club that admits per-day guests is **World Gym,** 834 Chestnut Street (tel. 592-9644). Opened in fall 1988, it provides an understanding staff, large Universal weight machines, free weights, and several aerobics classes daily. The cost is $15 per guest, unless your hotel has arrangements for reduced fees. It's open Monday to Friday from 6am to 9pm, Saturday from 9am to 5pm, and Sunday from 9am to 3pm. Another alternative closer to midtown is the **12th Street Gym,** 204 S. 12th Street (tel. 985-4092), a revamped version of a 1930s men's club with a pool, courts for squash and racquetball, and weights and aerobics rooms. It's open Monday to Friday from 6am to 11pm, Saturday and Sunday from 9am to 7pm. The basic rate is $10 per guest.

**HIKING**   **Fairmount Park** (tel. 686-3616) has dozens of miles of paths, and the extensions into Wissahickon Creek are quite unspoiled, with dirt roads and no auto traffic. Farther afield, **Horseshoe Trail** (tel. 664-0719) starts at Routes 23 and 252 in Valley Forge State Park and winds 120 miles west marked by yellow horseshoes until it meets the Appalachian Trail.

**HORSEBACK RIDING**   There are 80 paths of riding trails in Fairmount Park, the Wissahickon, and Pennypack Park within city limits, and Chester and Brandywine counties are famous for horsemanship, from fox hunting to the Winterthur Point-to-Point races. Unfortunately, insurance costs have made it unprofitable for most riding stables to allow visitors to rent horses. The only riding stable within city limits that does is **Harry's Riding Stables** (tel. 335-9975), Holmesburg Avenue near Pennypack Park. It's open 7 days a week from 9am to 8pm, and 7 or 8 horses are always available, with rates of $15 per hour for guided trail rides with Western saddles. The easiest directions from Center City are via I-95 north. Take the Academy Road exit, following the exit ramp to the left onto Academy until the first light; then turn left onto Frankford Avenue and continue for two miles. After a hill, there's an intersection with a railroad trestle that passes above Frankford. Before going under it, take the dirt road on the left and follow 300 yards to the white barn building on the right.

**ICE SKATING**   It rarely gets cold enough in Philadelphia for ponds and creeks to freeze over. Although the city operates several artificial rinks, your best bet for finding a rink near Center City is the **University of Pennsylvania Class of '23 Rink,** 3130 Walnut Street (tel. 387-9223). It's open daily to the public for about two hours in the afternoon.

**RUNNING & JOGGING**   Here again, **Fairmount Park** has more trails than you could cover in a week. An 8.2-mile loop starts at the front of the Museum of Art, up the east bank of the Schuylkill, across the river at Falls Bridge, and back down to the museum.

**SWIMMING**   Philadelphia has 86 municipal swimming pools, and many hotels have small lap versions. Municipal pools are open daily from 11am to 7pm and are free. Two of the best are **Cobbs Creek,** 63rd and Spruce streets, and **FDR Pool,** Broad and Pattison in South Philadelphia. Call 686-1776 for details.

**TENNIS**   Some 115 courts are scattered throughout **Fairmount Park,** and you can get a tourist permit for their use by calling 686-0152. You might also try the University of Pennsylvania's indoor courts at the **Robert P. Levy Tennis Pavilion,** 3130 Walnut Street (tel. 898-4741). Rates are $27 for two visitors until 4pm, $31 for two after 4pm.

# CHAPTER 8

# STROLLING
# AROUND
# PHILADELPHIA

1. **INDEPENDENCE NATIONAL HISTORICAL PARK & SOCIETY HILL**
2. **OLDE CITY**
3. **MIDTOWN, RITTENHOUSE SQUARE & LOWER BENJAMIN FRANKLIN PARKWAY**

**P**hiladelphia is probably the most compact, walkable major city in the United States, just as it was in 1776. It's fascinating to see the progress of the centuries and unexpected juxtapositions on a random walk, always noting that the nearer you are to the Delaware, the older (and smaller) the buildings are likely to be. The walking tours mapped out below are specifically designed to enhance your ability to cover the most worthwhile attractions and to recoup your strength along the way.

## WALKING TOUR 1 — INDEPENDENCE NATIONAL HISTORICAL PARK & SOCIETY HILL

**Start:** Visitor Center, 3rd and Walnut streets.
**Finish:** City Tavern, 2nd and Walnut streets; optional extension to Penn's Landing.
**Time:** 6–7 hours.
**Best Time:** Start between 9 and 11am to avoid hour-long waits for Independence Hall tours.

Start your tour at the:

1. **Visitor Center** in Independence National Historical Park, 3rd and Walnut streets. This handsome brick building was built for the 1976 Bicentennial celebration and maintains spotless restrooms and cool benches as well as providing pamphlets and maps of the park, free tickets (limited in number) for the Bishop White and Todd Houses (see below), and information about special tours or special daily events. The John Huston–directed film *Independence* is shown without charge every half hour. There are a small exhibition area, currently devoted to the Bill of Rights, and a substantial quality gift shop and bookstore.

   Just opposite the Visitor Center is the:
2. **First Bank of the United States** (1797), not open to the

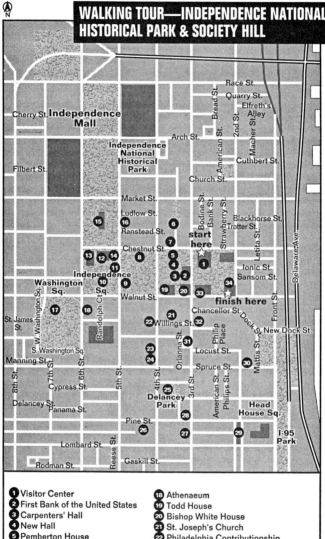

# WALKING TOUR—INDEPENDENCE NATIONAL HISTORICAL PARK & SOCIETY HILL

1 Visitor Center
2 First Bank of the United States
3 Carpenters' Hall
4 New Hall
5 Pemberton House
6 Franklin Court
7 Philadelphia Maritime Museum
8 Second Bank of the United States
9 Library Hall
10 Independence Square
11 Philosophical Hall
12 Independence Hall
13 Congress Hall
14 Old City Hall
15 The Liberty Bell
16 The Bourse
17 Washington Square

18 Athenaeum
19 Todd House
20 Bishop White House
21 St. Joseph's Church
22 Philadelphia Contributionship
23 Mutual Assurance Company
24 Old St. Mary's Church
25 Hill-Physick-Keith House
26 Old Pine Presbyterian
27 St. Peter's Episcopal Church
28 Kosciuszko National Memorial
29 Head House Square
30 Man Full of Trouble Tavern
31 Powel House
32 St. Paul's Episcopal Church
33 Philadelphia Merchants' Exchange
34 City Tavern

public but a superb example of Federal architecture, as old and as graceful as a Roman rotunda. The idea for this building derived from Alexander Hamilton. The reliance on the currencies of the 13 new states hampered commerce and travel, and he proposed a single bank for loans and deposits. The Bank started in Carpenters' Hall but moved here on the completion of the building. The mahogany American eagle on the pediment over the Corinthian entrance columns is a famous—and rare—example of 18th-century sculpture.

Behind the First Bank, the Park Service cleared much of the block (as throughout the Historic Park area), leaving historic structures and establishing 18th-century gardens and lawns. To the right, a walkway leads to the mid-block:

3. **Carpenters' Hall,** which was a newly built guild hall when the First Continental Congress met here in 1774 (see Chapter 7 for a fuller description). Just north of this, you'll find:

4. **New Hall,** a modern copy of a hall built in 1791 for rent by the Carpenters' Company. With the federal government based in Philadelphia until Washington, D.C., was habitable, the U.S. government took the space as the first headquarters of the War (now Defense) Department. This building now houses the Marine Corps Museum, since they were founded at Tun Tavern nearby; you can see uniforms and swords that fought on "the shores of Tripoli" as well as the medals that decorated those uniforms.

A few steps north on Chestnut Street proper is:

5. **Pemberton House,** another reconstruction. Joseph Pemberton, a Quaker merchant of sugar and madeira, had just built this fine Georgian home when the Second Continental Congress cut back on British imports, in the aftermath of the gunfire at Concord and Lexington. After Pemberton went bankrupt, the house was razed in 1862, only to be reconstructed a century later. The development of the infant U.S. army and navy are the subjects here. The basement features continuous showings of a military history of the Revolutionary War, which followed a slow pattern of British advances, defeats, and regroupings to the south. The main theater of battle moved from Boston in 1775 to New York, New Jersey, and Pennsylvania in 1777 and 1778, with a final bottleneck for the British at Chesapeake Bay in 1781. Pushbutton dioramas illuminate many of the crucial battles. Of course, most Americans don't realize that the war for the colonies was only part of a British global military effort in Europe and India, and it never engaged British attentions fully. The second floor's highlight is the model gun deck of a frigate, with instructions on maneuvering for a naval battle.

The other side of Chestnut Street is a handsome collection of 19th-century banks and commercial facades, including the 1867 **First National Bank** at no. 315 and the **Philadelphia National Bank** at no. 323. The Chestnut Street entrance to:

6. **Franklin Court** is nestled here (see Chapter 7 for a full description of this wonderful tribute to Benjamin Franklin's final home and spirit).

Virtually across Chestnut Street at no. 321 is the:

7. **Philadelphia Maritime Museum** (tel. 925-5439). It's been a

marvelous museum here for about 25 years, but it may be merging with the Port of History Museum at Penn's Landing (see Chapter 7). If it hasn't yet, it's a fine exploration of how the Delaware Valley influenced the history and trade of the region. The building itself is an unusual Victorian specimen, in yellow brick and granite facings. "Man and the Sea" on the first floor displays navigation and sailing tools from over 300 years and has a splendid collection of scrimshaw. A special exhibition features displays on the 1912 sinking of the *Titanic* and recent efforts to salvage relics and valuables from that ill-fated liner. Admission is $2.50 for adults, $1 for students and seniors. The museum is open Tuesday to Saturday from 10am to 5pm, Sunday from 1 to 5pm.

Walk west along Chestnut Street or back in the gardens, crossing 4th Street until you get to the mid-block:

**8. Second Bank of the United States.** Its strong Greek columns have corroded somewhat, but the bank still holds interest. The Second Bank was chartered by Congress in 1816 for a term of 20 years, again at a time when the country felt that it needed reliable circulating money. The building (1819–24), designed like the Merchants Exchange by William Strickland, is adapted from the Parthenon, and the Greeks would have been proud of its capable director, Nicholas Biddle. An elitist to the core, he was the man Andrew Jackson and his supporters had in mind when they complained about private individuals controlling public government. Urged by Henry Clay for reasons of political capital, Biddle asked prematurely for the renewal of the charter, making this the issue of the 1832 presidential election. "Old Hickory" vetoed the charter and won the election; this increased the money supply but ruined Biddle and the bank.

The federal government bought the building in 1844 for about half its original cost of $500,000 and used it as the Customs House until 1934, when the National Park Service appropriated it as a portrait gallery of early Americans. The collection contains many of the oldest "gallery portraits" in the country, painted by Charles Willson Peale and once displayed in the Long Room of Independence Hall. Sully, Neagle, Stuart, and Allston also are represented. The second floor (open in summer; ask a guard in winter) has an excellent selection of engraved scenes of old Philadelphia, portraits, and other temporary exhibits. These scenes gave National Park Service archaeologists a good idea of how the reconstructed buildings should look.

**REFUELING STOP** A **tea garden** in the adjoining holly garden, staffed by the Friends of Independence National Historical Park, provides ice cream and cool drinks from noon to 5pm from mid-May to mid-September.

Just west of the Second Bank lies:

**9. Library Hall,** the 1954 reconstruction of Benjamin Franklin's old Library Company, which was the first lending library of its type in the colonies. The Library Company is now at 1314 Locust Street (see Walking Tour 3, below); this graceful Federal building houses the library of the American Philosophical Society based across the street. The collection is entrancing, including Franklin's will, a copy of William Penn's 1701 Charter of Privileges, and Jefferson's own handwritten copy of the Declaration of Independence. The exhibits center on the history of science in America. The library's hours follow the Park schedule.

The pull of great government will lead you across 5th Street to:

10. **Independence Square,** where on July 8, 1776, John Nixon read the Declaration of Independence to the assembled city. You'll be at the back of the official trio of **Independence Hall, Congress Hall,** and **Old City Hall** on Chestnut Street between 5th and 6th streets.

On your right is:

11. **Philosophical Hall,** the home of the American Philosophical Society. The society is a prestigious honor roll of America's outstanding intellects and achievers founded by Ben Franklin. The building's interior is not open to the public, but look for traces of old Georgian springing into new Federal architecture, such as fan-shaped windows, larger windows, and more elaborate doorsteps. In Franklin's day, philosophers were more often than not industrious young men with scientific and learned interests, so the society included most intellectually advanced citizens.

To your left is:

12. **Independence Hall,** grand, graceful, and one of democracy's true shrines (see Chapter 7 for a full description). Ranger-led 35-minute tours depart every 15 minutes or so. The two flanking buildings, **Old City Hall** (Supreme Court Building) and **Congress Hall** were intended to balance each other, and their fanlighted doors, keystoned windows, and simple lines reward you from any angle. They were used by a combination of federal, state, country, and city governments during a relatively short period (this can get confusing).

13. **Congress Hall** (1787) held the U.S. Congress for 10 years; Washington departed public life from here. The House of Representatives met downstairs, and the place looks somewhat modern with wall-to-wall carpeting and venetian blinds. It's hard to get mahogany desks and leather armchairs of such workmanship now, though. Washington was inaugurated here in 1793 and John Adams in 1797. Look for the little corners where representatives could smoke, take snuff, and drink sherry during recess. Upstairs, the stair landing leads into the south-facing Senate Chamber, where 24 of the 32 leather chairs are original, including the canopied official's bench. Watching the House and Senate from the balconies became a popular social activity, and if debate was boring one could always admire the ceiling moldings. The carpet, a magnificent allegory of union, was reproduced after painstaking research.

14. **Old City Hall** (1790), at the corner of 5th and Chestnut streets, contained the only unaccounted-for branch of the federal government, the U.S. Supreme Court under Chief Justice John Jay. (Until the present City Hall anchored Center Square, this was the City Hall from 1800 to 1870.) The park uses the restored courthouse to describe the judiciary's first years.

Across Chestnut Street from this central trio is:

15. **The Liberty Bell,** once located in Independence Hall, was

moved for the Bicentennial celebration to the special glass pavilion across Chestnut Street (see Chapter 7 for a full description).

Just to the east of the Liberty Bell is:

**16. The Bourse,** a superb example of late Victorian architecture. It has been renovated as a mall in the form of two arcades surrounding an expansive skylit atrium. The Bourse, built from 1893 to 1895 as a merchants exchange, handsomely combines a brick-and-sandstone exterior with a cool and colorful interior.

**REFUELING STOP** The Bourse's **Great Hall, stores,** and **restaurants** are open Monday, Tuesday, and Thursday from 10am to 6pm; Wednesday, Friday, and Saturday until 8pm; and Sunday from 11am to 6pm. The Bourse is a great place to rest during a hot day of sightseeing in order to sample from the dozens of second-floor snack bars and to listen to the free lunchtime music.

Now cut through Independence Square to the greenery at the southwest corner. This is Washington Square:

**17. Washington Square** seems a little unbalanced since Independence National Park opened up the block to the northeast—but it's just as expansive and even more leafy than when it was the town's pasture. In the 1840s, this was the center of fashionable Philadelphia; but many handsome structures, such as Washington Square Church, have been razed to make room for chunky offices and apartment houses. Only the 1823 southwest corner Federals, the **Meredith-Penrose House** and its neighbors, give you a sense of what was lost. The square has also housed Philadelphia publishing for 150 years, with **Lea and Febiger** and **J. B. Lippincott** at no. 227. The massive white building on the north face has been redeveloped as the almost fully rented **Curtis Center:** The Curtis Publishing Co. once sent out the *Saturday Evening Post* and other magazines from here. The **Norman Rockwell Museum** in the corner section pays tribute to the *Post*'s frequent illustrator (see Chapter 7 for a fuller description). As you enter, admire that luminous mosaic mural *The Dream Garden:* Tiffany Studios executed a drawing by Maxfield Parrish, and the 1916 hand-fired masterpiece must be worth a fortune.

That solid, Italianate Revival brownstone (1845–47) on Washington Square East is the:

**18. Athenaeum,** home of an organization founded in 1814 to provide a library "connected with the history and antiquities of America, and generally disseminate useful knowledge." You can peek into a corner of virtually unchanged 19th-century society (see Chapter 7 for a fuller description).

If you wander closer to midtown from Washington Square, you might pick out a **large mansion** between Spruce and Pine streets on 11th Street. Joseph Bonaparte, brother of Napoleon, moved here in 1813 after the collapse of their empire—this was certainly a far cry from being King of the Two Sicilies! Joseph eventually wound up in New Orleans, but you might catch his portrait from life still at the Athenaeum.

Society Hill wasn't named that because only the upper crust of Philadelphia lived there in Colonial times, although they did.

The name refers to the Free Society of Traders, a group of businessmen and investors persuaded by William Penn to settle here with their families in 1683. The society didn't do very well—it went into receivership in 1723—but the hill did, and the name applies to the area east of Washington Square between Walnut and Lombard streets. Most of Philadelphia's white-collar workers, clerics, teachers, importers, and politicos have lived and worked here.

In 1945 nobody would have considered walking through the decrepit and undesirable neighborhood, despite the hundreds of Colonial facades. That's all changed now because of a massive urban-renewal project; a shell that then cost $1,500 now sells for $100,000, and it will sell for $300,000 after the interior refurbishment. Many new housing developments fit in discreet courts; they, too, use simple brick facades that blend with the Georgian exteriors superbly.

It's a good idea for you to know something about Colonial and Federal architecture as you stroll about the vital blocks because many homes aren't open to individual tours. Brick is everywhere, since English settlers found clay by the Delaware's banks—but the types and the construction methods have varied over 150 years. Generally, houses built before the 1750s, such as the **Trump House** at 214 Delancey Street, have two and a half stories, with two rooms per floor and a dormer window jutting out of a steep gambrel roof. An eave usually separates the simple door and its transom windows from the second level. Careful bricklayers liked to alternate the long and short sides of bricks, called "stretchers" and "headers"; this was called Flemish Bond, and the headers often were glazed to create a checkerboard pattern. Wrought-iron boot scrapers flank the doorsteps.

Houses built in Philadelphia's Colonial heyday soared to three or four stories—taller after the Revolution—and adopted heavy Georgian cornices (the underside of a roof overhang) and elaborate doorways. The homes of the truly wealthy, such as the **Powel House** at 244 S. 3rd Street and the **Morris House** at 235 S. 8th Street, have fanlights above their arched brick doorways; the **Davis-Lenox House** at 217 Spruce Street has a simple raised pediment. Since the Georgian style demanded symmetry, the parlors often were given imaginary doors and windows to even things out. The less wealthy lived in "trinity" homes—one room on each of three floors, named for faith, hope, and charity. Few town houses stood on individual plots; the **Hill-Physick-Keith House** at 321 S. 4th Street is the exception that proves the rule.

Federal architecture, which blew in from England and New England in the 1790s, is less heavy (no more Flemish Bond for bricks) and more graceful (more glass, with delicate molding instead of wainscoting). Any house such as the **Meredith House** at 700 South Washington Square, with a half story of marble stairs leading to a raised mahogany door, was surely constructed after 1800. Greek Revival elements such as rounded dormer windows and oval staircases became the fashion from the 1810s on. Three of the few Victorian brownstones at 260 South 3rd Street once belonged to Michel Bouvier, Jacqueline Kennedy Onassis's great-great-grandfather.

If you're here in May, don't pass up **Philadelphia Open**

**House,** which issues an admission pass to view the bandbox interiors of dozens of homes (volunteered by proud owners). Such details as marble fireplaces, folding interior shutters, hollow banisters (to hide the mortgage), and painted wood floors will leave you sighing to return. Call 215/928-1188 for information.

Of course, houses aren't all there is to Society Hill. Georgian and Federal public buildings and churches, from **Head House Square** and **Pennsylvania Hospital** to **St. Peter's** and **St. Paul's,** may make you feel as if you'd stumbled onto a movie set. But all of the buildings are used—and the area works as a living community today. Fine restaurants and charming stores cluster south of Lombard, too, especially around Head House Square (1803) at 2nd and Lombard streets.

Continuing on your tour, leave the Athenaeum and walk west one block on St. James Street, then go north on 5th Street and take a right turn onto Walnut Street for two blocks. As you walk down Walnut to 3rd Street, the restored row houses will catch your eye, with their paneled doors and shutters, bands of brick or stone between floors, and small lozenges of painted metal. These last are fire-insurance markers—all early American cities had terrible fire hazards, and Philadelphia, led by Benjamin Franklin, was the first to do anything about them. Groups of citizens formed such companies as the Philadelphia Contributionship, which suggested prevention strategy with leather fire buckets and lightning rods. The plaques of leafy green trees (on the Mutual Assurance Company) or four clasped hands (on the Contributionship) functioned as advertisements but also helped the firemen identify which houses they were responsible for saving. Now the houses belong to park offices and the Pennsylvania Horticultural Association, which maintains an 18th-century formal garden. At the corner of Fourth and Walnut streets is the:

**19. Todd House** (1775). Tours (for 10 at a time) are given on the half hour, and tickets by advance reservation are available gratis at the Visitor Center. John Todd, Jr., was a young Quaker lawyer of moderate means: His house cannot compare to that of Bishop White, but it is far grander than Betsy Ross's. You might think this building is a long step from the White House—but that's not true. Todd died in the 1793 epidemic of yellow fever, and his vivacious widow married a Virginia lawyer named James Madison, the future president. The Todds lived and entertained on the second floor, since Todd used the ground-floor parlor as his law office.

Farther down Walnut toward 3rd Street is the other park-run dwelling, the:

**20. Bishop White House,** at no. 309. This house is on one of the loveliest row-house blocks in the city, giving the park a life-size example of how a pillar of the community lived in Federal America. The town house sheltered the bishop for 49 years, and his family has restored most of their heirlooms here. Bishop White (1748–1836) studied for the Anglican priesthood in England, then returned home to tend Christ Church and founded Episcopalianism after the break from the mother country. He traveled abroad with Benjamin West and was Franklin's warm friend, which his upstairs library shows. White stayed out of politics as an expression of his belief in the separation of church and state. Since the guides do an excellent job, a tour isn't necessary in this guide. But notice the painted cloth floor in the entrance hall—after 20 varnishings, it survived muddy boots remarkably well. The tea salon has an unusual camelback sofa with scroll arms and a wooden children's puzzle with English royalty. And, in case you take the indoor "necessity" for granted, remember that outhouses provided the only relief on most Colonial property. The same innovativeness goes for the built-in bedroom closets, although there's no dearth of elegant wood chests and tables here. The library shows "modern" tastes, with Sir Walter Scott's Waverley novels, the *Encyclopaedia Britannica,* and even the Koran alongside traditional religious texts. The collection has survived intact.

Across the street, the park has purchased property and made a garden that exposes the side of:

**21. St. Joseph's Church,** the first Roman Catholic church in Philadelphia (see Chapter 7 for a description). It's much more intriguing if you enter through Willing's Alley and walk back to 4th Street and south half a block because an iron gate and archway conceal it well.

Not many tourists know about them, but the headquarters of 18th-century fire-insurance companies are open to the public, in the heart of Society Hill. In a neighborhood that was as moneyed and as crowded as this one, fire was a constant danger. Groups of subscribers pledged to help one another in case of fire—there were no fire departments in those days! Ironically, many companies required a complete inventory of the possessions before they would set premiums, and these inventories have guided modern restorers of run-down town houses. You can see the insurance plaques on the upper facades of many homes. In fact, the:

**22. Philadelphia Contributionship** (1836), 212 S. 4th Street (below Walnut Street), has used the "Hand-in-Hand" mark since 1752. This facade is all Greek Revival—with a gorgeous limestone entrance, columns, and balustrades leading to the front door. Architect Thomas Walter also designed the dome and the House and Senate wings on the U.S. Capitol. Entrance to the building is free, and it's open Monday to Friday from 10am to 3pm. The normal exhibition displays old leather fire-fighting equipment, desks with inkwells, and the original policy statement and list of members. If you call 627-1752 ahead of time, you'll get to view some of the gorgeous boardrooms, with their veined marble fireplaces and maple dining-room chairs.

Just below Locust Street on the same block is the:

**23. Mutual Assurance Company,** at no. 240. The company combines two splendid row houses built in 1750 and 1826. Mutual's firemark is a green tree, because when the Contributionship decided to stop insuring houses close to sidewalk trees in 1784, Mutual went for the arbor-loving market. It's well worth a tour—call 925-0609 to arrange one and enter through the garden on Locust Street. Such old Philadelphia families as the Cadwalladers, Shippens, and Wistars once resided here; the furniture (mostly Empire, with some Hepplewhite) and art are as outstanding as the pedigree. The back parlor of the Cadwallader House has famous portraits of

Washington and Franklin. Other attractions include silver by noted local smiths, painted stovepipe hats worn by early volunteer firemen, and beautifully painted paneled doors.

Just opposite the Mutual is **Bingham Court,** a 1967 adaptation within the Society Hill idiom of brick row houses. A few doors down 4th Street is:

**24. Old St. Mary's Church,** the most important Roman Catholic church during the Revolution (this was the "Sunday" church, as opposed to St. Joseph's weekday chapel). The interior is fairly prosaic, but the paved graveyard is a picturesque spot for a breather, with some interesting headstones and memorials.

The corner of Spruce and 5th streets is a good place to take a breath, with the town houses of **Girard Row** in front of you. Half a block to the west at 426 Spruce Street, Thomas U. Walter, the architect of the Capitol's dome in Washington and a master of Greek Revival, designed a Baptist church in 1830 that has been modified as the **Society Hill Synagogue** (run by Romanian immigrants at the turn of the century and by Conservative Jews more recently).

A half-block down 4th Street is the:

**25. Hill-Physick-Keith House,** at no. 321, possibly the nicest residential structure in Society Hill (see Chapter 7 for a fuller description). Take a few steps east on adjoining Cypress Street to reach **Delancey Park,** a delightful playground with sturdy activities and a group of stone bears that are perfect for photo props.

More Georgian and Federal church facades appear at the corners of 4th and Pine streets. One is Old Pine:

**26. Old Pine Presbyterian,** with its enormous raised facade and forbidding iron fence, didn't always look like a Greek temple, but that's what makes it worth seeing (it's free and open daily from 9am to 5pm). The Penns granted the Presbyterians this land in perpetuity, and the first sanctuary took shape in 1768. John Adams worshiped here when he was in Philadelphia. The double Corinthian columns, inside and out, were added in 1830, after the occupying British soldiers burned most of the interior. Everything is linear at Old Pine: The portico leads into a rectangle of pews, and slim pillars support a gallery with an elaborately carved rail of flowers and dentils. The altar will surprise you—it's just a dais backed by elaborate columns and entablature. You'll find it hard to believe that this filigree is of wood and not clay or plaster.

**Old Pine Community Center** on the block south to Lombard Street leads to South Street's funky shopping and nightlife district just beyond. Walk east on Pine Street to:

**27. St. Peter's Episcopal Church** (1761), an example of classic Georgian simplicity (see Chapter 7 for a fuller description). Farther east, at 301 Pine Street, is the:

**28. Kosciuszko National Memorial,** a double 1775 Georgian that housed this Polish engineer and soldier who turned the tide for American forces at Saratoga. He returned to the United States, exiled from Poland, in search of a pension from Congress and lived here in 1797 while pursuing this.

Now follow Pine Street to 2nd Street, the major north-south route through Philadelphia in Colonial days. Open markets were a big part of urban life. (People complain about railroad tracks near their houses nowadays, but think of the noise and smell a Colonial marketplace in dusty streets must have involved!) In fact, no Colonial native would recognize Market Street today without its wooden sheds that covered stalls from Front to 6th streets and its narrow cart paths on both sides. One place he or she would recognize, though, is:

29. **Head House Square,** built in 1803 in the middle of 2nd Street as a place where fire companies and shoppers could congregate. Head House itself, that brick shed with a cupola that once held a fire bell, trails a simple brick arcade between Pine and South streets. In those days, market took place on Tuesday and Friday at dawn. Butter and eggs were sold on the west side, meat under the eaves, and herbs and vegetables on the river side. Fish sellers were relegated to the far sidewalks (it isn't hard to imagine why). Now, in summer, craftspeople spread out their goods, especially on weekends.

Next door is **NewMarket,** between Front and 2nd streets, a home of the future that looks increasingly forlorn. Physically, NewMarket is a series of glassy cubes stacked around two courtyards. Culturally, it's disappointing: The most popular locations are still those located within the old Georgian facades on 2nd Street.

---

**REFUELING STOP   Dickens Inn,** 421 South 2nd Street, and several other Head House Square restaurants make excellent lunch or snack stopovers; Dickens Inn (open from 11:30am daily) has an English afternoon tea, as well as a tempting ground-floor bakery.

---

Now head up 2nd Street, perhaps cutting in to Delancey Street between 2nd and 3rd streets, north on Philip Street's quaint court, and back to 2nd on Spruce Street. Across the street from the 1765 **Abercrombie House** (one of the tallest Colonial dwellings in America) is the:

30. **Man Full of Trouble Tavern,** at 127 Spruce Street. This place re-creates a big part of Capt. James Abercrombie's life. It is thought that the tavern was built in 1760, but it is well known what kind of trouble the man had from 1842 on: "In this alley more than fifty years ago was an ancient sign with a very attractive design, having on it a man and his wife, the latter leaning on his arm. In the hand of the woman was a bandbox with a cat on top of it. The man had a monkey on his shoulder and a parrot in his hand." The Knauer Foundation has restored the tavern to its original appearance with Delft tiles, a cagelike bar, and tables with Windsor chairs and pewter candlesticks. The tavern bordered Little Dock Creek then, and sailors and dock workers ate, drank, and roughhoused here nightly. The attic held a mariner's flophouse—you'll wonder how because of the narrow gables called pent eaves. Look for the puzzle jugs, with their straws and holes built into the pottery; only one combination of holes covered and straw sucked yields liquid, and it's not easy even when you're sober. The tavern, its cellar, and its twin, the Paschall House, are opened by dames of the Colonial Philadelphia Historical Society. Admission is now by group appointment only.

Just up the hill are **Society Hill Towers** (1964), the I. M. Pei twins that signaled the 20th century and stick out like 30-story sore thumbs today. It's best to walk west back to 3rd Street, then north to a stunning block of row-house mansions including **Bishop Stevens** at no. 232, with its cast-iron balcony; **Atkinson House** at no. 236, which today conceals an indoor pool; and **Penn-Chew House** at no. 242, owned by the grandson of William and the last colonial governor of Pennsylvania. The one of these mansions that you can enter is:

**31. Powel House,** at 244 S. 3rd Street. This home of Philadelphia's last colonial and first U.S. mayor beats the Bishop White House by far (see Chapter 7 for the full details).

Across the street is:

**32. St. Paul's Episcopal Church** (1761), at 225 S. 3rd Street, founded because of another example of Philadelphia's religious tolerance. Christ Church on Market Street had a young clergyman, William McClenachan, who preached such radical notions as the separation of church and state. Since the High Anglican Church refused to license his speech, St. Paul's was set up as his "bully pulpit," and the money for the Georgian hall was raised through donations and lotteries. Among his other tasks, the sexton had to keep "goats and other animals" out of the churchyard. St. Paul's made the transition to Episcopalianism easily but soon fell into financial difficulties. Now it houses the headquarters of the denomination's community services, inside beautiful pre-Revolutionary wrought-iron gates and marble-topped enclosing walls. If you head for the second floor (open Monday to Friday from 9am to 5pm), you can still see most of the original chancel. The altar's rail pattern looks like a Chinese puzzle, and the bishop's chair has a carved wooden mitre.

Standing at the corner of 3rd and Walnut streets, you can't miss the:

**33. Philadelphia Merchants' Exchange** (1832), a masterwork by William Strickland (described in Chapter 7). It's not open to the public. Heading toward 2nd Street and the river, you'll cross one of my favorite spaces, a broad area of cobblestones covering Dock Street (Dock Creek in Penn's day) and the Delaware River beyond. The **Ritz 5** moviehouse on your left offers fine independent fare; the **Pasta Blitz** just beyond is the umpteenth restaurant trying to make it in this unwelcoming site. Soon you'll approach the reconstructed:

**34. City Tavern** restaurant and gardens from the rear. This was the most opulent and genteel tavern and social hall in the colonies and the scene of many discussions of the Founding Fathers. Unlike most of the city's pubs, it was built in 1773 with businessmen's subscriptions, to assure its quality. In fact, George Washington met with most delegates to the Constitutional Convention for a farewell dinner here in 1787. The park now operates the City Tavern as a concession, which serves breakfast, lunch, and dinner in summer (see Chapter 6 for a full description).

If you choose to continue toward the Delaware via the pleasant pedestrian extension of Walnut Street and the staircase at its end, you'll pass between the new **Sheraton Society Hill** hotel and the famed **Old Original Bookbinder's** restaurant, winding up more or less in front of the **Port of History Museum** on the waterfront. Consult the "Penn's Landing" description in the "Neighborhoods" section of Chapter 7 for more details.

## WALKING TOUR 2 — OLDE CITY

**Start:** Visitor Center, 3rd and Walnut streets.
**Finish:** Market Place East, 7th and Market streets.
**Time:** 3–5 hours.
**Best Time:** No later than 3pm, to avoid museum closings. If contemporary art and socializing is your interest, the first Friday of every month brings special late hours for all galleries, all cafés, and many historic attractions.

Olde City is an intriguing blend of 18th- and even 17th-century artisan row houses, robust 19th-century commercial structures, and 20th-century rehabs of all of the above featuring artist lofts and galleries. Walk out the south entrance of the **Visitor Center** and along the narrow lane adjoining **City Tavern** to:

1. **Welcome Park,** the site of the Slate Roof House where William Penn granted the "Charter of Privileges" (now at the Library Hall off Independence Square) in 1701. The pavement bears a massive and whimsical map of Penn's City, with a time line of his life and times on the walls.

   Next door is the **Thomas Bond House,** a restored 1769 Georgian row house that's now a bed-and-breakfast (see Chapter 5 for more information). Walk along the block-long **AMC Olde City 2** cinemas to:

2. **Front Street,** which actually lapped at the river's edge throughout Colonial times. A walk north brings you to **Hillary's Ice Cream** at the corner of Chestnut Street and the possibility of exploring Penn's Landing (see "Neighborhoods" in Chapter 7 for a description) via a beautifully terraced park. However, head back to the florid **Corn Exchange Bank** at 2nd and Chestnut streets, then turn right onto one of the liveliest block in the historic area.

---

**REFUELING STOP** The block of "Two Street" between Chestnut and Market contains good restaurants such as **Serrano's, Los Amigos,** and **Rib-It** (see Chapter 5 for details). My favorite is the quiet, cool seating for 40 at the rear of **Foodtek Market and Café,** with great hot and cold charcuterie. It's open on Monday to Thursday from 7:30am to 1am, on Saturday and Sunday until 2am.

---

Once you hit Market Street (High Street in Colonial times), you'll find a different world of sharp discount clothing and wholesale toy stores. The many alleyways between Front and 5th streets, with names like **Trotter Street, Black Horse Alley, Bank Street,** and **Strawberry Lane,** testify to the activities

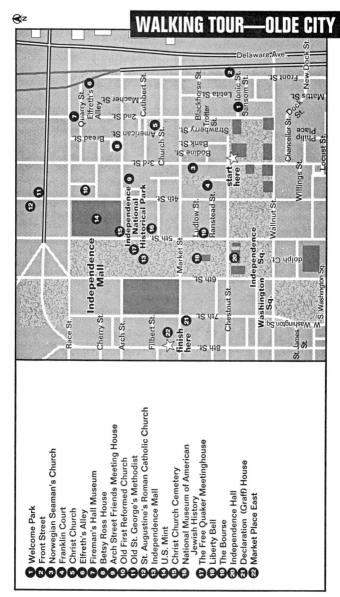

Delaware Ave.

start here:

Independence National Historical Park

Independence Mall

Independence Sq.

Washington Sq.

finish here:

and preoccupations of colonial residents. A particular favorite facade of mine is that of the:

**3. Norwegian Seaman's Church,** at 22 S. 3rd Street. This William Strickland 1837 gem with Corinthian columns and granite steps is now a nightclub called Revival. If you haven't taken Walking Tour 1, go now to:

**4. Franklin Court,** the final home and reconstructed post office of Benjamin Franklin between 3rd and 4th streets. Standing on Market Street, you'll find the graceful spire of:

5. **Christ Church** unmissable. Urban renewal removed the unsightly buildings that hid its walls from Market until the 1950s (See Chapter 7 for a fuller description of Revolutionary Philadelphia's leading place of worship and its restful benches and adjoining cemetery).

   It may be a bit early for another refueling stop, but the block of Church Street directly to the west of the church contains **Old City Coffee** at no. 221, a favorite place for marvelous coffee and light lunches. If by the time you get here the end of the day is approaching, duck underneath the Market Street ramp to I-95 at Front Street to reach **Panorama's** wine bar and bistro.

   Walk north along Front Street for four short blocks to get the flavor of 1830s warehouses, such as the **Girard** at 18–30 N. Front Street and **Smythe** at 101 Arch Street. If you continued north and east, you would come to the attractive new clubs and restaurants on the water, such as **Meiji-en, Rock Lobster,** and **The Beach Club.** Instead, take a left onto:

6. **Elfreth's Alley** (from 1702), the oldest continuously occupied group of homes in America (see "More Attractions" in Chapter 7 for a full description). The homes are tiny, and you can enter no. 126. Several courts are perfect for wandering.

   Back on 2nd Street with its china and restaurant supply stores, you might detour north for a minute to look at **2nd Street Art Building,** housing the Clay Studio and NEXUS galleries, or to visit the:

7. **Fireman's Hall Museum,** at Quarry Street, housed in an 1876 firehouse.

   Then head south to Arch Street, turning right onto it to the:

8. **Betsy Ross House,** at no. 239 (see Chapter 7 for full details). It's a short walk through the house, but there's a large garden. Directly opposite are the **Mulberry Market,** an upscale deli with seating in the rear, and **Humphry Flags** if you're feeling patriotic.

   Cross 3rd Street to the **Hoop Skirt Factory** at 309–313 Arch Street, a light 1875 factory renovated in 1980, and the charming **Loxley Court** just beyond, designed by carpenter Benjamin Loxley in 1741. It stayed within the family until 1901. On the south side of the street is the:

9. **Arch Street Friends Meeting House,** a simple 1805 structure with a substantial history (see Chapter 7 for details). You could keep walking straight west one block to Independence Mall, but I recommend that you take a slightly gritty walk north on 4th Street to:

10. **Old First Reformed Church,** at 151 N. 4th Street. Built in 1837 for a sect of German Protestants, the building survived a late 19th-century stint as a paint warehouse. Note that this church functions as a small and always full youth hostel during July and August nights (see Chapter 5 for details). Crossing under the gloomy piers of the **Benjamin Franklin Bridge,** you'll see:

11. **Old St. George's Methodist,** at 235 N. 4th Street, the cradle of American Methodism and the scene of fanatic religious revival meetings in the early 1770s. The bridge was in fact built farther south to preserve it. On the other side of the street, below Vine, is one more church:

12. **St. Augustine's Roman Catholic Church.** It's another

18th-century building, this one built for German and Irish Catholics who couldn't make it south of Market Street. Villanova University, and the Augustinian presence in the United States, started here. This building is actually an 1844 structure, built to replace the original, which burned down during anti-Catholic riots. Now, keep walking west along the bridge to 5th Street, then head south along:

**13. Independence Mall,** a swath of urban renewal that bit off more than the Historical Park could chew. At the upper end of the Mall (Florist Street) is the bicycle and pedestrian entrance to the Benjamin Franklin Bridge; biking and walking across the bridge make thrilling but time-consuming expeditions. It's best to head down 5th Street, stopping at the:

**14. U.S. Mint,** one of the three places in the country that churn out U.S. coinage (see Chapter 7 for its hours and description). Just south of the Mint is:

**15. Christ Church Cemetery,** the resting place of Benjamin and Deborah Franklin and other notables (toss a coin through the opening in the brick wall for luck), and also the:

**16. National Museum of American Jewish History,** at 55 N. 5th Street. The city of Philadelphia has a history of distinguished Jewish involvement in town affairs almost as long as the life of the town itself. Many of America's first Jews gravitated to Philadelphia because it was a city based on trade with Europe and the West Indies and with a legacy of religious tolerance. The museum, connected to the city's oldest congregation, commemorates this story (see Chapter 7 for a fuller description). You'll notice how much lower street level used to be by looking at the statuary outside.

In the Mall, a small building across from the Franklin graves is the:

**17. Free Quaker Meetinghouse,** run by the Park Service. These "Fighting Quakers," such as Betsy Ross, were willing to support the Revolutionary War; since this violated the tenets of pure Quakerism, they were read out of Arch Street Friends.

Now, recross Market Street to see the:

**18. Liberty Bell,** if you haven't seen it yet (see Chapter 7 for details). Near the Liberty Bell is:

**19. The Bourse,** a 19th-century exchange that now contains a food court and pleasant urban mall (a refueling stop described in Walking Tour 1). Reenter Independence Mall and you'll be in front of:

**20. Independence Hall,** with its two flanking buildings, **Congress Hall** and **Old City Hall.**

Continue west along Chestnut Street to 7th Street, and turn right onto a historic block containing the **Atwater Kent Museum** of city memorabilia, the **Balch Institute of Ethnic Studies,** and:

**21. Declaration (Graff) House,** a reconstruction of the lodgings where Thomas Jefferson drafted the Declaration of Independence. The latter is run by the National Park Service, with free daily admission. (All of the above are described more fully in Chapter 7.)

From the old to the new: Right behind Graff House on Market Street is a huge McDonald's designed for children; directly opposite it on Market Street is:

22. **Market Place East,** the converted and rehabilitated former home of Lit Brothers Department Store, a wrought-iron palace that's a block long (see the full description in Chapter 9). The below-ground food area contains an **Au Bon Pain** and **Pagano's** charcuterie. Quality stores include **Conran's** and **Einstein's Books** and **Toys That Matter.**

# WALKING TOUR 3 — MIDTOWN, RITTENHOUSE SQUARE & LOWER BENJAMIN FRANKLIN PARKWAY

**Start:** Visitors Center, 16th Street and John F. Kennedy Boulevard.
**Finish:** Logan Circle, intersection of 19th Street, Race Street, and the Benjamin Franklin Parkway.
**Time:** 6 hours.
**Best Time:** No later than noon, to avoid museum closings.
**Worst Time:** Sunday, when many stores are closed, and Monday, when most museums are shuttered.

This tour encompasses the confident heart of 19th-century Philadelphia. If you've already sampled the charm and excitement of historic Philadelphia, the downtown area and southwest of Center City may seem anticlimactic. But there's plenty to see here, too, starting with the massive French Renaissance City Hall. Center Square and its environs were farmland or parkland during the 18th century. But as commercial buildings and loft warehouses began to dominate Olde City, old Philadelphia families began to consider Rittenhouse Square to be the fashionable part of town. Individual dwellings, such as Hockley House (1875) at 235 S. 21st Street and the present Art Alliance Building on Rittenhouse Square, coexist with attractive row houses such as those at 18th Street and Delancey Place. Churches, the Academy of Fine Arts (at Broad and Cherry), the Academy of Music (at Broad and Locust), and such private clubs as the Union League (at Broad and Sansom) enhanced the Victorian life-style.

The 20th century has added international-style skyscrapers to Penn Center, notably the PSFS Building and such postmodern structures as I. M. Pei's Commerce Square (41 stories, at Market and 21st streets) and Helmut Jahn's One and Two Liberty Place (61 and 54 stories, respectively, three blocks east). But this is also a wonderful shopping, cultural, and restaurant area, catering to up-to-the-minute tastes. If you're here in May or June, don't miss the Clothesline Exhibit of paintings at Rittenhouse Square.

Start your walking tour at the:

1. **Visitors Center,** run by the Philadelphia Convention and Visitors Bureau at 16th Street and John F. Kennedy Boulevard. From every museum pamphlet in town to interactive displays and friendly guides, the Visitors Center has it all in a shiny wedding cake of a building that's open daily from 9am to 6pm. Half-priced tickets to many evening events are sold here as well.

   Passing by Robert Indiana's *LOVE* statue, you'll reach:

2. **City Hall.** You can't help knowing where City Hall is, at the intersection of Broad and Market streets. This fanciful, exuber-

ant hodgepodge graced with a huge statue of William Penn has free tours and elevators to the viewing area at Penn's feet. Until Liberty Place was built, Penn's hat was by custom the tallest point within city limits. Back on the ground, linger over the flag exhibits and historical placard in the courtyard; this spot was claimed as civic land by William Penn 300 years ago to house city offices, though it served as militia parade ground while waiting for the city to grow out to it. (See Chapter 7 for full details.)

Everyone wonders what that chiseled-looking building just north of City Hall with the single tower is—a church? No, it's the:

**3. Masonic Temple,** one of the world's largest (see Chapter 7 for a full description).

Continue two blocks up North Broad Street to:

**4. Pennsylvania Academy of Fine Arts,** founded in 1804. This 1876 building is now overshadowed by the Philadelphia Museum as "the" museum in town, but it hosts a wonderful blend of the best in old and new American art, in a wonderful and newly renovated High Victorian building (see in Chapter 7 for details).

Now backtrack to City Hall and head east through:

**5. Wanamaker's,** now a shadow of its former self but still an impressive department store. It features an enormous pipe organ; an atrium; and "the Iggle," a central statue of our national bird that has been a rendezvous for generations of shoppers (see Chapter 9 for details).

Back on Market Street, you'll pass the classic International Style **Philadelphia Savings Fund Society (PSFS) Building** skyscraper at 12th Street. Directly opposite that is:

**6. Reading Terminal,** once a commuter terminal but now the facade of the **Convention Center,** scheduled for 1993 completion. The **Reading Terminal Market,** mid-block just north of Market Street, is one of the country's great surviving urban food markets (see Chapter 6 for the delicious details).

Three blocks south, Locust and 12th streets are the center for:

**7. Philadelphia's littlest streets,** a group of wonderfully charming row houses tucked into alleys and courtyards. My favorites are the art clubs of **South Camac Street** between 12th and 13th streets and between Locust and Spruce streets, followed by **Manning, Sartain, Quince,** and **Jessup** streets, between 11th and 12th streets at the same latitude. If you care to continue two blocks south, you'll find **Antique Row** lining Pine Street with galleries between 9th and 12th streets.

The 1300 block of Locust Street has two wonderful collections. The finest collection of Colonial furniture and art in Center City won't be found at any museum but at the:

**8. Historical Society of Pennsylvania,** 1300 Locust Street (see Chapter 7 for a full description). The modern, connected:

**9. Library Company of Philadelphia,** at no. 1314, is the current home of Ben Franklin's original lending library. It contains 300,000 volumes, such as Lewis and Clark's records of their 1804 expedition. Grand old houses lie across the street at no. 1319 and no. 1321 Locust.

From here, walk past the Philadelphia Hilton and Towers to:

10. **South Broad Street,** once the undisputed cultural capital of the city, now punctuated with empty lots between the jewels. The 1980s dream was to revitalize this stretch as an unbroken series of theaters and performance halls, and indeed the Philadelphia College of Art at Broad and Pine has yielded to become the University of the Arts. However, future development is on hold. At Broad and Locust streets is the:

11. **Academy of Music,** modeled on La Scala in Milan. It is open for daytime tours or evening performances of the Philadelphia Orchestra, one of the best ensembles in the country (see Chapter 10 for details). Walk one block north (passing Philadelphia's most opulent health club) to the:

12. **Hotel Atop the Bellevue,** the current incarnation of a grand 1901 hotel. Thomas Edison designed the lighting fixtures; it's worth a peek at the former lobby, now the site for the **Shops at the Bellevue** and several restaurants (see Chapter 5 for full information).

    Keep walking north to the **Union League** at Broad and Sansom streets, the most evident of Philadelphia's many private clubs; this one was formed and constructed in the flush of Civil War sentiment for the Republican Party. Then backtrack to Walnut Street and turn left to:

13. **Rittenhouse Square area shopping.** The blocks between Broad and 18th are dotted with the city's finest independent stores (see Chapter 9 for a full listing).

---

**REFUELING STOP**    For a physical and intellectual pick-me-up, the second floor of **Borders,** the city's best bookstore at 1727 Walnut Street, has a comfortable espresso bar with racks of newspapers and magazines. It's open Monday to Friday from 7am to 10pm, Saturday from 9am to 9pm, and Sunday from 11am to 7pm. For more varied fare, try the legendary **Commissary** at 1710 Sansom Street, now mostly a charcuterie but with some rear seating. Both are between 17th and 18th streets. It's open Monday to Thursday from 11:30am to 10pm, Friday and Saturday from 11:30am to 11pm, and Sunday from 9:30am to 10pm.

---

14. **Rittenhouse Square** functioned as the city's center of social prestige roughly from 1870 through 1930, or until proper Philadelphians discovered that they could live in the Main Line suburbs permanently. Despite the construction of apartment houses to replace such mansions as **McIlhenny House** at the southwest corner, it still maintains a hold of elegance on the city, bolstered by the **Curtis School of Music** at Locust Street and the recent opening of **Rittenhouse Hotel** (though not by the jagged architecture it inherited). The park itself has splendid curving walks around whimsical fountains and decorative pools, with sunlight or winter chill dappling through the trees.

    South and west of Rittenhouse Square are unusual turn-of-the-century town houses ranging from severe Georgian to fanciful neo-medieval. A favorite "summary" street of styles is **Delancey Street,** between Spruce and Lombard streets. If you detour as far west as 20th Street, you'll be rewarded with the interiors and garden of:

# WALKING TOUR—MIDTOWN, RITTENHOUSE SQUARE & LOWER BENJAMIN FRANKLIN PARKWAY

1 Visitors Center
2 City Hall
3 Masonic Temple
4 Pennsylvania Academy of Fine Arts
5 Wanamaker's
6 Reading Terminal
7 Philadelphia's littlest streets
8 Historical Society of Pennsylvania
9 Library Company of Philadelphia
10 South Broad Street
11 Academy of Music
12 Hotel Atop the Bellevue
13 Rittenhouse Square area shopping
14 Rittenhouse Square
15 Rosenbach Museum and Library
16 Liberty Place
17 Penn Center (the former Suburban) Station
18 Logan Circle
19 Cathedral-Basilica of Sts. Peter and Paul
20 Academy of Natural Sciences
21 Franklin Institute Science Museum and Futures Center
22 Free Library of Philadelphia
23 Rodin Museum

**15. Rosenbach Museum and Library,** at no. 2010, a shrine of book collectors and lovers of literature (see Chapter 7 for a full description).

From Rittenhouse Square, head north on 18th Street to Chestnut Street, taking a right and following a block to:

**16. Liberty Place,** a tremendously inviting 1991 urban mall and superb family refueling stop at the second-floor food court. (See Chapter 6 for the cuisine and Chapter 9 for the shops.)

Walking east one block, then north one block, you'll see the Visitors Center. Look northwest, and begin your stroll along Benjamin Franklin Parkway.

The Parkway, designed and built in the 1920s, acknowledged a new desire for civic grandeur in Philadelphia as well as paid homage to the city wealthy as they migrated to the northwestern Main Line suburbs. The Parkway connects City Hall with the welcoming arms of the Philadelphia Museum of Art, just over a mile away, swirling through Logan Circle and its fountain en route. Despite its flags, parade of public art, and lawns, the parkway has seemed a bit too big for its britches. However, the last decade's explosive growth of the new corporate headquarters in town between Broad and 20th streets north of Market Street has solidified the many grand cultural institutions built on its edges. If you visit the cultural attractions, you can pick up a "Parkway Passport" offering discounts on most local restaurants—and vice versa.

Walking up from the **Visitors Center** at 16th Street and John F. Kennedy Boulevard, you'll pass:

17. **Penn Center (the former Suburban) Station,** a compact art deco terminal whose street level has been transformed into the inviting **Marathon Grill.** Be aware that an underground concourse linking the station to City Hall also contains dozens of shops, services, and food vendors. A left turn brings you onto the Parkway itself.

Two blocks up, the Parkway intersects with Cherry and 17th streets. On the Parkway's north side, **Friends Select School,** a leading Quaker-founded preparatory school, occupies new headquarters in the Pennwalt Building, while on the south side, **Pomodoro** dishes up Tuscan pastas and antipasti for hungry grazers. One block west on Cherry Street, **Dock Street Brewing Co.** dispenses American bistro fare and beer, freshly brewed on the premises, in a relaxed setting. A block farther, past **Friday's** and the rounded marble tower of the defunct **Palace** apartment house/hotel, lies:

18. **Logan Circle,** originally a square but converted with the Parkway construction. Ironically enough, this most corporate and institutional setting of all of William Penn's original city parks has the lowest buildings surrounding it. The highlight is the 1920 **Swann Fountain,** designed by Alexander S. Calder with evocations of the three waters (Delaware, Schuylkill, Wissahickon) that nourish Philadelphia.

At the eastern end of Logan Circle is the:

19. **Cathedral-Basilica of Sts. Peter and Paul.** Built in 1846, this sober Roman church with a copper dome made the statement that Catholics would recover and populate a newer part of Center City after the anti-Catholic riots of the early 1840s.

Continue walking clockwise around Logan Circle. The four-story **Four Seasons Hotel** was sensitively designed not to intrude architecturally; furthermore, the hotel renovated the Fountain in the mid-1980s and maintains its hothouse gardens. Afternoon tea at the **Fountain Café** within is a quintessential Philadelphia experience.

Just past 19th Street on Logan Circle is the:

20. **Academy of Natural Sciences,** displaying flora and fauna

from the world over, from dinosaurs to contemporary volcanoes (see Chapter 7 for details).

Next to the academy is **Moore College of Art,** with its street-level exhibition space open to the public. Taking up the whole west side of the Circle is the neoclassical facade of the:

21. **Franklin Institute Science Museum and Futures Center,** a top attraction (see the details in Chapter 7). Don't forget that even without admission you can eat at the entranceway **Ben's Café.** With a detour two blocks south on 21st Street, you'll come to the **Please Touch Museum** (also see Chapter 7).

To the north side lie both the:

22. **Free Library of Philadelphia,** with a wonderful Children's Library as well as research and circulating collections and an inexpensive rooftop cafeteria (again, Chapter 7 has the details) and the twin **Municipal Court Building.**

If you continue up toward the **Philadelphia Museum of Art** on the north side of the Parkway from the Free Library, two blocks up you'll come to the ancillary collection of the:

23. **Rodin Museum,** bequeathed to the city in the 1920s and renovated in 1989. It has a very pleasant outdoor sculpture garden in a leafy atmosphere (see the full description in Chapter 7).

# CHAPTER 9

# PHILADELPHIA SHOPPING A TO Z

**I**n Colonial days, Philadelphia was one of the most interesting shopping marts in the world—not quite the clearing house of nations but only a boat trip away. Cloth from England and Europe, porcelain from China, outstanding furniture from local craftsmen, and Ben Franklin's printing house all were available to the populace. Franklin's *Autobiography* tells of his surprise on coming to breakfast one morning to find a china bowl and silver spoon: "Luxury will enter families and make a progress in spite of principle."

He was right, of course, and Philadelphia has plenty of goods to help luxury enter your life. It's close enough to New York City to get high-fashion and international wares, especially in the specialty shops around Rittenhouse Square. Yet, unlike New York, it's walkable and comfortably proportioned for shoppers. Philadelphians stoutly defend the independent taste of the city, and sophisticated local artisans do a brisk trade. Also, remember that there is no sales tax on clothing; other items are taxed at 6%.

Most stores stay open during regular business hours on Monday to Friday, on Saturday, and later on Wednesday evening. Some are also open on Sunday.

## ANTIQUES

Philadelphia, say the "proper families," is one big attic that's full of the undervalued heirlooms and cast-offs of previous generations. Pine Street from 9th to 12th streets boasts about 25 stores, many of which do their own refinishing. Germantown Avenue in Chestnut Hill also has a concentration of shops. As in any antiques market, you'll have to bring a lot of expertise to any store and you'll have to trust your dealer. There are usually dozens of antiques markets every week in the Delaware Valley. Consult the "Weekend" section of the *Philadelphia Inquirer* for details.

### CALDERWOOD GALLERY, 221 S. 17th St. Tel. 732-9444.

This is an international resource for French art nouveau and art deco furnishings, which are beautifully displayed. The prices are reasonable compared to those in New York City.

### FREEMAN FINE ARTS, 1808 Chestnut St. Tel. 563-9275.

The dean of auction houses in town since 1805 stages a full auction every Wednesday (viewing on Monday and Tuesday). They specialize in most Americana. Special fully catalogued auctions for jewelry and fine furniture are held here several times annually; regular auctions include standard home furnishings and some fine pieces.

### GARGOYLES, 512 S. 3rd St. Tel. 629-1700.

In Society Hill, my personal favorite is Gargoyles, which has everything from toothpick holders to mantels and bars. Although much of the stock is American, there's also a delightful selection of English pub signs, dart boards, and the like.

Several large items have been salvaged from 19th-century buildings and businesses.

### JANSEN ANTIQUES, 1036 Pine St. Tel. 592-1670.
The displays of Victorian and art deco furnishings and jewelry here are unusually uncluttered compared to others in the neighborhood.

### M. FINKEL AND DAUGHTER, 936 Pine St. Tel. 627-7797.
Look here, one of the true anchors of the Pine Street neighborhood, for folk art, furniture, and painting in general and bright Amish quilts and needlework in particular.

### REESE'S, 928–930 Pine St. Tel. 922-0796.
This place is not quite as wonderful as the cigar-store Indian out front, and the help can be nearly as somnolent, but Reese's is one of the oldest Pine Street shops, featuring a large selection of china and silver.

### W. GRAHAM ARADER, 1308 Walnut St. Tel. 735-8811.
Arader has become one of the country's leading rare book, map, and print dealers in the past 15 years because of its aggressive purchasing and higher pricing. You'll find a variety of interesting items here.

# ART GALLERIES

Philadelphia abounds in public art. The first American city to allot 1% of public building funds for public use supports a plethora of artists and craftspeople for indoor beauty as well. The line between museums that exhibit studio artists, such as the Pennsylvania Academy of Fine Arts (PAFA), and galleries that promote sales is smaller here than in many other cities. The line between art and crafts is fine also (see "Crafts" below for more listings). Many of the less traditional galleries are setting up in the colonial district or on South Street.

### AIA GALLERY, 17th and Sansom sts. Tel. 569-3186.
This gallery alternates shows of known and unknown architects and craftspeople. Connected to it is an excellent bookstore (see below).

### DOLAN/MAXWELL, 1701 Walnut St. Tel. 665-1701.
Etchings, lithographs, and silk screens are sold here, as well as other works on paper by such major artists as Susan Rothenburg and Jasper Johns.

### THE EYES GALLERY, 402 South St. Tel. 925-0193.
The Eyes Gallery presents a cheerful assortment of Latin American arts and crafts, including Santos and retablos. Also included are one-of-a-kind articles of clothing spread over three floors.

### GILBERT LUBER GALLERY, 1220 Walnut St. Tel. 732-2996.
Here you can find superb Japanese and Chinese antique and contemporary graphics and art books. The gallery is branching into antique and contemporary Thai objects.

### GROSS-MCCLEAF GALLERY, 127 S. 16th St. Tel. 665-8138.
Quality exhibitions of primarily local printmakers, painters, and

sculptors are given here. Much of the work takes its cue from 20th-century reinterpretations of impressionism.

## HELEN DRUTT, 1721 Walnut St. Tel. 735-1625.

Among the private galleries, Helen Drutt has influential shows of crafted objects of fiber, clay, and metal—both beautiful and utilitarian. Winter hours are Wednesday to Saturday 10am to 5pm; summer hours are Wednesday and Thursday from 11am to 5pm and Friday from 11am to 4pm.

## JANET FLEISHER, 211 S. 17th St. Tel. 545-7562.

This is the city's undisputed doyenne of Native American and pre-Columbian artifacts and crafts, with some modern folk art as well.

## LOCKS, 600 Washington Square South. Tel. 629-1000.

This is another powerhouse gallery for paintings, sculptures, and mixed-media works. Gallery 1 is frequently devoted to group theme shows, and the smaller Gallery 2 usually focuses on a single artist.

## MAKLER'S, 225 S. 18th St. Tel. 735-2540.

Makler's presents the weightiest contemporary artists, such as Louise Nevelson and Jim Dine, in a somewhat elitist setting.

## THE MORE GALLERY, 1630 Walnut St., 2nd floor. Tel. 735-1827.

National and regional arts, from prints to ceramics, are presented here.

## NEWMAN GALLERIES, 1625 Walnut St. Tel. 563-1779.

This gallery provides a very strong representation of Bucks County artists and of American sculptors and painters in general.

## PHILADELPHIA ART ALLIANCE, Rittenhouse Square, 251 S. 18th St. Tel. 545-4302.

The three floors of local talent here are chosen by the alliance's committee of laymen and artists. Most of the material—pottery, sculpture, and hangings—already has a stamp of approval. Note that state and city budget cuts have caused a temporary closing in 1992, but there are plans to reopen in the future.

## PHILADELPHIA PRINT CLUB, 1614 Latimer St. Tel. 735-6090.

The Philadelphia Print Club is a private foundation that collects, promotes, and sells works done by most printing methods, notably lithography and screening. Tucked away below midtown, it's closed from June 15 to September 1. It sell cards and prints at Head House Square on summer weekends, though.

## ROSENWALD-WOLF GALLERY, University of the Arts, 333 S. Broad St. at Pine St. Tel. 875-1116.

This gallery features works not only by faculty but also by distinguished visitors. Student shows are held in May through July.

## SCHMIDT/DEAN, 1636 Walnut St. Tel. 546-7212.

Opened in 1988, Schmidt/Dean specializes in bringing younger regional artists to a younger audience.

**THE SCHOOL GALLERY OF THE PENNSYLVANIA ACADE-MY OF FINE ARTS,** 1301 Cherry St. Tel. 569-2797.

The building is a wonderful museum and school with exhibits that change frequently during the year. June is reserved for student shows.

**SCHWARTZ AND SON,** 1806 Chestnut St. Tel. 563-4887.

They are specialists in 19th- and 20th-century paintings, particularly those with Philadelphia connections.

**SNYDERMAN GALLERY,** 317 South St. Tel. 238-9576.

One of my favorites on South Street, this gallery offers beautifully sculpted wood furniture, glasswork, and jewelry. They try to keep up with the times, which means an abundance of brightly painted, sharp-cornered objects on display.

# ART SUPPLIES

**TAWS,** 1527 Walnut St. Tel. 563-8742.

A fine selection of artists' materials and studio furnishings can be found here, convenient to Center City. There are also some interesting decorative pieces and gifts.

# BOOKSTORES

**AMERICAN INSTITUTE OF ARCHITECTS BOOKSTORE,** 117 S. 17th St. at Sansom St. Tel. 569-3186.

Boasting some of the finest shelves you'll see anywhere, this bookstore also offers an excellent downstairs gallery that alternates shows of unknown and known artists and craftspeople.

**BARNES & NOBLE,** 1424 Chestnut St. Tel. 972-8275.

This branch of the fast-growing New York discounter has the same 10% off bestsellers, plus books for $1 and up. It's staff is efficient.

**B. DALTON,** Gallery II Mall. Tel. 592-8700.

This store stocks a particularly strong selection in fiction, books on computers and business, children's literature, and cookbooks.

**BOOK TRADER,** 501 South St. Tel. 925-0219.

If you're on South Street and feel like browsing or just resting, Book Trader has a fine paperback collection and benches, along with a resident cat. It's open until midnight on most nights. You can also find a good selection of out-of-print books and American fiction.

**BORDERS,** 1727 Walnut St. Tel. 568-7400.

Started by the Borders brothers in Minneapolis, this bookstore is a dream come true and has quickly become a cultural center of Rittenhouse Square. It features a great staff and a greater selection, computerized searches, hundreds of serious magazines and periodicals, attention to local writers, an active reading series in the evening, and even a second-floor espresso bar with newspapers! There's a great children's book section with toys and storytelling hours on most Saturdays.

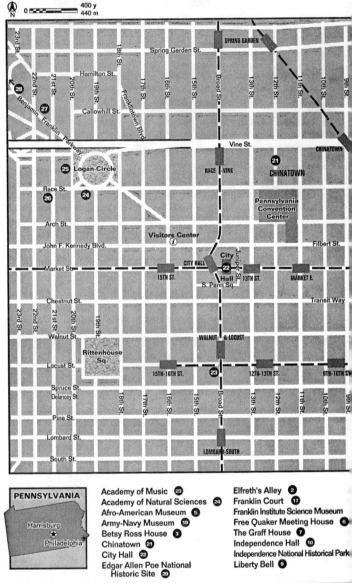

| | | |
|---|---|---|
| **PENNSYLVANIA** | Academy of Music ㉓ | Elfreth's Alley ❷ |
| | Academy of Natural Sciences ㉔ | Franklin Court ⑰ |
| | Afro-American Museum ❺ | Franklin Institute Science Museum |
| Harrisburg ★ | Army-Navy Museum ⑱ | Free Quaker Meeting House ❻ |
| Philadelphia ★ | Betsy Ross House ❸ | The Graff House ❼ |
| | Chinatown ㉑ | Independence Hall ⑩ |
| | City Hall ㉒ | Independence National Historical Park |
| | Edgar Allen Poe National Historic Site ㉙ | Liberty Bell ❾ |

## BRENTANO'S, The Shops at Liberty Place, 1625 Chestnut St. Tel. 557-8443.

Here you'll find a fine collection of bestsellers, a local-interest collection, classics, and glossy coverage of contemporary affairs.

## ENCORE, 609 Chestnut St. Tel. 627-4557.

Bestsellers are sold here at 35% off, the best discount in town. Nothing goes for full price, and you can often pick up exactly what you've been looking for. Additional Encore bookstores are located at summer weekends, although flea-market items seem to predominate there. **Head House Square** becomes a bustling bunch of booths all day Saturday and on Sunday afternoons from April through September.

## AGAPE, 1116 Pine St. Tel. 922-2804.

From a cramped storefront with a loft, Agape offers import and export items that are striking and sophisticated, with very low-priced specials on fine furniture and jewelry.

## ART A LA CARTE, 1911 Chestnut St. Tel. 963-0767.

This store features works on paper, clay, and glass.

## THE ARTISANS STORE AT LIBERTY, The Shops at Liberty Place, 1625 Chestnut St. Tel. 567-1355.

Currently one of the hottest stores in town, the Cooperative presents a collection of authentic native crafts from Appalachia, the South, New England, and the Midwest. A recent exhibition featured basketry, ceramics, painted wood toys, and fimo clay. Open on Sunday, their main gallery is located in the heart of the Brandywine Valley, at the junction of U.S. 1 and Penna. 100.

## THE BLACK CAT, 3424 Sansom St. Tel. 386-6664.

Next door to the White Dog Café, Judy Wicks has set up a charming arts-and-crafts store that's open until 9pm. Living-room knick-knacks are displayed in a living room and so forth. Also, there's a small number of antiques and near-antiques.

## THE COUNTRY SAMPLER, 1740 Sansom St. Tel. 563-9002/3.

Here you can find quilts, wood accessories and furniture, and needlepoint—just what the name implies.

## THE FABRIC WORKSHOP, 1100 Vine St. Tel. 922-7303.

This place is a bit out of the way, unless you're coming from the new Convention Center, but don't miss the Fabric Workshop for textile versions of Venturi and Red Grooms designs.

## MODERNE, 111 N. 3rd St. Tel. 923-8536.

This Olde City stalwart gives a slant to European art deco furniture. It offers a very good selection of American and French iron works—furniture and decorative items.

## OLC, 152–54 N. 3rd St. Tel. 923-6085.

OLC, in the Olde City, has 6,000 feet of sophisticated lighting and furnishings displayed in a museum-quality setting that's been cited by the American Institute of Architects.

## THOMAS MOSER CABINETMAKERS, 210 W. Washington Square. Tel. 922-6440.

Tucked away off Walnut Street, between 7th and 8th streets, is one of the country's great craftsmen of wooden furniture—or his store at least, since Tom Moser lives and works out of Maine. The beds, cabinets, desks, and chairs here are inspired by Shaker and other rural American designs, and the execution and finishes are wondrous. The items are not cheap.

## THE WORKS GALLERY, 319 South St. Tel. 922-7775.

The specialties here are ceramics, glass creations, and furniture transcending the boundary between craft and art. Photography is also tucked in between rooms.

## DEPARTMENT STORES

### STRAWBRIDGE & CLOTHIER, 8th and Market sts. Tel. 629-6000.

Strawbridges have run this department store for over a century, and it has quietly anchored the Market East neighborhood in the midst of bad times, and it will hopefully do so during the expected Convention Center boom. Now connected to the Gallery mall, it carries a full line over three stories; its prices and boutiques are moderately scaled, with frequent sales of 20% to 30% off. It contains an underrated but excellent food hall, too.

### WANAMAKER'S, between Market and Chestnut and 13th and Juniper sts. Tel. 422-2000.

Wanamaker's deserves special mention. This was one of the first of the great department stores in the country, and Philadelphians found the prospect of buying fine merchandise from soap to fireplaces tremendously exciting. President Taft saw fit to dedicate the building—that's how exciting it was. The present building (1902–10) fills a city block and is modeled ingeniously on Renaissance motifs, which give its 12 stories proportion and grace.

Ralph Lauren now has a first-floor boutique in Wanamaker's. The store also contains various snack bars to allay any hunger pangs that might arise while you're shopping. On the first floor, there's an Adrien Arpel salon, a chiropodist on call at the shoe salon, and an estate jewelry counter. On the mezzanine, you'll find a service center with a post office, a film developer, a travel bureau, a dry cleaner, and an optometrist. Carter Hawley Hale sold the store to Garfinckel's in 1988, and this Washington firm has shrunk retail from eight to five floors, with three stories of commercial offices on top. A five-story court presents Christmas shows with a massive 30,000-pipe organ; this court also hosts daily organ concerts at 11:15am and 5:15pm. What's on sale? See for yourself—and don't miss the bargain basement.

## DISCOUNT SHOPPING

### THE CAMBRIDGE CLOTHING FACTORY OUTLET, 1520 Sansom St., 2nd floor. Tel. 568-8248.

With a bread-and-butter type of styling, the Cambridge Clothing Factory Outlet offers discounts of a third or more. It's open Monday to Friday from 9:30am to 5:30pm, Saturday from 9:30am to 5:30pm, except in summer.

### FASHION DIRECT, 1737 Chestnut St. Tel. 972-0525.

Fashion Direct has a great selection of last year's—and sometimes this year's—styles for men and women, at discounts ranging from 20% to 60%. It helps if you know the designer names you like.

### HOUSE OF BARGAINS, 1939 Juniper St., at S. Broad St. and Passyunk Ave. Tel. 465-8841.

This South Philly institution for children's clothes boasts a remarkable assembly of brand names at from 40% to 80% off retail prices.

### NIGHT DRESSING, 2100 Walnut St. Tel. 563-2828.

Night Dressing carries Lily of France, Olga, Warners, and so forth, almost all at half price. New arrivals appear almost daily. There's a big selection of sleepwear and robes and some bathing-suit coverups. Another Night Dressing is at 724 S. 4th Street (tel. 627-5244).

## SHERMAN BROTHERS, 1520 Sansom St. Tel. 561-4550.

Here over 35 years and recently expanding into the suburbs, Sherman Brothers has the city's best collection of such fine men's shoes as Cole Haan, Allen Edmonds, and Bally. It also stocks difficult sizes. All shoes are discounted from 10% to 25% every day.

# FASHIONS

Philadelphia contains an ample selection of clothing stores for men, women, and children, with heavy reliance on seasonal sales and promotions aimed at tourists. Look for the more conservative styles in the many stores around Rittenhouse Square and in the department stores and the more sharply styled or contemporary fashions on South Street and in the malls. Buying clothes from the outlets of national stores, ranging from The Gap to Burberry's, could save you money because clothing comes without any state sales tax in Pennsylvania.

## CHILDREN'S FASHIONS

## BORN YESTERDAY, 1901 Walnut St. Tel. 568-6556.

Right on Rittenhouse Square, this store fits babies, boys to size 8, and girls to size 14. The fashions run the gamut from what was adorable in the 1890s to what is adorable in the 1990s. This is a great store for new grandmothers and doting aunts and uncles, with an attentive staff.

## THE CHILDREN'S BOUTIQUE, 126 S. 18th St. Tel. 563-3881.

This place features many all-cotton, color-coordinated outfits by local designers and a good selection of top-of-the-line traditional children's clothes.

## GAP KIDS, 432 South St. Tel. 629-1232.

Here you'll find high-quality, casual clothes that mix and match well—and can be exchanged or returned cheerfully at hundreds of locations nationwide. There's another location at 1718 Walnut Street (tel. 546-7010).

## KAMIKAZE KIDS, 520 S. 4th St. Tel. 574-9800.

Aggressively styled fashion wear is sold here. The stock ranges from tights to hair ornaments—everything the urban chic child needs. It also stocks incredible Halloween costumes. The items are not cheap.

## K.I.D.S. Children's Shoe Boutique, 56 N. 3rd St. Tel. 592-9033.

Somewhere between a postmodern carnival and a shoe store, this place is very convenient to Franklin Court and other Independence Hall sites.

## WANAMAKER'S, between Market and Chestnut and 13th and Juniper sts. Tel. 422-2000.

This store has an excellent children's department, with clothes ranging from onesies to dress for special occasions. There are frequent sales.

## MEN'S FASHIONS

### BLACK TIE, 1120 Walnut St. Tel. 925-4404.

If formal wear is a sudden necessity, sales and rentals can be found at Black Tie. It carries Lord West, After Six, Bill Blass, and other suave styles, as well as custom tailoring and accessories and shirts.

### BOTTINO SHOES, 121 S. 18th St. Tel. 854-0907.

Look here for sharper, more avant-garde European fashions.

### BOYD'S, 1818 Chestnut St. Tel. 564-9000.

Under the Gushner family, Boyd's has moved "uptown" to a beautifully restored blue-and-white commercial palace. It's the largest in the city, with 65 tailors on site, and has European and American lines of all types, as well as alterations for a variety of fine designers, such as Ermenegildo Zegna. Boyd's still has its valet and has added a café.

### BROOKS BROTHERS, 1500 Chestnut St. Tel. 564-4100.

Brooks Brothers won't steer you wrong on perfectly acceptable items for business and casual wear; slimmer men should head for the Brooksgate section because the regular styles are cut generously.

### DIMENSIONS, The Drexel Building, 15th and Walnut sts. Tel. 564-1132.

For its sheer ambiance, I have to mention Dimensions, which features contemporary menswear displayed in a magnificent Renaissance palazzo.

### WINDSOR SHIRTS, 1600 Walnut St. Tel. 546-1010.

Conservative and reasonably priced shirts for both men and women can be found here.

### WAYNE EDWARDS, 1521 Walnut St. Tel. 563-6801.

This stretch of Walnut Street is really the block for fashion. Wayne Edwards sports a slightly larger selection of contemporary styles than nearby Allure.

## WOMEN'S FASHIONS

A number of the following women's clothing stores could set up successfully in any fashion capital of the world.

### AMBITIONS, 212 S. 17th St. Tel. 546-1133.

Specializing in larger sizes, Ambitions carries a full selection of fashionable clothing and accessories.

### ANNTAYLOR, 1713 Walnut St. Tel. 977-9336.

This conservative retailer has recently stumbled by dropping the Joan & David shoe line and delving into cheaper garments, but it is working on a revitalization and a reemphasis on quality. Look for markdowns to rebuild trade.

### COMPAGNIE INTERNATIONALE EXPRESS LIMITED, 1730 Chestnut St. Tel. 563-1301.

This local shop of Leslie Wexner's Express empire has middle-priced contemporary styles and friendly help. The enticements are up front, with the cashiers far in the rear.

### DAN'S SHOES, 1126 Chestnut St. Tel. 922-6622.

Fully guaranteed and slightly discounted designer shoes are found here. It's more like a bazaar than a full-service store, but there are some real finds along with the regular stuff. There's another store at 1733 Chestnut Street (tel. 568-5257).

**DAFFY'S, 17th and Chestnut sts. Opening scheduled for late 1992.**
This frenetic retailer offers excellent value for house and near-name brands. Fine leather items are great bargains. It is a far cry from Bonwit Teller's, which occupied this site for decades until 1990, but hardly cut-rate merchandise.

**INTIMA, 1718 Sansom St. Tel. 568-6644.**
The premier (but pricey) lingerie store in Center City is Intima, with an extensive selection of items by French and Italian manufacturers. There's another location at 707 Walnut Street (tel. 238-7727).

**J. CREW, Liberty Place, 1625 Chestnut St. Tel. 977-7335.**
 This store offers a nice merging of casual with formal clothes, all brightly colored and softly styled, plus beautiful cable-knit sweaters. It's a meeting place for high-school and college-aged students.

**KNIT WIT, 208 S. 17th St. Tel. 735-3642.**
Knit Wit specializes in European and American sportswear and casual clothes, such as designer jeans, in a charged, dynamic environment. It also features a good shoe department and very interesting accessories.

**NAANA'S SOCIETY HILL TAILORS, 511 S. 4th St., between Lombard and South sts. Tel. 627-9251.**
Whether it's letting out that dress or an emergency repair, Naana's can take care of it in a hurry.

**NAN DUSKIN, in the Rittenhouse Hotel, 210 W. Rittenhouse Square. Tel. 735-6400.**
A Rittenhouse Square fixture for more than 40 years, Nan Duskin carries the creations of the finest European and American designers. It's the premier venue in town for national couturiers.

**ONE NIGHT STAND, 132 S. 17th St. Tel. 568-9200.**
Elegant designer dresses suitable for formal wear are for rent or sale here. Even the mayor's wife stops by. It's open Monday to Friday until 6pm, Saturday until 5pm.

**PHILIP MENDELSOHN, 229 S. 18th St. Tel. 546-6333.**
Offered here are stylish clothes for the mature woman with fashion sense. This place feels like a throwback to an earlier, pleasant era in Rittenhouse Square.

**PLAGE TAHITI, 128 S. 17th St. Tel. 569-9139.**
A selective store, Plage Tahiti has original but adaptable clothes. During various seasons, you can find excellent sales here, although the apparel isn't to everyone's liking. As the name suggests, French bathing suits are a constant.

**RODIER OF PARIS, 135 S. 18th St. Tel. 496-0447.**
This expensive, fashion-forward retailer is now back in Rittenhouse Square, after an untimely fling at The Bourse.

### TOBY LERNER, 117 S. 17th St. Tel. 568-5760.

With an intimate setting for clothes, accessories, and jewelry, this spot is in one of the most affluent neighborhoods in town—and the prices reflect this.

### VICTORIA'S SECRET, 1721 Chestnut St. Tel. 567-0510.

This very popular specialist in lingerie and accessories now carries a full line of women's clothing at excellent prices. It's always crowded.

## WOMEN'S, MEN'S & CHILDREN'S FASHIONS

### BANANA REPUBLIC, 1716 Walnut St. Tel. 735-2247.

This mail-order success story, combining safari retail and travel accessories and books, has moved into retail. There's another store in Chestnut Hill at 8506 Germantown Avenue (tel. 242-2882).

### BURBERRY'S, 1705 Walnut St. Tel. 557-7400.

Burberry's has all the suits, raincoats, and accessories suitable for a gentleman or a lady.

### THE GAP, 1524 Chestnut St. Tel. 564-3862.

The Gap features casual styles in predictable colors for men and women. As in Baby Gap, you know exactly what you're getting, and you can make an easy exchange or get a refund at any Gap around the country. Other locations are at 5th and South streets (tel. 627-7334), 1710 Walnut Street (tel. 732-3391), The Gallery at Market East (tel. 625-4962), and virtually all area malls.

### POLO/RALPH LAUREN, The Shops at the Bellevue, Broad and Walnut sts. Tel. 985-2800.

The new Polo/Ralph Lauren has its own private elevator and fabulous settings for the plushest suitings in town.

### URBAN OUTFITTERS, 1801 Walnut St. Tel. 569-3131.

Housed in a turn-of-the-century mansion on the corner of Rittenhouse Square, this store has been branching off from the conservative preppy look. The basement has an unusual children's, home-furnishings, and book selection.

## FLAGS

### HUMPHRYS FLAG COMPANY, 238 Arch St. Tel. 922-0510.

If Betsy Ross House has left you with an insatiable urge to trot out Old Glory, look no further than Humphrys Flag Company. This company has been manufacturing custom banners and state and foreign flags since the middle of the last century. It also has a complete list of pennants and award ribbons that are silkscreened and decaled in the shop.

## FLORISTS

Local flower stores abound. You can also call 24-hour service for FTD through **Flower World** (tel. 567-7100, or toll free 800/257-7880).

### BLOOMIES, 1200 Spruce St. Tel. 732-3262.

This florist is open late every day and provides prompt delivery for phone orders.

### FLOWER MARKET, Concourse of 2 Penn Center. Tel. 563-5478.

The Flower Market has cornered the Rittenhouse Square market. A dozen prize roses go for $15, and most of the world's standard blooms are available at good prices. Another store is at 177 S. 16th Street (tel. 569-0889).

# FOOD

 The **Reading Terminal Market** at 12th and Market streets, with its dozens of individual booths and cafés, has been recommended in Chapter 6.

### CHEF'S MARKET, 231 South St. Tel. 925-8360.

The premier gourmet store in Society Hill—or even the entire city—is Chef's Market, with a staggering array of charcuterie, cookbooks, and condiments. Would you believe this place stocks breads and cakes supplied by 20 bakeries?

### ITALIAN MARKET, 9th Street between Christian and Wharton sts.

The Italian Market comes straight out of another era, with pushcarts and open stalls of fresh goods and produce, cheese, and some clothes from Tuesday through Saturday (the end of the week is better). Many shops are open until noon on Sunday. Particular favorites are **DiBruno's** at 930 S. 9th Street for cheese, **Sarcone and Sons** at 758 S. 9th Street for bread, and the pound cake at the **Pasticceria** at 9th and Federal streets. You can always snack on fried dough or pastries along the route, as well as save money or pick up an espresso machine at **Fante's.** To reach the market, head five blocks south of South Street; SEPTA bus 47 goes south on 8th Street from Market.

### MARKET AT THE COMMISSARY, 130 S. 17th St. Tel. 568-8055.

In Center City, one gourmet favorite is Steve Poses' Market at the Commissary, which was a pioneer in the 1980s restaurant renaissance. You can have your carrot cake and eat it, too, and also pick up tins of many of the world's delicacies. The charcuterie section sells cold salads, breads, pâtés, and quiche. It's open Monday to Thursday from 11:30am to 10pm, Friday and Saturday from 11:30am to 11pm, and Sunday from 9:30am to 10pm.

### MARON'S, 107 S. 18th St. Tel. 988-9992.

The finest mints and chocolates in Philadelphia since 1850 are sold here. Maron's also prepares made-to-order gift baskets.

### MICHELFELDER'S SAUSAGE SHOP, below Suburban Station Concourse at 14th and Market sts. No telephone.

Michelfelder's has links of German and domestic wurst, plus lunch sandwiches.

### NUTS TO YOU, 24 S. 20th St. Tel. 567-7330.

Some people are crazy about nuts—and Nuts To You understands them. All nuts in this store come fresh-roasted, and dried fruits, candy, and chocolates round out the pickings at rock-bottom prices.

### PAGANO'S GOURMET, Market Place East, 701 Market St. Tel. 922-7771.

Pagano's stocks a large selection of cheeses, deluxe meats, exotic condiments, and breads and crackers. Gift packages and box lunches are prepared from $7.95. The original **Pagano's Cheesery** is at 1507 Walnut Street (tel. 568-0891). There's another Pagano's Gourmet in Penn Center Station Concourse, beneath 17th Street and John F. Kennedy Boulevard (tel. 557-0423).

### PETITE BOULANGERIE, 1418 Walnut St. No telephone.

A new entrant, Petite Boulangerie has four Center City locations for croissants, baguettes, and the like. The location listed above has some café seating.

### R&W DELICATESSEN, 19th and Walnut sts. Tel. 563-7247.

The deli nearest to Rittenhouse Square, R&W has plenty of fixings for do-it-yourself lunches, including hearty noodle pudding.

### RAGO, 258 S. 20th St. Tel. 732-0444.

A small gem of a store just north of Spruce Street, Rago is run by the same family that operates Fratelli Rago, a fine Italian trattoria three blocks away.

### STRAWBRIDGE & CLOTHIER, 8th and Market sts. Tel. 629-6000.

Philadelphia, like many American cities in the past decade, has imported that lovely French institution, the charcuterie. The Food Gallery at Strawbridge & Clothier, for my money, has a terrific assortment, if you're near Independence Hall.

# GIFTS

### AMY & FRIENDS, 2124 Walnut St. Tel. 496-1778 or 232-3714.

You have to put up with a fair amount of free-flowing disorder to enjoy this place, but there's a truly eclectic assortment of antiques and bric-a-brac, including Classic Writing, a boutique specializing in top-quality fountain pens.

### BERNIE ROBBINS CO., 1625 Sansom St. Tel. 563-2380.

Arranged for quick selection, Bernie Robbins Co. is a high-class catalog showroom, and the values on jewelry, technological wonders, luggage, and appliances are excellent. You can also order by mail.

### COUNTRY ELEGANCE, 269 S. 20th St., Tel. 545-2992.

Home accessories, along with a great selection of fine and antique linens, are sold here. It's open Monday to Friday until 7pm.

### CRABTREE & EVELYN, The Shops at Liberty Place, 1625 Chestnut St. Tel. 665-9184.

Crabtree & Evelyn, the very English emporium, purveys fine toiletries and comestibles for the discriminating. Their marmalade's famous, but those badger-bristle shaving brushes and those soaps make terrific gifts as well. There's another store at The Bourse (tel. 625-9256).

### DETAILS, 131 S. 18th St. Tel. 977-9559.

Sumptuous gifts, such as picture frames and stationery, are sold at the former Papier Cache.

### MINERALISTIC, 608 S. 4th St. Tel. 922-7199.

Crystals and semiprecious stones and pendants, along with New

Age tapes and the like, are sold at this store, at the intersection of South Street and Society Hill.

**TOUCHES, 225 S. 15th St. Tel. 546-1221.**
This is an upscale boutique with leather goods, boxes, perfume bottles, handmade jewelry, and frames.

**URBAN OUTFITTERS, 1801 Walnut St. Tel. 569-3131.**
Urban Outfitters specializes in campus-trendy furniture, clothing, health foods, kitchen equipment, and fabrics such as Marimekko. Entrees on Trays, a pleasant high-class cafeteria, adjoins the University of Pennsylvania location at 4040 Locust Street (tel. 387-0373).

## JEWELRY

Philadelphia is known for all types of jewelry—traditional, one-of-a-kind, heirloom, and contemporary. Most of the city's jewelers occupy two city blocks at **Jeweler's Row,** centering on Sansom and 8th streets.

**BAILEY, BANKS, AND BIDDLE, 16th and Chestnut sts. Tel. 564-6200.**
Established in 1832, Bailey, Banks, and Biddle has extraordinary silverware and stationery as well as jewelry. It's an enormous store (or museum, if you're not looking to spend).

**I. SWITT, 130 S. 8th St. Tel. 922-3830.**
Don't let the crotchety help at I. Switt scare you away; the store does beautiful traditional settings at reasonable prices.

**JACK KELLMER, 717 Chestnut St. Tel. 627-8350.**
With a magnificent marble showroom, Kellmer imports diamonds by the dozen and sells unusual gold and diamond pieces.

**J. E. CALDWELL & CO., Chestnut and Juniper sts. Tel. 864-8829.**
 This is another big and traditional store, founded in 1839. It stocks watches and silver as well as jewelry. It also does repairs, and the building has just been magnificently renovated.

**JEWELERS' ROW, between Sansom and Walnut sts. and 7th and 8th sts.**
This area contains more than 350 retailers, wholesalers, and craftspeople. Particularly noted is **Sydney Rosen** at 716 Sansom Street (tel. 922-3500). **Robinson Jewelers,** 107 S. 8th Street (tel. 627-3066), specializes in Masonic jewelry and watch repair.

**TIFFANY & CO., The Shops at the Bellevue, 1414 Walnut St. Tel. 735-1919.**
This fabled silver and jewelry store features exquisite service. Though many items are very expensive here, there are plenty of attractive items under $100.

## LUGGAGE

**ROBINSON LUGGAGE COMPANY, Broad and Walnut sts. Tel. 735-9859.**
Here you'll find a great selection of leather, along with discounted travel accessories and briefcases.

**TRAVEL-WISE, 132 S. 18th St. Tel. 563-7001.**

This Rittenhouse Square store carries gadgets and gifts as well as luggage.

# MALLS & SHOPPING CENTERS

## THE BOURSE, between 4th and 5th sts. and Chestnut and Market sts. Tel. 625-0300.

Just to the east of the Liberty Bell, this superb example of late Victorian architecture has been renovated as a mall in the form of two arcades surrounding an expansive skylit atrium. The original Bourse was built from 1893 to 1895 as a merchants' exchange, and it combines a brick-and-sandstone exterior with a cool, colorful interior. The Bourse is now a great place to rest during or after a hot day of sightseeing, especially because of the many second-floor snack bars. Brass ensembles and jugglers perform in the court during almost every lunchtime; you can view them from parasoled ice-cream tables or park benches in the loggias.

The Bourse seems to be throwing in the towel on most of its struggling retail stores, with a few mid-level survivors, such as **La Parfumerie** (with an enormous selection) and **Destination Philadelphia,** taking city-based merchandise to the limit. On one level above, about two dozen stalls offer a permanent street fair of ethnic cuisine. The Great Hall, the stores, and the restaurants are open Monday, Tuesday, and Thursday from 10am to 6pm; Wednesday, Friday, and Saturday from 10am to 8pm; and Sunday from 11am to 6pm.

## FRANKLIN MILLS, 1455 Franklin Mills Circle. Tel. 632-1500.

About 15 miles northeast of Center City on the edge of Bucks County (follow the signs from I-95 [take Exit 22 north] or from Penna. 276 [take Exit 28 south]), the former Liberty Bell racetrack opened in mid-1989 as Franklin Mills, the city's largest mall, with 1.8 million square feet devoted to 250 discount and outlet stores. The anchor tenants, who together have more than a million feet of the single-story center, are **Sears & Roebuck; Ports of the World,** a discount department store; **J. C. Penney;** and a discount pharmacy. There's parking for more than 9,000 cars. For entertainment the **49th Street Galleria** has bowling, roller skating, miniature golf, batting cages, and rides and games. (Open Monday to Thursday from 10am to 11pm, Friday and Saturday until midnight, and Sunday until 9pm). If you can't stop there, two ancillary malls are a 61-checkout-lane (that's right, 61 lanes) **Carrefour** supermarket/department store and a 30-store **Home and Design Centre.**

Franklin Mills is open Monday to Saturday from 10am to 9:30pm and Sunday from 11am to 6pm.

## THE GALLERY/GALLERY II, 8th to 10th and Market sts.

The Gallery and Gallery II are built on four levels accommodating more than 200 stores and restaurants around sunken arcades and a glass atrium. **Stern's** department store, at the 10th Street corner of Market Street, is struggling to fit in Gimbel's shoes. **Market Fair** has over 25 snack bars and take-out spots. **News Stand,** a popular bar and an intimate restaurant, is near the atrium at 9th Street, with its escalators and tapestries. Stores offer running shoes, books, pets, cameras, jewelry, fresh produce, toys, and all the clothing that you could ever need. **Strawbridge & Clothier,** one of America's last independent department stores still in family hands, connects over 9th Street with merchandise of slightly higher quality and prices.

The Gallery/Galleria II is open Monday and Tuesday and Thursday to Saturday from 9am to 8pm, Wednesday from 9am to 9pm, and Sunday from noon to 5pm.

## MARKET PLACE EAST, Market Street between 7th and 6th sts. Tel. 592-8905.

The century-old Lit Brothers Department Store was a sprawling assembly of wrought-iron facades that introduced hundreds of thousands to their first adult clothes. It has been recently and beautifully resuscitated. The ground floor has attracted classy tenants—including **Conran's** for home furnishings; **Einstein Books;** and **Toys That Matter,** a new favorite of 1990s families at the corner at 701 Market Street. There is garage space nearby.

Market Place East is open from 10am to 6pm Monday to Saturday and from 11:30am to 5:30pm Sunday. The food court and bars downstairs are open from about 7am to midnight most days.

## SHOPS AT THE BELLEVUE, Broad and Walnut sts.

The lower floors of the Bellevue Hotel have been turned into a very upscale collection of top names in retailing. Browsing here is quite low-key; you'll feel that the wares are displayed in a private club. **Polo/Ralph Lauren** is the third largest in the world, with three floors of mahogany-and-brass splendor and a private elevator. Other tenants include **Tiffany & Company,** with its extraordinary jewelry, silver, and accessories; **Pierre Deux,** with country antiques, table settings, and Souleiado fabrics from Provence; **Gucci,** with its own Walnut Street entrance for silks, cashmeres, leather, and their noble racing stripe; **Martin Lawrence Gallery,** with contemporary art; **Alfred Dunhill** of London; and **Neuchatel Chocolates.** Dining is at the **Palm Restaurant** or the **Broadway Deli.**

Shops at the Bellevue is open from 10am to 6pm Monday to Saturday (to 8pm Wednesday).

## THE SHOPS AT LIBERTY PLACE, Chestnut St. between 16th and 17th sts. Tel. 851-9055.

The Liberty Place development is the real thing: It's the handsome 60-story tower that supplanted City Hall as the city's tallest spire, and it contains 70 stores and stalls that together achieve an ambiance and a comfort level that are the finest in the city. It's beautifully designed and signed, with many street exits and entrances that curve and converge on a soaring, glass-domed rotunda with teal-blue and brass accents. Representative of the retailers are **Rand McNally** for maps and children's games; **Brentano's** for books; **The Coach Store** for luggage; **Compagnie Internationale Express** for casual clothes; **Handblock** for high-quality Indian clothes and fabrics; and **Jos. A. Bank** and **J. Crew** for traditional clothes. The second floor is a wonderfully convenient, reasonable court where you can eat on the run, with hundreds of well-kept tables and chairs around quality food stalls. Provident Bank operates an automatic teller machine inside near 17th Street, and the garage directly underneath holds 750 cars.

The Shops at Liberty Place are open Monday to Saturday from 9:30am to 7pm and Sunday from noon to 6pm.

## SOUTH STREET, just South of Society Hill.

This once-funky area is turning into big business. Because restaurants and nightlife now line South Street from Front to 8th streets, many of the 180 stores here are open well into the evening and offer goods ranging from the gentrified to the somewhat grotesque. Among the stores I recommend are these: **Queen Village Flowers,** 700 S. 2nd Street (tel. 925-0484); the **Works Crafts Gallery,** 319 South Street (tel. 922-7775); antique and contemporary fashions at **Xog,** 340 South Street (tel. 925-0907); terrific books and records at **The Book Trader,** 5th and South streets (tel. 925-0219); and smile-producing gadgets at **In General,** 634 South Street (tel. 592-7210).

## PRINTING

**THE PRINTER'S PLACE, 126 S. 16th St. Tel. 567-1400.**
If you need to reproduce material quickly, this store can handle almost anything, including color. There are two more locations: at 1315 Walnut Street (tel. 546-6562) and at the Penn Center Concourse (tel. 546-5666).

## RECORDINGS & MUSIC

Since the Philadelphia area has well-developed musical tastes of all kinds, the city has a wide selection of good stores.

**BARNES & NOBLE, 1424 Chestnut St. Tel. 972-8275.**
This stocks Center City's biggest selection of recordings.

**JACOB'S, 1718 Chestnut St. Tel. 568-7800.**
Jacob's is Center City's best source of sheet music for serious and pop musicians alike.

**NATHAN MUCHNICK, 1725 Chestnut St. Tel. 564-0209.**
Classical rarities are sold here.

**THIRD STREET JAZZ AND ROCK, 10 N. 3rd St. Tel. 627-3366.**
Jerry Gordon has one of the finest collections of jazz in the country. Also featured are new wave, Caribbean, and African music.

**TOWER RECORDS, 610 South St. Tel. 574-9888.**
The champion of South Street's recent stores has to be the Los Angeles–based Tower Records, which moved into the former Ripley Music Hall. Its philosophy is to stock virtually all current recordings at lower prices, and the Tower Records Classical Annex across the street at no. 539 has even lower prices. It's open 15 hours every day.

## SPORTING GOODS

**FINISH LINE SPORTS, 1915 Walnut St. Tel. 569-9957.**
This store has a great location right off Rittenhouse Square, but it's quite small and primarily for athletic shoes and fashion-conscious accessories. However, Finish Line is expanding into sportswear of all types.

**I. GOLDBERG, 902 Chestnut St. Tel. 925-9393.**
An Army-Navy paradise and then some, I. Goldberg provides at excellent prices the basic goods that you'll need for anything in the outdoors, with styles from the determinedly antifashion

to the up-to-the-minute. The selection is very large, but the help is harried.

## TILES

**COUNTRY FLOORS,** 1706 Locust St. Tel. 545-1040.
Some of the most elegant tiles in America, whether floor, wall, or trivet, are at Country Floors. The store is currently riding the French ceramic-finish boom but also carries a fine assortment of Spanish, Portuguese, Dutch, and Italian earthenware.

## TOBACCO

**HOLT'S,** 114 S. 16th St. Tel. 563-0763.
Holt's is renowned throughout the country for its selection of pipes and tobaccos. There are enough fresh cigars here to fill every humidor in Congress, plus an excellent pen selection.

## TOYS

**EINSTEIN BOOKS and TOYS THAT MATTER,** 701 Market St. Tel. 923-3622.
From Russian dolls to origami, from fossils to Babar the Elephant—it's all here for the 1990s family. The space is wonderful, and the staff creates a sense of festival with the constantly changing displays.

**KIDDIE CITY,** 1024 Market St. Tel. 922-3766.
Kiddie City is the urban mass-market toy (and child-needs) store par excellence. If you watch Saturday-morning cartoons, you'll recognize every doll, game, train, puzzle, and car in here. It also carries party equipment and some creative playthings.

**PAST PRESENT FUTURE,** 24 S. 18th St. Tel. 854-0444.
Past Present Future sells soft sculpture, custom and wooden handmade toys, and puzzles. I've seen plenty of adults whiling away some time in here. There's also a good selection of toys and gifts for adults, including craft jewelry.

## WINES & LIQUOR

After the repeal of prohibition, Pennsylvania decided not to license private liquor retailing but to establish a government monopoly on alcohol sales. You, or any tavernkeeper or restaurateur, can find liquor only in state stores (or at a vineyard within the state). They are usually open Monday to Wednesday from 9am to 5pm and Thursday to Saturday until 9pm. The selection has improved greatly in recent years. You cannot, however, buy chilled beer or champagne—just what's on the shelf. (Try a delicatessen or licensed supermarket for the bubbles.)

### STATE LIQUOR STORES

**OLD CITY LIQUOR,** 32 S. 2nd St. Tel. 625-0906.
Near Independence Hall, Old City Liquor looks—and acts—almost like a non-state store. It's open Monday and Tuesday from 11am to 7pm and Wednesday to Saturday from 9am to 9pm.
The following are some additional Philadelphia liquor stores. In the Independence Hall Area, try the **Bourse Building,** 5th and

Chestnut streets (tel. 560-5504); 32 S. 2nd Street (tel. 625-0906) or **Society Hill Shopping Center** (tel. 922-4224). In the City Hall Area, there are state stores at 1318 Walnut Street (tel. 735-8464) and 265 S. 10th Street (tel. 922-6497). Around Rittenhouse Square, you might try **The Wine Reserve,** 18th and Walnut streets, an upscale version of a state store, opened in early 1990. Consumers can browse freely among such opulent surroundings as a slate floor and a mahogany counter and shelves. Bottles of some 800 wines are stacked horizontally—a first in Philadelphia! In University City there's a state store at 4049 Walnut Street (tel. 222-3547).

# CHAPTER 10

# PHILADELPHIA ENTERTAINMENT & NIGHTLIFE

**1. THE PERFORMING ARTS**

**2. THE CLUB & MUSIC SCENE**

**3. THE BAR SCENE**

**4. MORE ENTERTAINMENT**

If you ask Philadelphians to name the biggest change in their city over the last 20 years, the explosion of entertainment and nightlife possibilities will rank right up there with Independence National Historical Park and the restaurant renaissance. From sound-and-light shows at Independence Hall to sound-and-light shows at Polo Bay to the Warwick's disco, there's enough pizzazz and activity in this city to fill months of idle evenings.

The city itself seems a little surprised with its newfound vitality, since Philadelphia's always been known for its sedate domestic pleasures. But with the gentrification of Center City neighborhoods and the preservation of a safe urban environment, such spots as Delaware Avenue along the river, Olde City north of Society Hill, and the northwest quadrant of Center City have joined South Broad Street and Rittenhouse Square as lively areas for café- or bar-hopping and live entertainment.

This doesn't mean that Philadelphia has let its preeminence in cultural affairs slide, even though recent disastrous city and state funding cuts have imperiled many operations. The Academy of Music presents a full season of the marvelous Philadelphia Orchestra and the financially struggling but artistically vital Pennsylvania Ballet. Two or three theaters offer road productions and preliminary versions of Broadway shows, and the Walnut Street Theater has been going strong since 1809. The city is rich in resources for all: movies, cabaret, dinner theater, and dance.

The best sources for what's current are the "Weekend" supplement of the *Philadelphia Inquirer* (it comes out on Friday) and a publication called *Welcomat,* 25,000 copies of which are distributed throughout Center City. Most hotel lobbies carry it, as does the Visitors Center, which is also an excellent information source. For monthly happenings, consult the bureau of the front of *Philadelphia* magazine.

## DISCOUNTS

For further inducement, check out **Upstages** at the Visitors Center, 16th Street and John F. Kennedy Boulevard (tel. 567-0670). It has half-price tickets for up to 50 events each week (open Tuesday to Saturday from 10am to 5pm). There's a small service charge. You can even call before you stop by, to see what's on.

Senior citizens can receive discounts of about 10% or $5 per ticket or more at many theaters, including the Annenberg Center, American Music Theater Festival, and Wilma Theatre. Concert halls generally make rush or last-minute seats available to students at prices under $10; these programs sometimes extend to adults as well. Groups can generally get discounts of 20% to 50% by calling well in advance.

# 1. THE PERFORMING ARTS

Music, theater, and dance are presented regularly all over the city. I have restricted the venues below to Center City and West Philadelphia, where you'll be most of the time and where the quality of entertainment tends to be highest. There's really no off-season for the performing arts in Philadelphia; when the regular seasons of the Philadelphia Orchestra or Pennsylvania Ballet end, the outdoor activities that make Philadelphia so pleasant take over.

## MAJOR PERFORMING ARTS COMPANIES

### OPERA COMPANIES

**OPERA COMPANY OF PHILADELPHIA, 1500 Walnut St., Suite 504. Tel. 732-5814.**

This company presents full stagings of five operas per year at the Academy of Music. The performances take place on Tuesday and Friday evening, with seating preference given to season subscribers. Such international opera stars as Benita Valente (who lives down the street), Theresa Stratas, and Plácido Domingo appear in about half of the productions. They have snagged Luciano Pavarotti to judge and host an annual International Voice Competition, with the winner receiving a role in a production the following season.

**Prices:** Tickets $12–$40.

**THE PENNSYLVANIA OPERA THEATER [TPOT], 1345 Chestnut St., Suite 1800. Tel. 972-0904** or 440-9797 for box office; TicketMaster 336-2000.

Barbara Silverstein offers two or three vital, dramatic productions sung in English at the Shubert Theater. Recent productions have included the world premiere of *The Sibyl* by Vincent Persichetti and Rossini's *The Barber of Seville.*

**Prices:** Tickets $20–$45. Half-price student tickets are available 30 minutes before curtain.

### CLASSICAL MUSIC

**ALL-STAR FORUM, 1530 Locust St. Tel. 735-7506.**

Moe Septee, Philadelphia's top concert impresario, brings recital soloists, chamber groups, dance troupes, and occasionally theater groups to the Academy of Music on weekday nights at 8pm or on Sunday at 3pm. The talent is world-class.

The All-Star Forum also presents the **Philadelphia Pops** in four series per year. Bridging the symphonic and the popular under acclaimed pianist Peter Nero, the Pops sells out for most performances.
**Prices:** Tickets $12–$40.

### CONCERTO SOLOISTS OF PHILADELPHIA, 2136 Locust St. Tel. 574-3550.

Marc Mostovoy has assembled a group of excellent New York visitors and homegrown Curtis graduates for seasons of chamber music. The concerts take place in Rittenhouse Square neighborhood churches, such as the **Church of the Holy Trinity** (tel. 567-1267) at 19th and Walnut streets.

### CURTIS INSTITUTE OF MUSIC, 1726 Locust St. Tel. 893-7902.

Philadelphia has a surfeit of really excellent musicians and programs, many of them springing from the world-famous Curtis Institute, which was led for many years by Rudolf Serkin. Curtis itself has a small hall that's good for chamber works, just off Rittenhouse Square; call 893-5260 for a schedule of the mostly free concerts, operas, and recitals.

### FREE LIBRARY OF PHILADELPHIA, 19th and Vine sts. Tel. 686-5322.

About once per month, the Free Library's Montgomery Auditorium presents another in an ongoing series of well-chosen soloists on Thursday at 8pm.
**Prices:** Free, on a first come, first served basis.

### MUSIC FROM MARLBORO, Port of History Museum, Penn's Landing. Tel. 569-4690.

This survivor of Rudolf Serkin's years in Philadelphia performs about once a month. The Port of History Museum site is also used on weekends by many smaller artists and organizations, such as the Philadelphia Chamber Music Society.
**Prices:** Tickets $10–$25.

### THE PHILADELPHIA ORCHESTRA, regular season at the Academy of Music, Broad and Locust sts. Tel. 893-1900, or toll free 800/223-0120 to charge tickets.

For many people, a visit to Philadelphia isn't complete without hearing a concert given by the smooth, powerful ensemble under Wolfgang Sawallisch. The orchestra achieved renown under Leopold Stokowski, then was led for 44 years by the legendary Eugene Ormandy and for 12 years by Riccardo Muti. The Philadelphia has built a reputation for virtuosity and balance that only a handful of the world's orchestras can match. (By the way, the score you hear with Walt Disney's noted film *Fantasia* was recorded by Stokowski and the Philadelphians, and the orchestra is suing Disney over videocassette royalties!)

The backbone of its year is the subscription schedule at the Academy of Music. The average season includes 86 concerts: 24 pairs of Friday afternoon and Saturday evening performances, 12 on Tuesday evenings, 14 on Thursday evenings, and a special series of 6 other pairs. The orchestra also offers nonsubscription and youth programs. In summer it moves to Mann Music Center for six weeks

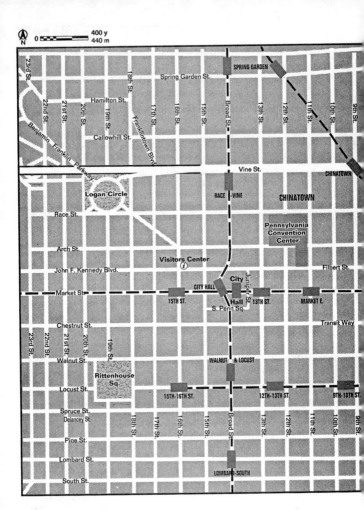

of free concerts (see below). More tickets to individual performances are available than in the past, with certain dress rehearsals open and fewer subscriptions sold.

**Prices:** Tickets $10–$45. Try to buy well in advance of the date. Rush seats for $5 are sold at 7:30pm for all Monday, Tuesday, and Thursday concerts. Unreserved amphitheater seats for $2.50 are sold at 1:30pm on Friday and 5:30pm on Friday and Saturday.

# THE PHILADELPHIA ORCHESTRA, summer season at

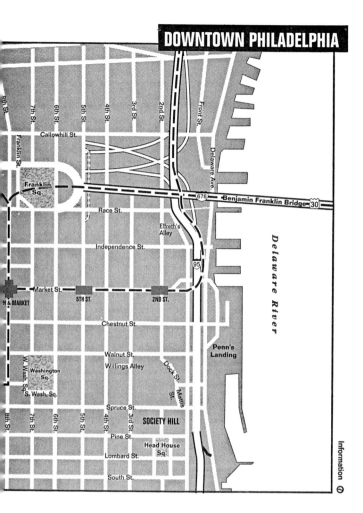

Callowhill St.

Franklin St.

Franklin Sq.

Race St.

Effreth's Alley

Independence St.

676 Benjamin Franklin Bridge 30

95

Market St.

H & MARKET      5TH ST.      2ND ST.

Chestnut St.

Walnut St.

Willings Alley

W. Wash. Sq.

Washington Sq.

S. Wash. Sq.

Spruce St.

SOCIETY HILL

Pine St.

Head House Sq.

Lombard St.

South St.

Penn's Landing

*Delaware Avenue*

*Delaware River*

7th St.  6th St.  5th St.  4th St.  3rd St.  2nd St.  Front St.

8th St.  7th St.  6th St.  5th St.  4th St.  3rd St.

Dock St.

Mattis St.

Information ℹ

---

**Mann Music Center, George's Hill near 52nd St. and Parkside Ave. Tel. 567-0707.**

⭐ During the six-week summer season at Fairmount Park, the orchestra's concerts at the Mann Music Center fill up quickly. Special SEPTA buses travel here from Center City, and there's plenty of free parking on Parkside Avenue. Concerts are on Monday, Wednesday, and Thursday at 8pm. You must have a ticket to be admitted as a seatholder, although tickets are free. To get them, write Robin Hood Dell Concerts, Department of Recreation, P.O. Box

1000, Philadelphia, PA 19105. Two's the limit, and requests made too far in advance will be returned.

If you haven't got tickets for seats, join approximately 15,000 others who sit on the grassy slopes above the orchestra. Don't forget the blankets and insect repellent.

**Prices:** Free.

### RELÂCHE, INC. Various venues. Tel. 963-0345.

This contemporary music group of about a dozen instrumentalists has expanded into copresenting world music or cutting-edge performances at the Annenberg Center, Painted Bride Art Center, Ethical Society on Rittenhouse Square, and elsewhere. Relâche strikes a refreshing balance between interesting and over-intellectualized choices, and has a particular affinity for young composers.

**Prices:** Tickets $8–$25.

## THEATER COMPANIES

### AMERICAN MUSIC THEATER FESTIVAL, 2005 Market St., One Commerce Square. Tel. 851-6450 or 567-0670 for box office.

Founded in 1984, this group presents music theater in all major forms—opera, musical comedy, cabaret, and experimental. American Music Theater also copresents a great cabaret series at the Hotel Atop the Bellevue.

**Prices:** Tickets $10–$40.

### ARDEN THEATRE COMPANY, St. Stephen's Alley, 10th and Ludlow sts. Tel. 829-8900 or UPSTAGES at 567-0670.

Arden is a small professional troupe that has carved a niche by presenting a mix of classics, such as Shakespeare's *Hamlet*, and adaptations of books into stage plays, such as Studs Terkel's *The Good War* and some of Kurt Vonnegut's stories. Arden performs in a new 200-seat theater, located on the site where Ben Franklin flew his kite in 1752.

**Prices:** Tickets $15–$17.

### PHILADELPHIA DRAMA GUILD [PDG], 100 N. 17th St. Tel. 563-7529.

PDG, quickly rising to national prominence under Mary Robinson, puts on five productions annually at the Annenberg Theater. Tickets are available from the subscription director at the above address or at the theater door. A recent season included top-quality productions of Molière, George Wolfe, Brecht, and Preston Sturges, following a smash world premiere of Lanford Wilson's *Redwood Curtain*. The season runs from late October through early April.

**Prices:** Tickets $9–$20.

### PHILADELPHIA THEATER COMPANY [PTC], Plays & Players Theatre, 1714 Delancey St. Tel. 592-8333.

New plays by American writers are the staple of the PTC. Most performances are Tuesday to Saturday at 8pm, with weekend matinees. It's a vital, enjoyable company. Call 735-0631 to buy tickets.

**Prices:** Tickets $10–$20.

### SOCIETY HILL PLAYHOUSE, 507 S. 8th St. Tel. 923-0210.

This playhouse presents distinguished history on a very small stage. It has been bringing *Nunsense* back as a staple for almost a decade, after previously offering more avant-garde work.

**Prices:** Tickets $10–$25. Look around town for twofers.

## WALNUT STREET THEATER, 9th and Walnut Sts. Tel. 574-3550.

Founded in 1809, the Walnut Street Theater continues its distinctive role in the history of the American stage. The regional Walnut Street Company as well as numerous local and touring attractions play here. It was renovated in 1971, and the orchestra pit can seat 50 musicians.

In the 1,052-seat theater, the resident company presents five plays from November through April; both subscriptions and single tickets are available. Each season, two musicals and one Shakespeare play hit the boards, in addition to classical and rock concerts, dance, and other events. In 1986 the company began a Studio Theater Season, presenting new and more experimental works in the 75-seat and 90-seat studio spaces at 825 Walnut Street, adjoining the theater.

**Prices:** Tickets $13–$35, with $5 student rush.

## THE WILMA THEATER, 2030 Sansom St. Tel. 963-0345.

The premier modern theater company in town has to be The Wilma Theater, which has grown to receive national acclaim and grants from the National Endowment for the Arts. A recent season featured new plays by Athol Fugard, Antonio Buero Vallero, Charles Ludlam, and Lanford Wilson.

**Prices:** Tickets $18–$22.

## DANCE COMPANIES

Local troupes vie successfully with such distinguished visitors as Alwin Nikolais, Pilobolus, and the Dance Theater of Harlem. Contact the **Philadelphia Dance Alliance,** an organization that includes most of the performing dance companies in the city, at 1315 Walnut St., Suite 1505, Philadelphia, PA 19107 (tel. 545-6344).

## AFRO-AMERICAN DANCE ENSEMBLE, Ile-Ife Humanitarian Center, 2544 Germantown Ave. Tel. 225-7565.

The Afro-American Dance Ensemble, inspired and directed by Arthur Hall, does everything from classical to modern but emphasizes African ritual dances, often with authentic costume. In summer you'll find them all over the city; Kennedy Plaza and Art Museum Plaza are two of the best locations for the program of outdoor arts presentations run by the city.

**Prices:** Tickets $10–$30.

## MOVEMENT THEATRE INTERNATIONAL [MTI], 3700 Chestnut St. Tel. 382-0606.

MTI—which has assumed operations at a tabernacle temple near the University of Pennsylvania campus—goes well beyond modern dance to present vaudeville, clown theater, mime, circus acts, and classical dance-drama.

**Prices:** Tickets usually $15.

## PENNSYLVANIA BALLET COMPANY, 1101 S. Broad St. at Washington Ave. Tel. 551-7014. Box office at Academy of Music 893-1930, at Merriam 875-4829.

The Pennsylvania Ballet almost went under in 1991 but was rejuvenated under young director Christopher d'Amboise, son of choreographer Jacques d'Amboise. The company performs at the Academy of Music and the Merriam (formerly Shubert)

Theater during the yearly season. Its Christmas-season performances of Tchaikovsky's *Nutcracker,* with the complete Balanchine choreography, is a new city tradition. Each of the company's dozens of yearly performances offers something old, something new, maybe something blue, and always something interesting.

**Prices:** Tickets $11–$25; *Nutcracker* performances $9–$45.

## MAJOR CONCERT HALLS & ALL-PURPOSE AUDITORIUMS

In addition to performances at the following major institutions, look for the many concerts presented in churches, especially around Rittenhouse Square; the city suffers from a dearth of medium-size concert halls.

**ACADEMY OF MUSIC, Broad and Locust sts. Tel. 893-1935 for general information,** 893-1930 for ticket availability.

In the early 19th century constructing an academy of music was a proposal much discussed by the cultured movers and shakers in Philadelphia. At the time, opera was the hallmark of culture, and Philadelphia lagged behind New York and Boston in the construction of a music hall equipped for it. Around mid-century the chosen architects told the investors that they couldn't build both an imposing facade and an acoustically satisfying interior. The group decided to focus on the interior, and the cornerstone was laid in 1852. Modeled on La Scala in Milan, it's still one of the best recording and concert halls in America and is used some 300 evenings annually. The marble planned for the facade has never been added, and the brick and glass seem to suit Philadelphia far better.

An outer entrance hall leads to a grand vestibule, the scene of countless receptions over the last 135 or so years. Inside, the curve of the hall prevents the concentration of sound along any one point, and the 3-foot-thick walls and original plaster help make the academy as resonant as the cellos of the resident Philadelphia Orchestra. The academy was refurbished in 1986, but it remains a symphony of Victorian crimson and gold, with original gaslights still flaming at the Broad Street entrance. Because the Orchestra has been unable to raise funds to build a larger hall down the street, the Philadelphia still plays some 100 dates here annually. Other days are given over to opera and ballet performances, travel films, and other events.

**Box Office:** Open Monday to Saturday from 10am to 5:30pm (8:30pm on event dates) and Sunday from 1pm on event dates. Tickets for any one event go on sale four weeks before at the box office. You can write for tickets from one month ahead of curtain time. The address is Academy of Music Box Office, Broad and Locust streets, Philadelphia, PA 19102; include a self-addressed stamped envelope.

**Tours:** Given most Tuesdays at 2pm, summer excluded, for $2.
**Prices:** Tickets $12–$45, depending on event.

**PAINTED BRIDE ART CENTER, 230 Vine St. Tel. 925-9914.**

It's hard to know what to call the Painted Bride Art Center, near the entrance to the Benjamin Franklin Bridge. It's an art gallery with contemporary tastes, but it also stays open for business and energy, in various forms—folk, electronic and new music, jazz, dance, and theater. Although its director claims that the room can hold 300, the official seat count for the main hall is 60.

**Prices:** Tickets $8–$20.

# THEATERS

At any time, there will be at least one Broadway show in Philadelphia, on the way into or out of New York. There'll also be student repertory, professional performances by casts connected with the University of Pennsylvania, small-theater offerings in neighborhoods of Center City, and cabaret or dinner theater in the suburbs.

## THE ANNENBERG CENTER, 3680 Walnut St. Tel. 898-6791.

The Annenberg Center, endowed by publisher and U.S. ambassador Walter Annenberg at the University of Pennsylvania, houses a complex offering high-quality theater, dance, and other performing arts as well as film screenings. It's located in the midst of the Penn campus and is easily reached by bus or subway/surface line. Two theaters offer performances every season, which runs from late October to early May. The **Harold Prince Theater** stages more intimate productions and usually presents the more avant-garde plays of the two theaters. The **Zellerbach Theater** can handle the most demanding lighting and staging needs.

Two nationally known festivals take place at the Annenberg. The American Music Theater Festival, held here since 1983, is a prestigious forum for sophisticated performances. *X*—the Anthony Davis opera about the life of Malcolm X—was presented here in workshop form, as was *Mowgli,* a musical adaptation of Rudyard Kipling's *The Jungle Book.* The Philadelphia Festival Theater for New Plays is now in its 11th eight-week season at the Prince under inspired leader Carol Rocamora.

The Annenberg also hosts a variety of other professional performers, such as the Philadelphia Drama Guild.

The Zellerbach Theater offers a range of special features, including signed performances and an infrared listening system. The entire complex is also accessible to the disabled.

**Box Office:** Open Mon–Fri 12–6pm, until 9pm on performance weekdays and Saturday, until 5pm on performance Sunday.

**Prices:** Harold Prince Theater tickets $14–$20; Zellerbach Theater ticket $8–$10 for balcony seats, $10–$13 for rear orchestra, $12–$15 for front orchestra.

## THE FORREST, 11th and Walnut sts. Tel. 923-1515.

Of the Philadelphia theaters listed here, the Forrest is the best equipped to handle big musicals, and it hosts several during the year, along with other short-running plays and concerts. Performances are usually on Monday to Saturday at 8pm and on Wednesday and Saturday at 2pm.

**Prices:** Tickets $15–$40, but the 1992 *Phantom of the Opera* production topped out at $100.

## THE SHUBERT, Broad and Locust sts. Tel. 732-5446.

The Shubert, belonging to the newly rejuvenated University of the Arts, hosts student performances and various nontheatrical enterprises. It's an ornate turn-of-the-century hall, renovated to some degree for uses never foreseen during the vaudeville era.

**Prices:** Tickets $5–$25.

## DINNER THEATER

**CAVANAUGH'S RESTAURANT, 119 S. 39th St. Tel. 386-4889.**
This University City stalwart restaurant and bar has gone in for weekend performances of ensemble productions like *A Deadly Affair*. Show runs last 6 to 8 months.
**Prices:** $20–$25.

**RIVERFRONT DINNER THEATER, on the Delaware River at Poplar St. Tel. 925-7000.**
The Riverfront Dinner Theater presents full Broadway shows such as *Pippin* and *Fiddler on the Roof* on a small but adequate stage.
**Prices:** Dinner-and-show package $20–$25, depending on day.

# FREE & OUTDOOR MUSIC

The city's Cultural Affairs Council and Department of Recreation coordinate efforts to bring a festive lineup of jazz, rock, folk, and classical music to places where people like to congregate in summer. You can hear anything from big bands to bongo drums on Monday at 8:15pm on **Rittenhouse Square.**

**Kennedy Plaza,** next to the Convention and Visitors Bureau at 16th Street John F. Kennedy Boulevard, features lunchtime entertainment, as does the Independence Mall Theater. On Wednesday in summer, the Old Citie Fife and Drum Corps marches throughout **Independence National Historical Park.**

The Philadelphia Orchestra plays at Mann Music Center for six weeks in the summer (see above). **Robin Hood Dell East** (tel. 226-0727) also hosts a full summer slate of performers on Monday, Wednesday, and Friday at 8pm. To be sure, not all the performers are top-quality musicians, but they're better than you'd expect for only $1 ($5 for reserved-seating with valet parking). If you send in a request early enough, there's a good chance of picking up a pair of tickets: Write or call 1450 Municipal Services Building, John F. Kennedy Boulevard and 15th Street, Philadelphia, PA 19102 (tel. 215/686-2254). The Dell is near East River and Strawberry Mansion drives.

## OTHER MUSIC PROGRAMS

Philadelphia contains many other institutions that offer the chance to hear music for the price of a museum admission or for free. For example, the **Wanamaker Department Store Organ,** a bewildering array of 30,000 pipes, bursts forth in powerful song every day at 11:15am and 5:15pm. The **Free Library of Philadelphia** offers Thursday concerts at 8pm.

The **Philadelphia Museum of Art,** 26th Street and the Parkway, presents Sunday concerts at 3:30pm in Van Pelt Auditorium. Museum admission is free until 1pm Sundays, so you can make a few hours of it. In addition, one of the city's most popular singles events is the museum's social on Wednesday, with drinks, music, lectures, and so forth from 5:30 to 8:45pm.

The **University Museum,** 33rd and Spruce streets (tel. 898-4000), offers an exceptional series of films and concerts on Sunday at 2:30pm. Children's films are shown on Saturday at 10:30am from October to March.

# 2. THE CLUB & MUSIC SCENE

The minimum legal drinking age in Pennsylvania is 21. Bars may stay open until 2am; establishments that operate as private clubs can serve until 3am.

## CABARET & NIGHTCLUBS

**BEVERLY HILLS BAR & GRILL, The Bourse, 21 S. 5th St. Tel. 627-0778.**
The best of the retro clubs, The Beverly Hills has given the Bourse a shot in the arm and features plenty of dining choices in a combination of hi-tech and Fiestaware, plus great dancing. Word has it that the music will be more contemporary in the future.

**ETHEL BARRYMORE ROOM, HOTEL ATOP THE BELLE-VUE, Broad and Locust sts. Tel. 893-1776.**
In collaboration with the American Musical Theater Festival, major cabaret stars such as Julie Wilson are presented in this classic setting every winter and spring. Old-timers will recognize this room as the Bellevue-Stratford's original home.
**Admission:** $25 cover.

**THE LOUNGE AT THE OMNI, 4th and Chestnut sts. Tel. 925-0000.**
This lounge is a very posh spot, with dark woods and Oriental carpets, a crackling fireplace, a piano trio, and large picture windows surveying Independence National Historical Park across the street. It stays open past midnight on weekends.

**MARKET STREET LIVE!, 701 Market St. Tel. 829-2401.**
This is the only bar mall concept in Center City; a single admission to the Lit Brothers renovation is good for most of the bars and the downstairs arcade of games. Bars include **Player's,** with a large-screen TV for gamesters; **Ltl Ditty's,** a sing-along bar with two grand pianos (open until 2am); a vast sports bar featuring Phillies slugger Mike Schmidt's memorabilia; and **Tooter's,** with live blues and rock.

**MIDDLE EAST, 126 Chestnut St. Tel. 922-1003.**
Dinner followed by belly dancing and eastern Mediterranean music makes a fine evening for scores of Philadelphians nightly. Councilman Jim Tayoun presides, and many of his family members help in various capacities. If you've never seen it, don't worry about taking the kids to see belly dancing: It's quite an art and as pure as the driven snow.
**Admission:** $10 minimum with show.

## COMEDY CLUBS

**COMEDY FACTORY OUTLET, 31 Bank St. Tel. 386-6911.**
Wednesday is open-stage night here, and local night is Thursday;

imported comedians from New York and Los Angeles are featured on other nights. The performances are on Friday at 8:30 and 11pm and on Saturday at 7, 9:15, and 11:30pm. This is a cash-only place.

### THE COMEDY WORKS, 126 Chestnut St. Tel. 922-5997.

This is a recent addition to the Middle East complex, and the biggest, with a recently opened Fun House restaurant (fun-house mirrors and Twister games on the floor) downstairs. It operates from Wednesday (open stage) to Saturday nights. Shows are on Friday at 8:30 and 11pm and on Saturday at 8 and 11pm. There is a separate $10 admission.

### FUNNY BONE, 221 South St. Tel. 440-9670.

Because of its neighborhood, the Funny Bone is a bit free-form. Shows are on Tuesday to Thursday at 8:30pm, on Friday and Saturday at 8:30 and 11pm, and on Sunday at 8:30pm. Admission is $8 on weeknights and $10 on weekends.

## FOLK & COUNTRY MUSIC

### BOOT N SADDLE, 1131 S. Broad St. Tel. 336-1742.

In the heart of South Philly, this cash-only place features live country music every Friday and Saturday night in the back, with seating at tiny tables. There's a large island bar in the front. It's open Monday to Saturday until 2am.

### D'MEDICI RESTAURANT, 824 S. 8th St. Tel. 922-3986.

On Friday and Saturday, Dave Morris and his band bring this otherwise sedate Italian restaurant in South Philadelphia to life with renditions of Sinatra, Mel Torme, Tony Bennett, and other neighborhood favorites. There's no cover charge.

### TRIANGLE TAVERN, 10th and Reed sts. Tel. 467-8683.

If you're in search of where Rocky Balboa would go to sing along with the band, go no further than this place, which couldn't be cheaper. The help really participates.

## ROCK MUSIC

### BACCHANAL, 1320 South St. Tel. 545-6983.

Live bands appear every night, with music ranging from reggae to rock. It's cash only and open daily until 2am.
**Admission:** $5–$8.

### CHESTNUT CABARET, 38th and Chestnut sts. Tel. 382-1201.

The Chestnut Cabaret, in the heart of University City, was once known primarily for nostalgia rock. It's now committed to bringing in a wider and better variety of local, regional, and even national acts on Tuesday to Saturday nights. It does not serve food.
**Admission:** Cover varies, but no minimum.

### J. C. DOBBS, 304 South St. Tel. 922-8713.

Dobbs features rock bands, both crude and smooth, every night until 2am. The upstairs serves food until 1am, and the air is always leaden. It's a hard-drinking place, with lots of energy when the band is good.
**Admission:** $5 at most.

### KHYBER PASS PUB, 56 S. 2nd St. Tel. 627-6482.

This is one of the most popular spots to hear jazz, country, folk, and rock nightly. There's live entertainment from 9:30pm until 1 or 2am, depending on the crowd and the day. Khyber Pass is named after the route the British took to get through Pakistan, and it's somebody's version of what a British overseas officers' club would look like. It does have a certain atticlike charm, nevertheless, and English ales and Irish stout are served.
   **Admission:** $1 Fri–Sat; other nights free.

### NORTH STAR BAR, 27th and Poplar sts. Tel. 235-7827.
   North Star, located near the Philadelphia Museum of Art, has pretensions to serving artists, with photo exhibits and poetry readings. Rock groups perform five nights a week in a recently glassed-in courtyard. You'll see an older bar as you enter. It's a very comfortable place to drink, and the spicy chicken wings are fine.
   **Admission:** $5–$8.

### PULSATIONS, Rt. 1, Glen Mills, PA. Tel. 459-4140.
   It's out of town a bit, but Pulsations in Glen Mills now features live music by name performers at least two days a week. Recent acts have included Joe Jackson and Guess Who. On other nights it's a disco with the latest gadgetry in sound and lights or the host of Chippendales-type exotic dancing. To drive there from Center City, take the West Chester Pike to U.S. 1 and head south on U.S. 1; you'll find Pulsations between the town of Media and Penna. 202.
   **Admission:** Cover varies.

### REVIVAL, 22 S. 3rd St. Tel. 627-4825.
   Featuring up-to-the-minute rock-video releases, Revival is heavily committed to such fare. Call to find out what local talent will be performing live on Sunday nights. Revival's open until 3am.
   **Admission:** $5–$10. Takes credit cards.

### SPECTRUM, Electric Factory Concerts, Broad and Pattison sts. Tel. 569-9416 or 568-3222; box office at Spectrum 336-3600.
   Most of the events that the Electric Factory sponsors, from Willie Nelson to Phil Collins, take place at the **Spectrum,** the city's main indoor arena, in South Philly. As with most rock concerts, tickets at the door are next to impossible to obtain. They're usually distributed through TicketMaster or Ticketron.

## JAZZ & BLUES

Philadelphia is one of the great American venues for jazz. June in particular is the month for presentations, with the Mellon PSFS Jazz Festival produced by George Wien and a jazz-oriented aspect of the American Music Theater Festival called Crosscurrents. For specific information, write or call Mill Creek Jazz and Cultural Society, 4624 Lancaster Ave., Philadelphia, PA 19131 (tel. 215/473-2880).

### BORGIA CAFE, 408 S. 2nd St. Tel. 923-6660.
   This subterranean bistro (the Lautrec restaurant perches on top) offers continuous music nightly from 9:30pm to 2am. Most of the contemporary keyboarders work in tandem with a bass, reed, or vocalist. On Friday and Saturday there's bar and snack service until 1:30am. The café's one of the few places in town that's open every night for jazz.
   **Admission:** $3 per set Fri–Sat; $3 per night rest of week.

**CAROLINA'S, 261 S. 20th St. Tel. 545-1000.**
This popular restaurant features a jazz trio on Saturday night. It's a favorite singles spot, with not bad bistro dining, though cramped.

**LIBERTIES, 705 N. 2nd St. above Fairmount Ave. Tel. 238-0660.**
A carved walnut bar and high-backed booths highlight this pub with a changing schedule of jazz trios. Live music is featured nightly from 8:30pm to 12:30am.

**MORGAN'S, 17 East Price St., Germantown, PA. Tel. 848-2640,** or 844-6067 for schedule. **Directions:** North on Germantown Ave. for 2¼ miles after intersection with North Broad St. East Price St. is one block beyond Chelten Ave.
Another place for serious jazz is Morgan's, an unassuming building in Germantown that happens to house top talent in a terrific environment.
**Admission:** $8–$15.

**ORTLIEB'S JAZZ HAUS, 847 N. 3rd St. at Poplar St. Tel. 922-1035.**
This is another Northern Liberties pub, with nightly sets at 9:30pm. Shirley Scott, Mickey Roker, or assorted quartets perform Wednesday to Saturday, with open sessions Sunday to Thursday. There's no cover charge.

**READING TERMINAL MARKET, 12th and Arch sts. No telephone.**
You wouldn't think it, but jam sessions on the second Friday of every month from noon to 2pm involve pianist Herman De Jong as well as noted city businesspeople, politicos, and bona-fide jazz musicians. This is a real local favorite.

**THE SALOON, 7th and Catharine sts. Tel. 627-1811.**
Deep in the heart of South Philly, The Saloon features Victorian antiques accenting a fine Italian restaurant. If you want to hear mellow music, head upstairs by the glossy mahogany bar. The Saloon bar is open Wednesday to Saturday until 12:30am. The drinks average $2.50.
**Admission:** Free.

**ZANZIBAR BLUE, 305 S. 11th St. Tel. 829-0300.**
This place features the best of the city's jazz bands. The ambiance is elegant, so you may wish to dress up for a visit. Zanzibar is open until 2am nightly; there's also a jazz brunch on Sunday.
**Admission:** $8–$10.

# DANCE CLUBS

## BALLROOM DANCING

**THE LIBRARY, 2 Bala Cynwyd Plaza, just off City Line. Tel. 667-3151.**
To get an education on how to run a successful singles disco turned ballroom, check out The Library, which swings nightly. The pretty crowd, mostly under 30, is on the trendy side. Tuesday and

Friday are prime times for singles; on Saturday couples and singles split the floor evenly. No jeans are allowed.
**Admission:** $5–$6, depending on night, plus 2-drink minimum.

## SOCIAL CLUB, 2009 Sansom St., 2nd floor. Tel. 564-2277.

There's no live entertainment, but Social Club's sound system is programmed with mambos, foxtrots, and swing. Most attendees are members, but nonmembers are welcome.
**Admission:** $10.

## DISCOS

The two hottest areas in town right now are Delaware Avenue, along the river, and the booming northeast between Logan Circle and the Museum of Art.

## AZTEC CLUB, 939 N. Delaware Ave. Tel. 574-5730.

One of the hot places along the Delaware, the Aztec is a cavernous room decorated with bamboo, mock Easter Island head carvings, and Aztec pillars. There's a huge buffet on Friday evenings. Live music and DJs are featured on most nights. All major cards are accepted.
**Admission:** $10–$15.

## THE BANK, 600 Spring Garden St. Tel. 351-9404.

The Bank, a taxi ride away from Center City, was created by the same people who started Chestnut Cabaret. It offers one of the city's largest dance floors, situated in a renovated 1872 Frank Furness–designed bank. Friday brings karaoke or Japanese sing-along.
**Admission:** $10.

## THE BLACK BANANA, 3rd and Race sts. Tel. 925-4433.

Even though this is technically a private club, nonmembers are admitted. You can dance to cool postmodernism until 3am. Videos are shown on the first floor, and the dance floor is on the second. American Express is accepted.
**Admission:** $15.

## CHRISTINE'S, Ponte Vecchio Ristorante, 121 South St. Tel. 925-9268.

Christine's, open every night, attracts a fairly well dressed crowd to its effects-laden dance floor. A male revue is featured on Wednesday, ladies night is on Thursday, and a beach party is held on Sunday. It's closed on Monday.
**Admission:** Free–$8, depending on night.

## CLUB METRO, Front and Market sts. Tel. 922-5676.

There's a neo-deco decor at this Top 40 dance floor. Three fish tanks are behind the main bar. Metro's the type of place that frequently hosts live radio feeds.
**Admission:** Free–$5.

## FRAN O'BRIEN'S, 4190 City Line Ave. at Kings Grant Ave. Tel. 473-0300.

Fran O'Brien's offers live music and creates one of the top singles atmospheres in the Northeast.

**Admission:** $5–$10.

### KATMANDU, Pier 25, Delaware Ave. just north of the Benjamin Franklin Bridge. Tel. 629-1101.

Katmandu's an outdoor island getaway complete with palm trees, white-sand beaches, world dance music, daiquiris, and waterfront vistas. There's a reasonably priced outdoor pit barbecue. The place broke the mold when it opened in 1988. You'll find huge crowds but plenty of nooks to separate them.

**Admission:** Free.

### MONTE CARLO LIVING ROOM, 2nd and South sts. Tel. 925-2220.

There's a brass plaque on the door stating that proper attire is required (coats and ties for men, dresses for women). The way to do the Monte Carlo is to dine romantically and well, then dance the night away at the piano bar and old-style disco upstairs, with a tinkling fountain illuminated in alternating reds and blues and sentimental artwork. The surfaces (including the ceiling) are very mirrored, with wood railings and flowered carpets leading to different levels. It's open Monday to Saturday from 6pm to 2am. There's dancing to continental crooners after 9:30pm, with a DJ playing Top 40 releases between sets.

**Admission:** $10, unless you've dined downstairs or are a member.

### NU BIARRITZ, 1415 Locust St. Tel. 545-8283.

This is a multilevel club that's open Wednesday to Sunday from 11pm to 3am. The dance floor is always overseen by a DJ. There are a game room and a fish tank upstairs. It's very popular late in the evening.

**Admission:** $5.

### PHOENIX, 7th and Arch sts. Tel. 625-2475.

This link in the chain of successful discos built up by Mark Blatstein is just three blocks from the Trocadero and is positioned for the over-25 crowd. It occupies a renovated cast-iron building in an area of parking garages and office buildings. There are lots of radio station tie-in evenings.

**Admission:** $5–$9, depending on evening and hour.

### QUINCY'S, at the Adam's Mark, City Line Ave. at Monument Rd. Tel. 581-5000.

The top choice in this flashy suburban-mall area is Quincy's, everything a club should be: Clean sounds emanate from good bands, there's lots of wood paneling and old brass, and there are backgammon tables galore. Quincy's also provides one of the best happy hours anywhere, with incredible buffet tables. There's a singles dance on Sunday from 5 to 10pm, with no cover charge.

**Admission:** Free–$10.

### ROCK LOBSTER, 221 N. Delaware Ave. Tel. 627-7625.

Located at the corner of Race Street, hence just north of the Bridge and on the Marina, Rock Lobster is a long-awaited blend of top nightclub/disco and good restaurant, with Neil Stein (formerly of the Fish Market) and Albert Taxin (of Bookbinder's) involved. Rock Lobster serves hundreds of moderately priced dinners nightly, in a 4,000-square-foot tent or in an al fresco setting designed to look like a Maine yacht club. Top local (occasionally national) pop/rock talent appears.

**Admission:** No cover until 9pm, then normally $5 Mon–Thurs, $7 Fri–Sat; higher when national acts appear.

## GAY DANCE CLUBS

### HEPBURN'S, 254 S. 12th St. Tel. 545-8088.

This is Philadelphia's only bar primarily for women, open nightly until 2am. Downstairs is a quiet bar, with etched glass and a community bulletin board. Upstairs are two bars and a crowded disco. No credit cards are accepted.

**Admission:** Free.

### KURT'S, 1229 Chestnut St., downstairs in the Adelphia. Tel. 751-0009.

This is a Center City spot with undeniable energy, both gay and straight. Wednesday brings a live band and an open-bar party; Thursday, belly dancing; and Friday to Sunday, laser dance parties. Lots of theme parties are held.

**Admission:** $5 Fri–Sat; other evenings free.

### WOODY'S, 202 S. 13th St. Tel. 545-1893.

Woody's party atmosphere also attracts many straights. The original bar is downstairs, and a sandwich counter has been added alongside. The disco adjoining the upstairs lounge features trompe l'oeil Atlases holding up a roof of stars.

**Admission:** $5–$10 Fri–Sat.

---

# 3. THE BAR SCENE

### BONJOUR, 701 S. 4th St. Tel. 592-0800.

Situated on the corner of Bainbridge Street, Bonjour is known for its French cuisine at reasonable prices and its unpretentious atmosphere. This is a fine singles bar, consistently crowded with natives from Queen Village. The service can be a problem, though, since the bar is long and narrow at the counter.

### BRIDGET FOY'S, 200 South St. Tel. 922-1813.

Bridget Foy's offers a nice, mellow atmosphere with no pressure to socialize if you don't feel like it, and the company to keep you entertained if you do. It's open every evening until 1am. Situated at the lower corner of Head House Square, the establishment features a lively sidewalk café in summer.

### CUTTERS GRAND CAFE AND BAR, 2005 Market St. Tel. 851-6262.

This is the quintessential 1990s bar: long, high, massively stocked, with businesslike high-tech systems and a friendly and elegant atmosphere. The destination, in the new IBM building at Commerce Square, makes it a fine post-business meeting place.

### SILVERI'S, 315 S. 13th St. Tel. 545-5115.

You'll find the best Buffalo chicken wings in the city here, along with pasta, burgers, and the like. The crowd is geared to singles, with high energy levels abounding.

### T. G. I. FRIDAY'S, 18th St. and the Parkway. Tel. 665-8443.

It's hard to believe that a place this obviously corporate in intent and atmosphere could make it—but it has become a favorite of the younger crowd that populates Logan Circle's new office towers. There's standing room only at the outdoor terrace on summer evenings for the happy-hour buffet and socializing.

## PUBS & WINE BARS

### BRIDGID'S, 726 N. 24th St. Tel. 232-3232.

This tiny, very friendly horseshoe-shaped bar near the Philadelphia Museum of Art stocks a superb collection of Belgian beers, including an array from fruit- to hops-originated brews. A tapas menu is also available at the bar.

### DOCK STREET BREWING CO. BREWERY AND RESTAURANT, 18th and Cherry sts., 2 Logan Square. Tel. 496-0413.

This is the epitome of the 1990s—a comfortable, moderate place that brews and sells only its own beers, nestled into a top corporate corner some 3 years old. Offered are up to six varieties of beer at $2.50 per glass, painstakingly brewed within the last month. You can even inspect the spotless fermenting vats to the right of the bar.

### HOULIHAN'S OLD PLACE, 18th St. and Rittenhouse Square. Tel. 546-5940.

Houlihan's Old Place isn't exactly old, and the decor is more that of Albert Hall with peppy graffiti than that of an Irish pub. But it's one of Center City's most active pubs, especially among young professionals and older students. The decor and noise level are determinedly eclectic and on the loud side. Mixed drinks start at $2.50. A substantial dining area serves lunch, dinner, and Sunday brunch.

### THE IRISH PUB, 2007 Walnut St. Tel. 568-5603.

Located on the other side of the square from Houlihan's Old Place, The Irish Pub packs in hundreds of good-natured professionals, of both genders and all ages. There are Irish and American folk music in the front, but you can get far away and a floor down if you wish. An incredible collection of business cards is displayed near the entrance.

### JEANNINE'S BISTRO, 10 S. Front St. Tel. 925-1126.

This is a more moderate effort by Jeanne Mermet, situated above her La Truffe. Guitar and violin music is offered on the weekend, though the bistro is open only until 10:30pm. The ambiance of plush pillows, padded bench seats, and candlelight is charming. About 20 wines are available by the glass at $4 to $6 each.

### MAGNOLIA CAFE, 1602 Locust St. Tel. 546-4180.

The best selection in the city for after-dinner ports, cognacs, and grappas and the like can be found at the rear of this fine Cajun restaurant. There's live Dixieland on Tuesday night. The prices are reasonable along the blond bar but can go up to $25 per glass.

### ODEON, 114 S. 12th St. Tel. 922-5875.

Odeon offers a fine assortment of both wines by the glass—the cruvinet holds 16—and fine beers, both U.S. and international. There are also more than 20 single-malt scotches. I recommend the bar as a dining spot, with its recent change to moderate bistro fare.

**PANORAMA, 14 N. Front St. at Front and Market sts. Tel. 922-7800.**

Panorama is at the rear of Penn's View Inn but separate from the moderately priced Italian restaurant. Its curving wine bar features 120 different selections by the glass. Most cost about $5. There's piano entertainment. Panorama is open Monday to Saturday until 1am, Sunday until 10:30pm.

**SAMUEL ADAMS BREW HOUSE, 1516 Sansom St. Tel. 563-2326.**

The Brew House was opened in the late 1980s as an offshoot of the Sansom Street Oyster House downstairs. Three beers are regularly brewed right here: a light ale, an amber ale, and a dark porter. The bar of aged wood and etched glass was imported from Great Britain.

**SERRANO, 20 S. 2nd St. Tel. 928-0770.**

Serrano is open only until 10pm on Monday to Saturday, but it offers a wonderful collection of brews in an intimate setting, on one of the Historic District's nicest blocks. The old wooden bar has antique stained glass behind it, and the wood fire is spiced. Try one of the local bewer's products, Stoudt's unpasteurized ($5.95 per bottle).

## PIANO BARS

**BARCLAY BAR, 18th St. at Rittenhouse Square. Tel. 545-0300.**

Barclay Bar has it both ways—a genteel propriety on the lobby side and an air of sophisticated mystery around the corner from a gorgeous 1935 Steinway. Special weekends devoted to songs by Cole Porter and the like crop up occasionally, too. The light meals make it perfect for an impromptu celebration or a classy meeting.

**DOWNEY'S, Front and South sts. Tel. 629-0526.**

Downey's is a terrific Irish pub with a contemporary flair. Many of the local professional athletes head here after a game to relax upstairs, downstairs, or at the café tables outside. The new upstairs bar has classy skylights set into the original tin-plate ceiling and the obligatory Irish coin nailed to the portal. The music's upstairs on piano and accompaniment nightly from 9:30pm to 1:30am. On Friday and Saturday and at Sunday brunch (11:30am to 3pm) a strolling string quartet punctuates the atmosphere.

**1701 CAFE, in the Warwick Hotel, 17th and Locust sts. Tel. 545-4655.**

Open 24 hours, 1701 Café offers plenty of smooth, sophisticated peace and quiet. There's something about comfortable chairs and marble-topped bars that draws in everyone from hotel guests to students. Of course, the cool music helps, played Wednesday to Saturday from 9pm to 1am and Sunday from 8pm to midnight. Light meals are available on the café side, and if you're at the bar you know where you stand, which isn't nearby. Jazz predominates.

**THE SOCIETY HILL HOTEL, 3rd and Chestnut sts. Tel. 925-1919.**

The Society Hill Hotel, a renovated 1832 shell, has a dozen rooms upstairs—but the bar has all of Society Hill excited. It's one of the few modern bars in town that's sophisticated but not glitzy, and the outdoor café makes it even more charming on a summer eve. (Why don't more places follow their lead and screw hooks into the undersides of tables and counters so that women can hang their purses and pocketbooks safely but conveniently?)

## GAY BARS

See also "Gay Dance Clubs," above.

### 247 BAR, 247 S. 17th St. Tel. 545-9779.

Animal heads and pine paneling mark this macho stalwart in the Rittenhouse Square area. There are pool tables and plenty of TVs for sports watching.

### THE VENTURE INN, 255 S. Camac St. Tel. 545-8731.

The quaint block has this charming bar and restaurant as a centerpiece. The dining room features candlelight and a fireplace, with intimate seating. Dinners are a real value. No credit cards are accepted.

# 4. MORE ENTERTAINMENT

## READINGS

**Borders Book Shop and Espresso Bar,** 1727 Walnut Street (tel. 568-7400), runs one of the country's top series of author readings in an elegant setting that's steps from Rittenhouse Square. In a recent month, authors included Anna Quindlen, Marilyn French, Nancy Lemann, Spalding Grey, Michael Pollan, and Meg Pei. Readings usually are at 7:30pm on weekdays and at 2pm on weekends.

## SPECTACLES

The **Benjamin Franklin Bridge** has been outfitted with special lighting effects by the noted architectural firm Venturi, Rauch and Scott Brown. The lights are triggered into mesmerizing patterns by the auto and train traffic along the span. Some summers **Independence Hall** is the scene of a 9pm sound-and-light show with 1776 as its theme.

## MOVIE THEATERS

Philadelphia, like the rest of the country, has seen three corporations—AMC, United Artists, and General Cinema—purchase most major movie theaters, using higher prices ($6 to $7.50) and frequent divisions into multiplexes as the sticks and beautiful renovations and expansion as the carrots.

## HISTORIC AREA

### AMC OLDE CITY 2, 2nd and Sansom sts. Tel. 627-5966.

This theater is very conveniently located in the Independence National Historical Park area. It's on Sansom Street, between Front and 2nd streets, and shows first-run films in a pleasant building with a parking garage attached.

### RITZ 5 MOVIES, 214 Walnut St. Tel. 925-7900/1

This is the single best Historic District Area choice for independent releases. It has five comfortable screening rooms and shows sophisticated—often foreign—fare. The first daily matinee performances cost $3.50—a real bargain. There are more screens in this part of town; Ritz has also constructed a fiveplex behind The Bourse and the new Omni Hotel at 4th and Chestnut streets (tel. 440-1180).

## CENTER CITY

### AMC PALACE, 1812 Chestnut St. Tel. 496-0222.

This house, close by Rittenhouse Square, shows two quality first-run releases at a time.

### TEMPLE UNIVERSITY CINEMATHEQUE, 1619 Walnut St. Tel. 787-1529.

This is Philadelphia's headquarters for rare and foreign films that aren't widely released. There are two screening areas, which present films seven times per week September through May on Sunday to Thursday at 7:30pm and on Friday and Saturday at 7 and 9:15pm. Admission is $3; $2.50 for students and members.

### ROXY SCREENING ROOM, 2023 Sansom St. Tel. 561-0114.

The Theatre of the Living Arts runs this room, which offers Center City's only cinemathèque of first-run and foreign films. Tickets cost $5; $3.50 for students and seniors.

Standard studio releases are offered at **Eric Rittenhouse 3,** 1907–11 Walnut Street (tel. 567-0320), and **Sam's Place I and II,** 1826 Chestnut Street (tel. 972-0538). Action films are screened at **Sameric 4,** 1908 Chestnut Street (tel. 567-0604), and **Eric's Place** 1519 Chestnut Street (tel. 563-3086).

## UNIVERSITY CITY

### ANNENBERG CINEMATHEQUE, 3680 Walnut St. Tel. 243-6791.

The Annenberg screens a documentary series Wednesdays during the University of Pennsylvania's academic year. Admission is free.

### ERIC 3 CAMPUS, 40th and Walnut sts. Tel. 382-0296.

This movie theater offers standard studio releases.

### INTERNATIONAL HOUSE, 3701 Chestnut St. Tel. 387-5125.

International House presents a fine series of foreign films, political documentaries, and the work of independent filmmakers. Admission is $3.

### WALNUT MALL, 3925 Walnut St. Tel. 222-2344.

This theater screens intelligent releases for the College Crowd from the United States and abroad. The popcorn is outstanding.

# CHAPTER 11

# EASY EXCURSIONS FROM PHILADELPHIA

**1. GERMANTOWN & CHESTNUT HILL**

**2. BUCKS COUNTY & NEARBY NEW JERSEY**

**3. MONTGOMERY COUNTY**

Philadelphians have never seen the city-country distinction clearly. The same boats that brought Penn's Quakers also brought the settlers of Germantown, an agricultural retreat that many wealthy Colonials called home in summertime.

Other pioneers fanned out into the Delaware Valley to the south (remember that the Penn family owned Delaware as well as Pennsylvania until the 1740s), Bucks County to the north, and what is now Pennsylvania Dutch Country to the west. Much of this area remains lush and unspoiled, although development-versus-environment struggles are becoming pointed. The major attractions of the countryside are historical: Colonial mansions and inns, early American factories or businesses, and battlegrounds of the Revolutionary and Civil wars. Besides the trips discussed below, you can find interesting excursions from Philadelphia in *Frommer's Delaware, Maryland, Pennsylvania & the New Jersey Shore* and *Frommer's Atlantic City & Cape May*.

## 1. GERMANTOWN & CHESTNUT HILL

### GERMANTOWN

Germantown, a district within Philadelphia's city limits, is far enough away from Center City stamping grounds to make it an excursion destination. The area was settled in the 1680s, by non-Quaker immigrants seeking a better life. They included people from Sweden and Holland and French Protestants (Huguenots). English Quakers soon moved into the area, as did German Mennonites, a Protestant sect now helping to rescue the neighborhood from late 20th-century blight. With such free-thinking religions, Germantown drew up the first protest against the Colonial tendency to enslave blacks.

Until well into the 19th century Germantown retained an agricultural ambiance, with farmhouses and shops along Germantown Avenue. Hundreds of simple fieldstone houses rest sturdily on their foundations even today—not only the 20 or so restored buildings, but also dozens more that have gone to seed under absentee landlords. Even though time has faded the handwriting, few other American streets have as much to tell about past American life at every level, from the nation's first summer White House to breweries. Many of these still bear scars from the Battle of Germantown, an attempt by the Revolutionary forces to recapture occupied Philadelphia.

**ORIENTATION**   Addresses of interest stretch approximately from no. 4500 to no. 6610 Germantown Avenue, a hilly 3-mile walk (once a Native American trail) in itself. In 1969 this portion was declared a Registered Historic Road by the U.S. Department of the Interior. Taking an automobile will ease your trek. On the other hand, if you start touring from Upper Germantown (as I recommend), it's all downhill.

**INFORMATION**   The Center City **Visitors Center,** at 16th Street and John F. Kennedy Boulevard (tel. 636-1666), offers a rudimentary map to start you off. The **Germantown Historical Society,** occupying a jumble of 19th-century houses at 5214 Germantown Avenue (tel. 844-0514), always has information and holds a mid-May open-house tour. The fastest route by public transport is the R8 commuter train to Chestnut Hill West; from Reading Terminal or Suburban Station, get off at Queen Lane (Middle) or Tulpehocken Avenue (Upper), four blocks west. By car from Center City, head north on the Schuylkill Expressway, and the Roosevelt Boulevard/U.S. 1 exit will bring you to the Wayne-Wissahickon turnoff in Lower Germantown. To return to Center City via public transportation, backtrack to Germantown Avenue to catch the no. 23 bus or catch the Chestnut Hill R7 or R8 commuter train at Wayne Junction, one block west of the avenue.

## WHAT TO SEE

The following listings are not arranged alphabetically but by location down Germantown Avenue toward Center City. A few restored buildings are open daily from 1 to 4pm. Most are open Tuesday, Thursday, and Saturday afternoon, at least from 2 to 4pm. Many are closed in the off-season; however, each has a curator/guide who will be glad to escort you on a private tour if you call or write far enough in advance.

### UPSALA, 6340 Germantown Ave. Tel. 215/842-1798.

Upsala (1755) was the first major mansion in Upper Germantown, and it was built and maintained by the same family until 1938. The details and colonial furniture are exquisite; dressed stone with painted trim substitutes for Philadelphia brick, but the Greek Revival portico fits right in. During the Battle of Germantown, American cannons that were set here shelled the British at Cliveden across the street (see below).

**Admission:** $2 adults; $1 children and seniors.
**Open:** Tues and Thurs afternoon 1–4pm. **Closed:** Jan–Mar.

### CLIVEDEN, 6401 Germantown Ave. Tel. 848-1777.

Georgian through and through, Cliveden was built in the 1760s for the chief justice of Pennsylvania, in the Palladian country-seat tradition used by Woodford and Mount Pleasant in Fairmount Park. Note the pockmarks of bullets from the Battle of Germantown. Cliveden was donated in 1972 to the National Trust for Historic Preservation.

**Admission:** $2 adults; $1 children and seniors.

**Open:** Tues–Sat 10am–4pm; Sun 1–4pm. The guided tour is obligatory.

### EBENEZER MAXWELL MANSION, 200 W. Tulpehocken St. at Greene St. Tel. 438-1861.

This house is a bit off the avenue, but it's an ornate and classic Victorian mansion (rare in Philadelphia) that's worth a visit, especially when bedecked at Christmas. There's also a public garden.

**Admission:** $2 adults; $1 children.
**Open:** Wed–Sun 1–4pm.

### WYCK, 6026 Germantown Ave. Tel. 848-1690.

Wyck combines the treasures of nine generations of the same Quaker family, but it's not too richly ornamented, since they were Quakers. The rear section is the oldest house (1690) in Philadelphia, and it's connected to the newer section by 1820s sliding glass doors and louvers by William Strickland that look contemporary.

**Admission:** $2 adults; $1 children and seniors.
**Open:** Tues, Thurs, and Sat 1–4pm. **Closed:** Winter.

### DESHLER-MORRIS HOUSE, 5442 Germantown Ave. Tel. 596-1748.

A 1975 renovation of a 1752 home, with a 1772 addition, the Deshler-Morris boasts an impressive history: General Howe stayed here during the British occupation of the city, and George Washington waited out the yellow fever epidemic of 1793 to 1794 here. The "necessary" in the garden seats 12!

**Admission:** $1.
**Open:** Tues–Sun 1–4pm; other times by appointment. **Closed:** Jan–Mar.

### LOUDOUN, 4650 Germantown Ave. Tel. 685-2067.

A commanding 1801 Greek Revival mansion, Loudoun is full of Hepplewhite and Queen Anne chairs and has an ingenious basement kitchen.

**Admission:** $2.
**Open:** Tues, Thurs, and Sat 1–4pm.

### STENTON, 18th St. and Windrim Ave. Tel. 329-7312.

After Cliveden, this is the best single site, though it's now 5 acres surrounded by an aging industrial area. It started life as the 1730 mansion for James Logan, a brilliant aide to Benjamin Franklin, and was the seat of a 500-acre estate. A log cabin, a 1790 stone barn, and other outbuildings linger on.

**Admission:** $2 adults; $1 children and seniors.
**Open:** Tues–Sat 1–4pm. **Directions:** Turn left off Germantown Avenue for four blocks, then turn right onto 18th Street.

**DINING** If you set aside Tuesday or Friday afternoon for the jaunt, the **Farmer's Market** at West Haines Street (near Wyck, or 3 blocks north of Chelten Avenue) will revive you with egg custard, cheeses, scrapple, and other Pennsylvania Dutch foods. It's open on Tuesday from 9am to 4pm and on Friday from 9am to 6pm.

# CHESTNUT HILL

Farther up Germantown Avenue lies Chestnut Hill, an enclave of suburban gentility—even exclusivity—with a historic "Main Street" flavor. It was once filled with chestnut trees, and it is still the highest point within city limits. Just to the south and west is Wissahickon Creek Park, an extension of Fairmount Park that was purchased and cleared of all commercial development by the city in the 1860s; the stunning rambles and walks have been compared to Alpine gorges. You can stop by the **Chestnut Hill Welcome Center,** 8426 Germantown Avenue, Chestnut Hill PA 19118 (tel. 247-6696), or simply ramble among the galleries, restaurants, shops, and boutiques.

## MORRIS ARBORETUM, entrance at 101 Hillcrest Ave. between Germantown and Stenton aves. Tel. 247-5777.

A 1932 gift to the University of Pennsylvania, this arboretum is an elaborately landscaped country estate as well as a collection of 3,500 trees and shrubs assembled for scientific study. The stone mansion is long gone, but maps indicating the Japanese Garden, English Park, and Wissahickon Creek meadow are available at the gatehouse. This place is great for families.

**Admission:** $2 adults; $1 students and seniors.

**Open:** Apr–Oct, daily 10am–5pm. Nov–Mar, daily 10am–4pm. Summer, Thursday until 8pm. **Directions:** Take Germantown Avenue north for .9 mile on Bethlehem Pike, then make a left onto Stenton Avenue; make a left on Hillcrest and follow it for .2 miles.

## WHERE TO STAY

### Moderate

## CHESTNUT HILL HOTEL, 8229 Germantown Ave., Philadelphia, PA 19118. Tel. 215/242-5905. 28 units. AC TV TEL

$ **Rates** (including Continental breakfast): $80 single, $90 double; $98 deluxe single, $108 deluxe double. Children under 12 free in parents' room. **Parking:** Free.

This stucco and cement hotel, built in 1899, was renovated and expanded to include shops and restaurants in 1983. It's comfortable, with first and second floor lounges, but the 28 rooms differ in size. On the premises are two pleasant restaurants: **J. B. Winberie** (tel. 247-6710) and **A Slice of Heaven** (tel. 248-3388) as well as a farmer's market.

## WHERE TO DINE

### Inexpensive

## CAMPBELL'S PLACE, 8337 Germantown Ave. Tel. 242-2066.

**Cuisine:** CONTINENTAL/AMERICAN. **Reservations:** Not required.

$ **Prices:** Main courses $7–$12 lunch, $6.95–$14.95 dinner. No credit cards.

**Open:** Lunch, Sat noon–5pm. Dinner, Tues–Sat 5–10pm. Bar is open until 1am.

This is basically a good neighborhood tavern for informed tastes, with a varied menu of pasta dishes, steaks, and Chinese wok cooking.

**UNDER THE BLUE MOON,** 8225 Germantown Ave. Tel. 247-1100.
    **Cuisine:** CONTINENTAL. **Reservations:** Recommended.
**$ Prices:** Appetizers $3.50–$5.25, main courses $13.75–$17.25. No credit cards. Check accepted.
    **Open:** Dinner, Tues–Thurs 6–9pm; Fri–Sat until 10pm.

The top choice in the neighborhood for over a decade, this restaurant offers unusual international dishes such as sesame-pecan chicken and a fabled duck. There's a sensible but interesting wine list.

# 2. BUCKS COUNTY & NEARBY NEW JERSEY

Bucks County, at most an hour by car from Philadelphia, is bordered by the Delaware River to the east and Montgomery County to the west. If you look at an early map of Pennsylvania, you'll see that many of the rural lands given by William Penn to Quaker settlers (as inducement for migrating) were in this area, and the population spread early along Native American trails and rivers. So it's no surprise that historic estates and sites, along with the antique stores and country inns they've spawned, abound. Many artists and authors, including Oscar Hammerstein II, Pearl Buck, and James Michener, have gained inspiration from the natural beauty, which has survived major development so far. Nearby New Jersey offers scenic routes for bicycling and walking as well as fine restaurants.

**GETTING THERE**    The best automobile route into Bucks County from Center City is I-95 (north). Penna. 32 (which intersects I-95 in Yardley) runs along the Delaware, past Washington Crossing State Park to New Hope, which connects to Doylestown by U.S. 202. By train, the R5 SEPTA commuter rail ends at Doylestown, with connections to New Hope and Lahaska.

**INFORMATION**    To find out more about the hundreds of historic sites, camping facilities, and accommodations here, contact the **Bucks County Tourist Commission,** 152 Swamp Rd., Doylestown, PA 18901 (tel. 215/345-4552). You can also write to or stop by the **New Hope Information Center,** South Main and Mechanic sts., Box 141, New Hope, PA 18938 (tel. 215/862-5880); it's open Monday to Friday from 9am to 5pm, Saturday and Sunday from 10am to 6pm.

## WHAT TO SEE & DO

**ANDALUSIA, State Rd., Philadelphia, PA 19135. Tel. 215/848-1777.**
    Andalusia, just off I-95 in Philadelphia, was the first mature Greek Revival mansion in America. It belonged to Nicholas Biddle, the haughty director of the Second Bank of the United States and the progenitor of generations of gentry. It was designed by the same man who planned the U.S. Capitol and the bank, Thomas Walter. The building is splendid both inside and out; there are very few mansions from this era as perfectly conceived and protected. The 250-acre estate also houses a grotto and a pump house for the water supply.

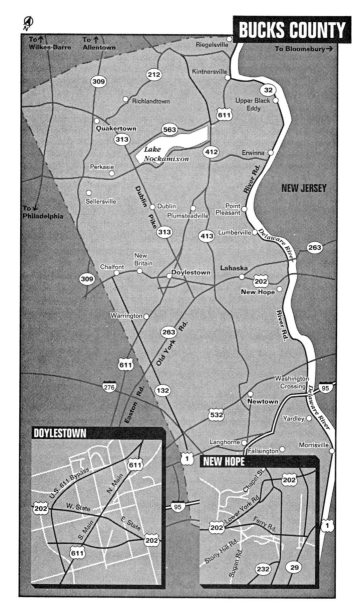

You must reserve the services of a house guide, made through the National Trust for Historic Preservation administration at Cliveden.
   **Admission:** $7 per person, with a minimum fee of $35.
   **Open:** Summer, Tues–Sat, by appointment only.

**SESAME PLACE, 100 Sesame Rd., Langhorne, PA 19047 (junction of U.S. Rt. 1 and I-95). Tel. 215/757-1100.**
At this hands-on family play park 30 minutes from Center City

and 12 miles north of Andalusia, kids climb through three stories of sloping, swaying fun on the Nets and Climbs or crawl through tubes and tunnels amid splashing fountains and showers of spray at Mumford's Water Maze. The kids will want their swimsuits for the Rubber Duckie and Runaway Rapids (locker rooms are provided). The Honkers, along with Big Bird and other Muppets, perform at the Circle Theatre. Indoors, the air-conditioned Computer Gallery has puzzles, Mix 'n' Match Muppets, logic games, and more than 70 computer activities for kids 3 to 13. Everyone will love the Rainbow Room, where every movement reveals a splash of stunning colors. There's even an Adult Oasis. Sesame Place is operated by Busch Entertainment Corp. under license from the Children's Television Workshop.

**Admission:** $16.95 adults; $18.95 children 3–15; $14.95 seniors over 55. Twilight admission $10.50. Second-day tickets $7.95 with validated first-day ticket. **Parking:** $3 per day.

**Open:** May to mid-June, Mon–Fri 10am–5pm; Sat–Sun 10am–8pm. Late June to August, daily 9am–8pm. Sept–Oct, Sat–Sun only 9am–8pm.

## PENNSBURY MANOR, Rt. Penna. 9 (Tyburn Rd.) from U.S. 1 (intersects I-95) or U.S. 13, Morrisville, PA 19067. Tel. 215/946-0400.

William Penn planned his very English plantation and manor at Pennsbury Manor, along the Delaware 24 miles north of Philadelphia on Route 32 (River Road). Penn's charter from Charles II deeded him all of what is now Pennsylvania and Delaware, which made him the second-ranking landowner in the colonies. (The first, King Charles II, didn't take landowning too seriously.) When Penn offered tracts for sale in the 1680s, he kept this section for himself. On it, he designed a self-sustaining (and obviously pre-Georgian) estate, replete with a smokehouse, an icehouse, a barn, an herb garden, a plantation office, and a boathouse. However, Penn spent much of his adult life in debtor's prison or England and didn't get to live in his domicile very often. The various dependencies and the manor itself were demolished but were rebuilt to the smallest detail in 1939.

Pennsbury Manor boasts the largest collection of 17th-century antiques in the state, spread over four floors of the manor. On a sunny day, it's a treat to inspect the carefully labeled herb garden, step inside the icehouse for a cool respite, and try to chase the guinea fowl (more popular than chickens in 1600s) around the golden brick paths.

**Admission:** $4 adults; $2 seniors and students 5–17; children under 5 free.

**Hours:** Tues–Sat 9am–5pm; Sun noon–5pm. Last tour at 3:30pm.

## FALLSINGTON, south off U.S. 1 at Tyburn Rd., Fallsington, PA 19054. Tel. 215/295-6567.

When Penn was in residence and wished to worship, he'd go to Fallsington, 6 miles north of Pennsbury Manor. This colonial village grouped around the Quaker meetinghouse has been preserved virtually intact. Many of the private homes have sheltered the same families since Penn's day. Some of the buildings have been restored for tourists; others are occupied but open on select occasions. Take Penna. 13 north to Tyburn Road (Penna. 9), then turn right and follow the road.

**Admission:** $1.

**Open:** Wed 1–5pm. Special Fallsington open-house days are the second Saturday in May and October.

## WASHINGTON CROSSING STATE PARK, Intersection of Pa. 532 and Pa. 32 (River Rd.) near I-95, P.O. Box 103, Washington Crossing, PA 18977. Tel. 215/493-4076.

A trip along the Delaware via Route 32, through Morrisville and Yardley will bring you to Washington Crossing State Park, 500 acres that are open year round. Most people know that Washington crossed a big river in a small boat on Christmas eve of 1776. This was the place, although the Durham boats on display in the boat barn used to hold 30. The state park is divided into an upper and a lower section separated by 3 miles; Washington left from the lower park. You can sip a glass of punch at **Old Ferry Inn** (1752), where he ate before the assault, and tour the bird sanctuary and the Memorial Building at the point of embarkation.

The **Wild Flower Preserve** in the upper park is really a 100-acre arboretum, flower garden, and shrub preserve rolled into one; it contains 15 different paths, each emphasizing different botanical wonders. The ferns come into their own in July and August; the flowers bloom in late spring. The **Thompson-Neely House** ($1 admission, good for the Old Ferry Inn also) is intact when General Washington, Brigadier-General Stirling, and Lt. James Monroe decided on the year-end push into New Jersey. Next to the Flower Preserve is the stone **Bowman's Hill Tower;** it will reward you (or the children) with a view of this part of the Delaware Valley, which would probably belong to the British Commonwealth if Washington's troops hadn't routed the Hessians in 1776.

An annual reenactment of the historic crossing takes place here on Christmas Day. A December-long series of events includes candlelight tours and riverbank parades. A complete program is available from the park.

**Admission:** Free to the Visitor Center and its 30-minute film. Tours following screenings of historic buildings are $2.50 adults; $1 children over 6.

**Open:** Buildings, Mon–Sat 9am–5pm; Sun noon–5pm. Grounds, Daily 9am–8pm or sunset.

## NEW HOPE & LAMBERTVILLE

Four miles from Washington Crossing, along River Road (Penna. 32), punctuated by lovely farmland (as opposed to U.S. 202's factory outlets), you'll come upon New Hope, a former colonial town turned artists' colony. It's somewhat commercial by now. The weekend crowds can get fierce, and parking is cramped, but once on foot you'll enjoy the specialty stores, restaurants, and galleries. Lambertville, across the Delaware in New Jersey, has rather pedestrian architecture but more scenic routes along the river and, many say, better restaurants.

Among the attractions of the New Hope area are the following.

## BUCKS COUNTY PLAYHOUSE, 70 S. Main St. (P.O. Box 313), New Hope, PA 18938. Tel. 215/862-2041.

This is the center of New Hope entertainment with summer theater that features Broadway hits and musical revivals. It's a former gristmill with a seating capacity of almost 500.

**Admission:** Tickets $13–$17.

**Open:** Apr–Dec, Wed–Sun evenings and Wed and Thurs matinees.

### NEW HOPE MULE BARGE, New and South Main sts., New Hope, PA 18938. Tel. 215/862-2842.

For an hour of feeling pampered, take a barge trip on the **Delaware Canal.** For a while in the early 1800s canals were thought to be the transport revolution in England and the eastern United States (in fact, an inland waterway still runs from New England to Florida). Coal was floated down this one in the 1830s from mines in the Lehigh Valley, and the barges are still pulled by mules. The barges run April through October and leave from New Street.

**Admission:** $6.95 adults; $5.50 for students; $4.25 children under 12.

**Open:** May 1–Oct 15, six launchings daily. Apr and Oct 16–Nov 15, reduced launchings on Wed, Sat, and Sun.

### PARRY MANSION, Main and Ferry sts., New Hope, PA 18938. Tel. 215/862-5652.

One of the loveliest old homes in town, this mansion was erected in 1984 by the elite of New Hope. The Parry family lived in this 11-room Georgian until 1966, and the rooms are decorated in different period styles of 1775 to 1900.

**Admission:** $4 per person.

**Open:** May–Oct, Fri–Sat 1–5pm.

### PEDDLER'S VILLAGE, U.S. 202 and Rt. 263, Lahaska, PA 18931. Tel. 215/794-4000.

Five miles west of New Hope, on Route 202, Peddler's Village looks antique, but the appeal to customers is timeless and most of the merchandise is contemporary. It's not a country market; the prices are marked up considerably, but the ambiance and convenience are attractive. **Jenny's** on Route 202 at Street Road (tel. 794-5605) is for elegant continental dining in an atmosphere of brass and stained glass. The specialties of the **Cock 'n' Bull** (tel. 794-7055) are a massive buffet on Tuesday and Thursday and the beef burgundy served in a loaf of bread that's baked in the hearth.

**Admission:** Free.

**Open:** Most stores, Mon–Sat 10am–5pm; Fri until 8pm. Special Strawberry Festival in May.

## COUNTRY WALKING & BICYCLING

Walking or riding along the Delaware River or along the canals built for coal hauling on either side can be the highlight of a summer. The two most convenient routes are the following.

In Stockton, New Jersey, take Route 263 just over the Delaware to Pennsylvania. Then park your car, cross the old bridge on foot or bicycle, and follow the towpath on the Pennsylvania side north toward Lumberville and its cute general store, 3 miles away. The **Lumberville Store Bicycle Rental Co.** (Route 32, Lumberville, PA 18933; tel. 215/297-5388) has all kinds of bicycles for rent at moderate day rates. It's open April to mid-October daily from 8am to 6pm.

The second route, just south of Lumberville, follows River Road south and west to Cuttalossa Road, which winds past an alpine chalet, creeks, ponds, and sheep grazing and clanking their antique

Swiss bells. **Cuttalossa Inn,** Cuttalossa Road, Lumberville, PA 18933 (tel. 215/297-5082) offers high-class cuisine in a spectacular setting.

## OTHER ATTRACTIONS

Other transport-based attractions of the New Hope area are a **covered-bridges tour** (call 215/345-4552 for information about this self-guided free tour); **river tubing** at Point Pleasant Canoe, up the Delaware from New Hope at Upper Black Eddy and Riegelsville (tel. 215/297-8181), for 2 to 4 hours of relaxing family fun; and a **steam railway** out of New Hope (tel. 215/862-2707).

## COOL FOR KIDS

### QUARRY VALLEY FARM, 2302 Street Rd., Lahaska, PA 18931. Tel. 215/794-5882.

On Street Road near Peddler's Village, Quarry Valley Farm is a working ménage of a hayloft for exploring, barnyard animals for petting, ponies for riding, and even cows for milking.

**Admission:** $4.50 adults; $4 children under 12

**Open:** Mid-March to December, daily 10am–5pm.

### RICE'S COUNTRY MARKET, Solebury, PA 18963. Tel. 215/297-5993.

Rice's Market is the real thing—a quality market of country goods and crafts. Amish wares are sold in the main building, along with antiques and collectibles; many outdoor stalls get taken also.

**Admission:** $5, including parking.

**Open:** Tues 6am–noon. Get there early. **Directions:** Route 263 south toward Peddler's Village (Route 202), right onto Aquetong Road for 2 miles, then a right onto Green Hill Road.

## WHERE TO STAY

New Hope and its New Jersey neighbor across the Delaware River, Lambertville, have earned reputations for their country inns and restaurants. The listings here only scratch the surface.

### Country Inns

### CENTRE BRIDGE INN, P.O. Box 74, Rt. 32, New Hope, PA 18938. Tel. 215/862-2048. 9 rms. AC

**$ Rates:** $70–$115 weekday single or double; $80–$125 weekend single or double. AE, MC, V. **Parking:** Free.

Situated beside the Delaware River 3½ miles north of New Hope, the current building is the third since the early 18th century. Many of the elegant guest rooms have canopy, four-poster, or brass beds; wall-high armoires; modern private baths; outside decks; and views of the river or countryside. Five rooms have TVs.

### EVERMAY-ON-THE-DELAWARE, River Rd., Erwinna, PA 18920. Tel. 215/294-9100. Fax 215/294-8249. 16 rms, 1 carriage house suite. AC TEL

**$ Rates** (including continental breakfast): $50–$70 single; $75–$135 double; $185 suite. MC, V. **Parking:** Free.

Thirteen miles north of New Hope on River Road in Erwinna lies this gracious historic inn. Combining privacy with a romantic setting overlooking the Delaware, Evermay once hosted the Barrymores for croquet weekends. The inn now offers rooms with luxurious antique furnishings. On Friday, Saturday, and Sunday, the formal dining room offers an excellent prix-fixe $45 dinner that's open to the public as well; reserve well in advance.

**ISAAC STOVER HOUSE, P.O. Box 68, River Rd., Erwinna, PA 18920. Tel. 215/294-8044.** 7 rms (5 with bath). AC
$ **Rates** (including full breakfast): $110–$125 midweek single or double; $150–$175 weekend single or double. AE, MC, V. **Parking:** Free.

With a sloping mansard roof and gingerbread trim, talk-show host Sally Jessy Raphaël's 1836 Victorian is full of charm. The rooms have such themes as the Emerald City and the Amore Room. It's set on 13 acres of meadows and woods.

**WHITEHALL INN, 1370 Pineville Rd., New Hope, PA 18938. Tel. 215/598-7945.** 6 rms (4 with bath). AC TV TEL
$ **Rates:** $110–$150 per night, single or double. AE, DC, MC, V. **Parking:** Free.

Four miles outside New Hope is this 18th-century manor house on a former horse farm, complete with a pool and tennis courts. Mike and Suella Wass serve magnificent four-course breakfasts, and their "innsmanship" is nationally known, with such touches as fresh fruit bowls and a bottle of local wine in every room.

## Hotels & Motels

**COMFORT INN, 3660 Street Rd., Bensalem, PA 19020. Tel. 215/245-0100,** or toll free 800/458-6886. 141 rms. AC TV TEL
$ **Rates:** $43–$58 single; $53–$68 double. AE, DC, MC, V. **Parking:** Free.

For moderate lodgings in Bucks County, this is one of the best choices, off I-95 about 20 miles from Washington Crossing and 5 miles from Sesame Place. The inn is a modern, bright four-story property with either two double beds or a king-size bed in each room. There's also an exercise room.

**NEW HOPE MOTEL IN THE WOODS, 400 W. Bridge St., New Hope, PA 18938. Tel. 215/862-2800.** 28 rms. AC TV
$ **Rates:** $45 single; $59 double. AE, DC, MC, V. **Parking:** Free.

Just a mile west of town is this motel tucked in a peaceful woodland setting off Route 179. For over 30 years, it has offered modern ground-level rooms with private baths and standard motel amenities. Open all year, it has a swimming pool that's open during the summer.

**ROYCE HOTEL, 400 Oxford Valley Rd., Langhorne, PA 19047. Tel. 215/547-4100,** or toll free 800/237-6923. 168 rms. A/C TV TEL
$ **Rates:** $125–$135 single or double. AE, DC, MC, V. **Parking:** Free.

This festive, modern 14-story hotel opened right across the street from Sesame Place in 1987. The soundproof guest rooms have oversized beds and quilted fabrics, many with extra sofabeds. Other facilities include a health club, a swimming pool and sauna, and a full-service restaurant.

## WHERE TO DINE
### Moderate

**KARLA'S, 5 W. Mechanic St., New Hope, PA 18938. Tel. 215/862-2612.**
    **Cuisine:** INTERNATIONAL. **Reservations:** Recommended for dinner.

$  **Prices:** Appetizers $3.50–$8; main courses $13–$19; lunch $3.95–$7.95. AE, DC, MC, V.
    **Open:** Sun–Thurs 11am–10pm; Fri–Sat 11am–4am.

In the heart of New Hope, next door to the Information Center, this lively and informal restaurant offers three settings—a sunlit conservatory with ceiling fans, stained glass, and plants; a gallery room with local artists' works; and a bistro with marble tabletops. The eclectic menu offers grilled rib-eye steak, veal francese, and chicken breast with Thai ginger sauce. The lunch items are tamer.

**ODETTE'S FINE COUNTRY DINING, S. River Rd. and Rt. 32, New Hope, PA 18938. Tel. 215/862-2432.**
    **Cuisine:** INTERNATIONAL. **Reservations:** Recommended.

$  **Prices:** Appetizers $4.95–$7.95; main courses $14.95–$24.95; lunch $6.95–$9.95. AE, DC, MC, V.
    **Open:** Lunch, Mon–Sat 11:30am–3pm. Dinner, Mon–Fri 5–10pm; Sat 5–11pm, Sun 4–9pm. Brunch, Sun 11am–3pm.

Surrounded by the river and the canal on the southern edge of town, this elegant restaurant has been an inn since 1794. The previous owner, Odette Myrtil, was a Ziegfeld Follies girl whose memorabilia adorns the place. The menus are seasonal and change every other month, providing nice twists on standard bases of steak, seafood, duck, and veal.

**THE SWAN HOTEL, Swan and S. Main St., Lambertville, NJ 08530. Tel. 609/397-2244.**
    **Cuisine:** CONTINENTAL. **Reservations:**

$  **Prices:** Dinner $25–$40 per person.
    **Open:** Dinner only, Tues–Sat 4pm–2am; Sun 2–11pm.

The Swan is actually not a hotel but a former bordello that's been turned into a local hangout. Anton's, the elegant restaurant connected to it, is full of corners and couches, with excellent cuisine that's served on Wednesday to Sunday.

# DOYLESTOWN AREA

The triangle where U.S. 202 (west of New Hope), Penna. 313 (south of Scranton), and U.S. 611 (that's North Broad Street in Philadelphia) intersect defines Doylestown, the county seat. It's a pleasant town just to walk around, but three interesting collections in town invite you indoors. They were all endowed by the same man, Dr. Henry Chapman Mercer (1856–1930). Mercer was a collector, local archeologist, and master of pottery techniques.

## WHAT TO SEE

**FONTHILL MUSEUM, E. Court St., off Swamp Rd. (Rt. 313), Doylestown, PA 18901. Tel. 215/348-9461.**

Not many people can call their home a castle, but Dr. Mercer could, and the castle even was built with reinforced concrete of his own design. The core of the building is an 18th-century

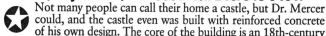

farmhouse, but towers, turrets, and tiles have been amassed beyond belief. All the rooms are of different shapes, and each has tiles of Mercer's collection set into the chamber.

**Admission:** $4 adults; $1.50 children.

**Open:** Mon–Sat 10am–5pm; Sun noon–5pm. **Closed:** New Year's Day, Thanksgiving, and Christmas. Guided tours of the interior are given from 10am to 3:30pm at 15-minute intervals; reservations are recommended.

## MORAVIAN POTTERY AND TILE WORKS, Swamp Rd., Doylestown, PA 18901. Tel. 215/345-6722.

Down the road on Penna. 313, the Moravian Pottery and Tile Works was Mercer's next big project. It's also made of his reinforced concrete, although it looks like stucco or even adobe. If you go to the State Capitol in Harrisburg, you can see over 400 mosaics from here that illustrate the history of Pennsylvania. The working potters at the kilns today turn out tiles and pottery for Bucks County and the in-house shop.

**Admission:** $2.50 adults; $1 students; $1.50 seniors; $4.50 family groups.

**Open:** Daily 10am–4pm. Tours are given every 30 minutes. **Closed:** Jan–Feb, Easter, Thanksgiving, and Christmas.

## MERCER MUSEUM, Pine St. at Ashland St., Doylestown, PA 18901. Tel. 215/345-0210.

Mercer Museum displays thousands of early American tools, vehicles, cooking pieces, looms, and even weather vanes. Mercer had the collecting bug in a big way, and you can't help being impressed with the breadth of the collection and the castle that houses it. It rivals the Shelburne, Vermont, complex—and that's 35 buildings on 100 acres! The open atrium rises five stories, and suspends a Conestoga wagon, chairs, and sleighs as if they were Christmas-tree ornaments. During the summer, a log cabin, a school house, and other large bits of American life are open for inspection.

**Admission:** Museum and library, $4 adults; $1.50 students.

**Open:** Mon–Sat 10am–5pm; Sun noon–5pm. Spruance Library (Bucks Country history), Tues 1–9pm; Wed–Sat 10am–5pm. **Closed:** Thanksgiving and Christmas.

## JAMES A. MICHENER ARTS CENTER, 138 S. Pine St., Doylestown, PA 18901. Tel. 215/340-9800.

Opened in 1988, this exhibition center is named for the noted author, Doylestown's most successful contemporary. The building itself dates from 1813 and once served as the Bucks County jail. The works of American artists predominate in the exhibitions here.

**Admission:** $3 adults; $1.50 students suggested.

**Open:** Tues–Fri 10am–4:30pm; Sat–Sun 10am–5pm.

## GREEN HILLS FARM, 520 Dublin St., Hilltown, PA 18944 (off Rt. 313 in Perkasie). Tel. 215/249-0100.

About 4 miles north of Doylestown, America and the East meet at the former home of Nobel prize–winning novelist Pearl S. Buck. Buck, who lived the first half of her life in China, bought Green Hills in 1934. She lived and worked here until her death in 1973, and the farm is now the international headquarters for the Pearl S. Buck Foundation, which helps needy children overseas. Your tour of the 1835 farmhouse will show you the two worlds Buck loved: In the spacious living room, hand-hewn ceiling beams and plank flooring encounter a Pennsylvania Dutch hutch; Chinese rugs; and Oriental wall hangings, including a Tibetan embroidery given to her by the Dalai Lama. The Treasure Room houses a collection of rare Chinese silk robes and small Asian objets d'art. You also can view the author's studio-office just as it was during her lifetime.

**Admission:** $5 adults; $4 children over 6.

**Open:** Grounds, daily to 5pm. One-hour guided tours, Mar–Dec, Tues–Sat 10:30am and 1:30 and 2:30pm; Sun 1:30 and 2:30pm. Visitors are welcome to use the on-site picnic tables. **Directions from Philadelphia:** Take the Penna. 611 Bypass from Center City, then take Penna. 313 West to Dublin; from there, make an easy left onto Maple Avenue.

## WHERE TO DINE

### Moderate

**DOYLESTOWN INN, 18 W. State St., Doylestown. Tel. 345-6610.**

**Cuisine:** AMERICAN. **Reservations:** Recommended.

**$ Prices:** Breakfast $3.25–$8.95; appetizers $2.95–$6.95; main courses $9.95–$17.95; lunch $4.95–$13.95. AE, DC, MC, V.

**Open:** Breakfast, Mon–Sat 7–11am, Sun country breakfast 8:30am–1pm. Lunch, Mon–Sat 11:30am–3pm. Dinner, Mon–Thurs 4:30–10pm; Fri–Sat until 11pm; Sun 3–9pm.

This in-town restaurant overlooking Main Street is a mixture of Victorian and modern. The menu offers a blend of contemporary and traditional fare, with broiled baby flounder, frogs' legs floating on biscuits, and chicken-and-vegetable pot pie. The upstairs inn has 22 rooms.

**SIGN OF THE SORREL HORSE, Old Bethlehem Rd., Quakertown. Tel. 215/536-4651.**

**Cuisine:** FRENCH. **Reservations:** Required. Jackets recommended for men. **Directions:** Go 10 miles north of Doylestown on Route 313. Take Route 563 north for 2 miles, then turn left onto Old Bethlehem. The restaurant is ¼ mile on the left.

**$ Prices:** Appetizers $4.50–$13.50; main courses $19.50–$24.95. MC, V.

**Open:** Dinner only, Wed–Sun 5:30–9pm.

This is the best restaurant in the Doylestown area, with a husband-and-wife team who have trained at the Cordon Bleu school. It contains three dining rooms in a 1749 building, overlooking the kitchen herb gardens. The menu is rich, with smoked sea scallops, lobster, and filet mignon—all served with fresh reductions and mousses. The ice cream is homemade with honey, not sugar.

# 3. MONTGOMERY COUNTY

Montgomery County is a region of rivers, hills, fall foliage, and Main Line suburban development. It's best known for Valley Forge, Washington's winter headquarters at the nadir of the Revolutionary

War, but it has everything from a Frank Lloyd Wright synagogue (Beth Sholom in Elkins Park) to Pennsylvania Dutch festivals (the Goschenhoppen Folk Festival held in mid-August in East Greenville).

**INFORMATION** I can't describe more than a few of the major attractions here, so call or write to the **Valley Forge Convention and Visitors Bureau,** P.O. Box 311, Norristown, PA 19404 (tel. 215/278-3558, or toll free 800/441-3549, 800/458-5600 in Pennsylvania), for particulars on recreation, annual events, campgrounds, and historic sites.

## VALLEY FORGE

### WHAT TO SEE

**VALLEY FORGE NATIONAL HISTORICAL PARK, Rt. 23 and N. Gulph Rd., Valley Forge, PA 19481. Tel. 215/ 783-1077.**
Only 30 minutes from central Philadelphia and a half-day excursion in itself now, Valley Forge was hours of frozen trails away in the winter of 1777 to 1778. The Revolutionary forces had just lost the battles of Brandywine and Germantown. While the British occupied Philadelphia, Washington's forces repaired to winter quarters near an iron forge where the Schuylkill met Valley Creek, 18 miles northeast. A sawmill and gristmill were supposed to help provide basic requirements, but they had been destroyed by the British. Some 12,000 men and boys straggled into the encampment, setting up quarters and lines of defense.

Unfortunately, the winter turned bitter, with 6 inches of snow and iced-up rivers. Critical shortages of food and clothing, along with damp shelters, left nearly 4,000 diseased and unfit for duty. Almost 2,000 perished, and many others deserted. Congress, which had left Philadelphia hurriedly, couldn't persuade the colonies to give money to alleviate the conditions. Nevertheless, the forces slowly gained strength and confidence, due in part to the Prussian army veteran Baron von Steuben, appointed by Washington to retrain the Continental Army under his revised and distinctly American "Manual of Arms." By springtime the Continentals were an army on which their new allies, the French, could rely. Copies of their huts, some of the officers' lodgings, and later memorials dot the park today.

Start your visit at the **Visitor Center** (tel. 215/783-7700), located at the junction of Penna. 23 and North Gulph Road. A 15-minute film depicting the encampment is shown here every half hour. Also at the Visitor Center is a museum containing Washington's tent, an extensive collection of Revolutionary War artifacts, and a bookstore.

If you pass along Outer Line Drive, named after the earthworks that served as a defense against possible British attack, you can't miss the **National Memorial Arch.** Triumphal arches have never been America's style, but the honor paid to the tough militia (most with uncared-for families in other states) is certainly well placed. Farther west, the route follows Valley Creek, passing Gen. Henry Knox's quarters (not open to the public) and an 1865 covered bridge (which is). The **Isaac Potts House** (1770), which Washington commandeered as his headquarters, has the same rustic, dressed-stone look as many Germantown houses. You can see his reception room, office, and bedroom. A park interpreter is always stationed here, along with a souvenir-and-food stand. The huts of the general's Life Guards huddle nearby.

A hilly inner loop shows the second line of defense, although Steuben's troops trained on the Grand Parade, a flat area to the east. Don't be confused by Fort Washington or Fort Huntington—a symmetrical earthwork counted as a fort in those days, with or without walls. If you're here in late April or early May, you'll see the magnificent dogwood blossoms.

That Gothic chapel (1903) houses the **Washington Memorial Chapel** (it's free, with Sunday carillon recitals in the bell tower at 2pm), next to the Valley Forge Historical Society Museum (see below). Like the memorial arch, the chapel seems to honor an American hero in a peculiarly European way, with flags and stained-glass medievalism.

**Admission:** Free; $1 adult admission to historic buildings.

**Guided Tours:** Auto-tape tour is $8 for 2 hours; tour bus service from the Visitor Center, $5.50 adults, $4.50 ages 5 to 16, toddlers, free).

**Open:** Daily 8:30am–5pm, later in summer. **Directions:** Access is from Exit 24 of the Pennsylvania Turnpike or Exit 25 of the Schuylkill Expressway (I-76) to Route 363. Follow the signs. By bus, take SEPTA no. 45 from the Visitors Center at 16th Street and John F. Kennedy Boulevard to King of Prussia Plaza, then take the hourly no. 99 bus to the park.

## VALLEY FORGE HISTORICAL SOCIETY MUSEUM, Rt. 23, Valley Forge. Tel. 215/783-0535.

The museum, next to Washington Memorial Chapel, has a large collection of Washingtoniana and the deposits of history, and the chapel cabin shop behind (open daily) vends homemade jam, bread, and sweets. I recommend the shoo-fly pie.

**Admission:** $2 adults; $1.50 seniors; $1 children 2–12.

**Open:** Mon–Sat 9:30am–4:30pm; Sun 1–4:30pm. **Closed:** Easter and Christmas.

## MILL GROVE, Audubon and Pawlings rds., Box 25, Audubon PA 19407. Tel. 215/666-5593.

Two miles north of Valley Forge (take Audubon Road, which parallels Route 422, and make a left off Penna. 363 just over the Schuylkill River), **Mill Grove** preserves 130 acres of wildlife sanctuary around the home of the young John James Audubon. Actually, Mill Grove belonged to his father, a French sea captain, who sent John James to supervise the estate. Soon after, he married the neighbor's daughter and moved to Kentucky, where he began his superb series of paintings of the birds of America. Now the fieldstone mansion with Georgian touches and a kitchen wing is decorated with murals of birdlife and Audubon's observance of nature. Outside, miles of walks among nature's calls and chirps make it easy to linger here for an afternoon. You're welcome to walk but not to picnic or pick.

**Admission:** Free.

**Open:** Museum, Tues–Sun 10am–4pm. Grounds, dawn to dusk.

## SHOPPING

## KING OF PRUSSIA COURT AND PLAZA, near junction of U.S. 202 and Penna. 363, ½ mi. south of I-276; 3 mi.

**south of Valley Forge National Historical Park via Rt. 422. Tel. 215/265-5727.**

People have always been drawn to King of Prussia because of its name. Now they stay because of the many hotels, restaurants, and shops in this community south of Valley Forge. The King of Prussia mall, called the Court and Plaza, is now one of the finest in the country, with 300 establishments in three separate sections. The major stores of the 130 include Bloomingdale's, Strawbridge & Clothier, and Herman's World of Sporting Goods. Choose from 15 restaurants, 12 shoe stores, 6 jewelers (including Bailey, Banks, and Biddle of Center City in Philadelphia), and 24 clothing stores.

**Open:** Daily 10am–10pm.

## WHERE TO STAY

### Moderate

**SHERATON VALLEY FORGE HOTEL, N. Gulph Rd. and 1st Ave., Valley Forge, PA 19406. Tel. 215/337-2000,** or toll free 800/325-3535. Fax 215/768-3222. 327 rms, 72 fantasy suites. AC MINIBAR TV TEL

**$ Rates:** $104–$115 single; $114–$125 double; from $150 suites. AE, DC, MC, V. **Parking:** Free.

This is a busy high-rise complex with rooms, suites, five restaurants, and two lounges, all of primary interest to get-away weekenders. The fantasy suites, ranging from Caveman, Wild West, and Pre-Raphaelite to Futurist, are remarkably popular.

**Dining:** 5 restaurants, including Lily Langtry's (see below) and Chumley's Steak and Sea Food.

**Facilities:** Health club ($15 additional) open until 12:30am, with Nautilus machines, racquetball courts, a whirlpool, a tanning bed, and a steam room; outdoor pool; dedicated no-smoking floors.

**Services:** Valet parking, complimentary newspapers.

**COMFORT INN AT VALLEY FORGE, 550 W. DeKalb Pike, King of Prussia, PA 19406. Tel. 215/962-0700,** or toll free 800/228-5150. Fax 215/962-0218. 121 rms. AC TV TEL

**$ Rates:** $75 single; $85 double. Weekend packages from $69. AAA and CAA discounts are available. AE, DC, MC, V. **Parking:** Free.

This inn is only a mile from the Valley Forge National Park, which makes it good for families. It has five floors. VCRs are built into the TVs.

**Facilities:** Coin-operated laundry, fitness center.

**Services:** Complimentary newspaper; free HBO.

## WHERE TO DINE

### Moderate

**LILY LANGTRY'S, Sheraton Valley Forge Hotel, N. Gulph Rd. and 1st Ave. Tel. 215/337-5459.**

**Cuisine:** AMERICAN/CONTINENTAL. **Reservations:** Required.

**$ Prices:** Lunch, $7–$13. Dinner, appetizers $4–$7; main courses $11–$18. Show $15. AE, DC, MC, V.

**Open:** Revue, Tues–Fri noon, 5pm, 8pm; Sat noon, 5pm, 9pm;

Langtry's has fairly reasonable and interesting dishes, within a packed-to-the-gills Victorian setting. However, the real attraction is entertainment straight out of Atlantic City, with revue-type showgirls, comedians, singers, and dancers.

# WEST OF VALLEY FORGE
## WHAT TO SEE

**RIDLEY CREEK STATE PARK, Penna. 3 (West Chester Pike) 3 miles past Newtown Square, Sycamore Mills Rd., Media, PA 19063. Tel. 215/566-4800;** and **COLONIAL PENNSYLVANIA PLANTATION, within park, P.O. Box 150, Edgemont, PA 19028. Tel. 215/353-1777.**
Ridley Creek State Park is about 15 miles west of Center City, 17 miles from the Valley Forge interchange, and 7 miles north of Media and I-95 via Penna. 352. It has two unusual attractions: the bonafide Colonial Pennsylvania Plantation, handed down straight from William Penn's charter; and a superb park with miles of picnic areas, playgrounds, and hiking and cycling trails. The plantation is the best example in the area of how a "yeoman," or common, family lived in virtual self-sufficiency on a colonial farm. It's staffed mostly by talented schoolteachers who come summer after summer to build wood fences, garden and grow corn, tend pigs and shear sheep, and weave cloth for clothes. Children love it.
   **Admission:** Park, Free. Plantation, $4 adults; $2 seniors and children 4–12.
   **Open:** Park, daily 8am–dusk. Plantation, Apr–June and Oct, Fri–Sun 10am–5pm. July–Aug, Thurs–Sun 10am–5pm.

**SKIPPACK VILLAGE, on Penna. 73.**
   Skippack Creek, which feeds into the Schuylkill near Mill Grove, runs along Penna. 73 near the junction of Penna. 113. To get to Skippack Village, follow Penna. 363 north to Penna. 73. The main entrepreneurs have refurbished about 40 Colonial and Federal manses as restaurants and shops. As you'd expect, antiques and collectibles rate high on the popularity list, but you can also pursue casual clothes and international dolls. The restaurants here include the moderately priced **Trolley Stop** (tel. 215/584-4849).

## WHERE TO DINE
### Moderate

**SKIPPACK ROADHOUSE, 4022 Skippack Pike (Rt. 73), Skippack. Tel. 215/584-4231.**
   **Cuisine:** AMERICAN. **Reservations:** Recommended.
**$ Prices:** Main courses $8–$12 at lunch, $13–$24 at dinner. AE, DC, MC, V.
   **Open:** Lunch, Mon–Sat 11:30am–2:30pm. Dinner, Mon–Thurs 5–9pm; Fri–Sat 5–10pm; Sun 4:30–8:30pm. Live entertainment on Fri and Sat.
This is an elegant, charming country roadhouse—with a white tile bar, mirrors, and fresh flowers—composed of six intimate dining rooms. The extensive blackboard specials of seasonal items include game and fresh fish and traditional meals of beef, chicken, and lamb.

# INDEX

## GENERAL INFORMATION

# SIGHTS & ATTRACTIONS

## PHILADELPHIA

**NOTE:** An asterisk (*) after an attraction name indicates that the attraction is an author's favorite.

# EXCURSION AREAS

# ACCOMMODATIONS

## PHILADELPHIA

### AIRPORT
Airport Hilton Inn (*M*), 76–7
Airport Ramada Inn (*M*), 77
Comfort Inn Airport (*I*), 78
Days Inn (*M*), 77
Guest Quarters Suite Hotel (*E*), 74–5
Philadelphia Airport Marriott Hotel (*E*), 75–6
Radisson Hotel Philadelphia Airport (*E*), 76
Red Roof Inn (*B*), 78

### CENTER CITY
The Barclay (*E*), 64–5
The Four Seasons Hotel (*VE*), 61–2
Holiday Inn–Center City (*M*), 68–9
Hotel Atop the Bellevue (*VE*), 60–1
KormanSuites Hotel and Conference Center (*E\*$*), 65–6
The Latham (*E*), 66
Philadelphia Hilton and Towers (*E*), 66–7
Philadelphia Marriott (*E*), 67
Quality Inn Historic Downtown Suites (*I$\**), 70
Ramada Inn–Center City (*I*), 70–1
Rittenhouse Hotel (*VE\**), 62–3
The Ritz-Carlton Philadelphia (*VE\**), 63–4
The Warwick (*M*), 69–70
Wyndham Franklin Plaza Hotel (*E*), 67–8

### CITY LINE & NORTHEAST
Adam's Mark Philadelphia (*E*), 78–79
Best Western Philadelphia Northeast (*B*), 80–1
Chamounix Mansion (*YH*), 81
Holiday Inn City Line (*M*), 79–80
Radnor Hotel (*M*), 80
Sheraton Inn Northeast (*I$*), 80

### HISTORIC AREA
Comfort Inn at Penn's Landing (*I$*), 58–9
Holiday Inn–Independence Mall (*M*), 55
Independence Park Inn (*M\**), 55–6
Old First Reformed Church (*B*), 59
Omni Hotel at Independence Park (*VE*), 53–4
Penn's View Inn (*M*), 58
Sheraton Society Hill (*VE*), 54–5
Thomas Bond House (*M*), 58

### UNIVERSITY CITY
Divine Tracy Hotel (*B$*), 74
International House (*B*), 73–4
Penn Tower Hotel (*M*), 71
Sheraton University City (*M*), 71–2
University City Guest Houses (*B*), 74

## EXCURSION AREAS

### CHESTNUT HILL
Chestnut Hill Hotel (*M\**), 239

### NEW HOPE
Centre Bridge Inn (*M\**), 245
Comfort Inn (*I\**), 246
Evermay-on-the-Delaware (*M*), 245–6
Isaac Stover House (*M*), 246
New Hope Motel in the Woods (*I$*), 246

Royce Hotel (*M*), 246
Whitehall Inn (*M\**), 246

### VALLEY FORGE
Comfort Inn at Valley Forge (*M*), 252
Sheraton Valley Forge Hotel (*M*), 252

**KEY TO ABBREVIATIONS:** *B* = Budget; *E* = Expensive; *I* = Inexpensive; *M* = Moderately priced; *VE* = Very Expensive; *YH* = Youth Hostel *$* = Special Value; *\** = an Author's Favorite

# RESTAURANTS

## PHILADELPHIA

### AFTERNOON TEA
Cassatt Lounge, Rittenhouse Hotel, 123
Dickens Inn, 123
Four Seasons Hotel, 123
Omni Hotel, 123
Ritz-Carlton, 123
Swann Lounge

### AMERICAN
Azalea (*M*\*), 118
Carolina's (*M*), 99–100
Catalina's (*I*\*), 103–4, 122
City Tavern (*M*), 85–6
Copacabana (*I*), 124
Cutter's Grand Cafe and Bar (*M*), 100–1
Diner on the Square (*B*), 107
Grill Room, Ritz-Carlton (*VE*), 119–20
Harry's Bar and Grill (*E*), 98
Jim's Steaks (*B*\*$), 93
Judy's Cafe (*M*), 88–9
Le Bus (*B*), 113
Lee's Hoagies (*B*), 117
New Deck Tavern (*I*), 112
Old Original Bookbinder's (*VE*), 83
Old Original Levis' (*B*), 93–4
Pat's King of the Steaks (*B*\*), 117
Philadelphia Fish & Company (*M*), 90–1
Reading Terminal Market (*I*\*$), 116–17
Rib-It (*I*), 106
Society Hill Hotel (*I*), 118
White Dog Cafe (*M*\*), 111

### BRITISH/ENGLISH
The Dickens Inn (*M*\*), 86–7
Grill Room, Ritz-Carlton (*VE*), 119–20

### CAJUN
The Magnolia Café (*M*), 101–2

### CHARCUTERIE
The Commissary, 124
Foodtek, 124–5

### CHINESE
Capital (*B*\*), 115
Golden Pond (*M*), 114
Harmony Vegetarian Restaurant (*I*\*$), 114
Imperial Inn (*I*), 114–15
Joe's Peking Duck House (*B*), 115
Ray's Coffee Shop (*B*), 115
Sang Yean Seafood House (*B*), 115–16
Susanna Foo (*M*), 103

### CONTEMPORARY AMERICAN
Jack's Firehouse (*E*\*), 98–9

### CONTINENTAL
Founders Atop the Bellevue (*M*), 120–1
Friday Saturday Sunday (*E*), 97
The Garden (*E*\*), 97–8
Palladium (*M*), 110–11
The Saloon (*E*), 108
16th Street Bar & Grill (*I*), 123
Zanzibar Blue (*M*), 123

### DELI/ROMANIAN
Broadway at the Bellevue (*I*), 122
Charlie's Water Wheel (*B*), 106–7
Famous Deli (*B*), 124

### DINER
Melrose Diner (*B*), 124

### DINING COMPLEXES
Bain's Deli, 121
Bassett's Original Turkey, 121
Boursa, 121
Chick-fil-A, 121
Food Court at Liberty Place (\*$), 121
Market Fair, 121
Mandarin Express, 121
Mentesini Pizza, 121
Nandi's, 121
Original Philly Steaks, 121
Reading Terminal Market, 121

### ECLECTIC
The Restaurant (*I*), 112–13

### FRENCH/BISTRO/CAFE
Au Bon Pain (*B*), 121–2
Ciboulette (*E*\*), 95–6
The Dining Room, Ritz-Carlton (*VE*),
    118–19
Jeannine's Bistro (*M*\*), 88
Le Bec-Fin (*VE*\*), 94–5
210, Rittenhouse Hotel (*E*\*), 120

### GREEK
Chef Theodore (*M*\*), 85

### HOAGIES & STEAK SAND-
### WICHES
Lee's Hoagies (*B*), 117
Pat's King of the Steaks (*B*\*), 117
Tacconelli's (*B*\*$), 117–18

**KEY TO ABBREVIATIONS:** *B* = Budget; *E* = Expensive; *I* = Inexpensive; *M* = Moderately priced; *VE* = Very Expensive; *$* = Super Special Value; \* = an Author's Favorite

# EXCURSION AREAS

## FROMMER GUIDES

| | Retail Price | Code | | Retail Price | Code |
|---|---|---|---|---|---|
| Alaska 1990–91 | $14.95 | C001 | Jamaica/Barbados 1993–94 | $15.00 | C105 |
| Arizona 1993–94 | $18.00 | C101 | Japan 1992–93 | $19.00 | C020 |
| Australia 1992–93 | $18.00 | C002 | Morocco 1992–93 | $18.00 | C021 |
| Austria/Hungary 1991–92 | $14.95 | C003 | Nepal 1992–93 | $18.00 | C038 |
| Belgium/Holland/Luxembourg 1993–94 | $18.00 | C106 | New England 1992 | $17.00 | C023 |
| Bermuda/Bahamas 1992–93 | $17.00 | C005 | New Mexico 1991–92 | $13.95 | C024 |
| | | | New York State 1992–93 | $19.00 | C025 |
| Brazil 1991–92 | $14.95 | C006 | Northwest 1991–92 | $16.95 | C026 |
| California 1992 | $18.00 | C007 | Portugal 1992–93 | $16.00 | C027 |
| Canada 1992–93 | $18.00 | C009 | Puerto Rico 1993–94 | $15.00 | C103 |
| Caribbean 1993 | $18.00 | C102 | Puerto Vallarta/Manzanillo/Guadalajara 1992–93 | $14.00 | C028 |
| The Carolinas/Georgia 1992–93 | $17.00 | C034 | Scandinavia 1991–92 | $18.95 | C029 |
| Colorado 1993–94 | $16.00 | C100 | Scotland 1992–93 | $16.00 | C040 |
| Cruises 1993–94 | $19.00 | C107 | Skiing Europe 1989–90 | $14.95 | C030 |
| DE/MD/PA & NJ Shore 1992–93 | $19.00 | C012 | South Pacific 1992–93 | $20.00 | C031 |
| Egypt 1990–91 | $14.95 | C013 | Switzerland/Liechtenstein 1992–93 | $19.00 | C032 |
| England 1993 | $18.00 | C109 | Thailand 1992–93 | $20.00 | C033 |
| Florida 1993 | $18.00 | C104 | USA 1991–92 | $16.95 | C035 |
| France 1992–93 | $20.00 | C017 | Virgin Islands 1992–93 | $13.00 | C036 |
| Germany 1993 | $19.00 | C108 | Virginia 1992–93 | $14.00 | C037 |
| Italy 1992 | $19.00 | C019 | Yucatán 1992–93 | $18.00 | C110 |

## FROMMER $-A-DAY GUIDES

| | | | | | |
|---|---|---|---|---|---|
| Australia on $45 a Day 1993–94 | $18.00 | D102 | Israel on $45 a Day 1993–94 | $18.00 | D101 |
| Costa Rica/Guatemala/Belize on $35 a Day 1991–92 | $15.95 | D004 | Mexico on $50 a Day 1993 | $19.00 | D105 |
| Eastern Europe on $25 a Day 1991–92 | $16.95 | D005 | New York on $70 a Day 1992–93 | $16.00 | D016 |
| England on $60 a Day 1993 | $18.00 | D107 | New Zealand on $45 a Day 1993–94 | $18.00 | D103 |
| Europe on $45 a Day 1993 | $19.00 | D106 | Scotland/Wales on $50 a Day 1992–93 | $18.00 | D019 |
| Greece on $45 a Day 1993–94 | $19.00 | D100 | South America on $40 a Day 1991–92 | $15.95 | D020 |
| Hawaii on $75 a Day 1993 | $19.00 | D104 | Spain on $50 a Day 1991–92 | $15.95 | D021 |
| India on $40 a Day 1992–93 | $20.00 | D010 | Turkey on $40 a Day 1992 | $22.00 | D023 |
| Ireland on $40 a Day 1992–93 | $17.00 | D011 | Washington, D.C. on $40 a Day 1992 | $17.00 | D024 |

# FROMMER CITY $-A-DAY GUIDES

| | Retail Price | Code | | Retail Price | Code |
|---|---|---|---|---|---|
| Berlin on $40 a Day 1992–93 | $12.00 | D002 | Madrid on $50 a Day 1992–93 | $13.00 | D014 |
| Copenhagen on $50 a Day 1992–93 | $12.00 | D003 | Paris on $45 a Day 1992–93 | $12.00 | D018 |
| London on $45 a Day 1992–93 | $12.00 | D013 | Stockholm on $50 a Day 1992–93 | $13.00 | D022 |

# FROMMER TOURING GUIDES

| | | | | | |
|---|---|---|---|---|---|
| Amsterdam | $10.95 | T001 | New York | $10.95 | T008 |
| Australia | $10.95 | T002 | Paris | $ 8.95 | T009 |
| Barcelona | $14.00 | T015 | Rome | $10.95 | T010 |
| Brazil | $10.95 | T003 | Scotland | $ 9.95 | T011 |
| Egypt | $ 8.95 | T004 | Sicily | $14.95 | T017 |
| Florence | $ 8.95 | T005 | Thailand | $12.95 | T012 |
| Hong Kong/Singapore/ | | | Tokyo | $15.00 | T016 |
| Macau | $10.95 | T006 | Turkey | $10.95 | T013 |
| Kenya | $13.95 | T018 | Venice | $ 8.95 | T014 |
| London | $12.95 | T007 | | | |

# FROMMER'S FAMILY GUIDES

| | | | | | |
|---|---|---|---|---|---|
| California with Kids | $16.95 | F001 | San Francisco with Kids | $17.00 | F004 |
| Los Angeles with Kids | $17.00 | F002 | Washington, D.C. with | | |
| New York City with Kids | $18.00 | F003 | Kids | $17.00 | F005 |

# FROMMER CITY GUIDES

| | | | | | |
|---|---|---|---|---|---|
| Amsterdam/Holland 1991–92 | $ 8.95 | S001 | Miami 1991–92 | $ 8.95 | S021 |
| Athens 1991–92 | $ 8.95 | S002 | Minneapolis/St. Paul 1991–92 | $ 8.95 | S022 |
| Atlanta 1991–92 | $ 8.95 | S003 | Montréal/Québec City 1991–92 | $ 8.95 | S023 |
| Atlantic City/Cape May 1991–92 | $ 8.95 | S004 | New Orleans 1993–94 | $13.00 | S103 |
| Bangkok 1992–93 | $13.00 | S005 | New York 1992 | $12.00 | S025 |
| Barcelona/Majorca/ | | | Orlando 1993 | $13.00 | S101 |
| Minorca/Ibiza 1992 | $12.00 | S006 | Paris 1993–94 | $13.00 | S109 |
| Belgium 1989–90 | $ 5.95 | S007 | Philadelphia 1991–92 | $ 8.95 | S028 |
| Berlin 1991–92 | $10.00 | S008 | Rio 1991–92 | $ 8.95 | S029 |
| Boston 1991–92 | $ 8.95 | S009 | Rome 1991–92 | $ 8.95 | S030 |
| Cancún/Cozumel/Yucatán 1991–92 | $ 8.95 | S010 | Salt Lake City 1991–92 | $ 8.95 | S031 |
| Chicago 1991–92 | $ 9.95 | S011 | San Diego 1993–94 | $13.00 | S107 |
| Denver/Boulder/Colorado | | | San Francisco 1993 | $13.00 | S104 |
| Springs 1990–91 | $ 7.95 | S012 | Santa Fe/Taos/ | | |
| Dublin/Ireland 1991–92 | $ 8.95 | S013 | Albuquerque 1993–94 | $13.00 | S108 |
| Hawaii 1992 | $12.00 | S014 | Seattle/Portland 1992–93 | $12.00 | S035 |
| Hong Kong 1992–93 | $12.00 | S015 | St. Louis/Kansas City | | |
| Honolulu/Oahu 1993 | $13.00 | S106 | 1991–92 | $ 9.95 | S036 |
| Las Vegas 1991–92 | $ 8.95 | S016 | Sydney 1991–92 | $ 8.95 | S037 |
| Lisbon/Madrid/Costa del | | | Tampa/St. Petersburg | | |
| Sol 1991–92 | $ 8.95 | S017 | 1993–94 | $13.00 | S105 |
| London 1993 | $13.00 | S100 | Tokyo 1992–93 | $13.00 | S039 |
| Los Angeles 1991–92 | $ 8.95 | S019 | Toronto 1991–92 | $ 8.95 | S040 |
| Mexico City/Acapulco | | | Vancouver/Victoria 1990– | | |
| 1991–92 | $ 8.95 | S020 | 91 | $ 7.95 | S041 |
| | | | Washington, D.C. 1993 | $13.00 | S102 |

# Other Titles Available at Membership Prices—
## SPECIAL EDITIONS

| | Retail Price | Code | | Retail Price | Code |
|---|---|---|---|---|---|
| Bed & Breakfast North America | $14.95 | P002 | Marilyn Wood's Wonderful Weekends (within 250-mile radius of New York City) | $11.95 | P017 |
| Caribbean Hideaways | $16.00 | P005 | | | |
| Honeymoon Destinations | $14.95 | P006 | | | |
| | | | New World of Travel 1991 by Arthur Frommer | $16.95 | P018 |
| | | | Where to Stay USA | $13.95 | P015 |

## GAULT MILLAU'S "BEST OF" GUIDES

| | | | | | |
|---|---|---|---|---|---|
| Chicago | $15.95 | G002 | New England | $15.95 | G010 |
| Florida | $17.00 | G003 | New Orleans | $16.95 | G011 |
| France | $16.95 | G004 | New York | $16.95 | G012 |
| Germany | $18.00 | G018 | Paris | $16.95 | G013 |
| Hawaii | $16.95 | G006 | San Francisco | $16.95 | G014 |
| Hong Kong | $16.95 | G007 | Thailand | $17.95 | G019 |
| London | $16.95 | G009 | Toronto | $17.00 | G020 |
| Los Angeles | $16.95 | G005 | Washington, D.C. | $16.95 | G017 |

## THE REAL GUIDES

| | | | | | |
|---|---|---|---|---|---|
| Amsterdam | $13.00 | R100 | Morocco | $14.00 | R111 |
| Barcelona | $13.00 | R101 | Nepal | $14.00 | R018 |
| Berlin | $11.95 | R002 | New York | $13.00 | R019 |
| Brazil | $13.95 | R003 | Able to Travel (avail April '93) | $20.00 | R112 |
| California & the West Coast | $17.00 | R102 | Paris | $13.00 | R020 |
| Canada | $15.00 | R103 | Peru | $12.95 | R021 |
| Czechoslovakia | $14.00 | R104 | Poland | $13.95 | R022 |
| Egypt | $19.00 | R105 | Portugal | $15.00 | R023 |
| Florida | $14.00 | R006 | Prague | $15.00 | R113 |
| France | $18.00 | R106 | San Francisco & the Bay Area | $11.95 | R024 |
| Germany | $18.00 | R107 | Scandinavia | $14.95 | R025 |
| Greece | $18.00 | R108 | Spain | $16.00 | R026 |
| Guatemala/Belize | $14.00 | R109 | Thailand | $17.00 | R114 |
| Holland/Belgium/Luxembourg | $16.00 | R031 | Tunisia | $17.00 | R115 |
| Hong Kong/Macau | $11.95 | R011 | Turkey | $13.95 | R116 |
| Hungary | $12.95 | R012 | U.S.A. | $18.00 | R117 |
| Ireland | $17.00 | R110 | Venice | $11.95 | R028 |
| Italy | $13.95 | R014 | Women Travel | $12.95 | R029 |
| Kenya | $12.95 | R015 | Yugoslavia | $12.95 | R030 |
| Mexico | $11.95 | R016 | | | |